THE FAMILIES OF
DUFF AND DIANA COOPER

SIR ALFRED COOPER
1838-1908
m.
LADY AGNES DUFF   (widow of Herbert Flower)
1846-1925

VIOLET (Letty)	DIANA m. ALFRED	STEPHANIE	HERMIONE	SYBIL
1888-1971	DUFF	1883-1918	1885-1923	1886-1927
m. 1 Hugo Charteris	1st Viscount	m.	m.	m.
Lord Elcho, 1884-1916	Norwich	Arthur Levita	Niel Arnott	Richard Hart-Davis
2. Guy Holford Benson	1890-1954			
1888-1975				

David, 12th and present
Earl of Wemyss b.1912

Martin, now Lord
Charteris of
Amisfield, b.1913

Nicholas b.1922

Giles b.1923

Jeremy b.1925

JOHN JULIUS
b.1929
Anne Clifford
b.1929

ARTEMIS   JASON
b.1953   b.1959

RUPERT   DIERDRE
b.1907   b.1909

A DURABLE FIRE

A DURABLE FIRE

The Letters of
Duff and Diana Cooper
1913-1950

Edited by Artemis Cooper

FRANKLIN WATTS Inc.
New York 1984

First published in Great Britain in 1983 by William Collins Sons and Co. Ltd

First United States publication 1984 by Franklin Watts, Inc.,
387 Park Avenue South, New York, NY 10016

ISBN 0-531-09827-3

Printed in Great Britain

For my grandmother
DIANA
with gratitude, admiration, and love.

But true love is a durable fire
In the mind ever burning;
Never sick, never old, never dead,
From itself never turning.

Walsingham,
Sir Walter Raleigh.

ACKNOWLEDGEMENTS

I should like to thank the following people for their kindness and help in the making of this book: Douglas Matthews, and the staff of the London Library; Mark Amory; the Earl of Bessborough; Lord Charteris; Lord Coke; Daphne Fielding; Mrs Edward Grant; the late Lord Head; David Herbert; Alistair Horne; Lord Howard de Walden; Peter James; Nigel Jaques; Patrick Leigh Fermor; Lady Lindsay; Laura, Duchess of Marlborough; Nigel Nicolson; Rosemary Peto; Sir Anthony Rumbold; John Ryle; Mr Sweeny; and the Secretaries of Buck's Club and the Travellers' Club.

I am especially grateful to my parents, for several inspired suggestions as well as constant help and encouragement; to Marilyn Goddard, who prepared the typescript; and to Alastair Forbes, Sir Rupert Hart-Davis, Stuart Preston and Hugo Vickers, without whose time, trouble, and expertise this book would be immeasurably the poorer.

Lastly I would like to thank my grandmother Diana. Not only for the fact that she made this book possible; but for the joy of her company, as I sat at the end of her bed and we talked about these letters, and the hours rolled happily away.

CONTENTS

INTRODUCTION

The letters of Duff and Diana Cooper to each other are kept in a tall, squeaky metal filing cabinet that my grandmother Diana always refers to as *The Olivetti*. As well as a large quantity of telegrams and post-cards, the Olivetti houses some two thousand letters, dating from 1913 to 1950. Several of them have already appeared in Duff and Diana's autobiographies, and in Philip Ziegler's biography *Diana Cooper*; but no individual letter can reflect the range and depth of the whole collection.

It was Philip Ziegler who suggested that I edit these letters, a suggestion for which I shall be forever grateful, quite apart from the help and encouragement he gave me as the book gradually took shape.

The letters divide themselves into three main groups, with a fourth much smaller one at the end. The first group, written between 1913 and 1917, are mainly Duff's love letters. These contain extravagant hymns to her beauty and heart-breaking descriptions of his passion and her cruelty, peppered with puns and funny stories and accounts of what he had for dinner. Diana was not, at first, the only person to whom he was writing love letters, and Diana was receiving hundreds from all the other young men who were in love with her. It was not until 1916 or so that the letters begin to tell that their love is turning to something deeper and more enduring.

Duff had begun his career in the Foreign Office in 1913, and when the war broke out, he and the other young clerks there were engaged on work too useful to the war effort to allow them to enlist. Duff did eventually get to the war, but not until April 1918. The second group of letters therefore covers Duff's active service in France, from April to October of that year. It was at this time that

[xi]

Duff and Diana, now seriously in love, begin to write to each other every day. The daily letter was of enormous importance. Anticipation of the mail was one thing that made life at the front bearable, and Duff – who knew that Diana was surrounded by dashing young soldiers home on leave – needed to know that he was still first in her thoughts. For Diana, if a letter did not arrive on time, it could only mean one thing: killed in action.

Duff was not killed in action, but returned covered in glory with a D.S.O. They were married in June 1919, having beaten her parents' opposition, and in 1923 Diana left for America to play the Madonna in Max Reinhardt's production of *The Miracle*. From November to March, for the next four years, Diana toured the United States with *The Miracle*, returning to England for the summer months. She and Duff wrote to each other every day. Diana is one of Nature's worriers. Constantly needing Duff's warmth and reassurance, she came to depend on these letters. And although the war was over, a letter's late arrival could still spell disaster: Duff was in the arms of another, or had been the victim of a fatal railway accident, or both. This is by far the largest group of letters, and spans the years 1923 to 1929.

Diana had gone to America to make some money, so that Duff could leave the Foreign Office and enter Parliament. Both these goals had now been accomplished, and this – coupled with the birth of their only child, John Julius – meant that never again would they have to be separated for such long periods. When they were apart for months on end, their whole relationship had been channelled into the letters. The reader can see their moods changing, little sub-plots developing; the letters weave themselves tightly together and can be read as a story. But from now on, the separations are comparatively short. There is not time to get into the rhythm of a correspondence like that of 1918 or *The Miracle* years.

For these reasons, the last group is the smallest, although it covers the longest stretch of time – 1931 to 1950. Now when they are apart, it is usually because Diana is abroad; she and Duff tried to take their holidays together but he was often too busy, and he never had Diana's passion for foreign travel. Her diary letters home tell of her daily doings in foreign parts, and these form the bulk of the last group.

In whittling this collection of letters down to a quarter of its size, I have based my selection on the simple criterion of whether I found a letter interesting or not, but the fact that this is a correspondence has sometimes imposed its own rules. If either Duff or Diana pick up a point mentioned in an earlier letter, for example, I have usually included the earlier one, even though I might rather have given the space to something else. When following a theme or a sub-plot, I have usually tried to keep it within its context, to avoid giving it an importance that might not exist in the letters. This does not mean, however, that every letter is given in full. I have cut out those bits for which there is no room, and those that seem to me boring, such as travel arrangements and lists of dinner guests. Any intrusions of my own are enclosed in square brackets.

Duff's handwriting is small, neat, sloping and very easy to read. Each letter is dated with the day, month and year, except for some of the early ones, written in sickness or the heat of passion. Diana's hand is not so easy to praise. The fact that she wrote in bed with a rather stubby pencil did not improve her curious calligraphy, and all effort goes into expression rather than presentation. As her writing gallops after her thoughts, there is little time for the intricacies of grammar, spelling and punctuation. The dating of her letters was sporadic, and frequently wrong: it was Duff – (with a sigh, I imagine) who corrected it, or inserted the right date neatly at the top of the page.

I have added or clarified the punctuation where necessary, and corrected the spelling – except when it seemed too breathtaking or inspired to change.

Violet, Duchess of Rutland was a beautiful woman and an accomplished artist. She had given her husband, the eighth Duke, four children before the birth of Diana. First was Marjorie, then Haddon – who died when he was only nine years old. Then came John, who became the ninth Duke, and then Violet, who was always known as Letty.

Diana was born in 1892. It is possible that she was not the daughter of the Duke of Rutland but of Harry Cust – poet, politician, and editor of the *Pall Mall Gazette*. He was brilliant, charming, fair-haired and very handsome, and his name had been linked with those of many society ladies of the day. That he might be her father was not an idea that unduly worried Diana, when she discovered it at the age of seventeen. The Duke's affectionate paternal love was what she had grown up with, she bore his name

[xiii]

and was part of his family. There was no reason for her to think of herself as other than his daughter.

The family lived in London, and when the Duke of Rutland inherited the title in 1906, weekends and holidays were spent at Belvoir Castle. Her education was sketchy; there was a lot of poetry by Browning and Meredith, and history by Shakespeare. In mathematics she learnt addition and multiplication, but subtraction has always been a problem, and long division remains shrouded in mystery. She was brought up with Viola, Felicity, and Iris, the daughters of Sir Herbert Beerbohm Tree, so the theatre was always a familiar world. She was taught to read by the age of four, and as she grew older she read voraciously.

From a podgy, affectionate child she grew into an extremely beautiful young woman. But Diana had an adventurous spirit, an appetite for life and a capacity for friendship that animated her beauty, increased it tenfold, and left the beholders dazzled. By the age of twenty-one she was the centre of a brilliant group of friends and admirers. We must introduce you to Duff, they said. Oh, you'll love Duff. He's so funny, so intelligent.

They met on the stairs of her parents' house in Arlington Street on an evening when the Rutlands were giving a ball. They found one another's company delightful, but it was not love at first sight – they grew into it gradually.

Duff Cooper was the youngest child and only son of a distinguished surgeon, Sir Alfred Cooper, F.R.C.S. Sir Alfred specialized in venereal and anal diseases, and wrote learned medical books about their symptoms and treatment, most alarmingly illustrated. His wife was born Lady Agnes Duff, the second daughter of the fifth Earl Fife. She had eloped with her first husband, been divorced, married her second, and been left an almost penniless widow before she married Sir Alfred. They had three daughters before the arrival of Duff – Stephanie, Hermione, and Sybil. Sir Alfred died in 1908.

After leaving Eton, Duff went up to Oxford and read history. He was a member of the Union and of several debating societies, but his success as a speaker was undermined by a reputation for wildness and high living. It was at Oxford that he met the young men who were to introduce him to Diana, and when they came down from Oxford to live in London, they formed a clique that they called the Coterie, with Diana at the centre.

It was a glittering set. There was Patrick Shaw-Stewart, who had a first in Greats, a Fellowship at All Souls, and was to become one of the youngest ever directors of Baring's Bank. Charles Lister, son of Lord Ribblesdale, was another intellectual and a committed socialist. Edward Horner did not share their mental brilliance, but he was good company, a valued friend, enormously tall and built to match. Alan Parsons was not nearly so robust. His asthma prevented him from going to the war in which most of his friends were going to die. He was amusing, sensible and extremely well-read, and he married Diana's oldest friend, Viola Tree. Julian Grenfell, who was to become one of the sad, heroic group of war poets, was also one of this set. Then there was Venetia Stanley, to whom the Prime Minister, H. H. Asquith, wrote long letters – frequently during cabinet meetings – about the doings of his colleagues.* She later married Edwin Montagu, whom Diana described as "interested in everything, and always plunged in gloom".

But among this group of friends, the most brilliant of all was Raymond Asquith. He was a few years older than the others, and his firsts in Greats and Law were crowned with a Fellowship to All Souls. He was called to the Bar in 1904, and married Katharine Horner (Edward's sister) in 1907. In 1913 he was adopted as prospective Liberal candidate for Derby. Diana had known Katharine for many years and they were very close, but she adored and admired Raymond above everything in the world, and he loved her. Katharine's nature was wise and generous: "I shall love and bless you always," she wrote to Diana after Raymond's death in 1916. "How could I have minded your loving Raymond and his loving you? It was in the fitness of things."

The Coterie met constantly, at balls and dinners in town and leisurely country house parties, and they cultivated all the pleasures of civilization. They took pride in their learning and conversation, and plays, prose and poetry were often read aloud of an evening. They indulged their high spirits in treasure-hunts, fancy-dress balls, and deliciously illicit evenings playing poker. They held riotous parties that went on till dawn, and their doings were written up by a shocked and delighted press.

Their company was always in demand by the great hostesses and the eminent politicians, but there were two rich, middle-aged

* These letters have now been published – *H. H. Asquith – Letters to Venetia Stanley*, edited by Michael and Eleanor Brock, 1982.

men who were particularly infatuated with Diana, and were only too happy to entertain her and her friends. The first of these was Ivor Guest, Viscount Wimborne, who was the Lord Lieutenant of Ireland from 1915 to 1918. Had she given him half a chance, he would have given up everything for her – she never did, but he remained her devoted slave, sending her fabulous presents and making the occasional pounce.

The second was George Gordon Moore, an American millionaire who reminded Diana of a squat red indian. Sinister stories were whispered about how he had made his money, but he was a magnificent host, and some of the Coterie's wildest parties took place at his house in Lancaster Gate. So long as Diana was there, he did not mind how long the party went on. But as soon as she left, the band was ordered to stop playing; the food and champagne were cleared away, and the lights were put out.

1913–1917

Diana to Duff, 1913   *Beau Desert*[1]

Mr. Duff Coowper – £2-2-0 for a ball ticket – Is it asking too much? Emphatically yes – but what can I Do? Give it you, you say – It never struck me you'd accept it. You will have to pay exorbitant interest in the future – not necessarily in coin should I stump up. I leave you for 2 days a choice.   Diana Manners.

Duff to Diana, 5 March 1913   *9 Berkeley House, Hay Hill*[2]

Dear Lady Diana, I adore the way you spell my name. Please always spell it so. It looks like a picture of a crocodile and is alone well worth two guineas. The ball was worth much more to me – three at least although there was no supper: it made an epoch in my life and will not be forgotten for days. I am wondering whether you got a letter which I sent on Friday to the house where we left you after the ball. You make no mention of it which seems odd as it was a charming letter, and perhaps the best part of it was a cheque – not for dancing but for poker. We must play again and dance again, please.   Yours, Duff Cooper – or as you so much more amusingly would write, Cooowper.

[In March 1913 Diana became ill while staying with the Beerbohm Trees in William Nicholson's house at Rotting-

[1] The home of Diana's sister Marjorie and her husband Charles Paget, 6th Marquess of Anglesey.
[2] Where Duff was living with his mother.

[3]

dean. Duff, who happened to be nearby with some Oxford friends, threw himself enthusiastically into the role of The Poet writing to his Ailing Mistress. The poems continued from Hanover, where Duff was studying German for his Foreign Office exams.]

Duff to Diana, 24 March 1913   Hillside, Rottingdean

A sonnet every few hours is my prescription for every malady. So here's another – deal kindly with it as you did the first. The poetry gambit is a trifle old fashioned in the twentieth century – but I like old methods best and I hope you will find the sentiments very affecting, and the numbers monstrous ravishing. In fact I should take it kindly if you would have an attack of the vapours on reading the verses.

Can't we play chess again with Nicholson's pretty men, or would the brain work send your temperature up like a rocket? Duff.

Diana to Duff, 1913   [Written on a torn envelope.]

Not Keats – O no – Honestly Duff dear you have excelled yr excess of beauty in line – Had I not anyhow swooned upon the midnight[1] I should probably have ceased like a blown candle on reading it at 1.a.m. In equal extreme it became to me as an Elexia – it filled sad veins with liquor.

I subsitute sonnet for bread in Christs prayer, and attribute the void days to God's pique at my not bending my knees. I have no means to thank. I send lilies – they are a bit pure for the season – but their morgue-element saves them.

Chess soon I hope – but my chains have lightened, and they are only silver-gilt.

Duff to Diana, 19 April 1913   86 Alte Döhrenerstrasse, Hannover

I hope you are still ill. I cannot bear to think of you as quite well, with a hat on. Also you will appreciate an unexpected letter from me so tremendously if it finds you in bed.

---

[1] Keats, *Ode to a Nightingale.*

[4]

Art thou still ailing, pretty one,
　　How dost thou dare be ill,
Now that the laughing Spring's be-
gun
　　　　　　Now that the sun
　　Makes promise to fulfill
All our wild hopes of summer fun –
　　Why art thou ailing still?

"Ailing" is a bad word, isn't it, but can you think of a better?
However let's go on with it.

Pitiful primrose, droop no more,
　　Hold up thy golden head,
For May is knocking at the door,
　　　　　　And all her store
　　Of garments white and red,
Her motley mummeries of yore
　　Are waiting to be spread.
Throw open wide the door to May,
　　Let her come into thee;
She shall with kisses charm away
　　All thine infirmity
　　　　　　So shalt thou see
　　How sweet it is to play
　　　　　　the livelong day
With such a joyous playfellow as she.

I think that will do for the present, so we'll leave it at that. By
the way I always meant to ask you whether you would marry me
or not. Probably not. I am mouse poor and should be a vile
husband. But there is only about one person as far as I can
remember whom I love better than you[1] but she won't marry me,
so I could promise at the altar to love you quite, to cherish you a
good deal and to endow you with nearly all my wordly goods
which wouldn't amount to much. I should in return require
implicit obedience and scrupulous punctuality. Think it over at
the end of the season.　　Yours almost, Duff.

---

[1] Katharine Asquith, 1885–1976.

[5]

Diana to Duff, April 1913   *16 Arlington Street*[1]

You wrecked your ship utterly, fond man, by confessing yourself a string of another's bow, (or belle.) There is no one I love
ecstatically – but if there was he would marry me, and that is the
attitude to take, and with conceit walks *succès fou*, so take my tip
and don't confess again.

My hands are like ice, so roughly speaking is the whole of me, so
cold that they freeze before they bite, the snakes I harbour in my
breast – but my heart is like Nebuchadnezar's raging furnace, in it
walk a few, yourself included, Christ in the middle.

He I have reason to believe is crazy about me – so I shall
probably marry the church. I love as much as I am loved & give
exactly what is given.

I think you are well out of it really. You did not know till now
that my feet are ever so slightly *web* – also I am somnambulist
when crossed – also very decadent and theatrical & inclined to
look fast – attributes no man likes in his wife.

I had rather you loved me – infinitely better than the woman
who won't marry you – but you never will. I know her and I know
her worth and 'pon my soul, you are right.   Bless you and write
to me again – Yours more or less, Diana.

Duff to Diana, 3 May 1913   *86 Alte Döhrenerstrasse, Hannover*

Your letter was like a spoonful of caviar in the desert, or a
spongeful of the best vinegar on the cross. But I am sorry you did
not fall to my 'second-best' gambit. I had never tried it before and
thought it might do. But I am happy to have a place in the furnace
of your heart, though I do not relish sharing it with the Son of man.
I think if you will compare us dispassionately the comparison is
bound to result in my favour. To begin with my hands and feet are
practically without blemish, and I have never been operated on
for appendicitis. In fact I am really as good as new, whereas he, to
put it mildly, is more than 'shop soiled'. But perhaps you like
scars. I believe German women are supposed to.[2]

As for your ghastly self-accusation of web feet, I will never
believe it until like St. Thomas I have thrust my finger into the
web. I don't mind your being a somnambulist as long as you don't

[1] The Rutlands' London house.
[2] Duelling scars were considered very dashing in Germany.

[6]

want me to walk *with* you, and I love you best for being decadent and looking fast. Think what fun if one's friends thought one was out with an actress when one was really with one's dreary old wife. I can imagine nothing better. So I have disposed of all your objections and as for loving you best in the world I think that might happen all too easily. I am really rather frightened that it will, for I feel that you would be terrible then and have no pity and that I might die of it, or perhaps go bad. (I meant to write 'mad' but 'bad' is funnier.)

Give me another spongeful of vinegar. I thirst.   Duff.

Duff to Diana, Christmas 1913   *Foreign Office*

Which would you like best for a Christmas present – a small china harlequin or a black velvet bag with a watch in it – very small, and heart-shaped? I have bought both and may mention that the cash value is about the same, but the bag looks worth more. Telegraph your answer tomorrow, there's a darling, and suggest whom I shall give the other to.   Duff.

8 January 1913

You never thanked me for my Christmas present, serpent's tooth of a child. 'Sharper than a serpent's thanks it is to have a toothless child.'

Duff to Diana, 20 March 1914   *Foreign Office*

Were you really angry with me this evening, Dikins? If so, I can't bear it. I've had a miserable day. Every thing has been wrong and everybody has been brutal. You are the only person who is ever kind to me and God knows how I love you, and if you think I am beastly to you it is the last bloody straw. I am going to dine with Eddie[1] now and we shall sob together. Why can't you always be with us, why can't we always all have fun. Partly, I think, because you and I are the only really delicious people in the world – the only two with whom I can find no fault. I suppose you are going away for Sunday. I am 'on duty' here. So if you don't go,

---

[1] Eddie Grant was a captain in the first war and in charge of foreign journalists in the second. He married Bettine Stuart Wortley in 1917, and Laura Waugh's sister, Bridget Herbert, in 1935.

[7]

please, please, please have tea with me here tomorrow or the next day, or lunch elsewhere. And forgive me my trespasses though I'm damned if I'll forgive them that trespass against me.   Duff.

Diana to Duff, undated   *Walmer Castle, Kent*

My angel Duff, Your tears of medicinal gum would have tamed and melted Barbarism itself. My steel heart flushed tenderer than our frailest meat.

You may have my hands all tomorrow – all tomorrow beginning for me at five at Arlington St. and as good as ending at seven thirty.   D.

Duff to Diana, 3 May 1914   *Foreign Office*

Shall I write you a love letter, Dikins? No, I fancy not. We have agreed, haven't we, that that would be a bore. And bores, with God's help, we will never be. So a love-letter it shall not be though a letter at all is proof of considerable affection, because this is the first I have written with my right hand and every word is agony. If you could see the pain that I am in you would, I feel confident, be delighted.

Last night, although not dressed for the occasion, you were looking lovelier than anything that my imagination, though far from sterile, has ever conceived. You were looking like – but no, this shall not be a love-letter – you were looking remarkably well. I promised you a long letter, and, by God, you shall have it though your promises to me are never kept and your ill-written, worse-spelt, pencil letters are as rare as Leonardos in my collection.

The thought that I shall see you tomorrow evening fills me with frenzy, though the fear that you will see me in trousers and *not* in breeches saddens and chastens and mortifies my corrupt affections. It is sad that the corpse of a dead Duke[1] should come between my well shaped calves and the anxious eyes of an expectant world. A live calf (especially if well shaped) is better than a dead Duke, I say.

[1] John, 9th Duke of Argyll, 1845–1914. He was the husband of H.R.H. Princess Louise, and had died the previous day. The Court went into mourning for a month, which meant the cancellation of all Court balls, where the gentlemen were required to wear knee-breeches.

There go the loves that wither,
  The old loves with wearier wings,
And all dead Dukes draw thither
  And all disastrous things.

—

Diana's heart is cold and white,
  There is no pity in her eyes,
She passes through the amorous night
  A scornful virgin of the skies.

—

I will give you another sovereign if you can tell me (first guess)
the authors of those two stanzas.[1]
  Lighten my darkness I beseech thee Diana, & by thy great
mercy change thy technique towards me and me only.   Duff.

Duff to Diana, 15 May 1914   *Foreign Office*

I was miserable about last night but it wasn't my fault, so how
dare you pretend it was. Under your thumb, you think, and so
adopt the brutal bludgeoning technique which Katharine practised: i.e. invitation to dinner at a quarter to eight – (all London
having first been ransacked) acceptance a matter of course,
refusal followed by Billingsgate.[2] Cheshire Cheese evening I
wasn't asked at all, should never have heard of it if I hadn't,
looking for dinner at 7.30, gone to find Denis[3] (my last resource as
I am yours) and nabbed him on the doorstep and wormed with
some difficulty the truth from him. Did I reproach you though?
Not a word, not a blow even, how dare you then turn on me so
venomously? Denis and Hamel[4] are your favourite men. I don't
complain, though to one of limited means it seems odd that
anybody should require *two* chauffeurs.

---

[1] The first stanza is from Swinburne's *The Garden of Proserpine*.
'And all dead years draw thither' is the original third line. The second stanza I have
been unable to identify.
[2] Shouting like a fishwife.
[3] The Hon. Denis Anson, 1888–1914.
[4] Gustav Hamel was a young Swedish aviator, whose good looks and dare-devilry
made him a great favourite of the Coterie.

[9]

Really Dikins, how beastly you have been to me lately, ever since, in fact, I have been divine to you. Send me a word to name your train to Sutton.   Duff.

Duff to Diana, 25 May 1914   *Foreign Office*

My darling, I have written you a poem to comfort you.[1] I think I was nearly as unhappy as you, but I can't cry – I have to burst into verse instead of into tears, which I don't think is nearly so pleasant.

I am rather shy of writing to you now because I am in love with you since this afternoon – I only loved you before – and one always writes boring letters when one is in love and sometimes ridiculous. I hate being ridiculous and hate much more being boring and I'm not quite sure that I like being in love. So I don't think I will say any more though I have a great deal more to say. Only I hope you will believe me when I say I am in love with you, because I don't think I've ever said it before. The climax of my slow decline into that state was strange and rather beautiful, wasn't it? I was beginning to think I had grown out of all emotions but on this day I have had more sorrow than I have had for long, and one moment of greater happiness than I have ever had. I am still trembling from both.   Duff.

If there is good news in the morning I think you had better destroy the poem – or perhaps, on second thoughts, you might only put it by.

Duff to Diana, 26 May 1914   *Foreign Office*

My very darling – Why should you call yourself unrepentant who have no more to repent than Christ upon the cross, for like him you were too charitable. If there was crime it was mine but I cannot think that there was any. I am old fashioned perhaps in believing that nothing that makes one very happy can be wrong. You gave, or perhaps I stole, what, if you never spoke to me again

[1] On the death of Gustav Hamel. He took off from Hardelot in France on May 23rd, heading for Hendon Aerodrome, and was never seen again.

would make me love you all my life. So it is perhaps almost waste of your time to speak to me again.

Nor did I regret the ungrand lovely channel for the tears and lilies that were between us seemed to make all things white and sweet.

The only fear I have of death is the fear of not remembering, for I have something so precious now that I could not bear to forget it.   Duff.

I have much improved your poem, as I found there was a line that didn't rhyme with anything. If you decide to let the world have a look at it I will send you the amended copy, which if you like you may send to *The Times* but under *your* name not mine as it is really yours.

This poem appeared in The Times on January 29th.

In Memoriam G.H.

> He was so young, 'twas hard to think him dead.
> And yet his thoughts were always otherwhere,
> His mind was holding converse with the skies.
> And on his brow their influence was shed
> Malevolent, for plainly printed there,
> The fate, which he foresaw, but could not fear,
> Shone like a prophecy to anxious eyes.
>
> He was too careless of all earthly things,
> Who made the bosom of the clouds his nest.
> He strove not with his kind, deigned not to share
> Their loves and hatreds. His heroic wings
> Supported him upon a higher quest
> Than they could dream of – and, when loneliest,
> He gazed around for dangers new to dare.
>
> The winds of heaven were his charioteers,
> He led the cohort of the Sky, and dared
> The elements, and the rebellious air
> Knew him for long her master, and his ears
> Heard thunderous melodies, and gladly heard.
> He knew the roads of heaven like a bird,
> And like a bird he fell, and none know where.

The murd'rous dawn broke on the waves, death-white,
Nature forgets her crimes; makes no amend,
But we who live and laugh – safe, shameful we,
Will bear in memory that last, fierce fight,
Fought by our fine, indomitable friend,
The final battle to the bitter end,
Alone with the blind wind and brutal sea.

D.C.

Duff to Diana, 30 May 1913   *In the train*

Nancy[1] & Edward[2] are dying to see who this is to. But for once
they shall *not* see and I shall *not* tell. Oh that bloody poem – how I
have suffered from it. Lady Cunard[3] read *selections* from it to Harry
Portman at lunch. *with* comment – "*He knew the roads of heaven like a
bird* – Like a bird – Oh but that's *sweet*, Duff. You're a great poet
you know. Don't you think Duff's a great poet Harry Portman.
Look at his profile."

I felt very miserable this morning with a lonely, weary, hopeless
heart and a twinge of rheumatism in the right shoulder.

I return on Monday not to the Foreign Office but to Berkeley
House, Hay Hill, a shorter walk for the messenger boys,[4] whom the
impatience of my passion that cannot brook the post's delays will
probably continue to employ. I wonder if the sun shines at Belvoir.
Never in Somerset.[5] Heaven's blessings on thine eyes.   Duff.

Duff to Diana, 9 June 1914   *Foreign Office*

I read your letter as I sat in my cold bath this morning, and so
much did it inflame me that the water boiled. I wonder why you
had a wretched evening. I should like you always to be happy even

---

[1] Nancy Cunard, 1896–1965. Daughter of Maud Cunard, see n.3. Briefly married
Sydney Fairbairn in 1916. Writer and champion of black peoples' rights.
[2] Edward Horner, 1888–1917. Son of Sir John and Lady Frances Horner, and brother of
Katharine Asquith.
[3] Maud Cunard, 1872–1948. She was born Maud Burke, an American heiress and a
great hostess. She married Sir Bache Cunard in 1895, but they separated in 1911. Nancy
was their only child. In 1926 Maud changed her name to Emerald.
[4] Many London houses took advantage of this service: A bell was installed that
summoned a messenger boy in a smart uniform, who would deliver letters and parcels on
foot for sixpence.
[5] They are on their way to Mells, the Horners' family seat since the time of Henry VIII.

when I am not there, though I have always found it difficult to imagine how anybody could be. Are you going to dine in Cavendish Square[1] and fancy dress tomorrow? Pray heaven you are. I have almost lost my first time rapture for dressing up, and shall wear tomorrow a dress which I had in the dark unlovely days before I knew you.

Why don't we now resume those evening readings which had so chequered though so sweet a life. Do you know Italian well enough to read Dante, if not we will read Malory, please.

Don't write too legibly or intelligibly as I have no occupation so pleasant as pondering for hours over your hieroglyphics, and for hours more trying to interpret your dark sayings. A clearly written simply expressed letter is too like the lightning. Good afternoon. Duff.

Diana to Duff, undated   *16 Arlington Street*

Duff – Its vitally important you should say you dined *alone* with Ruby[2] last night as when I got in I had a letter from Mother telling me I had been out with you, the which I have denied –   Diana.

Duff to Diana, 23 June 1914   *Foreign Office*

Suicide wears in my eyes an ever increasingly alluring aspect. A life spent in going from one place to another in order to see you, and seldom having a moment's conversation when I get there, is driving me to despair without in any way reducing my weight. Ceasing upon the midnight – with no, or practically no pain, is perhaps my best chance. But perhaps I shall feel happier after lunch. I generally do.

Do you ever feel good, Dotty? I must confess I occasionally do. Don't be alarmed. Nothing happens. The feeling passes off in a few hours and leaves me unaltered. I have it usually after having stayed up too late and drunk too much. Then I think I should like to live a simple life in the country and be a saint, a real saint with a

---

[1] No. 2 Cavendish Square, the house of H. H. Asquith, the Prime Minister.
[2] Ruby Peto. The only child of Col. Walter James Lindsay, she was a cousin of Violet Rutland and had been brought up with Diana and her sisters. In 1909 she married Ralph Harding Peto, 1877–1945, whom she divorced in 1923.

halo and a day of my own and taking precedence over half the people in heaven: I see myself getting good at prayer and fasting and becoming holy and beautiful and very thin. The feeling sometimes goes on till half way through lunch.

Goodbye, my darling – I hope that everyone whom you like better than me will die very soon.   Duff.

[The summer of 1914 marked the end of the golden age of the Coterie. As they took comfort in recalling it in the years to come, it seemed almost too good to be true, and never again would their life be so carefree, and so full of dear friends. Even so, it was not without tragedy. First came the death of Gustav Hamel, and then that of Denis Anson. There was a party on a pleasure boat on the Thames. Swimming was suggested – an idea that delighted Diana – and Denis was the first to dive in. He drowned in the treacherous currents, as did one of the bandsmen who leapt in to save him.

Shortly after the outbreak of war, Diana – whose mother had forbidden her to become a nurse at the front – became a voluntary nurse at Guy's Hospital. Although her life there is vividly described in her autobiography, it is barely mentioned in her letters to Duff – perhaps, she suggests, because she was talking to him of nothing else.

Duff was working hard too. For a while, he was doing an eight-hour shift in the cypher room before knocking off at four and beginning his normal day's work in the Commercial Department. Soon, however, he was transferred to the cypher room full time.

The war that was supposed to end by Christmas dragged on. When every month brought news of the death of another close friend, there seems to be barely time to mourn each individually, and numbness follows pain as the list gets longer.

First to go was Julian Grenfell, and then John Manners, Diana's remote cousin and Duff's childhood friend. Charles Lister and Billy Grenfell died in August 1915, and George Vernon in November. The following year took Letty's husband Ego Charteris, Basil Hallam, and – the greatest blow for Diana – Raymond Asquith. By 1917, with the death of Edward Horner and Patrick Shaw-Stewart, all their dearest companions were dead.

Morale had to be kept up, however, both at home and abroad. There was a continual stream of men coming back from the front on leave, and they had to be welcomed and fêted and given a good time. The weekend house parties and the London dinners and dances carried on; and the letters, at least for the first year or so, seem little affected by the war.]

Diana to Duff,   *Stanton Woodhouse, Rowsley*[1]
[?20] August 1914

Darling Duffety. I have had such acute pen-paralisise that – I am fearful of having lost you totaly.

It is with effort and suffering that I write now. It's all this war, I say – robbing me of all I love robbing you of all my care. I thank God for you perpetually – the only survivor (presumably) in this mamouth wreck. I admit I've grown pretty used to the war haven't you – insofar as reading letters before papers, taking care of ones body, squandering and pittering ones money – making continental plans etc. These died a Lazarus death for a few days, but custom has done a Christ – and brought them round in a jiffy.

O my sweet Duff I think I may be wandering – I would give so much to have you – it's for want of you that I seem to have lost my unequalled outlook and my commonest sense. You would restore it me, as your letters do for a spell. I adored the Maupassant more especially as it brought back the dear old fuddled chloroform days of Avon[2] – in fact Duff let there be no hesitation in your coming to me next Sunday – with a bottle concealed – and we'll do a little forgetting. Please come – perfect train 4 Saturday – perfect train 3 Monday or 10 p.m. Sunday. Imagine excess of hope – and it is half only of mine that you will gratify it.   Diana.

---

[1] A house near Haddon Hall that the Rutlands would take for the summer.
[2] Avon Tyrrell, the home of John, 3rd Baron Manners.

Duff to Diana, 21 August 1914

Sweet, painfully desired Diana. There is no hope. Sunday is exactly like any other day for me now, as I always when a child wished it could be. I work all through the Lord's long day, and it is but a pitiful consolation to be able to remind oneself that one is breaking a commandment. Fancy breaking the silly little fourth commandment when there are so many other really delicious ones to break. Upon my word I had rather make to myself any graven image, and ten thousand times rather devote the whole day to coveting my neighbour's ox. I don't know whether I shall ever get away from London, but in case I do in September warn me where you will then be. Or best of all come hastily to London – say you feel you must be where you can hear the latest news, and then we will go to the Hippodrome continually.   Duff.

Duff to Diana, October 1914   *Norton Priory,*[1] *Sussex*

My blessed, immaculate heart's blood, I have made you a beautiful passionate poem in the shape of an evening hymn, which please find enclosed. Parting with you yesterday morning was worse than having my heart torn steaming out of my chest, worse than the torments in the lowest circle of Dante's Inferno, worse even than getting up early in the morning.

Here I am surrounded by nearly the whole of my family – except, alas, Aunt Ida who never leaves London except for a fortnight in August when she goes to Tunbridge Wells. It is a very good thing to be with one's family occasionally – otherwise one is in danger of forgetting how much one hates them. Iris[2] also is here, and I make her sing to me all day of the unhappy fortunes of Marion Turner, who like Othello loved not wisely but too well.[3]

I really did enjoy Belvoir you know. That is the sort of party I like, and rather than disappoint His Grace I will really make an effort to let you see me again. You must I think have enjoyed it too,

---

[1] The country house of Duff's sister, Stephanie Levita.

[2] Iris Tree, 1897–1968 – poet, writer, romantic vagabond, and youngest daughter of Sir Herbert Beerbohm Tree.

[3] *Pity poor Marion Turner,*
Who ought to 'ave been Joe Bentley's wife –
First he got her into trouble,
Then he took away her life.

[16]

with your two stout lovers frowning at one another across the hearth rug, while your small, but perfectly formed one kept the party in a roar.

Into your hands I commend my spirit.   Duff.

> Mistress, who made of my proud heart
> One ruby for thy finger ring,
> Remember that to me thou art
> The only shrine for worshipping.
>
> So when my sad, forsaken soul
> Must pray or perish, then to thee
> I turn and try to show the whole
> Or half the hell that tortures me.
>
> Be gracious, Goddess, hear the prayers
> Which up to thee like incense rise,
> And granting one, repay the years
> Of my enormous sacrifice.
>
> White idol, though I cannot tell
> What sphere of all the spheres be thine,
> Yet be it heaven or be it hell,
> 'Tis some profounder world than mine.
>
> Oh favourably with mercy hear,
> Mysterious Goddess, visible,
> And graciously incline thine ear
> To thy converted infidel.

Diana to Duff, October 1914   *Belvoir Castle*

O my sweet Duff not any poetry of the most inspired has given me diviner emotions – and what I adore is the grand conceit it encouraged. No voracious, gloating Venetian mob bred so finished a 'strut' as I showed this morning. I read it first in my bath – and gave a jar of scent as incense to the reading of it – then it sent me straight back to bed where I shall stay till 7, feeling holier than holy and too severe for the eyes and rough hands of these – then I shall have another hotter and more suffocating bath and at once get into a purer and lovelier bed, and there stay till I dream involuntarily of luggage – and parents' nagging & two stout lovers, & the kitchen & taxis, & Belgian refugees, and wake forgetting your soul is on my finger, or the clay you have made me of, to face the same old humiliating struggle to tend & succour the sick.

More benefits you have bestowed – Congreve – a tasteful edition, and appreciated to the full – though not to be thanked for so rapturously as your letter. You will find me at Guy's Hospital, London Bridge from the end of next week onwards, and I shall be lonely and sick in the extreme. Two hours of your day I would like you to give – and all the letters you can write – it will take all your power to keep me proud. All my love – quickly write.   D.

Duff to Diana, 18 October 1914   *9 Berkeley House, Hay Hill*

Darling, My heart beats like a diseased one at the thought of seeing you tomorrow. Four o'clock, but where? Why not here as Lady Agnes[1] is from home? Anyhow please telephone and leave a message. I am shuddering with emotion at the thought of seeing you again.

'Gallop apace you fiery footed steeds',[2] I cry to the hands of my bedroom clock, forgetting for the moment that I never allow it to go in case its ticking should keep me awake.

When does the nurse's cap, so terribly like a nun's, come on and the tango curls fall off? And may I please be given one of the fallen curls – a wanton scented tress which I will treasure in a golden box.   Duff.

Duff to Diana, 3 November 1914   *Foreign Office*

My darling wonderful woman – How cavalierly one accepts the good things that the pitiless capricious fates do give one. This morning I am acutely, achingly conscious of the privilege that I have in knowing you, for in my sober moments, which are mercifully rare, I realize how truly you are the most remarkable woman of my generation. Sir Richard Steele said of the forgotten lady whom he loved at the beginning of the eighteenth century that 'to love her was a liberal education', which has always been quoted as the highest compliment paid to a woman and so it was

---

[1] Lady Agnes Cooper, 1846–1925, Duff's mother.
[2] *Romeo and Juliet*, Act II, scene i.

until I said, as now I do, that to love you is to love one's own age in its highest manifestation.

'*Enfant de mon siècle*' like Gautier, I have been more fortunate than him in finding the mate God meant for me. But God's schemes never quite come off and it seems highly improbable that I shall ever marry you, though two people so perfectly made to fit have never been turned out. But if you ever should happen to want a husband in a hurry – (and who hasn't occasionally?) be sure to ring me up. The devotion of a lifetime will always be waiting for you at 3446 Mayfair.

Diana to Duff   [*Written in bed with measles.*]
[*February 1915*]   *16 Arlington Street*

My lovely Duff, how sad I was from five onwards waiting – conscious that you would forget, and by forgetting miss the pains I took for you with my pierced body. A sad hour I gave to blinding myself with my beauty, knowing so surely I was acting for futility.

It is pleasant to think of the pure delight of two million germs lost in me – all treating this undefiled temple as an hotel, brothel, battleground, see-saws on my heart, 'I spy' among a hundred veins, or to whatever use their whims tempt them. Envy them Duffy. I envy them myself as Beardsley would say.

Dine tomorrow at Carlton with George,[1] and secure Pinafore Room[2] at Savoy.   D.

Duff to Diana [*February 1915*]   *9 Berkeley House*

Oh my measly love-bird, how you must weep to be the victim of so unaugust a malady. Don't think that I should be afraid to visit you, or that disease could ever turn me from you however loathsome it might be. In fact when I think of Saint Julian who lay with the leper, I am never able to help hoping that you may one day fall a prey to that distressing and – at one time, in the East, I am led to believe – almost universal complaint,[1] and that I shall then not

---

[1] George, 8th Baron Vernon, 1888–1915.
[2] The private dining rooms of the Savoy Hotel are named after Gilbert and Sullivan operas.

[1] A catchphrase originally taken from the testimonial included in every packet of *BROMO* loo paper, referring to the comfort it gave to sufferers from '. . . that distressing and almost universal complaint, THE PILES.'

miss my chance of emulating the Saint – and thus please God, myself and, dare I add, you, killing many glorious birds with one jolly little stone.

Oh the presumption of those halfwitted germs – it fairly staggers one. How dare they pasture in those luxuriant fields of firm white flesh that should have been all mine. Father, don't forgive them, for they know not what they do and that's what I hate about them.   Duff.

Duff to Diana [May 1915]   *9 Berkeley House*

Di. You have lain another victim prostrate. I am in bed with a feverish cold and exquisite earache. I adore being ill though I hate and fear pain, but what I say is – 'better even be in pain than not be ill at all'. They are giving me powders and medicine and pouring burning unguents into my ears so that I am as happy as King John.

Come, Sweet, and see me in the evening. Gloat over your handiwork. Taunt me with my disease and then my cup of happiness will be full.   Duff.

Diana to Duff [May 1915]   *16 Arlington Street*

Duff my rose, So the demon sepsis clutches your throat more cruelly and more poisonously than I ever might have. It's probably what at Guy's I used to call 'Dip' [diphtheria] in which case you should be inocculated at once and repeatedly. I had Raymond[1] to dinner last night – rather an amazing sight – a long course dinner on my bed, subdued lights, ballons and flowers emulating each other and a bottle of the boy.[2] Then as a climax my having to have half an hour's trunk-call with Her Grace – with Raymond on the bed – rocking at my moan of loneliness – it was quite 18th century enough. Today I am to go out – which seems disappointingly premature – but it saves anti-climax of gifts and mags, and enquiries.

Lady Agnes touched me to the quick last night with her "thought you'd like to know how poor Duffy is – he's very *bad*". Bless her for it.

[1] Raymond Asquith, 1878–1916.
[2] Champagne. Brandy was known as 'the old man'.

Sweet body, Your letter has just come, crossing mine. How divine your dinner sounds – But quite between ourselves wouldn't Duffy in his silk smoking suit have been rather in better taste than one of Kitchener's Khakis? And I should have so loved it. I havn't got Dip. because no temp. nor what my nurse calls 'scarlet' because no rash.

Later. Flowers just come from Her Grace. Thank her a thousand times. I needn't write to her, need I? Also a message to say that L.D.M. [Lady Diana Manners] is glad I am better. I'm *not* better. My temperature has gone up again my throat is agony I wish I was dead. The irony of us both being in bed and not being in bed together is more than I can bear. You are happier than I because you have the telephone, and you don't suffer hell every time you swallow – and I've always been so fond of swallowing. Pity me darling, and write to me – and when we are both better let us go away to recoup together at Margate or Brighton. What's your temperature? Mine's 100. Do write to me every 4 hours because I have my medicine every four hours.

Marjorie T.[1] has a sore throat too and so has Hazel,[2] but I mustn't boast.   Duff.

Diana to Duff   *16 Arlington Street*

My darling, I have now reached my zero. I could not get up early as she told me to rest and I could think of no excuse, and to crown these thorns with thorns, there the Duchess lies – prostrate with a head-ache – as atonement for having indulged in a little cocoa last night. We might have wandered on foot to Brighton without her noticing it, we might have sat long and securely in 88,[3] or have said 'Yak' to beasts at the Zoo, or broken the back of a nice book, or the back of a nice bottle. We *might* have done these things, and we *should* certainly have discovered some new and rare device of pleasure.

---

[1] Marjorie Trefusis. Born Marjorie Graham, she married Capt. the Hon. Walter Alexander Trefusis, 4th son of the 20th Baron Clinton, in 1911. They were divorced in 1919.

[2] Hazel Lavery, wife of Sir John Lavery, 1856–1941, the painter. She was the model for the Irish colleen, with harp and shawl, on the Irish pound note.

[3] 88 St. James's Street, Duff's flat.

All day I have sorted letters, sent a batch of yours to the Type –
and moped, & yearned, & thought sometimes that my wish would
be enough – so big was it, to draw you back.

O my dove, how vile it is when you leave me –   D.

Enclosed find £7.0.0.

Duff to Diana   *Foreign Office*

Darling. Save me from playing Bridge with Ruby[1] this afternoon.
Take me to a Cinema – Be kind to me. I was not ever thus nor
prayed that thou, shouldst take me to a cinema. I loved the garish
Bridge etc. but now, take thou me to a cinema.[2] I am so busy or I
would write to you for ever and ever and ever,   Duff.

Duff to Diana   *Stanway, Winchcombe*[3]

Darling. I left you last night with the mark of your fingers on my
face,[4] which I need hardly say I adored, and tingled deliciously for
hours. I cannot remember what lovely provocation I gave you for
so dear a blow but I hope it was passion not anger that moved your
hand. Bless you my sweet and bless your strong cruel hand.
Duff.

[After a dinner party in Brighton one Sunday, Diana
and Duff decided to go for a walk along the moonlit beach.
They both stumbled and fell down a rickety wooden
staircase on their way there, and Diana broke her leg. She
was able to diagnose it as a Pott's fracture, and pulled the

[1] Ruby Peto.
[2] 'I was not ever thus, nor prayed that thou
       Shouldst lead me on;
   I loved to choose and see my path; but now
       Lead thou me on.
   I loved the garish day, and, spite of fears
       Pride ruled my will: remember not past years.'
   – the second verse of *Lead Kindly Light*, by Cardinal J. H. Newman.
[3] The seat of the Earl of Wemyss.
[4] The incident took place at a rowdy party at the Cavendish Hotel. Diana, enraged by
Duff having said something insulting, slapped him hard enough to make his lip bleed. He
gave her 'the gentlest tap on the cheek', and she stormed out of the hotel.

wool over Her Grace's suspicious eyes by saying that she had tripped while getting out of the car.]

Duff to Diana, 6 July 1915   *Norton Priory*

Darling I can hardly believe that both your leg bones are broken. Look again, there must be some mistake. Also it sounds highly improbable that Arbuthnot Lane[1] should have been selected to operate. Remember I know something about the medical profession and I have always understood, as I have just telegraphed to you, that his speciality was not legs.[2] In fact I had heard that he was one of those ambitious people who look higher. I can only hope that he will keep his ambition under control during the course of the operation.

But, bar chaff, as Lady Lytton[3] would say, I do wish you could see the bruise on my knee, which was caused by our fall. It hadn't developed properly on Sunday but today it is marvellous – *yellow and black and pale and hectic red*[4] – at once sumptuous and august. In fact it reminds one of all the greatest writers in their greatest moments. No, it's not very painful, thank you, but rather stiff.

    Best love
        Duff.

Diana to Duff, July 1915   *Nursing-home in Manchester Street*

Angel Duff, I'm worth seeing – not me, my surroundings – 12 lots of floral tributes, (not including of course violets, lilies of the valley or anything wild). Some are shaped like harps with broken strings, there are anchors and dreadnoughts, and a not very seductive water-cress pillow with RIP on it. But I can't see any of them – neither can I see what I am writing, nor yet the grammer 'cos of 3 scents, 1 fruit, 2 chocolate boxes, 2 books. I stroke them all day.

[1] Sir William Arbuthnot Lane, 1856–1943, Senior Surgeon at Guy's Hospital.
[2] He specialized in diseases of the intestines. However, he did bring out a book in 1915 called *The Operation and Treatment of Fractures*.
[3] Pamela, wife of Victor, 2nd Earl of Lytton.
[4] Shelley, *Ode to the West Wind*.

[23]

My little silver fish with broken fins, my wine, my perfect Pommery, my pure pale Perrier Jouet, my snowy coon, my pampas grass, my bed of asphodel, my crazy little outrigger, my submarine, my dangerous marsh mallow, my button on the coloured cap of life, my duck, how are you.

Last night we dined with Montagu[1] and were once more faced with those little gobbets of lost moist lamb on tepid plates and Bongy[2] bald and unashamed. I drank like some great stag that comes down to a pool in the evening after having been hunted all day long. My face grew fiery red like the sun sinking in a fog, and then after more brandy it grew white and distorted and terrible like a waning moon looked at through twisted glass.

Her Grace says no visitors for seven days, but I know that she lies in her teeth, as sure as Iris lies with a Jew, and as I, alas, alas, lie alone.   Duff.

My darling heart, though you may doubt it I adored seeing you this evening, for I have now reached the stage when Grace or no Grace I am happy to be with you.

This is the third time that I have fallen into love with you. Oh see to it, my lily, that I do not fall out.

I wish I was more beautiful so as to be worthier of you. I should like to marry you and then go round the world to look for lovers lovely enough to deserve you. I should like to find a nearly perfect one, and bring him back and wash him and prepare him and tell him all about Aristotle and Alexandria and coach him in every engaging artifice of love, and then I would serve him up to you – a morsel for a goddess – and you would kill him in a fortnight and love me better than you did before.   Duff.

I shall wait longingly for you to telephone tomorrow.

---

[1] The Rt. Hon. Edwin Montagu, 1879–1924. The son of Lord Swaythling, a prominent Jewish banker, he pursued a successful career in politics that culminated in his appointment as Secretary of State for India, 1917–22. On July 26th 1915 he married Venetia Stanley, daughter of the 4th Baron Sheffield.

[2] Sir Maurice Bonham Carter, 1880–1960. From 1910–1916 he was H. H. Asquith's Personal Private Secretary, and served in the Air Ministry and the Reconstruction Ministry during the later years of the Great War. He married Violet Asquith (the Prime Minister's daughter) in 1915.

Duff to Diana, 22 September 1915 Stafford Hotel, St. James's Place

Darling – I never wrote to you yesterday. I wonder if you noticed. It was done – or rather left undone – partly as a stunt, partly to test my own self restraint, partly to test your love and partly because I couldn't for the life of me think of a damned thing to say. I let myself in last night for one of the most boring evenings of my life – Just look at my dinner table: Mrs. Duggan,[1] the Duke of Rutland, Maud Cunard, Me, Lady Randolph,[2] Lord Curzon,[3] Her Grace, and an Old Spaniard.

The total ages of the party exactly equal the most optimistic calculations of the German casualties on both fronts.

Duff to Diana, St. Crispin's Day, 1915[4]   *88 St. James's Street*

Darling, I am writing this in bed because the fire has gone out in my sitting room and although I would gladly die for you, I am sure you wouldn't wish me to catch cold.

I have never adored you so passionately as I did last night and never liked you so tremendously and been more happy in your company than I was this afternoon.

If only, my darling, you wouldn't pretend to disbelieve in my love for you, I would sit much more still of an afternoon, for talking to you I am far, far happier than talking to any one else in the world.

It is your tantalizing doubt that drives me to spasmodic and, as you find, boring demonstration. And really I don't see why you should aspire to out-Thom St. Thomas at his own particular stunt: I cannot alas allow you to thrust your hands into the wounds being, at time of writing, I thank God practically unpunctured, whereas if my hands show ever the slightest tendency to thrust, you are always down on them like a ton of bricks.

O my rose, my lily, my ripe nectarine, with the prayer on my lips that I may dream luridly of you, I say good-night.   Duff.

---

[1] Mrs. Alfred Duggan, a rich Argentinian widow who was to marry Lord Curzon in 1917 as his 2nd wife. She died in 1958.

[2] Lady Randolph Churchill, born Jennie Jerome, mother of Winston Churchill. She died in 1921.

[3] George Nathaniel, 1st Earl Curzon of Kedleston, 1859–1925. Later 1st Marquess (1921). Viceroy of India 1899–1905. Foreign Secretary 1919–24.

[4] 25 October 1915 marked the 500th anniversary of the Battle of Agincourt.

Take trouble about seeing me tomorrow, you haven't taken much today. And yet why should you? Why indeed. But it is long since we went to a cinema.

Diana to Duff [20] November 1915   *16 Arlington Street*

My darling – It's eleven and for two hours I can't stop crying – if only you were by me I would. O Christ the misery and the morphia not working.

O Duff save yourself – if you die, where shall I be – my *poor* George.[1] If only I could stop.

Duff to Diana, 21 November 1915   *88 St. James's Street*

Darling. I hope the morphia worked at last and that you slept and feel better this morning. How I wish that I were with you always to hold and comfort you. I cannot bear you to be unhappy.   Duff.

Duff to Diana, 29 January 1916   *Foreign Office*

Darling – on leaving you this afternoon I learnt from Wilkins[2] that Mr Horner was as he rather coarsely put it 'in the lavatory' so I quickly scuttled out of the house, bolted round the corner and precipitated myself bang into the capacious navel of His Grace who happened at that moment to be returning from lunch. A few moments amicable conversation regarding your health and that of the state and I passed on, speculating on his approaching interview with Edward, whom I calculated that His Grace would probably intercept half way between the lavatory and the bedroom of his youngest daughter: I enclose a telegram from Patsy[3] who you see is more imminent every moment. Telephone in the morning as to when I shall present myself. I adore you but I shall certainly be late for dinner.   D.

---

[1] George Vernon. Died of typhoid in Malta while on active service, November 10th. He sent Diana a dictated letter as he was dying. As he tries to sign his name, the pen trails off the end of the page.
[2] The butler at Arlington Street.
[3] Patrick Shaw Stewart, 1888–1917.

Duff to Diana, 20 March 1916

My Darling, My friend failed me at the last moment, telephoning from Tunbridge Wells about a missed train, so I dined, thank God, alone and was thus able to think about you with more concentration all the evening through.

There was nothing so remarkable about my dinner as to distract my thoughts from their absorbing subject. My soup, which was new to me, was made out of a sturgeon's fins but tasted like inferior turtle; a slice of salmon was followed by a Bordeaux pigeon whose slim, not to say emaciated, figure, was to me a subject both of envy and regret. Hardly had I decided to emulate by every possible means that swiftly swallowed bird, when a perfectly mature Gorgonzola made me forget my vows of perpetual attenuation, and encouraged me to drink two glasses of port in order that a bottle of claret, which had already insinuated itself into the sweet dim recesses of my body might not remain there without company.

Since then – for I keep nothing from you – I have drunk coffee and read Swift who was a very witty, clever chap but not good natured and happy hearted like you and me. A book of prose underneath a roof, a nice cold partridge, a bottle of Perrier Jouet (1907) and you, sitting very close beside me and doing anything in the world except singing, and I should ask, very politely, to be excused going to Paradise for the present. How strange it is that one is balked of Paradise at every turn by things going not quite right. Here am I under a roof, surrounded by books of prose, with Perrier Jouet (1907) within reach, but alas, you are dining out and alas, alas it is the close season for partridges. Thank God at least that my father devoted a small portion of an uncertain income, derived from curing people of unmentionable complaints, to the high object of having me taught to write, for how otherwise, in the name of heaven, should I spend the miserable hours that I pass out of your company?   Duff.

---

[1] cf. The twelfth quotation of the *Rubaiyat* of Omar Khayyam, translated by Edward Fitzgerald.

Duff to Diana, 6 April 1916 88 *St. James's Street*

Oh my one love, I have just had your letter and my heart is beating so fast that my hand shakes. I knew that you had tried to telephone last night because the exchange rang me up and when I answered said "They don't want you now", but I knew better, or thought I did and went to sleep happily, loving and blessing you.

You must not cry. It is our creed not to. We have lived so long with tragedy that we are only less bored with its purple than we are with its khaki. Let's have light comedy and loud laughter for the love of God. And if you must not cry for the failure of the world, which has let us down so damnably, much less must you cry for yourself who have remained so sweet and sane and beautiful and have been so adored by the living and the dead. 'Love like a lamp sways over all your days, and all your life is like a lamp-lit chamber.'[1] More than half your youth is waiting and it shall be more wonderful even than your 'salad days, when you were green in judgment'.[2] Oh yes, my sweetheart, we will have great fun when the world is good again and the fools stop fighting. More laughter is waiting for you and more lovers besides all the love of my life for ever and ever –   Duff.

Duff to Diana, 20 May 1916 88 *St. James's Street*

Darling, I have just come back from the station and am sobbing so frightfully that all the passers by are staring up at my window and Holbrook[3] is quite ashamed of me. Between sobs I am eating your nectarines, which I hate bitterly because they made me miss you – oh my love – this extra little disappointment has simply put the button on my misery's cap – Oh hell oh death I think I shall die of sorrow, and I'm sure to be sick if I eat any more nectarines but they *won't* keep till Monday damn them – what am I to do with them? If you were here you would tell me – You don't know how I longed to see you. Why did you say be there at half past nine? – I was there at half past nine and saw nothing but Wolkoff.[4] Holbrook is sending you the Brands Essence by post – it looks so nasty. I will write again when I am calmer.   Duff.

[1] Lord Alfred Douglas, *To Olive*, where 'your' is 'his'.

[2] *Antony and Cleopatra*, Act I scene v.

[3] Holbrook – Duff's manservant, promoted to butler when Duff got married. His service was characterised by a certain lugubrious efficiency.

[4] Count Gabriel Wolkoff, a friend of the Rutlands who was attached to the Russian Embassy.

[On July 1st came the news that Ego Charteris, Lord Elcho, had been killed in the Sinai. There had been many rumours, some hopeful, some less so – but now it was final. For his widow, Diana's sister Letty, it put an end to two agonizing months of uncertainty.]

Duff to Diana, 2 July 1916   *88 St. James's Street*

My darling love, Your little face was thin and sad tonight and I wished so to be alone with you and tell you how I loved you and how you must always think of me, when you are too unhappy, not as a passionate impatient lover but as a lovely velvet cloak to wrap you round and keep you close and safe and warm, away from the world's disasters. But I must not continue in this vein or you will laugh at me. Telephone on receipt of this. Oh how I love you.   Duff.

Duff to Diana, 3 July 1916   *88 St. James's Street*

My own darling – I am so sorry. Oh the cruelty of life. Your anniversary of disaster[1] comes true again. I am almost crying at the thought of you and poor darling Letty. I wrote to her this afternoon and told her to hope; now I have nothing to tell her except to give her my love and sympathy which are so useless. You know how little I shall enjoy my evening without you. Oh dear how miserable we shall all be.   Duff.

[For Diana, however, worse was to come.]

Diana to Duff, [?18] September 1916   *16 Arlington Street*

My darling Duff. I am glad you have got there & half hoped you would before you heard of Raymond's death – and perhaps get a week of careless holiday – but when you were stranded in Scotland I felt I must tell you before *The Times* did. O my sweet Duff I have tried so hard to sink all my misery and think only of holding Katharine up – but I can't do it. I went to her at Mells yesterday and did my best, but now I am back, and the wheel that has been revolving so fast in my brain that its outline was not visible – is slowing down for the slow consciousness to be felt.

---

[1] The anniversary of the death of Denis Anson, who drowned on this day in 1914.

[29]

I would really as soon be dead – 'Raymond killed – my divine *Raymond* – killed' has sung in my head for twenty-four hours – and tonight it's all coloured and true. Poor K. is like a dead thing only sensitive to torture – and what argument have I to put against her killing herself – when I hate to see her alive to such pain. She cannot possibly get right – her hold of energy was at best, and with all Raymond's stimulus, so slender. He taught her I think, how to *breathe* – she ought to give it up. Parents only impede their children – that's proved. She moans that she will deteriorate, and turn into a woman that Raymond meeting would not care to know – and then repeatedly "I shall become a *duty* to you –" so Duff darling – we shall both have a life's work in cherishing her.

I don't think you know how I adored Raymond – certainly he didn't – more perhaps than you – so had you not known him his loss might have been your gain – but knowing him there is no gain in possessing the world if he is not in it.

I have longed for you so much. Alan[1] has been good – he came with me in the train – but O I'm weary of the ships. The Hospital, I suppose, is a help – quite full, and 2 operations today – one by Lane – tell Vinny.[2] Give them both my dear love and tell V. that I think of how sad she will be – I that love her. As to you my Duff you know that whatever you feel I feel it for you – and love you always.   Diana.

Duff to Diana,   *Newton Lodge, Loch Maddy, The Hebrides*
[?20] September 1916

My darling, I have so much to say to you and the post goes today and I have to go out shooting in a few minutes. I havn't had a minute to write since last I wrote but I have been thinking of you a great deal and wondering how you were and longing to be with you. I thought we had insured against Raymond's death by always expecting it. Now it seems too bad to be true, too tragic, like the end of *King Lear*. If I could believe in God I should really think he had a grudge against us and meant to break up the Coterie – the old scoundrel – but he shan't. Darling darling I love you – they drag me away.   Duff.

[1] Alan Parsons, 1887–1933. He began his career in the Civil Service, and was Private Secretary to Edwin Montagu when the latter was Secretary of State for India. From 1925 to 1929 he was dramatic critic and gossip columnist for the *Daily Sketch*, and he worked on the *Daily Mail* from 1929–1933. He married Viola Tree in 1912.

[2] Venetia Montagu.

Diana to Duff, November 1916   *16 Arlington Street*

Duff dear. I cannot bear it at all. You will no longer help me with my moods – or be patient with my tired ways – you will not even let me lie quietly – without raging at the little I sometimes needs must deny you.

There is so rarely a night spent together that we do not make hideous with our complaints of one another. Tonight was a climax – and though I kept calm long enough to remind you not to rate me, it did not check your ill-temper but augmented it, and you ridiculed me till my heart shrank from myself – and then you stopped it beating by trying to step out of a fast taxi – and then you ground it to atoms by telling me I caused you all possible pain. So we will rest from each other for a little – and if possible return together restored to peacefulness.   Diana.

Duff to Diana, 16 November 1916   *88 St. James's Street*

Darling – Are you really not forgiving me? Are you teaching me a lesson? Oh, sweetheart I have learnt it – I learn so quickly. I wonder what you did this evening and how you spent today. I cannot bear not knowing where you are always and what you are doing.

It is just twelve o'clock and I am terribly tempted by the telephone at my elbow, but I have sworn to myself that I will not try to get forgiveness that way because it would be unbecoming, and also I am rather afraid it might only irritate you more. Yet I am tempted more than St. Anthony – What a subject for a picture or a poem – 'St. Anthony tempted by a telephone'. Edwin said the other day he wondered why 'rich' people didn't give themselves the pleasure of suddenly giving a poor friend £10,000. That is the kind of pleasure you could give tomorrow by suddenly forgiving me and letting me lunch with you. You probably won't, just as the rich never give people £10,000 and just as Edwin never gives one £10.   Duff.

["I continue to bombard Diana with letters," wrote Duff in his diary that day, "but I think she may keep this up till Sunday." He does not sound too worried, and sure enough she telephoned him on Sunday. They enjoyed the pleasure of reconciliation over lunch.

A separation longer than a few days was coming. The press had recently launched a vociferous campaign, criticising the civil service for holding on to men of military age when they were so desperately needed at the front. The young men in question were accused of cowardice, and the fact that they were obeying orders was no excuse. Duff was not much affected by these attacks since he was ready and willing to go to war, and the only cowardice he could accuse himself of was not being able to face telling his mother the news.

He was released from the Foreign Office in mid-June 1917, and joined the Officers' Cadet Battalion of the Grenadier Guards in early July. The training camp was at Bushey Hall in Hertfordshire, comfortably close to London, and Duff was rather looking forward to his summer. However, a rude awakening was in store. He had expected the long hours of rigorous physical training, but not the lack of comfort, civilization, and people of his own class. It was the first time he had been without these things, and he didn't like it.]

Duff to Diana, 5 or 6 July 1917   [*Bushey, Hertfordshire*]

My darling – I loved your telegram this morning and required its exhortation. I shall not see you for a long time. My proper uniform has to be made. The one I wear now is more shameful than a convict's. I sleep in a room with seven others, all of whom save one have risen from the ranks. They sleep at night in the shirts they wear by day. My bed, which I make myself, consists of a mattress in three parts and four blankets for whose rough male kiss I don't share Rupert Brooke's enthusiasm.[1] Either his blankets must have been softer, or the chins of his gentlemen friends less carefully shaved than mine. I have to walk half a mile through stone passages to a public washing place. I have with some difficulty found a man whom I bribe to black my boots and brighten my

---

[1] From *The Great Lover*, by Rupert Brooke, 1887–1915.
'These I have loved . . .
the cool kindliness of sheets, that soon
Sooth away trouble; and the rough male kiss
Of blankets.'

buttons. The food I will not attempt to describe. I shall grow nice and thin – at least not nice, but coarse and red and horrible. All this however I mind not at all compared with the separation from you. Just when I am bearing up and facing the discomfort, the thought returns that three summer months with you are being lost, and that I cannot bear at all and nearly sob to think of it – Oh darling. My only hope of the future is to get through this in three months instead of four and that will be difficult. It depends, I believe, on a man called Ebenezer Pike.[1]

If you see Scatters[2] ask him to tell his servant to send me my tennis racket, which he is reported by the Asquith servants to have brought from the Wharf. If he hasn't got it perhaps you would send me a new one – Good bye my angel – D.

Diana to Duff, 7 July 1917   *16 Arlington Street*

Darling Duff – Your letter has depressed me terribly – I picture your cross face and misfitting clothes, and enforced loss of self-respect, then fears surge, that you will take neither trouble or interest in it all or the others, therefore they will not adore you – and you will think this doesn't matter – it being temporary, and of course it does matter at last. To be thought and be keen, non grumbling and generally jolly by all is of vastest importance – as Raymond full well knew, and so got a throne in the Guards.

It was a nice morning. I was dusting in the ward[3] and on hearing the usual practise guns, looked out to see the blue radiance of a streakless sky, stained by 20 silver aeroplanes unscathed by torrents of anti-air craft shells. A scene of slight disorder followed – Mother screaming in the basement, surrounded by servants I had never seen – things from under sinks & stones that had never got above the courtyard, with light blind eyes, by Davis[4] demoralised – screaming "It's scandalous. Why

---

[1] Major Ebenezer Pike, M.C. 1884–1965. Became Commanding Officer of the First Battalion Grenadier Guards 1927–29. In 1917 he was correcting the examination papers of the cadets at Bushey. He was the father of the present Viscountess Esher.

[2] Lt. Col. Sir Matthew Wilson, 4th Baronet 1875–1958. Known as Scatters. He retired in 1912, but returned to fight in Egypt and win the D.S.O. Unionist M.P. for Bethnal Green, 1914–22.

[3] The Duchess had never liked the idea of Diana being at Guy's, and in 1916 she converted the Arlington Street house into the Rutland Hospital for Officers. Here Diana worked from late 1916 to May 1918.

[4] Marjorie's maid.

do they let them get right over the house" – and by Mr Conner of Gosford – (don't ask me why) lending tone but no calm or reassurance to the crazy group. Upstairs the wards were little better. Old fractured-thigh men – hitherto utterly helpless, I found scrambling back to bed from off the balcony. I believe the nearest bomb was Long Acre – but as usual, every soul says they were over them and their houses. I rang Leigh[1] up – "Mrs. Montagu I got right down to the cellar at once, Milady – they were dropping all round us, you see". Letty's maid – "Forty or fifty machines have just passed over the house". Charlie[2] (in Kensington) – "My dear, the whole fleet came *very* low, right over 97 Cadogan Gardens". I'm very tired. I'll write of this place tomorrow – it won't be much fun. I told Scatters to send your racket at once. Love me.   D.

Diana to Duff, 8 July 1917   *Rowsley*[3]

My darling. I have been through a lot in this place. It was here that I have seen twelve hot years fade into cold winters, here been infected almost to suicide by Marjorie's virgin melancholly – here was born and here died that regretable friendship with Ruby – (this style is getting like A. Lincoln's) one would think with such records the place would hold no ghost of sentiment – and yet the twenty days of heat, and baking, & Grenfells & Ego – blot out all the years of horror. The place is crowded too with objects of my own – that I loved before I became anti-possession, and though I have no courage or even great desire to retrieve them, it enrages me to see them put to mean uses.

I had a low dark room which I equipped, in years, with necromancer's and alchemist's properties. Curious bottles, coloured and crusted with irridescent sediments from elixial experiments, that now are scoured and used for tooth-water. Delicate gold scales that were hung for allegory above my mirror – now have to work and determine whether fish weigh more or less than a mean lb., a painted ivory ship is only produced should the baby

[1] The Montagus' butler.
[2] Charles Lindsay, 1862–1925, eldest son of Colonel Charles Hugh Lindsay, and brother of the Duchess of Rutland.
[3] See p. 15.

whine,[1] and George Meredith's palsied head is made a nursery picture. Its all made me very sad – but I am thankful that you were never here – to make it more poignant.

This morning as it happens all sorrows were forgotten in the ecstatic cruelty of draining the water out of a pond, and scampering about in black slush catching the fainting trout – hundreds of them – and putting them six at a time into very small buckets, and thence into a well in the garden For them it was the end of the world. Ours may end like that, for the wantoness of a so-called God – however it was very enjoyable, and the little frail and feminine Lady Granby saw red without even the qualm of conscience I felt. There was a discussion at dinner about you. I gave them a slight picture of your day (throwing a faint red) at which mother spat out "Do him a lot of good to rough it a bit", upon which John and Charlie let fly at her – no need for me to utter. "He doesn't want any good doing – only make him brown – he can beat the world at tennis, billiards –" etc etc. I don't know how many points they did not attack her with, plus all our own favourites.   Diana.

Duff to Diana, 10 July 1917   *Bushey, Hertfordshire*

My darling – after writing to you yesterday I was led away to be inoculated, from which I have suffered no ill effects but am excused some of the more violent duties of this place for today and tomorrow.

This morning I suddenly found myself to my confusion being familiarly addressed by an Officer who on closer inspection proved to be Basil Hambro. I have of course to stand to attention when speaking to him and call him 'sir'. He was very kind.

Your letters are a continual joy to me – I read them many times, but I don't want what is a joy to me to become a burden to you. Never, darling, write unless you feel inclined to or reproach yourself for long silences. I know how hard it is to write in London. Here it is so easy but there is nothing to say.

---

[1] Diana's brother John, Marquess of Granby and later 9th Duke of Rutland, 1886 –1940, had married Kathleen Tennant (Kakoo) in 1916. They were living at Rowsley at the time with their firstborn, Ursula. Although Diana was sad at the changes in Rowsley, it was John – when he became Duke – who lovingly restored Haddon Hall, that had lain empty and abandoned for over two hundred years.

Darling, I had hardly written the last sentence when they brought me, as though in answer to it, yet another letter from you – written from Rowsley but posted from London at 2.a.m. this morning so I conclude that you are back. It made me cry to hear that John & Charlie had spoken for me – God bless their hearts, and give them long lives and plenty of port. I've no doubt the view that roughing it will do me good is widely held. I don't share it. The only way in which roughing it can do anyone good is by making them more appreciative than they were of luxury. But that it is impossible for me to be. I have drunk champagne pretty regularly during the last four years, but every evening I have looked forward to it with keener anticipation, for the same period I have worn a lot of clean linen and slept in the same, but my taste for it which was originally somewhat stronger than Doctor Johnson's has only increased with years. When I return to these things I will, if only to please Her Grace and vindicate her opinion, try to drink a little more champagne and be a little longer in bed but I cannot promise her to enjoy either more after the first week than I did before. Bless you darling – You are my Holy Ghost, my comforter.   Duff.

Duff to Diana, [*undated*]   *Bushey Hall Golf Club*

My dear sweet love – It has rained ever since I left you which is beginning to depress me. My heart is heavier than air which it should never be and my brain is like a lump of cold, damp suet with no raisins in it and no jam. Therefore forgive me if I do not try to tell you how beautiful you are and how I love you. It is terrible to have a lover who neither writes you poems nor sends you pearls. I wish I were a poet, but oh how much more deeply do I wish that I were rich to command pearls and the world were at peace.

Oh the rain, the rain – I wish there were less water and more wine.   Duff.

Diana to Duff, 11 September 1917   *Vice Regal Lodge, Dublin*

Too tired to read this thro' probably its ghastly

My sweet. A wearier journey I never remember taking. A little modified in horror by my perfect new clothes and an oily sea but interminable and the prospect of arrival offering no relief. Yet once there, a line of Wicklow Mountains – a charred house the rebels had been burnt out of – rows and squares of gentleman's houses of the best epoch – and best of all, a slap up bouquet and perfect letter from the Vice-Roy[1] – encouraged me a lot. I went straight up to dinner at the Vice-regal in grandest *tenue* and alone. Perfect I thought it – don't believe a word against it. Forty people to dinner – many Convention[2] men. Labour ones and Peers, red ties and diamond stars. The Laverys – McEvoy[3] – Leonie Leslie[4] – A.E.[5] in fact a court as one would choose one.

Her. Ex,[6] ugly, but clothed and weighed down with jewels to improve. He vulgar but very graceful. Vulgar from being unlike *the* King, but not unlike a king. The table and its pleasures was a treat, all gold and wine and choicest fruits – one conventioner had never tasted a peach before. The footmen too, such beauties – battling with their silver cords, blinded by their powder. "Gentlemen, the King" was nice and the curtsey in the wide vistaed door a positive *volupté*. After dinner talking to the conventioners was the order. Many of them blindish, and quite unintelligible smoking great gift-cigars, and one played up and referred to someone, Ld. Oranmore[7] in fact, who was looking prosperous and well-being, as, "Sure he's as stout as the lamb of God".

Think of me at all times, my dear one.   Diana.

Duff to Diana, 16 September 1917   *Cassiobury, Watford*[8]

Darling, you are naughty never to tell me your address in Ireland. I like my letters to arrive fresh the next morning like eggs and butter, and not go stale and positively stink before they reach you. Tell me too your plans. I don't feel comfortable unless I know exactly where you are always and what you are going to do next.

[1] Ivor Guest, 1st Viscount Wimborne, 1873–1939 – see introduction, p. xvi.
[2] In July, Bonar Law assembled "A Convention of Irishmen of all parties, for the purpose of producing a scheme of Irish self-government."
[3] Sir John Lavery and Ambrose McEvoy (1878–1927), both fashionable portrait painters who had painted Diana several times.
[4] Lady Leslie, 1853–1943. The sister of Lady Randolph Churchill.
[5] The Irish poet G. W. Russell, 1867–1935.
[6] Born the Hon. Alice Grosvenor, daughter of 2nd Baron Ebury, she married Ivor Wimborne in 1902. She was known as Queen Alice in her vice-regal days.
[7] Geoffrey Browne, 3rd Baron Oranmore and Browne, 1861–1927, and a representative peer for Ireland. Member of the Irish Convention 1917–18.
[8] House of the 7th Earl of Essex.

Diana to Duff, 17 September 1917   *Vice Regal Lodge, Dublin*

My darling. A divine letter from you this morning, much needed for your sake – one of your happiest I thought, although less of the song of praise than the one before – I adored it too. I came here yesterday – and was ushered straight into Ivor's study. He was in a state of extreme nervousness, all dithery, and tossing down endless Vermouths – babbling of how this visit was a dawn, and going to be so strategically carried out that it would form a basis, (supported apparently by Her Grace, and Her Ex *couchant*[1]) of an easy and unsuspected relationship. I argued that to start off with a closeted *tête-à-tête* was ill advised.

Then after the dinner's pomp and Lord Oranmore, my regular neighbour for rank's sake, a long jaw with His Ex. writing petitions to be allowed to as he put it 'come and say goodnight' after the others were asleep. Imagine the madness – with the court's eyes skinned – so having at last wrenched a promise of continence out of him, I went confidently to bed and sleep, only to be rudely awakened by the noise of him fumbling with my furniture. He went after a moderate tussle and threats of my leaving the Vice Regal at dawn.

Diana to Duff, 27 September 1917   *[Written on the train returning from Chirk Castle, Wrexham]*

My darling. Such fun – how I have ached for you. First Hugo[2] left – leaving tears in our eyes – for he was the vitality of us all. Then Margot[3] asked a wretched woman called Lovat down, rather lovely of the Levine continental type with a perfect figure – a man's woman essentially. I took an unreasonable dislike to her, on that score I suppose, and gloated on her bad skin – but Christ what clothes – white cloth swathed and gleaming to travel in, and at dinner a miracle – she got off with both her men at dinner. Just as we were going in to the drawing room – Viola [Parsons] said to me, "*Credo che e Hugo vestito da donna*". I looked and banished the thought – for her neck had such a curve of elegance, while Hugo's has thickened with long wearing the Baroness's yoke – but in

[1] *Couchant* as opposed to *rampant*, presumably meaning that both Lady Wimborne *and* Diana's mother would be acquiescent.
[2] Hugo Rumbold, 1884–1932, stage designer.
[3] Margot Howard de Walden, born Margherita Van Raalte. She married the 8th Baron Howard de Walden in 1912.

another minute there was a shout of laughter, and everyone screaming out their suspicions, and evidences and congratulations to Hugo who had stammered for the first time, & confirmed the wild guess. O Duffy he was wonderful and so lovely – Viola had a love *crise* for him – kissing him, and really worshipping – I can see it might become a lovely vice, – this normality with Sappho's lyre in his hands – and no ambidextrous mistress might find pleasure till her lover almost deceived her eyes – when he, Hugo did it with his woman across Europe at 21[1], he must have been divine & no mistake – now of course he is a bit old, and I could see, poor love, that he was perpetually looking in the glass & sighing for his faded looks. He undressed later and was found to be wearing chiffon chemise and satin stays. Last night more dressing up – Margot as Hugo – not bad in uniform, Viola as the artist Steer – an amazement, with paunch & subtle make up – & Hugo coming in at 9.30, utterly unrecognisable as a blind buffed [drunk] waiter offering one meat again after the sweet – hiccuping – amazingly witty, but revolting too.

This morning I left and arrived at the hospital to find not a sheet of glass left in any window – and a crata the size of half a tenis court ten yards away in the park. Another bomb fell in Piccadilly – its Hell. Yours, my darling,   Diana.

Duff to Diana, 30 September 1917   *Bushey Hall Golf Club*

Darling – I loved your account of Chirk, the quarrels and the delicious Maupin[2] incident. I cannot bear to have missed anything so epoch making. The last period of a captivity is traditionally the most intolerable – and so I am finding mine. Yesterday so bored was I that I took a taxi and a companion to St. Albans to look at the dullest cathedral in England, and to have tea in a new hotel. This afternoon I have followed the sun about in a chair on the lawn and nearly finished *The Soul of a Bishop* at a sitting. If only

[1] Hugo was well known for the fact that he loved to dress up as a woman, and was very good at it. The story was that Baron Emile d'Erlanger sent his wife Catherine abroad when he discovered that she and Hugo were having an affair. Her maid, who had been their go-between, was sacked, and the Baron decided he would choose his wife's next maid himself. He chose a woman he thought very suitable who was in fact Hugo in disguise, and he and the Baroness travelled triumphantly round Europe together.
[2] *Mademoiselle de Maupin*, 1835, a novel by Théophile Gautier. Dressed up as a young squire, Mlle de Maupin wins the hearts of a poet called d'Albert and his mistress, Rosette.

Wells could keep his hands off God and politics and the other things which he thinks matter, what a pure source of delight he might become. This book is to my mind half nonsense but illuminated with lovely flashes of humour and scenes of exquisite comedy. I have just laboured through another novel called *The Loom of Youth*[2] which you must avoid, as it would bore you terribly. Nothing bores me or it would.

I have one commission for you to perform during the month or more that still separates me from London. I want you to procure me a bed, anywhere and at any price but of suitable dimensions for my bedroom. Will you do this for me, darling? The more I rough it and the uglier my surroundings, the more I reflect upon beauty and comfort. How do you spend next Saturday to Monday? I must stay here but perhaps if you have nothing to do you might come down for one or other of the days. It seems forever since I saw you – Bless your beauty.   Duff.

Diana to Duff, 9 October 1917   *16 Arlington Street*

My darling. This is bad news I hear. It is muttered that you stand a chance of not passing this coming time, and in consequence remaining some more months at Bushey? It hurt me terribly when it came to my ears, I love your record to be brilliant.

I shall find complete consolation, if you do fail, in remembering that the further from London, the further from the War – but Duffy my darling how should any cause be given for such a vile whisper – does your brain work slower, are your limbs stiffer, or is it the manner of disinterestedness that bitched Edward [Horner] in his Cambridge course? God, I never can put down my white wash implements for a minute. I told my damned informer that I had just heard, from somebody in authority, to the exact contrary. Anyway I love you whatever they say – but it has worried me terribly all day. I had to walk from Marble Arch–home, alone, absolute flooding rain at seven at night – thinking all the way how terrible everything was – and that really if I fell down I should not get up again. Then I dined out with Michael,[2] quarrelled on every

---

[1] *The Loom of Youth*, by Alec Waugh (1917). It caused a fearful fuss at the time, being the first book to suggest – very mildly – that homosexuality was a feature of the English public school.

[2] Michael Herbert, 1893–1932, younger son of Sir Michael Herbert who had been Ambassador in Washington and his American wife.

point – his manners were so vile, without a grain of initiative, and sleepy too so I left him in a pet – and there's a good chance of it being a permanent one.

Can't you wire Adela,[1] suggesting Sunday? Another thing about your bed, do you want single or double? Empire? 4 post? a box mattress on the floor & stuff behind like mine? What, in God's name? I shall love doing it.

Duff to Diana, 10 October 1917   *Bushey Hall Golf Club*

Darling – How silly you are to believe that I could fail in anything. Be assured that such rumours as you hear are only due to the nicety with which I calculate the very minimum of trouble one need take in order to achieve some tiresome business, and am then careful to take no more. But that you should be worried on my account is terrible and I pray you not to be.

Don't you read my letters, or didn't you get the one in which I told you that Adèle as far as I know is in France. So we can't go there on Sunday – where shall we go? In some haste and great love – Duff.

Diana to Duff, 31 December 1917   *Belvoir Castle*

My love – I look very much like being prisoner till Monday – unless I could get to Taplow[2] on Saturday, where of course I should be dispatched with pounds of tea by Her Grace. Can you think of some rare device?, some snare for Ettie?[3] My strategy is rusty: but I can face this life really – if it wasn't for you, and solicitude for Katharine I could almost cease chafing. The standard of conversation at meals is the worst. Queenie[4] said at lunch she had a war joke. Mother thought she said 'wardrobe' & laughs still over that slip – the joke was "This isn't Armageddon, its

---

[1] Adèle Essex. Born Adèle Grant, a New Yorker, she married the 7th Earl of Essex in 1893, as his second wife.

[2] Taplow Court, Buckinghamshire. The home of Lord and Lady Desborough.

[3] Ethel Anne Fane, who married William, 1st Baron Desborough, in 1887. Always known as Ettie, she was a famous hostess and great beauty. Her sons Julian and Billy Grenfell were killed in battle in 1915, and her youngest son Ivo in a car accident in 1926. She died in 1952.

[4] Lady Victoria Manners, 1876–1933, daughter of the 7th Duke by his 2nd wife. She painted water colours and wrote about art for the *Connoisseur*.

Armageddes"[1]. Mildred[2] didn't think it much better than I did, so she capped it with a story of a man who was heard to say he didn't care about meatless days, but he couldn't face the tartless nights, *whereupon* Mother flounced from the table banging the door.

[After passing his examinations at Bushey, Duff had six months of soldiering as an officer at Chelsea Barracks before he was sent to France. Then came the sad news that Patrick Shaw-Stewart was dead. Unlike his friends Rupert Brooke and Charles Lister he had survived the Dardanelles, but was killed in France early in the new year.]

Duff to Diana, 4 January 1918   *Taplow Court*

My darling – I am thinking so much about you and wondering how you feel. The anxiety for you helps me to forget my own misery. After writing to you last night, I went to the Ritz to dine with Lionel.[3] Michael came and then William Rawle with the terrible announcement. It came to me like a blow on the head with a bludgeon. I dived into champagne endeavouring to face it. We played cards till four – Hugo, who came after dinner, losing, and I ending after terrible variations some £10 to the good.

I tried to telephone you but couldn't – so I thought it best to telegraph, though I hate to bear or send bad news. We travelled down [to Taplow] with Rosemary,[4] Diana[5] and Casie,[6] and told them the news. They hadn't heard it and didn't know whether Ettie had. Arriving here we found she was up in her room which looks as though she did know. I hope so.[7] We have had tea and the

---

[1] Auckland Campbell Geddes, 1879–1954. Created 1st Baron Geddes 1942. Was director of National Service from 1917–1919.

[2] Mildred was the wife of Robert Manners, second son of the 7th Duke by his second marriage. She had a false hand, into which she would stick her needle, to hold it steady while she threaded it.

[3] Lionel Tennyson – 3rd Baron Tennyson, 1889–1951, grandson of the poet.

[4] Rosemary Leveson Gower.

[5] Diana Wyndham – daughter of the 4th Lord Ribblesdale and sister of Charles Lister. In 1913 she married Percy Wyndham, who was killed in action a year later.

[6] Monica Grenfell, Lady Desborough's daughter. She served as a Red Cross nurse in France during the War, and in 1924 married Air Marshal Sir John Maitland Salmond.

[7] Patrick was a very close friend of Julian and Billy Grenfell and, his own parents being dead, Ettie and Patrick loved each other as mother and son.

women have melted away, leaving Michael and me. I am very tired and in no mood to find words for my sorrow. I wish we were together. To talk to you now would be better than tears.

> 'There is nothing left remarkable
> Beneath the visiting moon'[1]

is a phrase that runs in my head, but the association of our darling Patsy with Cleopatra is too funny and makes me laugh. I find it difficult to maintain interest in life – if it were not for you it would be impossible, and I should indeed 'Encounter darkness like a bride'[2]. I have an uneasy feeling that Patrick would wish me to write something about him – and I don't think I can do it. Do you remember that quotation from Swift in Morley's *Recollections* – to the effect that he was of the opinion that there was no greater folly than to form a too great or intimate friendship which must leave the survivor miserable.[3] I feel that in my bitterer moments but I know it isn't true. For what should I do now if I had not you – oh my love, my love.   Duff.

Diana to Duff, 5 January 1918   *Belvoir Castle*

My darling – First in my heart an unceasing sigh for my blessed Edward – so that although Patrick's death is agonising, I am truly numb to 'lesser woes' – or is it that we are really only beasts and mind the loss of bodies that one loved, and beauty that delighted one. How coldly I write – and yet you know I loved Patsy – and had a greater sense of duty towards him than to anyone. How I tried, on his last leave to fulfil my resolution of gaiety, enthusiasm for him, festivity – and how ill I succeeded, I shudder to think of it. For the first time I think of the dead man himself, and not the spoilation of my life or another's (this reads colder still). He did love his every action and petty interest, moments that we found unbearable to him were life, and therefore to be eagerly enjoyed or profited from in some way.

I wish most terribly that you were with me to hold and melt me – but then holding you fast I might forget and forgive our torturers in blind thankfulness that you were there.

---

[1] *Antony and Cleopatra*, Act IV scene xv.

[2] *Measure for Measure*, Act III scene i.

[3] Quoted from Swift's letter in answer to a friend in Ireland, who had written to tell him that Stella was dying.

I want melting – it's dreadful to feel like a frozen limb, incapable – paralysed, ugly too, very – and with forbodance of pain at the thaw. Beloved Duff, how sad do you feel? pray God I hear from you tomorrow. Is Taplow still on? How was he killed? I'm such a child in hope – and as before, think it may all be a torturing mistake.

My darling, I long for you – I did love Patrick, oh why am I so changed to stone –   Diana.

Diana to Duff, 5 January 1918   *Belvoir Castle*

My angel Duff – The motor goes to Grantham at eight – so I write to you on the doubtful chance that this may come to you as you wake. I wrote this morning, but could do nothing before you left but I had rather you were at Taplow – Ettie will be wholly miserable and sympathetic – and how the strain of having you and not having you would have broken me. I feel you need more love and encouragement than I do – comfort there is none – and cannot bear not to be giving you all I can.

I wrote you a marble-hearted letter this morning, and later found myself cold and tottering and ashen, and had to resort to brandy – since then the agony of Patrick's not returning has been in crescendo. That two months should rob us of both Edward and Patrick should be enough to finish me, so any energy or interest that is left to me – were it not for you, my darling, who keep every part of me alive. If this could apply to you there is a vein of consolation in it. Patrick would so hate to be dead, which gives one an additional moan, for I have never felt this about the rest of our procession.

> 'As flies to wanton boys are we to the Gods
>   They kill us for their sport'[1]

My darling – I love you.   D.

[1] *King Lear*, Act IV scene i.

Duff to Diana, 21 January 1918   *88 St. James's Street*

My darling love – I hope you have such a day at Brighton as we have here – Mild and balmy – *Vorfrühling* – too good to be true and much too good to last. It has blown away my cloud of depression – but oh I do wish that you were here to share it or that yesterday had been such a day.

I slept most of the journey up last night and finished *Some Hawarden Letters*.[1] They end with George Wyndham and with references to Diana.[2] It made me feel old, too old, that a book which begins with Ruskin and Carlyle should end with a boy who was at school with me and a girl whom I knew as a child. Our generation becomes history instead of growing up.   Duff.

---

[1] A collection of letters to Mrs. Mary Drew, Gladstone's daughter, from 1878–1913 (1917).
[2] Diana Wyndham – see p. 42.

April–October 1918

[On the eve of his departure for the front, Duff had a farewell dinner with some of his family and friends before returning to Chelsea Barracks. From there, he and the other soldiers in his draft were to march to Waterloo Station. The officer who was to lead the march was found to be much too drunk to do so, and the task fell to Duff. "The band played nearly all the way", he wrote. "I felt proud, romantic and exalted." Diana followed him to the station, and there they said goodbye.

With Duff at the front, Diana felt she could not bear the pressures of home life and her hidden misery – hidden because Diana was extremely secretive about her love-life. She was determined to go back to nursing at Guy's. The impersonal vastness and the long working hours would dull the pain, and she would be spared the irritating supervision of her mother. It was a short break, though – the Duchess soon had her back at Arlington Street.]

Diana to Duff, 28 April 1918   *16 Arlington Street*

My darling love, I can think only of you and of your beauty and sereneness to me, and of all my extravagent dreams and demands that you have fulfiled. I adored your glorious spirits. Your salute to Maitland[1] deserves a page of praise. I blessed Monty for being too drunk to lead a dog to the water.

I am terrified that I clung and clamoured about you too much. A bright trite mask might have helped you more. Ettie's attitude haunts me yet, my angel – it seems unnecessary with you – you

[1] Lt. Col. Mark Maitland, 1882–1972, Acting Commanding Officer of the 5th Battalion Grenadier Guards.

needed no courage and it was heaven to be true. Many of my tears were sheer love unmixed with pity and desolation. I loved to feel them fall and feel the strong tide of love within me. My link with life, my love, my youth. This is a blessing and a sigh and a great pride signifying only my complete love.　Diana.

Write a love-collins to Vinny. I will write now to your Mother.

Duff to Diana, 28 April 1918　　　　　　*Victoria Hotel, Folkestone*

Darling my darling –
　How I loved you last night – how dreadfully I loved you. I couldn't think that I was going to the war, I could only think that I was leaving you. Will you love me as much when I come back. Please do.
　I slept stertorously from London to Folkestone and on arriving here went to a comfortable bed and slept till ten – and am now seizing a short moment between a late breakfast and an early lunch to write to you. The hardships of war are cruel.
　It was really rather lovely last night at the station, wasn't it? A picture for our gallery and deserving to be hung among the best. Which are our best? Long ago by the sea on the first night at Bournemouth – one earlier still, before the war, at Sutton – but I haven't time now to catalogue them – the Serpentine has a place, and a coffee stall in the East India Road. Tell me some more – and tell me your favourite. Good bye, my little love, my heart and soul, my brains and blood and marrow. I adore you.　Duff.

Diana to Duff, 30 April 1918　　　　　　*16 Arlington Street*

Darling Duff, It all went off far worse than I hoped. When Her Grace came in I started bravely enough with "Now, darling, about Guy's" and then God! hands up, shrieks, gasps for restoratives, so I withdraw into my own pleasant sheets' warmth and sent Letty to calm her and they wrangled, poor souls, till three, but I fear never got any quieter; though Letty put the fear of madness or suicide on her, unless I was humoured in every way. I long to know how much she connects this intolerance, this great remonstrance and inability to be even civil, with love or sorrow for you. But now this morning the continuance of scenes and ravings make

[50]

me waver, yet if I waver now I shall always waver so I must try: my determination I find greatly strengthened by your absence, darling. It's rather sad but so understandable – so much was tolerable with you to dally and philander secretly with, so much I was content to forfeit in sops. Now it seems any single straw will break my back.

Wimborne's reign is over,[1] they say and Ireland is to be governed by a triumvirate. He will be more in my hands or maybe he'll join the Grenadiers.

Today, that wooden legged virgin Oc[2] 'takes over', poor ignorami! Admission of impediments themselves in marriages is a thought better than omission of good legs – though perhaps Oc's were never great shakes.

I love you with every atom of myself. Poor baby, are you cold?   Diana.

11 p.m. I have had it out with Mother. She was pathetic, tamed, and bleated of the loneliness of her life but I didn't waver and shall probably leave next week. She thinks it is a penance; for what? too much life, or too much love, or too much suffering.

Duff to Diana, 4 May 1918   [*Havre*]

Oh my darling, how rich I was this morning with three whole letters from my love. One written apparently on Saturday night just after leaving me – most beautiful – one on Sunday and one on Tuesday, so I feel that I have all the back numbers now which I have been worrying about since I got Monday's letter.

Your fears about your own behaviour during those last hours are so groundless. I have no time to tell you how fine I thought it and how it strengthened and emboldened me like a rare unaccustomed wine. I was prouder than Napoleon when he put the crown on his head with his own hands, as I felt your arms about me and kissed your tears. When we arrived here we found that the party who left London on Monday morning had arrived before us, which seemed annoying but I thought that not even 36 extra hours of the greatest happiness in London would have weighed in the scale against the beauty of our sublime goodbye. The others left in

---

[1] Lord Wimborne was succeeded by Field Marshal Sir John French.

[2] Arthur Asquith, ('Oc') – 1883–1939 – lost a leg at Gallipolli in 1915. This was the day of his marriage to Betty Manners, daughter of John, 3rd Baron Manners.

taxis after breakfast with no men, no music, no magnificence.

I have written to Lady Herbert[1] but I can't think what to do with her little cross. It is charming and on a very nice thin chain but what on earth am I to do with it? In *The Idiot*[2] they all wear one round their necks but I'm not quite such an idiot as that.

Now, baby, I must try to carry on your education even at this distance. In the first place you mustn't put at the top of your letter '12 p.m.' because it signifies nothing – 12 can't be p. or a. because it's m. itself. You must say 'noon' or 'midnight'. In the second place you mustn't ever say 'ignorami' when you mean more than one ignoramus. It would bore you if I explained why but take my word for it. Oh darling, how I love you, long for you, hunger and thirst for you – how pointless I am without you – how you complete and satisfy, make and magnify me.   Duff.

Diana to Duff, 1 May 1918   *16 Arlington Street*

My darling love,

My spirits today are a little heightened by the amazing arrival of the grenade-embroidered chemises and faun-haunted night gowns – Mars by day, Pan by night.[3] If I had had them at Wilton my cup would have been nearly full. They are so lovely, nestling bombs – and mad pursuits round thighs.

Diana to Duff, 3 May 1918   *Belvoir Castle*

Sweetheart – It's you in all the world I love the best, but I must check the soppiness of my letters – on looking back at them, in my mind not at the drafts, they seem to have been volumes of outworn out-pourings, stalest sentimentalities thrust upon you because they were fresh to my cold stagnant heart. So from now I must narrow my material down to the trivial daily occurences. Take this morning – I went into Father's room about 12 noon. I have not seen anything like it – on the stage even – for 10 years. All the Brumell in him was out and rampant – four torn and contorted ties lay dead around him, he was tugging at a 5th, tugging first to get it tied, tugging then to get it off, then tugging at his studded collar till

---

[1] The American mother of Michael and Sidney Herbert, née Lelia Wilson.
[2] By Dostoyevsky.
[3] cf. Swinburne, *Atalanta in Calydon*.

apoplexy point – and all, as he said, all this wouldn't happen "if I wasn't as weak as a baby after my illness." He at last was suited, but (honestly) so drenched with perspiration that he was obliged to change; then wrapt in a muffler, warmly hatted and cloaked he hobbled down the centrally heated passages to his study, leaving directions for the ties to be burnt.

After lunch, John and I and Kakoo took a 20 mile drive and divested a church, filled with Manners tombs,[1] of any texts, cloths, hangings, church furniture in general, dating after 1700, and left it mutilated like Rheims; the new Vicar came in, cassock-ed, lean and hungry, in the middle. "May I introduce myself as Lord Granby," was all he got from John perched about 20 feet up bestriding an alabaster Duchess, barefooted as a Mahometan at his rites and photographing the Earl's face. I had a happy inspiration of saying all the sham Gothic was German, so God's flabberghasted vicar helped us with a will to piecemeal his furnitures, and was intimidated into giving permission for ex-humation of any corpse in his keeping that John may fancy to have a 16th century ring or spur on its dusty extremity. The drive thro' the forests was terribly sad first because of the new leaves you know, so anxious and frail and you away from me, secondly because every straight fine trunk has the governments nasty numbered stamp of condemnation upon it.

Michael came over for the night – he was sweet and very good with Mother. He is rather upset as he thinks his lot are to be sent in a fortnight to France with their training half done.

I forgot to say, how vile I thought him for going to his mistress and not seeing you off, but let that . . . Christ, I broke off because of Mike and what could I have meant, 'pass' no doubt. Anyway it's 2 a.m. and he has just stalked into my room on some fairly plausible pretext of being 'called' tomorrow. Mother is divided from me by the frailest of partitions, and now as he crept out again I heard him crash into the night watchman, dressing-gowned, towsled and candled as he was. What reputation have I left? No word from you yet since Folkestone and no news of yr Battalion, tho' Wade[2] rings up daily without orders, seeing my anxiety – perhaps you will be saying the same at this moment.

---

[1] St. Mary's, Bottesford – but the distance from Belvoir Castle to the church is four miles rather than twenty.

[2] Kate Wade came to Diana as her maid in 1916, and stayed with her for forty years.

My dove, my love. I have found a photograph of self aged five for you, too big to send; – also the enclosure to make you smile – self as Princess Katherine in *Henry V*. I love. you.   Diana.

Diana to Duff, 9 May 1918   *Guy's Hospital*

My darling, I have endured great physical pain today, hip and thigh, calf and foot. Wards claim one from 7.30 a.m. to 8 p.m., and with the exception of ¾ for lunch and ½ for tea, during which I hung my legs in cold water just to calm them, one is not off one's feet. I don't remember it being so torturing last time – do you? perhaps novelty and patriotism stiffened my sinews. It was one of our spring days – but one must lead the leisured life to appreciate weather, I'm glad to say; once busy it matters little except to one's general spirits. The poor don't notice it at all. Another thing about the poor that amuses me is that when friends, or chiefly relatives, come to see them sick – they as often as not sit in a complete silence for an hour and a half, rather self-consciously too, occasionally broken by "Feelin' very poorly, dear?" or some such rhetorical remark. But what *amazes* me about them is their lack of question or curiosity about themselves. They are all afraid of cancer – they have all got it. They have the words 'Diagnosis – Carcinoma' written over their beds, big. They say as a rule "What is glands, not cancers are they?" I say "O no, dear, not cancer" and there they leave it. There is a lovely woman of thirty-five not unlike me, with a glimmering skin and breasts like the Milo's, but if you touch them it's like touching stone, so they were both removed today, and yet she doesn't ask what's wrong.

Duff to Diana, 10 May 1918   *B.E.F. France*

Darling – Such beautiful days yesterday and today – too beautiful to be spent happily without you. I went to a lovely wood – long avenues of trees all ending in vistas of blue sky seen through a gothic window of leaves. It was the sort of wood you like with no undergrowth only a carpet of bluebells which Buchanan[1] called hyacinths and I didn't like to contradict him. Then we went to a

[1] Capt. J. N. Buchanan (D.S.O., M.C.), 2nd Battalion.

café with a terrace hanging over a cliff looking down on a wide plain and we drank a bottle of cider which as Buchanan said really tasted of the apple and I assented. You can imagine how I missed you all the time. Today Buchanan goes up to his battalion so once more I lie alone.

What do people say about General Maurice?[1] It seems to me he might have found some rather more important lies to tax Lloyd George with while he was about it. The average soldier – I mean officer – is a perfect Gallio[2] with regard to politics and has no opinion except that the politicians are wrong and the soldiers right – quite ignoring that the soldiers are as much divided among themselves as the politicians. They can't even take the trouble to read Maurice's letter and I have had to explain a dozen times what it's all about.

What news of the Indians?[3] How you must be longing for Alan's return. I shan't expect so many letters then. Good bye, dear angel.   Duff.

Diana to Duff, 12 May 1918   *Guy's Hospital*

Vinny [telephoned to say] the Anglos had arrived, and we were to dine at eight-fifteen at the Savoy. I have seldom suffered from greater nervousness darling – wasn't it silly. I looked so aged and different. I wore that dissatisfying penguin dress. I was in a haze of emotion and wine. I told them, I thought inspiredly and rather self-committingly, the prose picture of your departure to the wars. They told me stories of Leigh[4] and stories of how Alan's tooth had been extracted that morning at Boulogne, and Edwin gave a graphic picture of his Vision of the Old Bird [Asquith] – a vision of a great sack; an upright, righteous, patriotic, fine, worshipful sack – but being shoved and flung about and goaded by Margot and Mckenna and Runciman and all the Old Gang, and told to strike, and be a man, and look up, and in Edwin's opinion his epitaph

---

[1] In April 1918, Major General Sir John Frederick Maurice, 1841–1912, Director of Military Operations at the War Office, publicly accused the Prime Minister Lloyd George of misleading the country by falsifying the number of British troops in France.
[2] Acts xviii. "And Gallio cared for none of these things."
[3] Edwin Montagu and Alan Parsons. They had just returned from India, and so were called "the Anglo-Indians".
[4] Edwin's manservant.

should be 'Here lies the body of H. H. Asquith, who married Margot Tennant, but was Prime Minister for ten years.'[1]

I drove home at nine-thirty alone[2] (you could not have let me do that – O God to have you) a little fuddled in an open taxi. The flash lights were playing magically and I found myself addressing a very complicated and exacting prayer to the Power of Lives aloud, to the effect that you might not be killed, or might be restored very quick to my very arms, that nothing should touch your face or arms, at least not both arms, but I didn't mind your leg or rib, and so on for ten minutes before I caught myself. My lover, my lover, it's sad to be alone.   Diana.

Diana to Duff, 13 May 1918   *Guy's Hospital*

My darling, 3 letters this morning – one sad one from the sad sea-shore – one *heavenly* one about yr realisation of my love for you which I thought had always flamed on my forehead like the morning star.[3] Another sylvan one, of woods as *I* like them unthicketed, and of the sea as *I* like it glimmering smooth – it gave me pleasure. I believed you had thought of me – by that proof. Buchanan was right – bluebells are wild hyacinths; Hyacinth's blood died the flower purple, and that flower was not a cobby Dutch annual, but a pretty wild flower.

Today, in consequence no doubt of my night out, I dozed off after the bell had rung and woke again to my panic when the watch indicated the hour Home Sister takes her estrade seat above the breakfasters. To come in behind her is punishable. I clapped my uniform over my nakedness, took no look in the glass and ran 300 yards to the hall holding and tugging at my ungartered stockings. Providence had made my watch two minutes fast, so I thought myself safe as I sank into my chair exactly beneath Sister's empty chair. But my table of twenty started sniggering, I hoped at my flaming flurry and pantings, then when twenty mouths had whispered it to me I found I was collarless – always

---

[1] Asquith's first wife, Helen Melland, had died in 1891, and in 1894 he married Margot Tennant, 1868–1945. The candour for which she was known in her youth grew harsher as she grew older, and both she and the Prime Minister suffered from the effects of her unhappy nature and the nervous illnesses she was prone to.

[2] The hospital gates shut at ten.

[3] *cf.* Milton, *Lycidas*.

ridiculous, you know, think of yrself stalking into Ava's[1] with a bare neck, and a stud like a star. I was distraught as my great flashing nape was the first thing Sister's eyes must rise on, after grace. But a grubby choking collar was handed me through three hundred hands beneath the table from Nurse Philip Sidney sitting in an inconspicuous place – and I swept into port very weary. No. 2 can no longer remember when she has washed and starts loading herself with soaps and brushes as soon as I have got her back to bed. She will speak no word more, and because her arms are swollen, I have tied her two hands up to a rod above her bed, till she looks a crazy 'Kamerad'. Can the poor mad thing be sleeping? She can't, I know.

I went to see Alan at Mulberry[2] this afternoon. Mrs. Crockford was tackling, but not coping with innumerable massive deal cases. What will they be full of? from samples I have seen, cheap tin trays and objects the same as those that decorate the mantles of every Colonel's home in Cheltenham – brass work, red and yellow idols, signed photos, hunt trophies, pussypussypussies for the staircase walls. Alan told me that Venetia's letters were so unbelievably dreadful that no one an inch less besotted with love than Edwin could have tolerated them. Beginning always with the worn gambit of "darling, I wrote you a frightfully good letter, but have already lost it, so must write another one, a bad one. Last night I dined with . . . ." then follows a long long succession of dinners and their guests, without even a peroration of love; nothing in fact that Edwin could not give Alan to read.

Duff to Diana, 16 May 1918   *In the train*

Darling – After I left you yesterday I went almost with you to the churches we wanted to see [in Rouen]. At the first – Saint Patrice – there was such a crowd witnessing first communions that I could hardly get in. So I went to Saint Ouen where a service was also going on – but there was plenty of room and the church is most beautiful inside. I felt I could become a bore about churches. One of the little girls – I suppose the best – *la rosière* – made a long oration. She said it beautifully – enunciating every word distinctly

---

[1] Ava Astor. She and her first husband, John Jacob Astor, were already divorced when he went down with the *Titanic* in 1912. In 1919 she became the second wife of the 4th Baron Ribblesdale.

[2] Mulberry Walk, Chelsea, the home of Alan and Viola Parsons.

and laying no stress on any as though the whole had no meaning. There is a charm in the sexless voices of the young not because one likes sexlessness but because one likes birds, in spite of oneself, and although they get up too early.

Then I strolled back to the Cathedral because I wanted to see some tombs there which I hadn't been able to see in the morning. There was a large one of two cardinals which I had hoped would be more like the Bishop's,[1] and there was a very lovely one of the husband of Diane de Poitiers[2] – good late renaissance – alabaster divided as it were into two stories (I mean *étages*, not *histoires*). Above, the gentleman appears on horseback and in armour, very fine with smiling female figures at his head and feet representing Victory, Glory etc. Beneath him is seen a small almost naked man, one cloth twisted round the lower part of his body, his head thrown back as though in death agony and his face *mesquin* and ugly – at his head kneels Diane quietly praying, at his feet a virgin with a happy laughing child. I remember that he was a very ugly man and small as he here appears. Diane ordered the tomb. How well those people lived and with what pomp and fantasy they died. The heat is so lovely and I have just had a beautiful wash and feel clean and cool and fresh. I must hurry or the train will go. You darling.   Duff.

Diana to Duff, 21 May 1918   *16 Arlington Street*

My darling, I have just come in and found your letter – a rare thing to do at this hour. I hesitated to open it, seeing that it's anticipation makes my morning's work thinkable. It has left me in great doubt where to address this one as you are hovering between battalions. Tonight I had the great pleasure of 'taking prayers' in the ward. Sister mumbles them, like [George Gordon] Moore might. I thought of yr *rosière* and annunciated. I thought of Patrick and looked up from the book. I thought most superstitiously of you, as I prayed to the 'only giver of Victory who can save by many or by few' which I find a lovely line. Last night a new patient came in unexpectedly – the nurse rushed to me shouting "What do you think we've got in". I guessed a hun, or a hermaphrodite or a

---

[1] *The Bishop Orders his Tomb at St. Praxed's* by Robert Browning.
[2] Louis de Brézé, Grand Seneschal of Normandy, and husband of Diane de Poitiers. He died in 1531.

dog-faced woman. "No", they whispered breathless, "an *actress*" and a poor furtive little widow actress she was, with a blue ribbon in her modest night-dress instead of an unbleached calico ward-gown. She threw off her blanket in the middle of the night (the one *next* to her – as the heat is abnormal and the ward has eight *calorifés*) and the night people declared she had done this as the House Surgeon came in so as to 'catch him'. She walks in Romance and Sir Alfred Fripp[1] shows unusual interest in her. My tender Duff, good night. I need not say keep warm and keep cool has the wrong meaning.   Diana.

Duff to Diana, 21 May 1918   *B.E.F. France*

One word, darling love, before I go to the battle. I am starting in a few minutes – and am going to ride there. I had always imagined a long exhausting march to the trenches, but it is pleasant and romantic to be able to ride there comfortably after tea. I had a thirst for poetry this morning, having brought none with me. I found a volume of Rupert Brooke. It hadn't my favourite about your brown delightful head but had the 1914 soldier sonnets which on rereading I find good but a little cheap. Far the loveliest and the one which I tried to learn by heart this morning and have already forgotten begins – *These hearts were woven of human joys and cares.* Read it and tell me what you think. Gunther [2nd Lt. G. R. Gunther, M.C.] goes with me to the Battle. He looks like Chu Chin Chow in his steel helmet but I look lovely in mine, like the relief of Ladysmith or with Kitchener to Khartoum. Bless your beauty, my angel.   Duff.

Duff to Diana, 22 May 1918   *In the trenches*

Darling – Yesterday evening after tea Gunther, another boy called Jingles, [2nd Lt. G. G. Inglis Jones] the Commanding Officer [Lt. Col. A. Thorne D.S.O.] and myself set out on horseback for the trenches. A pleasant enough ride but rather too warm owing to the number of things one was carrying. As we got nearer the battle and the guns became louder, my horse grew rather nervous and began shying at each shell hole and I was terrified of falling off. At

---

[1] George V's personal surgeon, 1865–1930.

last we got off them and left them with two grooms. We then had a few hundred yards to walk to Battalion Headquarters. There we descended into the bowels or into one bowel of the earth – an incredibly deep dug-out with rather uneven steps down into it which I thought most unsafe. At the bottom we found Harry Lascelles[1] who is 2nd in Command of this Battalion. He was looking extraordinarily elegant, beautifully clean and rich, a perfect type of the 'tenth transmitter of a foolish face' which I always see him as. I felt ashamed to be covered with perspiration, very untidy and wearing camouflage i.e. a private's uniform. There was another elegant young man with him called Fitzgerald [Lt. E. G. A. Fitzgerald, D.S.O.] and the table was stewn with papers and periodicals like *Country Life* and the *Burlington Magazine* which one associates with the houses of the rich.

Thence I was led by a guide to my own Company. 20 minutes walk over green fields while the sun was beginning to set most beautifully. At last we arrived at a dug out – an ordinary shallow cinema one, and here I met my Captain face to face – nobody more surprised than my Captain, as he had expected someone else of the same name. It was then 8.15. He called for dinner for two which was immediately produced. Quite good soup, hot fish tasting like sardines but larger, no one knew what they were – cold beef, pickles and peas, prunes and custard – plenty of whiskey and port. It was still light when we finished and I was sent on to the very front line of all in order that the officer there might come back and dine. The front line proved extraordinarily unalarming – and it was rather thrilling to think that there was nothing between oneself and the German Army.

I have had to censor a lot of letters, which has put me out of conceit with letter writing – so I shall read till dinner or lie and think of the chicken we are going to eat. I have reread this letter and am ashamed of it. I think like Machiavelli that one must be clean and comfortable and well dressed in order to write well. Duff.

Diana to Duff, 23 May 1918   *16 Arlington Street*

My darling, I resolved tonight to glean you some information

---

[1] Capt. Viscount Lascelles, D.S.O., 1882–1947. He married H.R.H. Princess Mary, later the Princess Royal, in 1922, and in 1929 succeeded as 6th Earl of Harewood.

about the state and scandal and have come home jewelless. I dined next Edwin, Viola, Hugo [Rumbold], Nellie,[1] Alan, Vinny and Birrell[2] – the last asked who had heard from you. It is a source of endless astonishment to me this blindness of our *proches* [near ones] to our love. Venetia answered she had heard from you once and asked if I had heard from you *lately*. With what dignity must we have lived before them, and yet I have been afraid of our free behaviour lately. We have lived our lives together quite perfectly, my darling, with refinement, and blatancy unseen. We have lain on Westminster steps and in many gardens. We have sat joined rapturously before a thousand people, screened by a fluttering curtain at theatres. We have driven a hundred miles at least in *delicto flagrante* and yet we are beyond suspicion.

Almost every night I tramp home over the London Bridge, tonight I bowed my head against the freezing gale and felt like 'one more unfortunate'.[3] I felt lonely for you. How much greater have fears grown since I ran from that storm at Torcello – when all commented and scoffed or loved.   Diana.

Diana to Duff, 24 May 1918   *16 Arlington Street*

My dearest, I have had my worst day. It is cold and dark. I changed my ward and was sent to one in the pent of the roof. There was bed after bed of burnt children of three and four, on whom I was made to practise the new treatment of very hot melted wax poured on their raw surfaces; the pain is excessive, and they scream like tortured not babyish things. They are held down while it is done. The few remaining beds were occupied by four little girls each with such virulent gonohreah that gloves are worn to tuck them up.

All afternoon I felt sick and fighting with a wish to ask for removal, knowing that it was bad for me to give under. At the tea half hour, feeling terribly weak, I found in its pigeon hole a letter from you and for the first time for years I cried and cried with joy, and then my darling its news, when other petty woes had done their worst, overthrew me and I collapsed with the misery of you

---

[1] Nellie Romilly, née Hozier, sister of Clementine Churchill. She married Colonel Bertram Romilly in 1915.
[2] Rt. Hon. Augustine Birrell, 1850–1933 – politician, lawyer, essayist, and writer.
[3] The opening words of Hood's poem *The Bridge of Sighs*.

in the battle, and that I must drag on not hearing from you for days, and that the torture of mind must go on indefinitely. I'm happy to say it dismissed any false-conscience that had been forming like fetid fungus that grows even on me when you are not there to keep me clean of such mustiness, and I flew to the office and asked to be moved – an unheard-of presumption – but darling, you unwillingly inflict me with more than I can combat without burdening myself with my own burdens. I have no admiration, but great pity, and a great great love for myself. I am glad you rode, and that Gunther went with you. I have one advantage over Steffie [Duff's sister] in that I do not have to retire for an hour daily to think on you – but manage to do it day and night with no effort, and in all companies. So if this simple method is to keep you safe you are strongly accoutred. Keep warm, baby.   Diana.

Duff to Diana, 25 May 1918   *B.E.F. France*

My darling – I didn't write to you yesterday. It rained all day and my body and soul were damp and dank and there was nothing to say. We all got rather drunk at lunch and argued about Napoleon, one of my brother officers maintaining that Napoleon was not what he called a clever man.

We got rather drunk at dinner, too, and argued about Asquith and Lloyd George. One of my brother officers maintained that Asquith was 'all in with the Huns' and he believed that Mrs. Asquith was a 'female bugger', that being as near as his limited vocabulary allowed him to get to Sapphist. He sounds dreadful but is really sweet – of the Denny [Denis Anson] type – with red hair and a large nose and a slow smile. He is acting Captain. My other brother officer said that Lloyd George was not what he called a clever man. Soon after dinner we were relieved. This meant a long and tiring march in darkness and mud. Also a shower of flying bullets at first but we managed to dodge 'em. Then we arrived at our new quarters – a good way back – and there we found our kits waiting for us and all prepared by our servants who had gone on in front. It was a great luxury to take off clothes and boots and get into a sleeping bag and have nothing to do all night. But there was a far greater joy than this waiting for me

– two letters from Mother, one from Sybil,[1] one from Venetia and *four* from my angel. I felt so rich that I only read two of yours and kept the other two for the morning, with the result that although I was very tired I kept waking in the night and wanting it to be day. We were not to be called till ten but at nine I could bear it no longer so I drew a chink in the curtains and read the other two.

Your letters, darling, are most beautiful. I will have them printed one day with the contemporary spelling.

I have finished *Doctor Thorne*[2] and have only a little more Gibbon standing between me and literary starvation. Lots of books are on their way but none have reached me. Perhaps they may soon. We are here for three days living in a construction which as a child one would have thought quite heavenly and would not have crashed one's head against a beam every time one stood up. I never fail to do so. There is nothing to do. We are supposed to be resting, but it is a noisy spot. Some of our own guns are close behind us and make a hell of a row. The Germans quite rightly in my opinion are trying to silence them and drop shells all round. I'm glad to say the Germans are shooting pretty accurately and I trust will continue to do so, as should they drop their shells a bit short they would interfere with us. Champagne for dinner tonight. Hooray – I have a lot more to say but the letters are going.

Good bye, my own white beauty. I love and long for you to an extent that I have no time to find words to express.   Duff.

Duff to Diana, 28 May 1918   *B.E.F. France*

Oh, my beloved, the joy of last night. Five letters from you. I wrote you yesterday praise of your letters but I felt it had been vilely inadequate when I read these wonderful five. There were three of ten days ago completing the series, and two recent ones – and all five seemed to me even more than ordinarily beautiful. They made me laugh out loud and they almost made me cry. I loved the story of Nurse Philip Sidney and the collar. I loved your prayer to the Powers of Life. But more than all I loved your words of love, your longing for me and your loneliness. Let not your love languish, darling, as long as I live. I am afraid that if I'm away for a long time it must grow less as regret does for the dead. I know the

---

[1] Duff's sister, who married Richard Hart-Davis in 1904.
[2] One of the Barsetshire novels of Anthony Trollope, published in 1858.

miser's feeling when I think about your love – the greed for and glory in wealth and the horror of spending.

My two companions have gone and been replaced by two others. One – the Company Commander,[1] I like – fat with a wine red face and a passion for port, but a soft voice and shy manner. He was at Eton with me but seems years older. The other I hate. His face is brick red and wine has played no part in the painting of it – bricks rather, laid by his father – or perhaps his grandfather, whose trade it must have been. He talks with the affected refinement of a schoolmaster but is not quite sure of his 'ou' sounds. He is terribly keen and knows his job though he is only about nineteen and is thank God by a month my junior in the regiment.

After dining with these two last night and reading your letters we left the spot where we were and came back to the battle. An hour's march during which we were shelled a good deal, but I with your five letters in my pocket could think of them only and felt happy and proud. The usual night of restlessness, though I did manage a few hours sleep, then a beautiful red dawn which was accompanied by a terrific bombardment which funnily enough hurt nobody. All this morning enemy aeroplanes have been buzzing round exactly like mosquitoes. We fire at them, they go away, we never hit them – and a quarter of an hour later back they come humming triumphantly, and the same thing happens again and again. Now I have just come up to the front post of all to relieve Brick Red for a couple of hours while he has his lunch. I think Wine Red will wait and lunch with me. I am lying in a little cave which reminds me very much of our Brighton cave – the same size, the same white chalk – not like our sandy cave at Bournemouth. A most beautiful black and white butterfly has just settled here. I have never seen one like it. It is very modern – or perhaps just a little *démodé*. It reminds me of a dress you used to have – I can't describe it – one evening that you wore it was an evening that we danced at the St. James's Palace Hotel and we quarrelled because I didn't want you to drive home with Michael, and I gave you scent the next day. Good bye, Baby.   Duff.

[1] Lt. E. R. M. Fryer, M.C., known in Duff's letters as Wine Red.

Duff to Diana, 30 May 1918   *B.E.F. France*

Darling – I am much warmer and much happier now – for many reasons.

1) The sun has come out and the larks have started singing. The larks are marvellous here. Everywhere else in France they are shot by the *Français sportifs*, but here since neither the English nor the Germans ever can hit anything they are perfectly safe with the result that the front line has become a regular bird refuge. As one has anyhow always to be awake at dawn, which as you know is their favourite hour for kicking up a row, one doesn't mind the little buggers as much as one does when living in civilisation. 2) The weather turned out really warm which it hasn't been this last week. 3) At the happy hour of lunch came a letter from my angel – the first one addressed to the third Battalion. 4) We are going to be relieved this evening.

Oh, baby darling, what a good little creature you are to write so often. If I am here for four months or more you cannot keep it up and I shan't expect it and I hope you will never force yourself to do so when disinclined. The first night that I went out on patrol I felt I must give my servant your address to send my things to, my letters and diary should anything untoward occur. I was so shy that I had to drink half a bottle of whiskey before I could bring myself to it. He took it quite naturally, but I have felt rather shy of him ever since.

Sweet love, I want you more than I want peace or comfort or home or life. Every hour of the day and night I want you – in every wretchedness but more in every joy. Tell me in every letter that you love me and that your love doesn't grow less with absence as I fear it may. Tell me whom else you love and how much less you love them. Keep for me a chart of your love's temperature.   Duff.

Diana to Duff, 31 May 1918   *16 Arlington Street*

My dearest love, Here is the last day of this desolate month – a month of our best youth – our beauty's blazon, of hot days and warm nights, of trees in white and pink, and birds and leaves again new to the senses, and all its goods have been wasted in the desert

[65]

air. Olga[1] was there in a bad anxiety about the Billing case.[2] I told her I knew her name and address was bound to come out; she stands I honestly believe but a small chance of being overlooked, as she comes under 'alien', 'vice', and 'house of ill repute'. It's not unlikely that my name is heard of soon. The nurses are just the same as your subalterns – they ask me all the time about the case and are totally ignorant of any significations. They have a dim vision of Sodom and Gomorrah, which is built for them by the word vice, but even that is hazy.

Sister Clynical was married today. We were told we could attend the ceremony instead of lunch, so there was a rush for Southwark Cathedral if only to avoid the smell of the fish. Sister Clynical had a guard of honour consisting of Sister Lazarus, Sister Eyes, Sister Kitchens, Sister Out Patients, Sister Pan & San and Sister Officers. It was lovely. I wanted you – blazing sun making new perspectives through the beautiful pillars, and three hundred austerely dressed women and staring blue sisters, and then green trees and confetti.

Such a good ward maid came back to see me yesterday. She had been here in 1914 and had left a month ago to have a baby – her attitude could hardly be improved upon. "Never 'ad one?" she said to me, "O you are a dirty worm Di. Any'ow I done my bit and sharked the little bugger on to a 'Jesus loves me' institute. Don't know 'is faver, don't care neiver." She was never going to see it again, she said, but all quite incidental. "I'm not an ice-man. I likes a gay life". It's the 1st of June as I didn't finish this last night. I was so dog tired, and there was no letter, nor is there one this morning, so my agony begins again. My darling love.   Diana.

---

[1] Born Olga Loewenthal, she changed her name to Lynn. A well-known singing teacher of lesbian inclinations, she was too small to perform on stage; but she was enormously popular, and acquired several wealthy and influential patrons.
[2] An article appeared in a propagandist magazine run by Pemberton Billing M.P., 1880–1948, shockingly titled *The Cult of the Clitoris*. The Germans, said the article, had made a list of 47,000 people in high places who practised unnatural vices, and who were therefore vulnerable to blackmail and so potential German agents. Several of them, it said, would be going to see that lascivious play *Salome* by Oscar Wilde. Maud Allan, the dancer who was to play the leading role (and who had performed it before in 1908), brought an action against Billing for criminal libel.

Duff to Diana, 2 June 1918   *B.E.F. France*

My darling – there was another letter from you last night forwarded from the 1st Battalion. You are the best and bravest, most
beautiful and perfect mistress in the world.

I was rudely awakened at three this morning by a gas attack.
Fumbling for my gas mask in the darkness and trying to hold my
breath the while I got a whiff or two but am none the worse. It was
not the very deadly kind I think but the kind which produces
symptoms like a cold in the head, sometimes bronchitis or at the
very worst pneumonia. Perhaps it's a pity I didn't get more of it.
Has Orpen[1] any pictures of men in gas masks? Something might
be made of the effect, which is a mixture of ridiculous and ghastly
and sometimes reminiscent of Longhi.

I think you may have misunderstood me when I said I was
going to the battle. It is the phrase one uses here when one means
going to the front line. The actual battle now going on is very far
from here. I am nearer to that behind which a certain rash
intruding old man was once taken for his better and fared worse.[2]

There is a terrible shortage of port suddenly which doesn't
affect me much as there is plenty of whiskey and my companions
don't like it. My poor Wine Red captain is almost expiring as he
says that port to him is as petrol to a motor. I don't mind the Brick
Red one now as I have him well in hand, and we call him by an
obscene nickname.

How thrilling the Maud Allan case. The best I ever read. Tell
me all that everyone says of it.
            Duff.

I have written to Katharine.

Duff to Diana, 3 June 1918   *B.E.F. France*

Darling. No one here speaks or thinks of anything but the Billing
case. Even my Commanding Officer – the most regular of regular
soldiers – greeted me when I met him for the first time today not

---

[1] Sir William Orpen, the Irish painter, 1878–1931. He was to be the Official Painter of
the Peace Conference of 1918.
[2] *Hamlet*, Act III, scene iv. Hamlet stabs Polonius, who has been hiding behind the *arras*.

  'Thou wretched, rash, intruding fool, farewell!
  I took thee for thy better.'

[67]

200 yards from the front line trenches with – "What did you think of Fripp's[1] evidence. I should have thought he knew more about clap." The general feeling is that anybody who is anybody is in the book and that it is very second rate to be in the 53,000 and not in the first 47. I havn't had a letter from you since it began – I expect to find one when I get back this evening. What with Margot [Asquith], Haldane[2] and Mrs. Keppel[3] and Neil Primrose[4] I think we may congratulate ourselves that our friends are well represented. I expect you are in the book alright, although I should think it confined itself more to officials, and I flatter myself that even a junior clerk in the Foreign Office may have crept in – 47,000 is a large number. I do so long to be in London now in order to hear what people say about it.

Tonight I go some way back and tomorrow still further – and after that further still, so you needn't worry for a week or two – as except for air raids which are only rather more frequent than in London, I shall be safe enough. But at the same time hope is temporarily extinguished of that nice wound which we should all so much enjoy.

Later

I found 2 letters from you when I got back to dinner. I am delighted about His Grace's Garter.[5] It's quite the best thing Lloyd George has yet done. Shall I write and congratulate him? I am also glad about old Jennie[6] getting another run. Bless your darlingest.   Duff.

Diana to Duff, 3 June 1918   *16 Arlington Street*

My darling one. Work was over by nine tonight and unable to endure the wait for last post, I went and took a swim with the nurses. Today my last day, I am rather glad to find myself so very

---

[1] Sir Alfred Fripp (see note p. 59). He said that *Salome* (of which he had only read extracts) was written deliberately to corrupt, and was indeed capable of turning susceptible members of the audience into sexual deviants.
[2] 1st Viscount Haldane, 1856–1928, a close associate of H. H. Asquith's. As Secretary of State for War he had been largely responsible for the modernization and strengthening of the Army prior to 1914.
[3] Alice, Mrs. George Keppel, the intimate friend and mistress of Edward VII.
[4] The Hon. Neil Primrose, born in 1882, was the youngest son of 5th Earl of Rosebery. He was killed in Palestine in 1917.
[5] The Duke of Rutland had just been made a Knight of the Garter.
[6] Lady Randolph Churchill, who was about to marry her 3rd husband, Montagu Porch.

popular with them and the patients. They bring me bunches of very tired flowers when they have their half holliday and rush home to Peckham – and the young girl patients wink at me to wash them, and lie to get me. It *is* nice. No. 2 has gone to the infirmary, but No. 12 who has lain lost in her own dirt since I have been here, literally crawling and weighing 15 stone and spitting unintermitantly has suddenly developed a disease, incurable, called fetid brochitis – which makes it quite impossible for any one to tend her unless we burn an incense cone by her bed. Every few hours she puts on a gas mask snout filled with the strongest possible disinfectant, and breathes it for an hour; this she thinks is a treatment, but its only for the staff's sake. All the fluid in her lungs, all she spits has gone bad inside her. Could anything be worse? So I'm glad I'm going tomorrow – though there will be many disadvantages and I have been, as it were, left very much with you in this ordered place, and once out of it, they will be buzzing and questioning and no regular time for my little duties to you. A lovely letter from you tonight – terrifying – my darling – the patrols I do not like. Do not be afraid of my love waning – 'by Love's best arrow with the golden head'[1] its very improbable.

Then tonight too I get a terribly disquieting letter. Mr. Billing at the door I think. It reads – *128 Harley St*: "Dr. R. W. Alan is the possessor of certain information in regard to a case now much before the public of which it is very desirable that Lady Diana Manners should also become acquainted imediately. If she cares to call sometime before two p.m. Monday Dr. Alan will be pleased to convey it to her." I shall of course not go – but I think I'll show it to Edwin tomorrow.

All that I love in one frail bark[2] – Good night, keep warm, baby.   Diana.

Duff to Diana, 5 June 1918   *B.E.F. France*

Darling, I think I forgot to thank you for the little Shakespeare Comedies. Bless you for it. We had a sergeant in our Company called Shakespeare – he was killed the other day. The morning of

---

[1] *Midsummer Night's Dream*, Act I scene i.
[2] From the epitaph of Penelope Boothby, a little girl whose grave lies at Ashbourne, Derbyshire:

> Her parents ventured all
> On this one frail bark
> And the wreck was total.

the gas attack.[1] I cannot bear to miss your Shakespeare matinée. How lovely you will look.

Aunt Ida is dead. She died very slowly of cancer and to the last she wore a huge pyramid of red hair dressed in elaborate little curls, chiefly artificial and partly dyed. They longed to release her from it but didn't dare. Wasn't it splendid. Do you remember the old lady in *Dombey and Son*?

Diana to Duff, 5 June 1918   *Belvoir Castle*

My very dear one. I got up as early as usual with the dutiful resolve to catch an early train. My God – it is lovely – trees, and grass and flowers at their most florid wealth. It is difficult not to resent it all – There is a lot to resent legitimately here – First the noise of aeroplanes incessantly teasing one – secondly the reproving voice of the grownups, repressing the energy of children. Marjorie's, Letty's and John's, are all here and there is always a babble of repression – and commands for them to do something just different. No wonder they grow up to chaff against this accumulation of contrariness (and contrariness on the part of the adults is exactly what it is) – no wonder they can never cease from it – when their foolish tongues have wagged disapproval for so many years without opposition.

I ran through my *Salome* last night. I can see nothing abnormal, no more can Her Grace – she thinks it lovely – chiefly because I made her read it aloud in French, which she managed wonderfully well. She mentioned incidentally – and true to her school – that she did not believe in that vice amongst women. Lord Albemarle is said to have walked into the Turf and said, "I've never heard of this Greek chap *Clitoris* they are all talking of". It is said that either the Primroses or the Derbys[2] are going to take action to prove that Evelyn Rothschild and Neil were never in England together in that year[3] – also that Neil never knew Mrs. Stuart-Villiers, who by

[1] In 1949 Duff wrote a book called *Sergeant Shakespeare*, which sought to prove that Shakespeare had served in the army in the Low Countries under the Earl of Leicester.
[2] Edward Stanley, 17th Earl of Derby, 1865–1948. His daughter Victoria was the widow of Neil Primrose.
[3] Mrs. Stuart-Villiers, one of the most important witnesses at the trial, had said that Neil Primrose had shown her the book of 47,000 names in the presence of Evelyn Rothschild. The two men both died in action in 1917.

the way is Lord Tredegar's mistress.[1] She thinks she is my double and has that conjunction of elephants for a chaperone.

I'd advise them to leave Neil unexhonerated – Much worse is bound to crop up – and it's always better to wrong the dead than the living.

A perfect but not unhumourous letter from father today, addressed to his "very gallant daughter Diana" and saying he is "a very unworthy recipient of such high honour". Poor love. My whole love – 　Diana.

Duff to Diana, 6 June 1918　　　　　　　　　　　　*B.E.F. France*

My own darling – It is nearly three days since I had a letter from you and I am quite sick for want of one. It isn't your fault angel but that of the post which has somehow gone wrong these last days. I expect I shall get one this evening. The result of the Billing case has made me positively angry – "I was not angry since I came to France. Until this moment" – (I fear I misquote – do I?[2]) Really I feel that a country is not worth fighting for or preserving in which a Billing is still to be allowed to libel, a democracy which can produce 12 idiotic jurymen still allowed to rule, and a judge as utterly inept as Darling[3] allowed to administer the law. But I suppose one should be grateful to Billing. He has kept the whole army amused for several days and provided a topic of conversation to officers who can never find one for themselves.

I have such a nice billet now – a large low room to myself. A soft mattress on which to stretch my sleeping bag – two large low windows opening on a wild overgrown garden with trees at the back of it so that when I open my eyes in the morning I see nothing but green. But I leave tomorrow – for greater safety but less comfort I fear.

Good bye – my baby – my love, my beauty. I think of you so continually and with such great love.　　Duff.

---

[1] She had been Neil Primrose's mistress, and at the time of the trial was Pemberton Billing's.

[2] By one word. It should have been "instant". *Henry V*, Act IV, scene vii.

[3] Mr. Justice Darling, 1849–1936, was universally condemned for having grossly mishandled the trial. Billing was found not guilty of criminal libel against Maud Allan, because *Salome* was 'proved' to be a degenerate play.

Diana to Duff, 7 June 1918   *Train*

I spent the afternoon preparing food for a picnic which John begged for, in his endeavour to direct their energy away from the child torture. It was such a lovely tea, in Frog Hollow. The garden is exactly like a transformation scene at Drury Lane – azalias and syringa & asphyxiating smells, there were petit pains filled with chicken and lettuce, and mayonnaise – and feathery jam tarts, and cucumber. I thought I would make a meal just like it for ourselves – and somehow we should be in that garden together – for no breeze can reach it and the flowers meet accross the paths and you would kiss me as we walked – and I should not be afraid and always looking back.

The train is full of a North country Accrington family going to Peterborough for a day's jaunt, and the train stops every few minutes, and they are so anxious for every minute is of value to them, they are trying to pass the agony over with jokes – chaff, and they find a little consolation by occasionally saying "Well, we moost remember we've a war on and be contented" but they can't keep their watches in their pockets, or their heads from craning out of the window.

Duff to Diana, 8 June 1918   *B.E.F. France*

Darling – I didn't write yesterday – it was so occupied in moving to our new habitation. Remember the largest farm you have ever seen and then imagine one just twice as big. A perfect rectangle with a great pool in the middle. In front is a gentleman's house – or at least a gentleman farmer's house – with two large rooms downstairs and a multitude of little bedrooms above. At the back is the largest barn in the world and down the sides are outhouses of every description. It must have been so lovely when it worked. Brigade and Battalion H.Q. are both living in the house. I could have lived there but preferred a tent to myself under a tree to sharing a room. The whole of my Company are in the barn and the company's officers mess with Headquarters. This is a doubtful advantage as although one gets rather better food and drink, one is afraid to speak in the presence of the great. However I think I can arrange a side table where the lowly and meek shall be able to whisper their own particular obscenities and giggle to their hearts' content. We are supposed to be here for a month's rest though I

[72]

doubt there being much rest about it. We shall be training all the morning and playing compulsory games in the afternoon. Added to which the Commanding Officer has just informed me that he wants me to give a lecture to the Battalion on the working of the Foreign Office – its uses etc. Oh darling – how do you think I shall do it? Well I expect – but imagine the terror of an audience composed of one's superior officers, one's contemporary officers – two Commanding Officers and gaping privates. However a bottle of brandy fifty years old has just arrived from Steffie, and that may help me through. Don't worry my beloved about my drinking too much. For one thing there is not so very much to drink, and for another the effect of this open air life is to make one's head like a rock, on which one could build a house or found a church. I havn't been drunk once since I left Havre – not even the night that Lascelles went up the line and left three quarters of a bottle of his own brandy which nobody appreciated but me.

Duff to Diana, 12 June 1918   *B.E.F. France*

My beauty, my darling, my flower, such a lovely letter came from you today telling me about tea in Frog Hollow and the family from Accrington. I sometimes feel that to be with you again were too great a happiness ever to come true.

Last night I went to dine with Adderley.[1] Then we played cards and oh my mistress don't be angry with your seven and seventy times sinning lover. We didn't play the forbidden game [poker], but that far worse one which you call 'Mr. Dodd' – and I lost a lot – almost as much as when we played it with Ruby's Americans. Walking home I thought only of your frown and remembered only how divinely you had consoled me on that other occasion. It would sound silly were I tell you that I didn't play rashly and that fortune was incredibly jadish – but such was indeed the case. Think darling that it is insurance money, and then you will not think it thrown away.

Paris leave has been abolished – I suppose because everyone is leaving Paris. They have substituted for it Boulogne leave which is not much good to anyone.

---

[1] Capt. Peter Broughton Adderley M.C., 1891–1918, Scots Guards.

Read Sonnets XCVIII and CIX and think of me[1] – sweet sweet heart.   Duff.

Duff to Diana, 15 June 1918   *B.E.F. France*

My darling – We went for a route march this morning. I had to go on with two men two hundred yards ahead of the Battalion to lead the way which had been carefully explained to me on the map. Of course I went the wrong way as I did when leading Mr. Asquith and Princess Christian. At least I thought I had gone the wrong way and turned back in panic and a scene of confusion ensued. The band who were immediately behind me stopped playing one by one and

> 'Those behind cried 'Forward'
> And those in front cried 'Back' '[2]

– and I discovered too late that I had been right all the time. Of course I was thinking too much of you and wondering whether there would be a letter when I got back. They come at luncheon now which is a very agreeable time. I normally read Mother's and any others there may be and *The Times*, and keep yours till afterwards, when I retire with them and a cigar to my tent. Today darling there were two which was miraculous, especially as you say in one that you hadn't written yesterday. Yet I got one yesterday.

Diana to Duff, 15 June 1918   *16 Arlington Street*

I am utterly wretched – all my misery of weeks has given way before a new agony or the proof that you don't think of me. I fit all my actions to your whims, neither forgetting to date my letters, nor not to eat chocolates in the open street. I beckon no new lovers, I take no pains to fetter the old, I even read for you and bone your meat – all this for someone who is as remote as God, & who I may not see again though living on. Could you not think at the time how much I would mind. Why think Mr. Dodd legal, and poker

---

[1] "From you I have been absent in the spring"
(XCVII)
"Oh never say that I was false of heart"
(CIX)

[2] Macaulay, *Horatius*.

[74]

illegal to my code? To be a transgressor within the law is so vile and without courage.

Queen Elizabeth when she dubbed Knights said 'Be faithful, be brave, be fortunate'. I found it in a book yesterday & thought I would wish it you tonight. It seems an irony now, when, you prove faithless to me, frightened and surrounded by bad stars. I shall not write for a space.   Diana.

Diana to Duff, 16 June 1918   *16 Arlington Street*

My darling love – I wrote last night in anger and rage. It is dissipated like night's dew by a sun of love, and these messages, that are my pleasure, must accumulate till a letter of repentance from you wipes out the last vestige of my sorrow for your infidelity. You are all my world and thoughts – if I war with them, it is civil war and I am no ground for passengers – no home for myself. I had thought of punishment in a viler shape – for example, announcing my face's disfigurement in a taxi accident, a change of allegiance – a note from Vinny telling of my mortal condition – but I was afraid of a future Wolf Wolf, and you not running like the French run to help me in my misfortune – besides the labourer in me is long dead.

I have become Commandant and secretary of this Hospital, and write officially for two hours a day. In this hand? with this spelling? Certainly. I continue tomorrow – My darling I love you –   Diana.

Duff to Diana, 24 June 1918   *B.E.F. France*

My darling. I dined alone tonight. You know that I love dining alone sometimes and that when I do so I think of you all the time. It was a lovely evening after a rainy day so that the air was full of smells, and birds singing. I walked out through the pinewoods to the Restaurant Champêtre. As I went I said *The Statue & the Bust* [Browning]. When I came to *the silver line that streaked her hair, and, worn by the serpent's tooth, the brow so puckered the chin so peaked*, I couldn't help thinking of darling Katharine which made me sad. There is so much grey in her hair now.

I had my dinner in a little room with a window looking on the pretty garden. Two nurses were in the room when I arrived but

[75]

they went at once and I had it to myself. The garden was so beautiful and full of flowers and quiet. There was no one there. I wanted you so much that I said your name aloud and called you 'love' and 'darling'. I was sad but not unhappy and I pictured very vividly bringing you there on some far distant happy day. I had *The Brothers Karamazov* with me but I read little of it, preferring to drink my claret and to think of you. One of my companions turned up with the coffee and broke my dreams. Trying to make the best of circumstances I probed him to discern whether he had any knowledge or any interests in life. I found that the only thing he really cares for is butterflies, or at least – as he was careful to explain – only British butterflies. So I made him tell me about them. Do you know that there are some which migrate to England from Northern Africa – or at least he says so. Imagine those delicate little creatures travelling all that way. It is as though we were to fly to the moon – I think he lies. There are two kinds that do so – and one is called the Clouded Yellow and the other the Painted Lady. Isn't it fun? I told him about the one I saw in the trenches which was like your dress and he said that it was called the Marbled White. I might become a butterfly bore but I shan't.

Try to remember when you next write to tell me where you dined tonight, Monday night. I was thinking so hard of you and trying to see you. I guessed the Gate[1] as a likely chance.   Duff.

Diana to Duff, 25 June 1918   *16 Arlington Street*

My only thought. I dined with Beavercrook[2] and found the Edwins, Nellie [Romilly] and McEvoy my fellow guests – the latter with hair hun-cropped and full Major's Khaki on.

Money and one's needs was the dinner talk – Edwin wanted £60,000 for his debts, Nellie £8 for a new bath – I asked and hoped for £1000 for the brave boys in hospital, at which Max rose and walking to the telephone rang up the *Daily Express*, ordering the sub-editor to make an appeal for the said £1000 tomorrow. Does he pay a man to receive such messages between eight and twelve as fudge – or is it true? I am bamfusled – It was a genuine call, for he took House of Commons news off him too.

---

[1] Edwin and Venetia Montagu's house, in Queen Anne's Gate.
[2] William Maxwell Aitken, Lord Beaverbrook: 1879–1964. Known to Diana as Max, 'Beavercrook' or 'Crooks'.

On Thursday I go to Leicester to act Britannia with words and without rehearsal – my bones have begun to soften. Tomorrow I shall be incoherent. Thursday night happy even though shamed. My darling I want *you* most. Your happiness next.   Diana.

Diana to Duff, 27 June 1918   *16 Arlington Street*

A letter from you this morning, my blessed Duff, as I was starting, writen on a Monday night after dining at the Pré Catelan. I was at the Montagus – you were right – I love to think of you calling my name aloud to the oaks & rills. It is a way I have always had since you left me – daily I call upon you, tremblingly as a rule. The butterfly news I loved too. Painted Ladies are so brave – do many fail in the flood? I'm sure they do – the marbled queens, too – like my dress. I started very early with mother – for Leicester and have had a shocking day – standing for hours on a rock as Britannia in clashing reds topped with Lady Wolverton's helmet. Adèle [Essex] told me she had an *élite* helmet, and as no shop had more to offer than bashed paper ones, and Clara Butt's[1] from which my feet peeped beneath, I asked her for the loan, and lovely it was. I thought my voice was marvellous resounding, and with reserve behind it, but I couldn't manage to feel much conviction or message in such words as "Who will protect the little children, and the old folk?" I'll send you photographs that were done, surrounded by my defending elements, a sister Moon like Jennie Porch dressed to kill and a sun of the huge large-paunched male type – not gorrilla but young Brighton perfumed school. I had flowers and crowds at the door and 3 cheers, and mother slouching behind with the hand luggage so I felt most like Miss Janis[2] touring.

Shall I do Juliet, or part of her for charity? Viola wants me to, I don't know whether to risk it. Advise. It couldn't be good, though severe coaching from Martin Harvey[3] would help a lot, but it would be terribly exciting and good for me to do something of

---

[1] Dame Clara Butt, 1873–1936. Six foot two inches in height, she did much valuable War work and sang stirring patriotic songs dressed as Britannia.
[2] Elsie Janis, 1889–1956. In 1918 she was in France, entertaining the troops of the A.E.F.
[3] Sir John Martin-Harvey, 1863–1944. Knighted in 1921, he was with Henry Irving's Company for fourteen years and then became manager of the Lyceum.

which I am truly frightened. Half the pleasure would die as I missed you, and a lot of fear too. My darling – where are you – be fortunate.   Diana.

Duff to Diana, 29 June 1918   *B.E.F. France*

Darling. While I was writing to you at that station yesterday the train went on and I was left looking foolish. However I stepped into the road and with my usual luck in these matters was presently picked up by a swift motor car and arrived triumphantly at my destination half an hour before the train.

Oh my darling, my Diana – the joy of my arrival. So many letters and such good ones. It was a shame sweetheart that you were defeated in your effort to chastise but really it would have made me too miserable. I should have said with Cain 'My punishment is greater than I can bear'. Dear love I do repent me – I swear by thyself I do and I know of nothing holier to swear by. Indeed even at this distance my love still grows. You ever seem to me more marvellous, more perfect as a companion, more inspired as a correspondent never failing nor slackening in interest and sweet variety, more adorable as an ideal and a divinity and as a mistress more desirable. I think about you continually, especially when I ought to be thinking of other things – so that I am a better lover than soldier.

30 June 1918

Eminent Victorians and *Frenzied Fiction*[1] came today. The fools had forwarded them to Hardelot where they must have arrived the day I left. Thank you darling for sending them. I do love reading the volumes you have read and marked.

Duff to Diana, 2 July 1918   *B.E.F. France*

We have had a most exhausting day – we marched about seven miles – I leading the battalion again, and leading them right this time, thank God. We went to a charming bathing place in the grounds of a château. At least it would have been charming for you and me but for a battalion of perspiring men it was inadequate.

[1] *Eminent Victorians* by Lytton Strachey and *Frenzied Fiction* by Stephen Leacock were both published in 1918.

Anxious to bathe before the water had been too polluted, I plunged in with my wrist watch on my arm. Now it won't go so I am sending it to you to be seen to. Will you be sweet and have it done as soon as possible. It is vital here to have one and will be more vital next week. Then I had to pay the company – and finally worst of all to inspect their feet – an experience which would cure the most confirmed pediphilist that ever bit boots.

Nor are my labours even now finished for after dinner I have to go and watch an imitation raid. Isn't it damnable – I long for the peace and quiet of the comfy line. The Commanding Officer has got the prevalent disease which pleases me because he is one of those people who doesn't believe in illness. I cannot give you a better idea of him than by telling you that the fact of my jumping into the water with my watch on has amused him and made him laugh more than anything ever before. Bless you. I have no time and never shall have to tell you how much I love you.   Duff.

Duff to Diana, 4 July 1918   *B.E.F. France*

My one darling – Three letters came from you this morning so you do love me after all. Lovely letters from Breccles[1] which made me laugh and one from Alan that made me cry. I cried at Alan's description of your sweetness, your beauty and your love for me. He expresses fear of my not fully realising the last. Perhaps I don't. One can hardly sometimes realise the greatest fabulous wealth, and I feel about your love as about a miraculous fortune that has come to me, which makes me proud and happy all day long and over which I ponder and gloat more avariciously than ever the maddest miser over his heap of gold. And it is true that I never knew how great it was until I came abroad. Imagine then the miser's joy, when, counting his shekels for the thousandth time, he finds that there are twice as many as he thought before. Alan goes on very charmingly to urge our marriage and makes me think of Shakespeare and Mr. W.H. He will not admit impediments. And certainly it does seem wicked that so great and unimaginable a joy should be hindered by the miserable shortage of crumpled Bradburys.[2] Tell me truly what you think about this and about the

[1] Breccles, Norfolk – the home of Edwin and Venetia Montagu.
[2] Pound notes. Bradbury was the Chief Cashier whose signature endorsed each one.

irreducible minimum. I think I asked you once before and you didn't answer.

I thought of sending you Alan's letter but I can't spare it, so I will quote a little. "Diana is too lovely at present – lovelier and younger I think than I have ever seen her, and Duffy she does love you so much – perhaps you don't realise it and will be glad to have me tell you, but it really is true and you should be very proud of it. She thinks of you all day, watches the post eagerly for your letters and loves to talk about what you are doing and what you have done and will do with her" (I cried –) "I wish you would marry her, Duffy. She would take you at once if it were practicable. And can't it be made practicable? I don't suggest that you should do what I did – which is to marry on £400 worth of debts though I would like to point out that even a crushing burden like that is not a fatal obstacle to a happy marriage. But I wish it could be made possible, your marriage couldn't fail" and more in needless but pretty praise of your qualities and assurances which God knows are unnecessary to me of how perfect a wife you would make. "She is not only the most beautiful woman in the world but also the best, the most warm-hearted, the most gentle, the most loyal. Is all this to change and wither after marriage? Surely it can only blossom the more etc." Damn him, he appears to think I am hanging back. He can't think that really but is only carried away by his own verbosity.

You surely, darling, have never doubted how madly proud and wildly happy I should always have been and always will be to marry you under any conceivable conditions, how little I should mind poverty, how gladly I should renounce all my extravagances and vices, break my champagne glasses, throw away my cigars, tear up my cards, sell all my books, the first editions first, study the habits of buses and the intricacies of tubes to obtain that inconceivable honour. You don't believe this – you shake your lovely head, your pale eyes look reproaches for past transgressions and too recent ones but, oh my best, you can surely see how different it would all be then. Believe, believe me how gladly I would spurn the delights and live laborious days[1] – and indeed what could it matter then how the days were spent.

But what would Her Grace say, and His Grace too? Though two old people with three legs in the grave between them should surely

[1] Milton, *Lycidas*.

never be allowed to hinder us. So I propose to you again. It is just five years since I did so first – by letter from Hanover in fun, do you remember. I can still remember your answer. I wonder what it will be this time. Whatever it is, my life, it cannot make me love you more.

It was sweet of Alan to write, wasn't it? Perhaps he showed you the letter, in which case I shall look silly. You were writing to me near him at the time. He described you stretched under an apple tree. My jewel, my beauty.   Duff.

Diana to Duff, 8 July 1918   *16 Arlington Street*

My beloved angel, such a wonderful letter this morning about our marrying. It was my cure, my wings, my darling Duff with me. I feel it may be so. I know I cannot be as happy without you, but these dread days indicate less than ever a means. After all I'm living on those who are bound to keep me now that you cannot be with me, and when you are here I shall anyway live with you in the dark nights, so I am not more unfortunate than others, though sometimes it is all like wine being spilt (also fruit).

In a sense the world shapes to hide our possible squalor, no one shall have motors since we cannot, there shall be fewer servants all round, and food is not to be bought, but wine shall flow which our guests' other hosts lock up and so they'll love us best, and never pity our poverty.

It was very sweet of Alan to write such incense. I remember his scribbling away at Breccles and when I asked him "What was the matter", he said he was telling you about Edwin's swallowed-fly which I had already done. Write to him very sweetly darling – someone told him you always were bored with him and it's upset him so.

On reaching the last page it isn't what I meant to write. I wanted to be tenderer and more loving than ever before in return for the divine beauty and generousness and unselfishness of your letter and instead its trite and facetious. My darling you know that I would marry you and love you for years, and that I would fly to you with the jubilance and excitement of a child to a fresh lover – but, so far, for you and me there is no betrothing, no nothing – only stolen days and nights and perfect as they are, young in our love as they have kept us, one day we will boast to the world instead. Your letter gave me many castles to build all day. I do not dare allow them – they will tempt this Fortune who will whirl you out of life and my sight in revenge for my forgetting her.

I love you, love you.   Diana.

Write quick to A. if not nice enough already, then again now. I think it so extraordinarily sweet of him. He must only have thought of making you happy. He doubts your love less than I do, blessed one. I did not tell him you quoted.

Duff to Diana, 8 July 1918   *B.E.F. France*

Sweet darling heart – No mail today from England, which made everyone cry but none so much as me – *nulli flebilior quam mihi*[1] – I have just written to Alan on the subject of his letter to me. I have told him that God knows I never needed prompting and that the decision rests only with you. And I have pointed out to him the arguments against – your arguments and the world's for I have none – the arguments of the star against the moth, of King Cophetua's best friends against the beggar maid, of all which I am probably more sensible than you; so don't think, darling, that I wish to force your hand and you may if you like and find it easier ignore the matter in your letters altogether. I only feel that in a collapsing world it would be a great bid for happiness which the fates don't seem likely to bestow on us unless we fight for it. As for the pecuniary aspect – while the war goes on it hardly matters – everyone lives from hand to mouth and from lunch to dinner. Afterwards there will surely be work to be done, or shall we say jobs to be got, in the securing of which our combined talents could not fail us. People have started on less and lived happy ever afterwards. But there – don't let me bother you. Your answer will probably be the traditional one of the Old Gang[2] and I can't quarrel with it.

I have nearly finished the *Eminent Victorians*. He tries to be detached and dispassionate but he doesn't succeed. You can feel reading the book that he is pleased that Miss Nightingale grew fat and that her brain softened, and he is delighted that Gordon drank. I must say that he makes me like both better than I did

---

[1] cf. Horace, Odes, I, 24.
[2] 'Wait and see'.

before, partly out of opposition. Dr Arnold of course is a bit too much.

You never tell me, you naughty child, whether you are learning what I told you to learn out of the *Dream*. I have learnt to where Demetrius and Helena come in and don't know whether to go straight on or to jump to 'I know a bank'.

Good bye, my love.   Duff.

One last word about that Victorian book. Isn't the last sentence typical of the whole and isn't it poor? 'At any rate it had all ended very happily in a glorious slaughter of twenty thousand Arabs, a vast addition to the British Empire and a step in the peerage for Sir Evelyn Baring.' How neat, how cheap. I am sure Lytton Strachey must be a very thin man who doesn't drink. I think he might marry Elizabeth[1] and produce real worms. And yet I'm so sorry I've finished his book and would at the moment give £5 for another like it. But I always love books about the Victorians.

My dear, have you seen the *Morning Post* these days about Edwin's report.[2] It is really too insulting but rather funny. On Monday it says that when the Indians ". . . see Mr. Montagu coming to India they argue with themselves: 'Why does the British Raj advance this person of ignoble birth?' – for there is unhappily a prejudice against the Montagu type in India . . .

Mr. Montagu is to them merely a symbol of the decadence of the British Empire."

Does Edwin read it and wince, or read it and laugh, or not read it? Good bye, baby. Are you going to marry me?   Duff.

Diana to Duff, 9 July 1918   *16 Arlington Street*

My darling, Your letter today asks me for a picture – rather queer as I have been inundating you with them these last days. I send you another today – for the sake of the romance in it. She was a spy – her prettiness you can believe, her hair is of an acid peroxyde colour and her skin frail. She told her beads while Orpen painted

---

[1] Elizabeth Asquith, 1897–1945, daughter of H. H. Asquith by his second wife Margot. She wrote novels and poetry, and married Prince Antoine Bibesco, a Roumanian diplomat who was a close and loyal friend of Marcel Proust.

[2] The Montagu–Chelmsford Report on India, which Edwin Montagu and Lord Chelmsford had recently completed.

her the day before she was shot, crying terribly. The story is told but not believed that she asked to be allowed to dress properly for her execution, so her maid was allowed to go to the cell taking with her an unequalled sable and chinchilla coat, and a pair of white satin mules. She asked for no bandage, no cords for her hands and begged for short warning. When it came she let the furs slip from her naked body and lie like a vanquished animal round her feet. Like that they shot her. No doubt she had a little hope and faith in her beauty earning her a reprieve.

Duff to Diana, 11 July 1918   *B.E.F. France*

My darling – No letter from you today which worries me because you were ill when you last wrote. This morning I distinguished myself as an advocate. I had to play the part of Prisoner's Friend at a Court Martial. The man had written a letter containing military information. Everyone knew he had done it and he had previously confessed as much to his Company Commander and the Commanding Officer. However, by legal quibbles, by successfully objecting to half the evidence and by a brilliant oration, I secured his acquittal. Nobody more astonished than the prisoner. So after the war, darling, I go straight to the Bar and shall soon become as rich as Isaacs.[1]

I am going on with Gibbon. Here is what I read this morning about the conversion of Clovis and liked. "The mind of Clovis was susceptible of transient fevers: he was exasperated by the pathetic tale of the passion and death of Christ, and instead of weighing the salutary consequences of that mysterious sacrifice, he exclaimed with indiscreet fury 'Had I been present at the head of my valiant Franks, I would have revenged his injuries'."

How will new legislation about Aliens affect Olga. I have never known exactly what her position is. Will she be expatriated, poor little pimp? I have read *The Two Gentlemen of Verona* – a pleasant play with a very weak ending and no purple patch.

> *Oh how this spring of love resembleth*
> *The uncertain glory of an April day.*[2]

Beauty.   Duff.

---

[1] Rufus Isaacs, 1st Marquess of Reading, 1866–1935. Lord Chief Justice, 1913–21, and Viceroy of India, 1921–6.
[2] *Two Gentlemen of Verona*, Act I scene iii.

Diana to Duff, 13 July 1918   *The Wharf, Sutton Courtney*

My darling, I have touched the apex of wild despair. The party is Cynthia [Asquith], Mary [Herbert], Beb[1] Hugo R[umbold], Sidney Russell-Cook, Eliza [Elizabeth Asquith], 2 Mackennas,[2] 2 Asquith and from ten to twelve after a parched dinner Mary and I and Hugo and Beb sat in a fireless room in the Mill House. At dinner Beb had relieved the monotony a trifle by turning to Mrs Joshua and saying with intent about a German battle "We won it, no you did, no I think we did."[3]

On returning to those three clostrophobied little rooms the old boy turned me out into the rather cold garden, to a seat where we spent an hour in acute mental and physical discomfort. He is on my nerves terribly. God knows I hold a small enough brief for sincerity and what Mother calls realness, but his cross question-ings and invitation of confidence and star lit talks are so laughably rhetorical. Whenever he sees me he automatically remembers Raymond (and only then I think) and then invariably after a short flimsy transition link he murmurs a mouthful of clichés. I got very tired of racking my brain what to say next and of defending my face from his fumbly hands and mouth, and I tell you with shame my darling, I put up a poor fight and a poor mental output.

Wade I loved this morning because she volunteered some reminiscences of last years Wharf and reeled off the guests, all with the purpose I think of saying when she reached your name "How is Mr. Cooper, milady, has he been much in the front line?" I said "yes, he has" curtly with 10,000 beams raying towards her from my heart. I love you.   Diana.

Duff to Diana, 14 July 1918   *B.E.F. France*

My darling – A wet day but a letter from you which is better than sunshine. I can't bear the story about Orpen's spy. It quite worried me until I dismissed it from my mind, as the lady did the story of the Gospels, with the comfortable reflection that it all happened long ago and let's hope it isn't true.

---

[1] Herbert 'Beb' Asquith, 1881–1947, 2nd son of H. H. Asquith by his first wife. He was a barrister, and married Lady Cynthia Charteris in 1910.

[2] Rt. Hon. Reginald McKenna, 1863–1943, Barrister. Entered Parliament in 1895, and held the posts of Home Secretary (1911–15) and Chancellor of the Exchequer (1915) among others. He married Pamela Jekyll in 1908.

[3] Mrs. Joshua's maiden name was Hirsch.

I love the pictures you have sent me. The little round head is most beautiful and fits into a place designed for stamps on this little writing pad, which I have always with me and all the others fit in behind the writing paper very secretly.

Carstairs[1] is here now. You probably know and dislike him. I like him – here at any rate – as Brummell liked certain people at Bath but not in London. Duff.

Duff to Diana, 15 July 1918   *B.E.F. France*

There were two letters from you this morning, my beloved – and there was also Orpen's picture of the spy. I am so wretched about her. I do hope she wasn't quite as pretty as that. I had rather a thousand Nurse Cavells[2] had been shot. Tell me all you know about her.

This monotony goes on. I must eat less – the insidious whisper *à quoi bon?* shakes my resolve at every meal. But it would be sad if in a war where many have lost their arms and legs and some their lives I should be so careless as to lose my figure. I kiss your bluest vein.[3] Duff.

Duff to Diana, 17 July 1918   *B.E.F. France*

My Pleasure – There was a letter from you today which made me happy. I will answer it. I don't think we need bother much about Henry James. I have read *What Maisie Knew* but never quite found out exactly what she did know though I hope for her sake, poor little bitch, she knew a bit more than I did about the story. Patrick always made rather a point of Henry James, but Patrick's dead.

I have learnt the whole of Act 2, Scene 1, of *Midsummer Night's Dream* except the conversation between Helena and Demetrius, but I think I shall learn it. As you go into my room it is on your right under the Duke of Wellington by the screen, fourth shelf from the top. Oberon has the Dolphin fun but Titania has the little

---

[1] Carroll Carstairs, an American soldier. He and Duff took Paris leave together in October 1918, a time described in Carstairs' book of war memoirs called *A Generation Missing* (1930).

[2] Edith Cavell, 1865–1915, matron of the *École Belge des Infirmières Diplômées*, was shot by the Germans on October 13th 1915 for harbouring British, French and Belgian soldiers and helping them to escape.

[3] *Antony and Cleopatra*, Act II scene 5.

bit about the boy's mother which I love. However I know it all so you can say the parts you like – even 'Didst thou not lead him through the glimmering night' – I love those lines, and I love the idea of a fairy mistress aiding and abetting her favourite's amours and encouraging his rapes and infidelities.

I think I should like to read the Aga Khan's book[1] – but why do you suggest Ivar Campbell's poems?[2] They were published nearly a year ago and I read them ten years before that. I have most of them in the author's manuscript. I sat by while they were written and one verse – and that to my mind the best in the book – I wrote myself. So don't send me them.

How silly of Alan not to show you my letter. I wonder why. It was written for your eyes as all I write must be and all I do. You say I must not love you less. Oh, my darling, fear anything but that. Surely I have more grounds of fear than you have – for you still live among wine and roses and love, surrounded by the ardent youth of England and the still more ardent middle age and eld, while I see nothing but dusty veterans lumbering about in sweat and lice. But even if I were on Calypso's isle with Helen to wait at table and the Sirens coming in to sing after dinner I can imagine no enchantments or enchantresses which could lure me from my fidelity.   Duff.

Duff to Diana, 18 July 1918   *B.E.F. France*

The real captain of this company isn't Wine Red – but another man whom I don't much like and who came up just now and looking at my writing case said, "I suspect that little round thing in the stamp case of being a photograph". I confessed and blushed and felt pleased, pleased to have your picture spoken of even though the speaker was ignorant, and knew not what he said. I am glad he is going down after lunch to where I came from. His name is Tufnell, [Captain N. C. Tufnell] he suffers from piles, he is apt to get nervous and when nervous is rude.

Now I *must* have lunch. Good bye, my angel.   Duff.

[1] The Aga Khan, 1877–1957; *India in Transition* (1918).
[2] Poems by Ivar Campbell, 1890–1916, with a memoir by Guy Ridley (1917).

Duff, I am so despicable and awful. I find tonight after a dinner and dance at Ava's that I have grown bitter and evil-tongued about other people, pointing out Ruby's feet, Mrs. Dudley Ward's[1] paint, Ava's face pleats to comparative strangers. I sat between Wolkoff and Sidney Russell Cook – the latter has constituted himself my lover. I am glad because he makes a pretty show and because I have not raised a lid to allure him, but I cannot do even as much to keep him, and he does not stir a spark of interest in me. He is undoubtedly a *spintria*[2] I think, but so is his own father with an Adam house in the Isle of Wight.

Beaverbrook took me to see a private view of a German produced film, unreleasable because of its origin, but of such gross commonness and vulgarity that I think it should make fine propogander. Nothing I have seen or heard has bred more hate in me of the enemy – old men's lips and fat women caught bending. Crooks also produced from his pocket a wireless they had just intercepted from Germany making tremendous propergander of His Grace's prayer for rain.[3] "Ld. Rutland gives us to understand," it runs, "that the harvest in England is even worse than our highest hopes, all crops are dried up . . ." etc., and many enlargements. Poor Dad. Two letters today, I tremble for tomorrow. I adore you so.   Diana.

We leave here this evening and go up to the front line where we remain for 48 hours so when you get this we shall be there no longer. I shall be glad to leave this spot. There are too many large fat rats whose bulk I suspect of being due to a series of supper parties with the British army. And as for the flies – whatever other faults he may have had, I consider the favourite pastime of the Emperor Domitian to have been both laudable and sanitary.[4] I

---

[1] Born Winifred (Freda) Birkin, she married the Rt. Hon. Dudley Ward in 1913. She was a great favourite of the Prince of Wales during the late twenties.

[2] The *spintriae* were the young boys and girls, well-trained in exotic sexual deviations, who entertained the Emperor Tiberius in his palace at Capri.

[3] On July 9th, the Duke of Rutland sent a letter to *The Times*, urging all churches to start praying for rain. This letter earned him the title of 'The Damp Duke'.

[4] "At the beginning of his reign Domitian would spend hours alone every day catching flies, and stabbing them with a needle-sharp pen." – Suetonius, translated by Robert Graves.

very likely shan't have time to write for two days so don't wonder or worry.

Do you like Hutchinson.[1] Mother met him in the train and he said that you had told him I should soon be coming on leave. I wish it were so. Since I have been out only one officer has gone from this Battalion. So you may imagine I am pretty low on the list. Goodbye, my only love, my only joy, goodbye.   Duff.

Duff to Diana, 21 July 1918   *B.E.F. France*

Darling – I should be justified in not writing today as I have so little time for sleep but I can't sleep happy until I have written. We arrived here [the front line] last midnight and I slept until nearly three. It is now ten a.m. Two bottles of port arrived for me this morning, which cheered us up enormously especially as we had already received two bottles last night – the first we have seen for weeks. Wine Red's eyes glistened and he said "With four bottles of port in hand I regard the day as won." He doesn't drink whiskey, poor lamb, and has been having toothache, which combined with our rather uneasy and very muddy position had begun to depress him. We take it in turns to walk round which takes some time to do. I did it early this morning – from five to eight. The morning began with clouds and a shower – the kind of morning Milton thinks of in *Il Penseroso* – and then the sun came out fitfully but very prettily through the clouds, making strange yellow lights and the air smelt fresh and sweet, which it has not done lately. Also the larks sang as though they were mad with joy. I came back soon after eight and with great difficulty got one mug of water to shave and wash in, which means one less mug of water to drink till tomorrow night. And now I am having a glass of port and writing to you and waiting till 11 when I go on duty again. My feet are cold and wet and my legs are muddy but my hands are clean and my face is smooth, clean enough to touch your hands, smooth enough to kiss your face.   Duff.

Duff to Diana, 23 July 1918   *B.E.F. France*

We were relieved last night and reached our present home safely. It is a beautiful dug out, safe, spacious and airy. I felt ill last night

[1] St. John Hutchinson K.C., 1884–1942. Barrister and liberal politician.

[89]

and couldn't sleep – nor have since – although I have been looking forward to sleep for so long. And I thought of you and worked myself into a fever – a real fever – of jealousy. I thought of other people's arms round you and others' awful ghastly mouths – a waking nightmare – and I wondered and like a flagellant tortured myself with the speculation how much you would tell me of any folly that wine and loneliness and melancholy might induce you to. Then I imagined – nearly mad by then – your falling or tripping into the proverbially greatest folly and asked myself whether you would tell me that. I pictured you remorseful – a lovely picture – deciding at last upon confession. My imagination was taxed. Then the final and fiercest problem, my reception of that letter and my reply. First solution – no reply – dead silence for evermore – sending back further letters unopened – a cruel ugly attitude. I blushed for myself taking it.

Second solution – a laughing answer – hope you liked it – wonder you never tried before – was it really the first – how many years wasted – hooray – better late than never, don't think I mind – shall call when next in London, best wishes and bless your heart. More subtly cruel, and I rather admired myself in the attitude but knew that I could keep it no longer than standing on one leg.

My third solution was so beautiful that it made me cry – regretting – owning my regret was largely selfish – forgiving – asking who was I to forgive – thanking – rather humbly for the charity of the confession – loving – not as much, but by so much more as Jesus loved the repenting sinner and the lost lamb. I had almost sobbed myself to sleep with the beauty of my final attitude when it was three o'clock and time to stand to. Then when your letter came this morning and I read "Duff I am so despicable and awful" – I thought I was in for it and took another glass of port: and it was only – Oh lovely baby – that you had abused this woman's feet and that one's face, so that my lovely pardon remains unwritten – but it is still up my sleeve. I laugh but you will understand everything I mean – will understand that I am a little tired and a little feverish – that I want to know always everything you do, who drives you home, who tries to kiss you, who succeeds, to whom in your more wretched and too too few moments of passing ecstasy you yield a little and perhaps shut your eyes and think – oh, my conceit – of me.

I begin to rave – this letter is too long. Know only this that you are everything and the only thing I care for in my world and whenever I am in danger or think of death, I shudder to think of making you unhappy and of not seeing you again.

Love me, trust me, think of me as much as utterly as always as I love, trust and think of you.   Duff.

Duff to Diana, 25 July 1918   *B.E.F. France*

My desire – We came back last night marching some distance under a full and most suggestive moon.

Here we found our kits awaiting us and we had the joy of going to sleep with our boots off, inside our pyjamas and our own little bags and slept till ten like Gods in heaven. We are pleasantly situated on the top of the largest rise in rolling country so that we see for miles and the air is fresh. We are here for six days and can do hardly any work because we are in sight of some Germans miles away. I sleep with Wine-Red in a very well constructed little dwelling, quite safe with yards of concrete on the top – made by Germans so it's sure to be good – and we have a separate sitting room. I am reading *The Moonstone*[1] which you wouldn't like but I love because it is two of my favourite things, Victorian and a detective story.

Your interview with Edwin is sad. I think their troubles are unworthy of them both. If Edwin's only trouble is Venetia's lack of interest in politics tell him not to be an ass – if it is rather her lack of interest in him tell her not to be an ass but if necessary to simulate – if it is debt tell them both not to be bloody fools but to sell Breccles which they need never have bought. But really it surpasses my belief that a pair so wordly wise and so money wise starting married life two years ago in affuence can *really* now be in financial difficulties. We must remember how Edwin invariably magnifies misfortune and foresees disaster.

Darling – We must try to be philosophic about time. We must put away impatience with a grand gesture – trust in our love and think of days as moments and years as hours – and see all the obstacles dividing us which after all are only time and space and circumstance and people as very small and insignificant compared to the magnificence of ourselves. Then we shall be happy and quiet.   Duff.

[1] By Wilkie Collins (1868).

[91]

Duff to Diana, 26 July 1918   *B.E.F. France*

It is so pleasant here – more like one's old-fashioned ideas of war – standing on the top of a hill and seeing the battle fields all round you. We can see miles of the country held by the enemy which looks much closer from here than it does from the front line. And ten miles away we can see – and lovely it looks through glasses – the ruins of the cathedral which once graced the hiding place of the rash old man.[1]

I don't expect to like the Beresford book you say you've sent me.[2] I have read reviews of it. I don't like the very new novelists and the very new poets. They make me think of Osbert[3] and Elizabeth [Asquith], of mean restaurants and bad wine. I came across a book of poems by Alec Waugh[4] lately which I thought miserable. These new poets – all that I have read – seem to me especially bad about the war. They can't see anything in it but lice and dirty feet and putrid corpses and syphilis. God knows that nobody living loathes the war more than I do or realises more fully the waste and folly and universal unrelieved unnecessary harm it does. But there is romance in it. Nothing so big can be without it – and there is beauty too – I have seen plenty from our parting at Waterloo until today. And those poets ought to see it and reproduce it instead of going on whining and jibing. And the ones that don't whine say it is all so glorious because we're fighting for liberty and the world set free and to hell with the Hohenzollerns and the Yanks are coming. This attitude of course is even more tiresome than the other. I think Rupert Brooke might have continued to do it alright. He started well. God bless your body –   Duff.

Diana to Duff, 9 August 1918   *Breccles Hall, Norfolk*

My darling sweet, No letter today. I am terrified that you may be among filth and stench and in no mood to do more than unsensitise yrself. I have had a laborious day of bicycling to and from town and to and from shoots. Edwin insists on staying out till 10.30 p.m. which makes the servants bad-tempered and really

[1] Arras. See page 67.
[2] *God's Counterpoint* by J. D. Beresford (1918).
[3] Osbert Sitwell, 1892–1969. Poet, novelist, essayist and critic.
[4] *Resentment: Poems* by Alec Waugh (1918).

now its a mute point which is the most moodily unreliable, he or his wife. Tonight I played chess with Edwin and got left behind with him, he drew me on the sofa and said "Must you go to bed? or will you stay and love me a little." – "I must go to bed, but I always love you". "Not in the way I want though." silence and an almost imperceptible drag away on my part. "Go to bed then" – and he sprang up, walked sharply to his room and banged the door. I think Venetia refuses him and he is half mad with desires. Poor baboon. I've told Viola she must sacrifice herself. My darling, leave looks more and more remote. How is it bearable. I do want you.   D.

Diana to Duff, 11 August 1918   *Breccles Hall*

My light, I have been lying on a wide sofa since dinner while Edwin read aloud a story by Galsworthy (the first one: I have sent it you today) that I had read before. I made him read it, because I wanted the others to be engrossed that I might be free to enjoy your complete empire over me. I was so happy – half a bottle of champagne had put you nearly out of harm's way. These rooms are lit by a few spare candles and my limbs in this demi-light seemed to flow with peculiar grace, and my green film cloak to foam and curl round them like Aphrodite's birth-waves.

I ordered my waking dream and it was obedient, so that my greatest imaginings of joy seemed realisable in a fairy way. I wanted you to see me, almost as greatly as my eyes wanted you; and I wanted your love to transcend its own clear maximum immeasurably. I wanted you to take me up in your arms to a prepared bed, and above all I wanted to yield you there all my treasure at a price of pain, and that that price should be high that you might know the zeal of the giving.

If I could have written then, I could have made your soul aflame as you read: but Edwin's voice wound up and there has been an hour's good nights and Bradshaw talk, and Alan's asthma has claimed my attention as a hypodermic expert, so I offer you this tribute, cold, from a hand trembling once again with apprehensions, and inevitable reaction.

I should go to Ashby[1] tomorrow, reluctantly – but wait still for a word from Lady Wimborne. My dear one, love me.

[1] Country house of Lord Wimborne.

Alas! I didn't send you Boufflers[1] or the other. I am so glad you like it. I adored it. In a hundred years shall we be read? I fear not, but all's one.   D.

Duff to Diana, 11 August 1918   *B.E.F. France*

These last two nights I have spent crouching and crawling. As I lay flat on the dun wet ground I pictured your party at dinner – Birrell fingering his port glass benignly meditating a roar, Edwin, stomach thrust forward with sunken chin and listening eyes, Scatters holding the table and the attention of all with infectious smile and slightly frog-like expression of lust, Venetia fingering her hair, speaking seldom and with quick assurance while watching with anxiety the servants, the food and the wine, you leaning forward and from side to side like the conductor of an orchestra calling at will for the right sound from each instrument, yourself bright and animated and beautiful as the Mother of Love. That you see is what I am thinking of when I ought to be thinking of the enemy and of a thousand other things. We have a password when we go out on patrol and last night I nearly gave them "Diana" but I was too shy to. Would you like to think of fierce men crawling about No Man's Land in the darkness, and whispering your name to one another when they meet?

This afternoon in lovely sunlight and heat I went for a little crawl by myself and had rather fun. I found an arm sticking out of the earth. I don't know what impulse made me take off the glove. The arm had been there a long time and there was little left but the bones. The hand was beautiful – thin and delicate like the hand of a woman and the nails had grown long and even like a Mandarin's nails. How much the flesh may once have hidden the beauty of the framework you couldn't tell, but it must always have been a small hand and I think the owner must have been proud of it because gloves are not usually worn at the war. It gave me no feeling of disgust or uneasiness but rather content to find that beauty can still hang about the bones, surviving the corruption of the flesh, and staying with the body until the bitter end of complete annihilation. The hand was raised and the fingers curved in rather an affected gesture. I wish I could have kept the glove. My brother

[1] *The Chevalier de Boufflers, a Romance of the French Revolution* by Nesta H. Webster (1916).

officers were amazed at my lack of squeamishness in removing the glove from a corpse – and yet they would think nothing of treading on a beetle. How different we are. Thank God we are not as other men.

When I came in from my crawl I found a hard case to deal with. Some stretcher bearers carrying down dead and wounded this morning had during their absence been despoiled of their few belongings by their brave companions. It is apparently understood that when a man is killed or wounded his comrades instantly pounce on his belongings, but to take those of the stretcher bearers too was considered a bit hot.

And oh, I hadn't finished the story of my crawl. I finished by getting back into our own trenches at a sentry post without being detected by the sentry which shows how clever I am and how bad is the British Army.   Duff.

Diana to Duff, 16 August 1918   *Breccles Hall*

My treasure-house, You must not again miss a day's letter. I love you too utterly now to bear the anxiety, only a word however tired and it saves me a sea of troubles. I did not hear of you from Tuesday at Ashby (which I counted as Monday in London) till Friday and against all reasoning I thought you dead, and my joy dead with you. I woke, as I foretold you I would, at first dawn, and by nine was crying. The smoke grimed vault of Paddington at eleven seemed, as William met me with one fluttering letter, suddenly a pleasuance and shining with peace and light. A sad letter but very beautiful, my darling. What a strange impulse to unglove the dead hand. You could only have done it alone, and I wonder how you told them you had done it, or why you told them or perhaps you never did. It makes a great impression on me. I have thought of it all day. Your expression of it, I think, is chiefly the reason for this.

The train [to Breccles] took two hours longer than scheduled, on account of most of the U.S. Army, and ill mannered curs they are, jeering and booing and even insulting us as we passed their windows. The hundred German prisoners drawn up further on I found far decenter. The relationships of the Monts [Montagus] is worse daily – he had preceeded us, and was out shooting when we arrived, and returning in the middle of dinner beaming and keen with an evening walk, and many kills, he kissed my hands first then Viola's fervently and in fond anticipation of Venetia's at last, but smilelessly she did not let it meet his lips and with an irritated gesture asked a gruff question about a baillif. I am not magnifying, and I am terrified.

I have thought of your hands, since your letter, and their long beauty and naughty nervousness that I have so often reprooved, and the faint scar on one, and the art and cunning and sense in both – and this minute I want the touch of them – fleet and jealous loved hands.   Diana.

Duff to Diana, 14 August 1918   *B.E.F. France*

I read Eddie's memoir of Rupert Brooke yesterday.[1] It is well done and will live with the poems as one of the curiosities of literature. The poems themselves on re-reading I find never quite first-rate. There is no whole poem, or sonnet even that I want to know by heart. How beautiful his funeral sounds. I envy Patrick who commanded the firing party. I bet he was thinking all the time of his next word of command. I don't think he cared particularly for Brooke. We don't make new friends easily. We had too many. I don't think I have made a friend since Oxford – have I? It is perhaps a pity but I think it is better not to lower the standard. What Rupert Brooke says about his friends[2] might very well with a few alterations be applied to ours. I get on well enough with the boys here and like them but feel no affection for them and no pleasure in their company. I had as soon dine alone as dine with any of them. I feel very much, only rather more kindly, what Gibbon felt about the officers in his regiment.[3] I may have quoted that to you already so I won't do it again.

Reading about Rupert Brooke makes one half in love with easeful death.[4] It is very becoming to die young, but to be on the

---

[1] The *Memoir of Rupert Brooke*, by Edward Marsh, was written a few months after the poet's death in 1915. It was published with Brooke's *Collected Poems* in 1918.

[2] "... there is no man who has had such friends as I ... so prone to laughter, so strong in affection ... so stern with vices and so blind to faults and folly, of such swiftness of mind and such strength of body, so apt both to make jokes and to understand them." Quoted in the *Memoir*, see above.

[3] "The loss of so many busy and idle hours was not compensated by any elegant pleasure; and my temper was insensibly soured by the society of our rustic officers." Edward Gibbon, *Memoirs of my Life and Writings* (1796).

[4] Keats, *Ode to a Nightingale.*

[96]

safe side you need a background of sea and mountains and isles of Greece. The plains of Picardy and the flats of Flanders aren't good enough. But there are consolations for the deaths of the light foot lads. Think of Julian growing more like Lord Desborough and John growing more like Lord Manners. Twiggy [Anderson]'s charm was going and would all have gone with the beauty of his face and the swiftness of his feet – and oh what would have happened to Denny [Anson]? However it is a profitless speculation and cold comfort. And it is better to be a live Lord than a dead Lieutenant.   Duff.

Duff to Diana, 15 August 1918   *B.E.F. France*

Darling – A very slow letter came from you today. It was written on the ninth. It told of Edwin's overture which made me shudder a little. And it shocked me that you should tell Viola to sacrifice herself. Damn the man – he's got a wife and if he can't tame her let him pay a mistress. Don't let's be too tolerant of silly weakness in our friends.

I have finished two books today. The Aga and the Corsican [i.e. Napoleon]. Odd the glamour which clings to the latter – do what one will to away with it. I hate him really but read any scrap about him with interest.   D.

Duff to Diana, 16 August 1918   *B.E.F. France*

Oh my love – Such a letter from you this morning. It made my heart beat, my eyes swim and my head reel. I stretched out my arms for you – for you as you lay in abandonment to me in the dark room while Edwin read. Oh my dear love, my very heart's blood, the thought of you is with me all day and I sleep with the desire of you. Every day that passes I count as one day nearer to you. We should have passed mid-channel now.

I wonder what your plans are and whether you are still at Breccles? I like to think of you in the country these hot days – driving to market through the fields of poppies, living calmly as it were in retreat and thinking a lot of me. Oh, I forgot you may be going to Ashby [the house of Lord Wimborne] – a lovely setting for you too, but the weather rather warm for struggling with old gentlemen. I have been looking today at the *Confession* of the wife of

[97]

Sacher Masoch – a disappointing squalid little book.[1] She didn't enter into his ideas of fun at all and hated whipping him which he made her do daily – he also insisted on her having lovers and he would dress her to receive them and then make her kick him out of the room.

Good-bye, my heart. I love you more and more and more which I could have sworn was impossible – and you must love me more, *much* more than you do – and tell me so continually – and exaggerate a little when you tell me. You are my drug, my madness, my solitary desire.   Duff.

Duff to Diana, 18 August 1918   *B.E.F. France*

My beloved – Yesterday morning came a message from Sidney borne by a motor bicyclist with a side car urging me to get into the latter and lunch and dine and sleep and go the next day to Katharine and Rosemary.[1] There were difficulties as the battalion was suddenly moved the day before yesterday and to use an army slang phrase for which I have no alternative, there is 'wind up'. This means that everyone is excited, some people nervous, no one knowing what is to happen, everyone full of ideas and rumours.

Diana to Duff, 20 August 1918   *16 Arlington Street*

My angel, It's all true what is said about love – the enobling power of it. Tonight as I drove home alone – my thoughts were of my nightly happy duty. This duty is the first I have ever found to be a fine pleasure and an unselfish one too in its search for expression and words to give you satisfaction. This evening I feared a little to have nothing to tell, save the twice-told – thousandth told, tale of devotion. The fear was a proof of zeal to please you. All my home life has been a wish to please authorities (supported by a benefit to be derived from the success of it) and only through deception was it achieved. How serene, in contrast, is the belief that the nearer my utterance is to truth, the more joy will it breed. When before has one framed truth or striven for a more convincing way of declaring it?

[1] Wanda de Sacher-Masoch – *Confession de Ma Vie* (1907).
[2] Katharine Asquith and Rosemary Leveson-Gower were working in a hospital in St. Omer.

[98]

The day ended with a dinner at Mulberry and a calm un-accountably pleasant 'droning through' of old German operas. The pleasure was augmented by constantly remembering that you were missing nothing.[1] It is only when you are there that there is anything to miss – there's a theme for an Elizabethan minor soneteer to labour at. It's very late, I adore you – Diana.

Duff to Diana, 20 August 1918   *B.E.F. France*

Darling, my darling – One line in haste to tell you that I love you more today than ever in my life before, that I never see beauty without seeing you or scent happiness without thinking of you.

You have fulfilled all my ambition, realized all my hopes, made all my dreams come true. You have set a crown of roses on my youth and fortified me against the disaster of our days. Your courageous gaiety has inspired me with joy. Your tender faithful-ness has been a rock of security and comfort. I have felt for you all kinds of love at once. I have asked much of you and you have never failed me. You have intensified all colours, heightened all beauty, deepened all delight. I love you more than life, my beauty, my wonder.   Duff.

Diana to Duff, 22 August 1918   *16 Arlington Street*

My adored Duff, The days I have dreaded almost most are upon us. Your letter of the ninth came on the twenty-second, together with one – of so much love and tenderness written on the twentieth, that it frightened me more than any warning. I have not known what to do with my easeless self. Telephoning unceasingly to Osbert[2] for news, which he never had, and even lunching with him. Bed all the afternoon in despair, and up at seven to go and meet Katharine. Every means of locomotion is on strike, so for 10 minutes I wrestled with a man in the pub to take me to Victoria – at last he consented on condition of high payment and instant dismissal. Suddenly half way down St. James's he stopped and asked me if I was the young lady who went rowing with the officer on the Serpentine some months ago, and gave him some sweets for

---

[1] Duff was tone deaf.
[2] Osbert Sitwell was in the Grenadier Guards from 1912–1919.

his children. Then I started crying, and he said he'd wait up for either of us all night, and I poured out my misery of fear to him – relieved to find anyone to whom I could. K. never came, though I wanted for two trainloads of uproariously happy people. It was a cruel disappointment – for she might have heard some news. I feel so certain the Guards are in, though Osbert clings to the chance that the 3rd Army is all we have heard to suggest it, but *I* have your love letter. I went down to Mulberry Walk for an hour and found Alan engrossed in his typed anthology of London, dedicated elaborately to Viola, Diana and Duff (another rain of tears). I can't write any more; Phyllis[1] has come to sleep and worries me.

23 August. After a night of conflicting dreams, the morning paper endorsed my belief. Osbert on the telephone is still daft. I have nowhere to turn. O God – to find you now.   Diana.

I hope if you are unscathed you have not been too wretched and worn, my darling. It flits through my head as an extra terror all the time.

Diana to Duff, 23 August 1918   *16 Arlington Street*

Nothing can describe what these days are like. There is a new Compton Mackenzie,[2] which I pounced onto thinking to have found a dope, but I can't fix my distraught mind. You have not dealt very faithfully with me in not telling – though God knows your letter did tell enough. I met that ominous Gordon Ives today and crossed the street to belabour him with questions. He said the something [2nd Guards] Brigade had been engaged, and added 3rd Grenadiers casually. My darling love, I hope so terribly, if you are safe, that you are pleased and satisfied with yourself – state of mind and action. One's emotions and mental attitudes never fail to surprise – in crises – so I can hardly guess yours, but I think, my darling, you will have made a lovely and inspiring figure, and your reckless gambling spirit will not have deserted you. I have chucked Ivor Churchill[3] and Nellie [Romilly] this evening, not facing anything, but tomorrow I must face that seat of your pleasures

---

[1] Phyllis Boyd, 1894–1943. She married Comte Henri de Janzé in 1922.
[2] *Early Life and Adventures of Sylvia Scarlett* (1918).
[3] Lord Ivor Spencer Churchill, 1898–1956, younger son of the 9th Duke of Marlborough.

Wrong Wilton.[1] How shall I endure it alone? I moaned away to Alan at lunch. He sees the outcome of all this as a leg wound and a decoration. Why haven't I got that happy eye? I love you desperately.   Diana.

Diana to Duff, 24 August 1918   *Wilton Park, Bucks.*

My darling darling Duff, If you could but give yourself a voluntary wound there, in the thigh. I should love you less, but even then it would be heaven to have you again. Of a truth, Duffy, my tired body is aweary of this great world. Look at this notepaper – it is like returning to a grove where Pan and Bacchus paid court to Eros, and finding the gods dead and the grove laid waste, and a mocking shadow of beauty reigning over a waste heap. The same bed tries to rest me, the same clock ticks minutes that will bring no ecstasy in the passing of time.

I made myself conspicuous tearing across the Ritz from Her Grace's table to ask Victor Cunard[2] if he had heard a word about the Division, and ringing up the War Office Casualty Department to ask for you under my own glaring name. I am glad to let them learn my love, and get seasoned to it. I must give Mother her due – she wrote me a letter of sympathy being, thank God, speechless on the subject. O my love, my dove, my peace and my restlessness, keep as safe and whole and brave and shining as I want you.   Diana.

Diana to Duff, 25 August 1918   *Wilton Park*

My sweet, When I put out my light last night after writing, all command of thought vanished, a surging mind vanquished my hope of sleep and a realisation that I had neglected any formation of plans for eventualities. I thought of you desperately, maybe mortaly ill in France, and how my coming to you should be accomplished. I had to settle everything then – my first step, who I should make my appeal to? A.J. Balfour?[3] Cowans?[4] Beaverbrook? a

[1] A house near Beaconsfield, Bucks, taken by Ava, Lady Ribblesdale. "Right" Wilton was the house of the Earl and Countess of Pembroke.
[2] Victor Cunard, 1898–1960. Nephew of Sir Bache Cunard.
[3] Arthur James Balfour, 1848–1930. Foreign Secretary and Prime Minister. Later Earl Balfour.
[4] Lt. General Sir John Steven Cowans, 1862–1921 G.C.M.G. He had been Quartermaster General of the Forces since 1912.

threat of suicide if they opposed, and how it should convincingly be phrased – my luggage and what it should include, V.A.D.'s clothes, officer's khaki, in case – whose? Frankie de Tuyll's[1] in London, and [he's] my size. *Money* – easily asked of Crooks – £50. my *letters* to Mother – all the wording of a frank and total confession, not to be sent till I was entrained. I know (and still know) they cannot keep me from you – then finally my finding you and holding you. It all possessed me too much – a turbulence, not to be quieted by sitting at the open window, or smoking, or will-power, racked me. Seven struck before I slept, and today I have felt a trial to my companions and a sore disappointment to Ava though a little calmed by a morning and evening anonymous enquiry to the War Office.

Perhaps this may be all a prophecy. I calculate you went in the twenty-first and that by now bad news would have sought me out, but how vague are one's conjectures. Its all impenetrable. I think to hear from you Wednesday if all is well. My darling, I write these silly papers about myself, when I should be encouraging you and praising you and convincing you of my courage and belief and hope in you. No one but you among the fighting millions is thought of so continuously or adored more.   Diana.

Duff to Diana, 1 a.m., 23 August 1918   *B.E.F. France*

Had no moment to write. Am safe, well and happy. Have no moment now. Telephone to Mother to say all is well. I have been wonderfully lucky for 2 days but 3 letters from you 10 minutes ago crowned my luck. I adore you. *Don't worry*. Probably shan't be able to write tomorrow. The Germans are charming and always surrender.   Duff.

1 a.m. 24th
Couldn't post yesterday. All worry over now, am safe *out* of the battle. Great fun today. Very sleepy. Will write tomorrow. Have written Mother.   Duff.

---

[1] Son of Baron Carlo de Tuyll and his wife Louise Emily Harford, who later married the 9th Duke of Beaufort.

Diana to Duff, 27 August 1918   *16 Arlington Street*

My dearest one, The light of everything is changed with a letter from you this morning. I am mad with relief and pleasure. I did not write yesterday because Katharine arrived at last, and I lay talking with her till 5.30 this morning. Today too comes horrible news of Lance Page's death – the entire tragedy to my poor old Podgie the imagination fails to encompass[1] but in the huge selfishness of my happiness I cannot think of it.

I can hardly wait for your next letter, my love, my darling. O the delight and the elation of this morning. Will write tonight. Your scribble of safety, I must tell you, is in the style of a demented man. Is it 'shock'?

Diana to Duff, 28 August 1918   *The Manor House, Frome*

My darling Duff, No letter today but I can't complain. Tomorrow I shall be twenty-six. I'm not really sorry – there is a time for everything and these last years I could not endure again and besides with every year one is a little less tramelled and more courageous, and independent of everything but love. Thank God we age together – it would not be unlike him to have showed favouritism and caprice over this point too.

I have worked out what I think is a dignified money-making plan for my future, entailing the minimum of work. It is a nursing home run by me and Katharine backed by Bouch,[2] Moore, Crooks, Baker,[3] Haldane etc. on the Manchester St. lines. No nursing home fails, at least very few, and it seems to me that we start with tremendous advantages a) by being closely allied with the medical shining lights and surgeons b) by having ready made in my own possession very superior nursing and medical equipment i.e. beds, theatre accessories etc. Sister White[4] should run it on a high salary and K and I would take turn about light superintendence and doubtless coin money. Its a bid for freedom too without any notoriety of convention breaking for Their Graces

[1] Lance Page was the only son of Mrs. Page, Diana's old governess.
[2] Tommy Bouch, 1882–1963. He wrote Diana poems, and was Joint Master of Foxhounds of the Belvoir Hunt.
[3] The Rt. Hon. Harold Baker, 1877–1960. Originally a barrister, he was the Liberal Member for Accrington 1910–18, a member of the Army Council in 1914.
[4] Sister White – head sister of The Arlington Hospital for Officers. She was Chinese, and therefore called Sister Chinese White.

to take exception too. I need a little encouragement. Tell me how it strikes you.

Why do I not hear from you? Your Mother telegraphed today 'Alright glorious news' otherwise I should wonder more. The Compton Mackenzie is so perfect I'll send it tomorrow. We are teaching the children 'Ill met by moonlight'[1] – its maddening how doubly quick they are to us, they learn only by ear and can't forget. The baby mouths struggle with ravished Perigouna and Ægle, yet they are questionless.   D.

Duff to Diana, 25 August 1918   *B.E.F. France*

My own and only darling – I have so much to say, so much to tell you, so much to thank you for, so many lovely letters to answer, and their beauty to comment on that I feel like St. John when he completed his Gospel in despair of ever writing all he had to say. Oh to hold you now in my arms for two or three days and nights without interruption and breathe into your own soft conched ear all that I have to tell.

I am going to shirk telling you of the first day of the battle by sending you the rough copy of the official report I had to send in.[2] Please don't show this to anyone except in great and *safe* confidence. I fear it may not convey much to you. There was, you know, from the start at five a.m. until about ten-thirty, a thick mist. One couldn't see a yard.

The second day we remained where we were in boiling sun under heavy shell fire suffering from thirst. I have been thirsty all my life but never quite so thirsty as that. We thought to be relieved that night and lived on the hope. But as night came on we learned first that we were not to be relieved and then that we were to make another attack at four a.m. My platoon of 30 was then reduced to 10 – and at the last minute as we were forming up for the attack I discovered that my sergeant was blind drunk – a dreadful moment. But it was followed by some of the most glorious of my life. A full moon, a star to guide us – a long line of cheering men, an artillery barrage as beautiful as any fireworks creeping on before us – a feeling of wild and savage joy. It is a picture that will hang in my gallery for ever, and will come next in value to three or four

[1] *A Midsummer Night's Dream*, Act II scene 1.
[2] See *Old Men Forget*, p. 82 *et seq.*

dozen in which you figure. The whole battalion won their objective under the scheduled time. I was the first of my Company in the German trench. I boast like a Gascon but it was what the old poets said war was and what the new poets say it isn't.

And then, darling, but this is a secret, I am covered with glory. When first I realised this, the Commanding Officer speaking to me in terms that made my head swim, my one thought was that the Chevalier de Boufflers had thought by obtaining military glory to render himself in the world's eyes worthier of Madame de Sabran. And I wondered how a medal would weigh in Her Grace's scales – lighter than a leaf I feared – certainly lighter than a strawberry leaf.[1] Personally I am as proud as a peacock though I have an affectation of modesty that is very deceptive. I love to bring home glory to my mistress so that she may sew medals as well as grenades on her chemises and tie her hair with their attendant ribbons. But to tell truth my success was very largely due to the favours of that fickle goddess whose smiles I have so often courted at the green table where she so often withheld them, biding her time for this even more valuable occasion. Darling I haven't begun to write to you, to tell you what I want to say, to thank you for letters and books and lovely pictures, but I want this letter to go tonight and I rather want now to go and listen to the band and gossip about the battle, so I will go on tomorrow – my only love, my darling.   Duff.

Duff to Diana, 27 August 1918   B.E.F. France

My darling – I have your letter telling me of your first day's anxiety – the first I fear of several. Poor sweet sad heart – but now I trust you know the happy truth. The incident of the taxi driver is so beautiful that it must have lightened that dark day. Bless his kind grateful heart and remembering eyes. That was the day you cried waiting for me at the flat. Cast your secrets upon the Serpentine and you shall find them after many days.[2]

Now I am waiting for a horse to carry me to Details. So if the Battalion does go in again which is possible I shan't go with them. I confess very reluctantly to the faintest tinge of regret should this

[1] The ducal symbol.
[2] *Peter Pan in Kensington Gardens* (1906) by J. M. Barrie. cf. Ecclesiastes, Chapter XI verse i: 'Cast thy bread upon the waters: for thou shalt find it after many days'.

occur. I have come to be a little – only a very little – sentimental about my platoon, and don't quite like to think of the ten survivors going back to the battle without me. As we were coming out on Saturday evening marching peacefully and very slowly over these quiet uplands where men didn't dare show themselves three days before, lit by a perfect sunset, the tired men crooning popular songs as they went, the Commanding Officer and the Brigadier rode by. And I heard the Commanding Officer say "That's Duff". The Brigadier came up and praised me till I blushed and sweated. He said the whole Brigade had done marvellously but that my platoon had simply shone. I wished so then that you could share my content that moment for my happiness was marred by knowing that you were probably miserable.

Darling, your letters lately have seemed to me even more beautiful than was their wont. Such happy phrases, and such lovely words. I don't think love was ever told more beautifully.

Don't, darling, repeat to anyone all the boastful stories which my vanity makes me tell you. It is not my vanity only but my desire to make you share all my joy. My love, my life.   Duff.

Diana to Duff, 30 August 1918   *16 Arlington Street*

My lovely gallant Duff, If you had told me of a heart, grey and shaking with dread of pain, or of stabbing men that they might not ask for help, I would love you no less – nor am I in any way astonished – well, yes I am a little surprised in Fortune's attitude, knowing her hostility to me. You have blamed me for having so little belief in the capacity of those I love, and yet I was as sure of you in this respect as I might be of the sun's shining, so all my jubilance has gone to join yours and I soar above tragedy today in thinking of your delight and sudden tyranny over people's opinion of you. I see you as a tried Mars, my angel, and would delight in Vulcan's net, if it held us enlocked for many days.

I can not cease to read your letters and account. I had, strangely enough, had such a vivid picture of a railway backgrounded action – did I write to you to that effect? I love the Commanding Officer for pointing you out as 'Duff'. I love to think of your men's pride in you as you reached the guns, I love to think that even strangers will admire you as I do, and I dread to think of your disappointment if it all gets forgotten, as many such things have, without ribbons for your love's hair, to proclaim your bravery.

I tried to discover where there was room in those 3 terrific days for your spirits to sink, and the evening of the 22nd looked a likely time. If someone does not write to me of you I shall mind: Sidney[1] at least might. Tell me, sweet, the chances of recognition – what it might be: M.C.? or only 'mentioned'? Tell me when such a thing will be settled. If you were only here to be crowned and praised by me; no I think you are better there, among your regiment's tributes, if you were with me, exploits and success and medals and arms, all would be lost and sunk in my ineffable love that distinguishes so little what elements go to form my adored.

Tell me truly any succeeding and belated appreciations and commendations. Write like a Peacock of Gascony – it delights me. I told Katharine and Vinny and Alan under seal of secrecy. Why should it not be known if you are not quoted as informer? Tell me when I may brag. Diana.

Diana to Duff, 2 September 1918   *Vice Regal Lodge, Dublin*

My darling darling. No letter again today – I blame you at last – surely you know how I rely on you to give me daily vitality and incentive – you must have neglected.

It is going to be difficult to see my ten days through in this place. I dreaded it would be. I spend nearly all the day resting in bed, and trying to sleep away the waits. Tonight's dinner was between two strangers who I cross-questioned on the different virtues of guns – Machine, Lewis, Waxer etc. – they *did* enjoy themselves, as Lady Horner might say – but for me it was effort intensified to keep attention focused – with only the vision of Corpl. Harrison & Corpl. Harris[2] to enjoy and keep me in touch at all, at all. The Liffey will brag in the possession of me unless tomorrow relieves my anxiety for your life & your love. Diana.

Diana to Duff, 3 September 1918   *Vice Regal Lodge, Dublin*

My darling – I have had a true grievance – I got a letter tonight dated the thirtieth, and my last reached London Thursday and was of the twenty-sixth – so either the mails have gone crazy or it is

---

[1] Sir Sidney Herbert, 1890–1939, eldest son of the Rt. Hon. Sir Michael Herbert and his American wife, Lelia Wilson. Brother of Michael Herbert.
[2] Who had distinguished themselves in the attack with Duff.

true that you have been bewildered and puffed out of touch with me – and very soon your deeds will be forgotten, and more than probably never recognised, and you'll regret the forfeit of a fraction of my love. My blessed, I forgive you – and really today I feel so sad about Brassey,[1] who loved you so. Poor little thing – with a life spent in preparation alone.

I'm not very happy here – and feeling so ungregarious. Every night I loose a little packet at chemin de fer – detestable it is, and I see it as glasses and rugs, & lace sheets being taken from you and me.

Duff to Diana, 6 September 1918   *B.E.F. France*

Oh you silly wicked faithless little doubter. How dare you question my unfailing love which is ever growing and ever fresh. And how naughty of you to throw my braggings and vainglory in my face and say that it is all I think of. And how stupid of you not to guess that the biggest battle of the world may interfere a little with the post. I don't think I have missed writing a single day – and there is not so very much to write about, except my own fortunes and my love of you. And because I have dared to intrude the former subject once or twice – not lately I think but in the first days after the battle – what an outcry, what a hullabaloo!

Poor baby – must I tell you ten times on every page of every letter that I love you only, utterly and more than all – that my only ambition is to please you and my only joy in achievement is to lay it at your feet. I must say that I never thought to see you jealous of my devotion to military renown. I suppose now if I tell you I have been reading some stories by Balzac which I have enjoyed very much you will cry that I think more of Balzac than of you. Darling, you will have long since got many letters and have laughed at your own fears. The post is still I hope keeping something from me. I have nothing between the twenty-eighth at Mells when you hadn't heard from me – (at least only once) and the thirty-first in Ireland. But perhaps you were thinking too much of something else on the twenty-ninth and thirtieth – glorying in your beauty and your lovers – to find a moment to write to me. Angel – I love you – all you do, all you feel, all you are. I adore your childish jealousy – you lend grace to any quality that you assume, and

[1] Gerald Charles Brassey – born 1898. Lieutenant in the Coldstream Guards. Killed in action August 27th.

beauty to any failing you fall into. You could make shop lifting charming and food hoarding romantic. You have my heart in your hands.   Duff.

Diana to Duff, 4 September 1918   *Vice Regal Lodge, Dublin*

My darling. Mine is the fault – me to be forgiven; why don't I trust you more, the two belated letters came this morning – and made me so happy.

Lord Londonderry[1] continues his attack, and has now reached the gambit of open discussion as to whether he could make me happy – he thinks he could with arts, arts of tantalizing with good things – and a spice of tyranny – its easy to parry and he's light in hand – but I haven't the inclination for him. I've only the inclination to think of you – my sweet – its a wonder really that I kid them all into belief of my attention.

Duff to Diana, 9 September 1918   *B.E.F. France*

My darling. I am with the Battalion again but don't be alarmed. We are back in support now and we believe that the Division will be relieved in a few days. We drove up this morning in motor lorries – a long drive and we were late for lunch. We had six officers gassed the other day – three of them above me for leave and another has gone down to hospital ill who was also above me. So the prospects are improving. We had no post yesterday and our move today has I fear deprived us of another. We are pretty comfortable here living in houses in a trench and have our kits with us.

And now a lovely post has suddenly arrived. (Why do I say suddenly – how could it arrive gradually?) Two letters from my darling. One very naughty one taunting me with being puffed up with deeds which will soon be forgotten – and another apologetic one – hardly apologetic enough for such naughtiness. You darling with you silly little doubts and jealousy – which make me love you more – perhaps you know it. I wonder if you could adopt a line which would make me love you less. Even if for some reason I

---

[1] Charles Stewart, 7th Marquess of Londonderry, 1878–1949. In the course of a long political career he was twice Secretary of State for Air. Lady Londonderry was a brilliant hostess, and had a snake tattooed on her ankle.

hadn't written for a day or two mightn't there have been any other cause than being puffed up and bewildered as you say with conceit. When your letters don't come isn't it always the post that I accuse? Now I will answer your letter.

First Lord Londonderry – there are few whom I could better pardon you for casting eyes on. There is no one whom I would sooner look like. Tell me how the intrigue progresses. Next your losses at cards and what you see them as. Oh darling I lost some £30 the other evening at Bridge, but now that you have given me this new view of losses be sure that I will never risk again more than a door mat or a servant's fire irons. It was a lovely thought of yours my darling, and will cure me for ever of my wicked gambling.

How was I to know that Venetia had sent me that over-ripe melon? Wine I cannot face unless it was the same brand as Mother sends me. She never takes the trouble to write to me nor has answered my last letter. I rather resent the sloth of those who salve consciences by gifts instead of letters and expect pages of thanks. I resent it because I know the spirit that prompts it, a spirit on which I always acted myself in those days of civil life. However I will write to her to bless her.

Duff to Diana, 10 September 1918   *B.E.F. France*

Darling. I had another belated and naughty letter from you this morning beginning "I blame you at last". If you were in my arms I could punish you. All this afternoon I have been thinking of my leave, imagining the first hours, debating the best hour for arrival, envisaging our meeting. Mother will be our only problem, bless her.

I send you back [Ettie's] letter which is charming. She is a perfect woman as I always told you and loves you and me. I have had some delightful letters from her since I've been in France – but not lately. I don't know why she hasn't written to me for so long. She must be puffed up with pride about something. Good bye my treasure love my only darling   Duff.

Diana to Duff, 6 September 1918   *Vice Regal Lodge, Dublin*

My darling. Your mother wrote this morning enclosing a letter from Streatfeild[1] – it's all very great – and fine for us all. Strange that such an eventuality never occured to me before. I set no values on the hope, and so didn't hope, and yet now it seems this is what's made me happiest since you left. Such luck (forgive me darling) is so seldom touchable by us – that our whole strength of hope is negatively directed – and not death is all we pray.

Perhaps I put your triumphs too much on luck. I really in my heart think it is all your due, but in a strange kind of defence for the others I find myself declaring for chance. In valour weren't they all Herculeses? but they had little to flaunt. Darling – I love you.   Diana.

Duff to Diana, 10 September 1918   *B.E.F. France*

Darling. You can only have a short letter today – not because I've been busy all the morning, not because there's been no post yet so that I have nothing to answer, not because I'm going out to tea with Peter Adderley who lives some way away, nor yet because the post goes early and I have no time – no – it is because I am so puffed up and bewildered with conceit and pride that I want to sit quiet for an hour or two and think about myself.

Oh little Miss Lackfaith, little Lady Jealousy, Doubtful Countess Petulant, Marchioness of Pouts, Duchess of Malice, Queen of my heart. God bless you, God kiss you since I cannot.   Duff.

Diana to Duff, 14 September 1918   *Belvoir Castle*

My darling. It has been a dreadful day of loss of nerve & hold & manners. Straight rain, no taxis, and a loss of mackintosh, started my humours, and a lunch with Mother, Harry[2] and Claud[3] chez Ritz, didn't improve them. War and peace were discussed, and

---

[1] Colonel Sir Henry Streatfeild, 1857–1938, was Colonel commanding the Grenadier Guards from 1914–19. He had sent Duff a letter of congratulation, on having won the D.S.O.

[2] Henry Linday, 1866–1939. Youngest son of Col. Charles Hugh Lindsay and brother of the Duchess of Rutland.

[3] Sir Claud Russell, 1871–1956. He was a diplomat, and the first man ever to propose to Diana.

the boycott of Germany, in the future. Mother's argument was that no rising hungry tradesman should buy a stock from Germany or sell his rotting goods to her – another time admitting she would gladly sell her Gobelins for £200,000 to a hun, seeing that it would be taking money from Germany – and then she started gloating & gluttening over American war-lust, reprisals, no prisoner taking etc, also the 'deaf ear to terms' touch – and I, arguing meekly, was told I had not realised the war. Even this empty worn old phrase coming from her, sitting opposite, secure & unimaginative, with her son safe, & nothing on earth to lose or fear for – was enough to make me afire in colour and brain till I flew at her and Harry, & embarrased Claud. How dare she say such things to me, with my old world lost & my new world out of grasp, & winged to leave me? How abject a pacifist she would be if John was not on the staff in France.

Duff to Diana, 16 September 1918   *B.E.F. France*

My darling. We moved yesterday and are now in much more comfortable quarters and not appreciably nearer the war. The sound of our own guns is the only inconvenience and we have all our comforts. We had a beautiful exhibition of aerial warfare last night. A German aeroplane with all our search lights on it, flying very fast and trying to dodge the implacable lights which followed faster. It flew madly from side to side like a huge bewildered silver moth. Above it were our own machines in the darkness so that we could not see them except when they fired when they seemed like a star appearing for a moment on a background of stars. And they shot tracer bullets which came like red rockets out of the darkness all aimed at the poor moth, which suddenly turned into a ball of fire and fell blazing and a low cheer came up from the dark trenches all round us.

It is still warm and pleasant and I prefer our new position, but the barren desolation of this country is appalling. Before the battle we had within a mile or two of the front line, corn fields and trees and villages. Here there are none of those in any direction – only an endless waste. What villages there are consist literally of a heap of ruins. I thank God I was never fool enough to care for ruins, and certainly without ivy they are the very ugliest and most disheartening sight on earth. Good bye my pretty mistress   Duff.

Duff to Diana, 19 September 1918   *B.E.F. France*

My beloved. Two letters from you today which thrilled me with
pleasure. I love you beyond control. They were beautiful letters. I
have no time this evening to tell you of my love. But you mustn't
cry darling or be frightened by anything you see in the papers. I
will in future always tell you what I am doing. Nor must you be
frightened by the caprices of the post these days.

   Bless Dudley Coats[1] for his praise. I met him that morning in
the mist before I – but no – I mustn't refer to the battle or you will
say I am getting puffed up again. Such a beautiful sunset this
evening. With me to see beauty is to think of you. I *must* write and
thank Venetia for that melon.   Duff.

Diana to Duff, 19 September 1918   *16 Arlington Street*

My dearest one. I am hoping desperately that you are well out of
this – but the loathed comuniqué talks of Guards Division being
engaged. By dinner time I felt so impossible, that the dear drug
[morphia] was resorted to, so calm has come – but no pleasure. So
maybe I am undone.

   Such a silly letter today my Mr. Duffident. Do you really think I
shall find you blunted and disillusioning? Do not you know the
oldest adage, about love's blindness? It is as true as all it's other oft
sung atributes. In my present state – you can be nothing wrong.
You never could, even when you strove to, by reading my diary –
and losing the money we might have spent jointly, and behaving
like a terrapin, and cheeking me, and in all your thousand crimes
that I sometimes punish trivially. Besides now my eyes are more
blind, with long watching and salt tears. So you shall lie silent – or
say the silliest things, and if the while I feel you are happy – I shall
be satisfied. Love is satisfied with very little, bless it – Antony was
satisfied by one kiss even after the loss of Actium – Titania with an
ass. So no more fears my sweet. I've given a lot of thought to my
meeting you first. I can't go to the station with Vinny and Alan &
the crowd. I should like to be at 88, but then how am I to bear
waiting there alone – if you are late – a dreadful thought. The hour
too? night light before dinner – after dinner? It is more likely to be
in the middle of dinner at Queen Anne's – not bad either. Such

---

[1] Muir Dudley Coats, 1897–1927; in the Scots Guards during the war.

cheers and toasts and hero-worship, and adorable anticipation and desire of leaving the kind house, and kissing you alone. I mustn't go on, its exciting to folly but tempting to Provvers. I want you, I want you as much as I did when you steamed away from me months ago, with spring and warmth & life & love in your train. Sweet heart Good night.   Diana.

Duff to Diana, 21 September 1918   *B.E.F. France*

My darling. Your letters have taken to coming in pairs again – bless them. There were two today. I have written to thank Venetia for that melon. Aren't I good. I write continually to Katharine but she doesn't answer. She must have taken a dislike to me. More officers are coming out to us which is good. I really ought to get to Paris soon. If you were married to me you could meet me there – why aren't you pray?

Duff to Diana, 25 September 1918   *B.E.F. France*

Darling. A beautiful letter came from you in the dead of night. I think yours are the loveliest letters ever written – and I hate to think of yours to me being lost by any misadventure. Light they could not see for many years, but after many years they might give light for ever. Should they ever fall again into your hands you must give them to Alan, together with all your other ones at 88, and he should make a book of them to be published when his youngest child is dead. But how I envy him the fun of annotation. I think – and I'm sure he would agree – the original spelling should be preserved. Sweet love, are your eyes big with drugs and blind with love and tears and watching? I would drink the drugs from them and kiss away the tears for I don't like blind love. Let it be keen and critical and see the imperfections and yet love.

Tomorrow before dawn I fight a battle. I only fear death when I think of you because you are all that I cannot bear to leave in life. Apart from you I could be absolute. You must be brave and must remember that battles terribly disorganise the post. My Diana – Duff.

Read no forebodings in the first pages – I have none.

[114]

My soul. I write for the second time today. I feel nearer you when I write and as if I was holding you to me with greater hope & force. I scarcely know myself anymore – all old egoisms have been dissolved away by this heat of passionate concentration for your safety and content and glory.

I cannot any longer be free from the terror of any pain physical or mental, for you. I would bear twice the desperate dread that bows me, to ensure your not knowing a moments apprehension. If God were only more of a jew I would be blind & maimed – a loathed toad even by dint of many bargains – to save you my love in life – my darling Duff.

I read a letter from you tonight – a veiled adieu, and cried a drenching patch on Alan's shoulder. He shall not have my letters. No one must know me as you have and shall. It is I that must edit them, and if I must be old it is I that shall read them to the envious young – flauntingly, exultantly – and when they hear yours they'll dream well that night, and waking crave for such a mythical supreme lover and regret that they are born in the wrong age – as once I did before I saw your light, crying for Gods and wooers.

The war will not have been all calamity if it protects you, for it will have shown me my own heart and emotions undreamt of.

———

Duff to Diana, 27 September 1918   *B.E.F. France*

Darling, I have fought another battle and am none the worse. I havn't done anything to be puffed up about this time you will be glad to hear, but we did what we had to do promptly and effectively and laid one of the corner stones of a great battle. It was rather fun. We started in darkness after a wet night and there was a good deal of death about at first. Then the sun rose beautifully, and the enemy fled in all directions – including ours – with their hands up, and one had a glorious victorious Ironside feeling of Let God arise and let His enemies be scattered. And then they came back again over the rill and one was terrified, and had a ghastly feeling of God is sunk and His enemies doing nicely. But we shot at them and back they went and God arose again. This happened three times. And now the battle has rolled away and I am tired, tired and wondering where I shall be tonight. I am so dirty. It was a shame to keep us three days in the line before fighting. The

Germans hate the war even more than we do – thereby proving once more their superiority.

Duff to Diana, 29 September 1918   *B.E.F. France*

My darling. No real post from England today or yesterday which is very sad. I cannot do without your letters at all. My name has been sent in for Paris leave and I hope to be off in about a week. Oh my darling if only you could be there. If only, if only.

We have just got yesterday's *Times* which tells of our attack. I do hope you haven't had too much anxiety. I have written every day but fear you won't have heard every day.

It will be rather fun for me to go to Paris, won't it? I adore the place for its own sake and the thought of real luxury – baths and bath salts – sheets and linen sheets – good food and good champagne which I havn't hardly tasted for five months – lying in bed as long as I like – all this seems too good even to happen. As for the other pleasures and temptations of Paris – I confess that I shall feel very shy of telling you how I resist, or rather how I·yield to them. I think I shall hush up and say no more about it than I would of any of the other little harmless necessary but unmention-able workings of nature. But you must tell me what you think or rather what you feel about this. Paris leave doesn't really interfere with English leave at all I find. There is a rule but it is disregarded. Also it is rumoured that English leave is to be increased to three weeks instead of a fortnight. Perhaps you would tire of me in three weeks – would you? Oh darling – I want you – come to Paris. I cannot have real fun without you – only shadow fun, shadow wine, shadow love.   Duff.

Diana to Duff, 2 October 1918   *16 Arlington Street*

My divine Duff. I'm on the crest of my spirits. Ask me how many letters I have from my love today, and I will say five with a famished voice. One before the battle and four since. One warns me of Paris leave, and shows indecision of how or whether you shall tell me all of it. You never have full faith in me, my darling – or you would know that my desire is your inclination. Tell me as much or little as you enjoy to confess. You know that I want your happiness above my own and that I delight in your shadow love (keep it shadow) but that from your arrival in Paris I absolve you from all letters, sincerety, superficial thoughts – 'rush into the folly', baby darling. Tell me nothing or all. I shall love you the same. I only warn you against getting drunk because Paris is a sink of English scandal and its a rumour, though not a habit, that I want killed, and it bids fair to be so, since you 'made good'. If I was forced to voice a whim it would be that a) you absented yrself from felicity with my own 'caste' – Rose, Diana, Laura etc. b) that with help of every known device you keep your body clean for me. c) That you do not gamble – but where these scruples count as a ha'pth of tar, your boat must not be spoilt.

This letter will read like Polonius's to Laertes so let it break, and I'll write at the same time to the Battalion in case you miss a post. My dearest – good night.   Diana.

Duff to Diana, 5 October 1918   *B.E.F. France*

My darling – I didn't write yesterday but this will catch the same post as if I had so you lose nothing. And I didn't hear from you yesterday either.

I have just been sending home your letters – 145 of them. I hated to part with them but it had to be done. They couldn't stand the war bless their hearts. You see they were nearly always in damp places which is very bad for them. When I re-read them I often find that they have shut up again as though they had never been opened – like flowers that shut in darkness and only open to the sun. And then they cling to one another so that they can hardly be separated and grow limp and sad, and the marks of your little pencil grow fainter and fainter.

You mustn't wonder if you don't hear for a day or two because I believe letters take longer from Paris. You know that I shall write.

Two letters from you since I wrote this morning and good news about my Paris leave. All being well Carroll Carstairs and I start tomorrow at cock crow, should reach Paris in time for dinner and stay at the Ritz until about the sixteenth. My love, I think I shall miss you more in Paris than here – for I always miss you most when I am happiest. And I won't pretend that I shan't be happy in Paris – for I shall be – radiantly I expect.

Good bye baby. Don't cease to think of me because I am safe in

Paris – or doubt for a minute that I shall be faithful to you in my fashion.[1]   Duff.

Duff to Diana, 7 October 1918   *Hotel Mirabeau*
                                              8 Rue de la Paix Paris

My love, my life, my light. I am missing you terribly, for I am enjoying pleasures which only you could share.

Carroll and I left the war at daybreak yesterday and arrived at Amiens in time for lunch. It was delightful there – such a spirit of joy and victory abroad as made the eyes water. The streets full of parties of inhabitants returning – staggering under their household goods and carrying the canary in their right hand – all so happy to find their own house standing, and that of their neighbour blown to hell. We had a gargantuan lunch and visited the cathedral which has been hardly the least damaged. I met Sidney [Herbert] in the street but he was with his Colonel and could only speak for five minutes. We arrived here at about half past nine to find the Ritz and every other hotel crowded so we came here which is really very nice and I can watch the Rue de la Paix from my first floor windows. We had a little supper and a bottle of champagne in our sitting room, played a game of cards and went peacefully to bed ·expecting to sleep for ages. But either the unaccustomed comfort of soft bed and linen sheets intervened, or else the bright keen air of this beloved city awoke me. At all events I could not sleep after seven, but lay and read and breakfasted and was happier than any king that I have read of. My book was the *Histoire Comique* of Anatole France. I had never heard of it and it's hardly worthy of him, but quite worthy of me.

When I at last got up and went out I was almost intoxicated with delight. And oh my darling I did want you – I love Paris next to you in the world, and I long for you to be with me so that I could show you how and why I love it. The sun was shining and everybody in the street looked beautiful and familiar although I didn't see a soul I knew. I met a nigger and thought he was the Aga Khan – a dwarf and could have sworn it was Olga. I was shaved and curled and made beautiful and lunched at the Ritz with Carroll, his brother and another Grenadier – Carroll's brother is

[1] Ernest Dowson, *Non Sum Qualis Eram.*

of course ghastly – but thank God Carroll knows it and warned me before lunch. "I've asked my brother to lunch; I'm afraid he's much more American than I am." He was, and I argued with him about peace and nearly insulted him.

And then my angel came the crown to all my glory. Two letters from my mistress and very, very lovely ones – I have nothing to confess at present. I have told you everything. Perhaps my greatest pleasure has been my bath this morning. You have never been really dirty so imagine what the joy must be when in that state to get into a bath of water which looks cleaner that what one is accustomed to drink.

Sweetest sweet heart we will come here when we are married and walk slowly about the sunny streets, and linger for hours before the shop windows, and you will enjoy everything that I enjoy and I will enjoy you.

My bird, my pretty, my little love, good afternoon.   Duff.

Diana to Duff, 11 October 1918   *16 Arlington Street*

My precious Duff. Such excitements since I wrote this morning. As I went on duty this morning William (our own dear ally) coming up, met my eyes with a look of panic and appeal for several seconds, so unusual in a menial, that I asked him if he was well. At ten he called Sister White down to His Grace's room and there raved to her madly – mad. Trembling incoherently he tried to explain what he could not. He had dreamt of me he said, and it had upset him terribly. He asked if he was a criminal? and if so what was his crime? He wanted to die before he did worse. It was due to the pictures he had seen as a little boy. He wanted to explain it to me, and could'nt. Sister sent him to bed, quieted him a little and sent for the cook's husband to come and keep an eye on him. The whole story is like a lodging house shocker. By one our beloved William, neglected for a few minutes by the cook's husband, had found a penknife in a drawer and forced its flimsy rust into his throat narrowly missing the Carotid. After this he was born away to a mental institution, and I feel really sad at the loss of him, he loved us both so much. Till now it has been a pointless story for you but the interest begins and ends when I tell you that he went on after his throat was pierced murmuring "Duff Cooper, Duff Cooper – that little moustache. Has he really got the D.S.O. Sister? It's very fine isn't it." So this is why it has made such an impression on me – poor man – its real horror. The theories are many as to the cause of this defect. Is it sexual restraint? or V. disease? he often raved – "women come to me, but they dont want me" Is it fear of abnormality, preying? I have nursed a similar case. I must go and see him tomorrow.

Such a day for the other servants. They are mad and totally disorganised with the stimulus of crime and tragedy – and the gold was gilded when news came that Marjorie's house-maid was on the Irish boat.[1] Wade had seen her once at Beau Desert but she was not allowing this paleness of acquaintanceship to hinder her grief. She snuffed me into my clothes, and finally burst into a flood of pleasant tears, and refused to hear of hope though no lists of survivors is published yet.

Duff to Diana, 13 October 1918   *Hôtel Ritz, Paris*

My darling – just after I had written yesterday – a lovely letter came from you and two more this morning forwarded from the Battalion.

Last night we dined at the Café de Paris where I fell into temptation and was not delivered from evil. We went on the Zig Zag in increased numbers and then to a rather pleasant illegal dancing place where there was music, wine and sandwiches, then to a very pretty flat from which I returned this morning with the proverbial milkman from whom I was able to buy butter for breakfast. As I was lying in my bath Carroll came in and said "The War is over." And really it would appear to be so, and now we can be married and live happy ever after.

Orpen spent the evening with us yesterday. O you silly baby to have believed his story of the Belgian spy. The lady in question is living in Paris and is Orpen's mistress. He says she was feeling a little tired the day he painted her. He deliberately invented the story in order to advertise the picture, and got into some trouble

---

[1] The Irish mail boat *Leinster* was torpedoed and sunk on October 10th by a German submarine. Over 450 lives were lost. The disaster caused particular indignation since the Germans were suing for peace at the time.

with the War Office for having done so.[1] I am so glad it isn't true –
I had often thought of it since you told me. Good bye my best
beloved –   Duff.

Diana to Duff, 13 October 1918   *16 Arlington Street*

My only love. The papers this morning intoxicated only me. How
disinterested the English are. I assure you that I walked out with
an honest expectation of bursting – and gaity, of conductors
asking their passengers their views, of more loungings at street
corners and civility from taxi-men – but both among the People
and at the Ritz the crowd wore the same look, and talked as
detachedly as they did when Paris was near being held by the
enemy.

I prophesy the laying down of the German arms almost immediately – if only to disappoint the Foch schemes. Besides what
men will fight, feeling they may be the last to be killed; peace
perhaps declared, and the news not penetrated?

I dined alone with Alan at Mulberry Walk and enjoyed it very
much as we talked exclusively of you. I love him, because with all
his encouragement and unselfishness he thinks he minds terribly
the loss of me – or your jealousy or break with him. Alan has been
all I had that knew my heart, these months, and in consequence I
have seen a great deal of him. He knows your return will rob him –
so resolve to be generous and fond.

How confidently I always think of you, my darling – it is
ridiculous, really. You are made of moods, as I am. It is easily
possible you may find me less desirable, when unfamished and
unweary. The disadvantages of marriage may crowd the glamour
out, if it approaches. It is not a year ago that you asked me if after
all more problems might not be solved by living together than not
– with a tone of paradox and much doubt. Yet I'm not frightened
of your return – there is so much to lavish on you anyway at first –

---

[1] See p. 83. The story is told in Orpen's biography by P. G. Konody and S. Dark:
'Orpen never supposed that the story would be taken seriously. But it was. And this and
other irregularities caused him to be sent home, and it was only by the insistence of Lord
Beaverbrook, then the head of the Ministry of Information, that he was permitted to return
to the front in July 1918.' The painting, originally called *The Spy*, had to be retitled *The
Refugee*. Many people thought this was the story of Mata Hari's execution, which took place
on 15 October 1917. But Mata Hari went to her death wearing a pearl-grey dress, a straw
hat, and a pair of very good shoes.

for the rest I must remember the possibility and I have seldom not detected your thoughts. I hope you'll love me.   Diana.

Duff to Diana [*undated*]   *Hôtel Ritz, Paris*

Dear heart. Life here is becoming hourly more difficult to keep up with – and minutes to write to my mistress more difficult to find. I must work backwards to tell you all I have done. Last night I dined with Carstairs and his mistress – a truly beautiful creature. There was a fourth – a friend of hers who turned out to be a recently discarded mistress of Cecil Higgins – and it was when I discovered this that I noticed that, although she was not bad looking, she had a horrible look of Mrs. Higgins.[1] However she took a great fancy to me and I don't blame her. I was charming last night and succeeded in being amusing in French. I made the dinner, I made the theatre, I made the supper and then I was carried off and raped by Mrs. Higgins.

I had two very exciting letters from you yesterday The tragedy of William horrified me – I cannot bear tragedy of any sort. The tragedy of the allies refusing to make peace at this moment is sickening. But I have so much to say on that subject that I will not embark in case I never stop – But if you meet anyone who wants to bet about the duration of the war and who does not think it will be going on this time next year invest all that I have against him – but no – *n'en parlons pas* – Good bye my love.   Duff.

Duff to Diana, 15 October 1918   *Hôtel Ritz, Paris*

Then followed dinner – Carroll and the same two women as the night before. His was still very pretty but hardly worth the thousands, literally thousands, he is wasting on her. The other lady who was looking far more like Mrs. Higgins than ever, with a dash of Don Q. (she wore a sombrero) filled me with fear. She is rather intelligent, and the night before had spurred me to brilliance, but this evening her conversation reminded me of Elizabeth and had precisely the same effect of reducing me to complete silence and almost shrieking boredom. We went to a music hall where there was a nigger band which it was proposed to

---

[1] Later Mrs. Arthur Fowler, who became a great friend of Diana's in America.

bring back to the last mentioned lady's flat to play to us. This final threat, accompanied by the prospect of ultimate rape, gave me the strength that helps the desperate weak.[1] Feigning a need of nature, I slipped away and at once bolted home. And oh I cannot tell you my delight to be sitting comfortably in my little room – the door well locked – writing to you of whom I have been thinking all the time. I wished particularly that you were here just now when the telephone rang and I sat and laughed at it but didn't answer.

My only love and only joy – never have you been more present to me than during these Paris days. There is no shadow love. Black vice there is – which can be illuminated by the false thinking of starved appetite. But my appetite however starved is soon satiated, nor can it ever drive me to feed on anything but fine food tastefully served – and I do believe that it has never made me think falsely. (I quarrel with 'tastefully' in the last sentence – what should the adverb be? 'Delicately' perhaps – but not quite) The telephone rings again. I feel quite panic stricken – but they can't get me – the door is locked and I will fight to the last. Oh my love, my darling – this night I have ended by writing a long letter to you I have enjoyed the most of my nights in Paris.   Duff.

Duff to Diana, 19 October 1918   *B.E.F. France*

My darling. After writing to you yesterday evening I had a very good dinner and then we went to see Orpen with whom we talked and drank for some time. He is a very pleasant little man. After a very good night's sleep we left this morning in Orpen's car – he with us – and were back at Details in time for lunch. Tomorrow we go on up to the Battalion who are a long, long way away.

I am now the next in the Battalion for leave. It may come any day. I think myself it will not come for about three weeks. It may be sooner or later. Have all in readiness. Brick Red who has just gone on leave had an amusing adventure the other day, which I wish had happened to me. There was a complete village in No Man's Land where it was suspected Germans still were. He was sent out with a patrol at night to investigate it. Finding a light in a cellar he surrounded the house and cautiously crept down to the cellar where an old lady – French – fell on his neck and led him to another cellar where there were a lot of pretty girls who all kissed

[1] Meredith, *Modern Love.*

him and fêted him – the first allied soldier they had seen for four years. The village remained in No Man's Land and the next day a little girl of 14 who appeared in the streets was shot at by the Germans and wounded three times. Some of our men carried her into our lines and she is now dying in the casualty clearing station near here. Really the Germans are very ill natured and they do make people so cross.

Oh my love, think of my leave and Breccles.   Duff.

Diana to Duff, 24 October 1918   *16 Arlington Street*

Today I sold produce & orchids & made a great quantity of money – £100 from Bouch – £25 from Crooks – £150 from [Vincent] Caillard. I was proud but then beaten with fatigue and despair as I read an evening paper proclaiming Wilson's impossible note[1] – making it only possible for the Germans to die hard and honourably – when the alternative is the same with dishonour. British killed from today, I consider murdered – and the overthrown lengthened out for three years. Then, worse, I read of the 3rd Army's part in yesterday's attacks and a famous Division's fine work – and I turned sick remaining so till now, when returning from Lady Ridley's bud ball next door, partially calmed by darling Ivo [Grenfell], I find a letter which liberates my soul from hell – and my darling, my darling it announces my heaven. Write news of it every day. I don't want you to walk in on me unprepared, I must lose no flavours of anticipation. Ivo thinks he is going to France next week – speaks of it with an illumined King Arthur expression. Is it true? What is more, Moore is back – Gawd.

I *do* love you – be very careful baby.   Diana.

Your Mother was so sweet and came with a pound to the Red Cross shop. I flung her in some partridges – she's so excited – Sidney as gloomy as ever. I adore you Duff.

[1] President Wilson said he wanted an unconditional surrender from the Germans, with no 'unfruitful diplomatic conversations'.

1918–1922

Winter 1918

[Duff returned to England at the end of October, and his reunion with Diana was everything they had both hoped it would be. Their love, tempered by the ordeal of the war, was stronger than ever – and now this irresistible force was to meet a seemingly immovable object.

That the Rutlands should oppose the alliance of their daughter to an impecunious, untitled clerk in the Foreign Office was understandable, and Diana and Duff were prepared for it. They were, however, taken aback by the outraged hysteria it occasioned in the Duchess, to whom the news came as a complete and very unpleasant surprise. Had Diana once expressed her love for Duff in front of her mother, who was a creature of sentiment, then at least the Duchess would have seen the motive. But Diana talked to her mother in a voice that was cold and distant with embarrassment. The Duchess did not believe that they loved each other; she saw only a horrible estrangement growing between her daughter and herself, that Diana was trying to make final by marrying a man of whom she could never approve.]

Belvoir Castle

My darling one. I thought the article fine[1] – the man in Manchester, and the 'real soldiers', the right line and no mistake. I made

---

[1] On December 29th, Diana had formally launched Lord Beaverbrook's new newspaper, *The Sunday Express*. She had also been commissioned to write a series of articles for it. These were written by Duff, but appeared under her name.

about two trifling alterations – such as 'brilliant' instead of 'bright' in one place – but not so as you'd notice it, and I crossed away the fancy-ball bit. I'll send it to Blum[1] today. We must do the Drug one next. Sunday expects.

So much for the bright side of life – and now follows the misery. The situation has been impossibly tense. There is a general recrudescence of the topic all round and Mother talks to Letty, Kakoo, John, Charlie, Henry, Mildred, Bouch. I talk or am talked to by Letty, Kakoo and Bouch. Last night arranging the dinner table on Her Grace's lap – I said, hardly thinking, "Don't put me next to Godfrey Thomas, I'm so tired." The consequence was Mother had a despairing blue all the evening. How could I guess that this young potential bridegroom for Letty was, in Mother's eyes, a keyhole out of Hell[2]? That I was down on her programme to seduce him from his widow, or that my act only served to illustrate my perpetual disregard for her wishes. All this she explained to me over a far card table where she was playing Patience alone. I started with an apology for the misunderstanding and seeing we were getting quickly to the main point, I hoped to push on to it – but she switched off onto cancer, and her near death – till I had to retire.

On reaching my bed room very tired I found a note from John asking me to go to him in his tower – it was midnight then – but I toiled up and talked to him for two hours. His argument was that I must wait a year. And I at last swore that I'd put it to you – I could hardly endure it but if it is to be forced upon us by entreaty – humble entreaty – and the face of Mother's health, I don't see how we are to stand out. Suppose we love each other less in a year? God, what a conspiracy of cruelty it is. True – you could get perhaps more money by then. O Duffy I could not stop crying till four, and I feel so hopeless this morning. Strengthen me Duffy – I feel in despair. Perhaps I shall come up Saturday – with the gang. I hate you to be lonely too – Hazel [Lavery] should be about – also Ava is running Wilton again so buttonhole her at the earliest opportunity. Dont forget a job, it would be a great thing, and a great argument and a great comfort if that find could be hastened.

[1] R. D. Blumenfeld, editor of the *Daily Express*, 1902–1932.
[2] There was just a chance, in the Duchess' mind, that Diana would fall for Godfrey Thomas – who had been originally earmarked for the widowed Letty – and so avert the hellish possibility of marriage to Duff.

Fuss does pay. O Baby darling, be exemplary for I am being so tortured and beaten here.   Diana.

Duff to Diana, 1 January 1919   *Foreign Office*

My Darling – Your letter this morning rather depressed me. I hate you to be unhappy and how deeply and viciously I hate the people who make you so I can't say. I have no faintest fear that love would suffer from a year's delay – were it to do so that would be an argument for waiting rather than against it. But I do feel that we have only a handful of years of youth and joy and passion and that we shouldn't be expected to give up one of them at the whim of a mad woman.

There is no single sensible argument in favour of waiting except the financial one – and that we have surely satisfied ourselves that we can surmount. And at the end of the year all the same trouble would begin again. John may undertake that it wouldn't, but he as you know is powerless to prevent it. Meanwhile the situation would be absurd. When people are made to wait a year they are supposed not to see each other during the interval, which is logical but for us impossible – I think. I am sure it is the moment to be firm. Everyone in the world agrees with me outside Belvoir. Be brave and pitiless my utter love, for I am haunted with the thought of frustrate ghosts, cold statues and dreary busts. I love you so.   Duff.

Duff to Diana, 2 January 1919   *Foreign Office*

Darling, another unhappy letter from you this morning. Pray God you escape from prison on Saturday. What devils they are.

I feel strongly that there is a tide in our affairs and that now is the moment to take it at the flood. There is nothing – not one thing – to be gained by waiting – and everything – heaven itself to be lost. We must be firm. We have years of certain happiness before us and so very little in the way. It were wicked to let such a hindrance rob us of such a joy. We must not be afraid to crush it. The bitter journey to the bourne so sweet.[1] Nor is it cruel to refuse to be swayed by pity. Too often many lives are ruined out of pity

---

[1] Coventry Patmore, *A Farewell*.

[129]

for one – and the pitied the most ruined of all. What sort of life does Her Grace hope to have during the next year if we wait.

[However cruel the prospect of waiting another year might seem, there was not really much choice, since neither Duff nor Diana wanted to cause a scandal by breaking off relations with her parents. In fact, Diana did not commit herself to waiting a full year. She decided to bide her time for six months and then re-open negotiations.

In an effort to clear the air and take Diana's mind off Duff, the Duchess took Diana to Paris, where the Peace Conference was to be formally opened on January 18th. Statesmen had been gathering for weeks before, and the British Delegates were all quartered in the Hotel Astoria and the Hotel Majestic.]

Duff to Diana, 13 January 1919   *Foreign Office*

Darling. It never rains but it pours. I was greeted on arriving here this morning with the news that I was to work in the Commercial Dept – temporarily at any rate. I was afraid it would happen as there really wasn't enough to do in the other. It may be only for a week but once people get into this Dept. they never get out. The immediate cause is that Alec Cadogan[1] who has been in the Commercial for four and a half years has become Cecil Harmsworth's[2] secretary.

I am now more anxious than ever to get a job and get out of the whole damned place. No work could conceivably bore me more than the Commercial Dept. So give Edwin and Crooks no rest on the subject of jobs.

Darling I shall miss you so. You are hardly yet gone, and already I feel a gloom darker than the fog fallen upon me.   Duff.

---

[1] Rt. Hon. Sir Alexander Cadogan, 1884–1968. He became Permanent Under-Secretary of State for Foreign Affairs, and then Representative to the United Nations 1946–1950.
[2] Cecil Harmsworth, 1st Baron Harmsworth, 1869–1948. He was Parliamentary Under Secretary of State, Home Dept. 1915–19, and Foreign Affairs 1919–22.

This morning our spirits were at a very low ebb – no telephones work in Paris, so no plans could be crystalised. Mother's hopes were to drop cards on Foch, Wilson, Derby, Clemenceau, Poincaré, Balfour[1] & others – but there are no taxis.

Crooks and Venetia turned up just as we were turning out. Its a disgusting case – her face lights up when that animated little deformity so much as turns to her. They are living in open sin at the Ritz in a tall silk suite with a common bath, and unlocked doors between while poor Ted is sardined into the Majestic,[2] unknown and uncared for. The Majestic is the most impossible arrangement known, they say. If you ring up Arthur Balfour, they keep you waiting an hour, and finally answer that the name is not on their list. Nothing is done as there is nothing to do. The delegates walk into their offices, and seeing no papers or work stroll out into the very cold wet streets – and say when you meet them that they have got a lot before them – while Americans and continental rovers at the Ritz say 'we have to be here – its the greatest week, no moment, of the world's history.' Alan is for home I hear, he not being employed for one hour in the day. We lunched at the babbling Ritz with a man who Mother picked up by stealing his table, and ended by letting him pay the bill. I dined with Crooks and the Montagus at the Ritz Grill. The shocking, shocking Crooks said to me, "Don't you think she's very attentive to Edwin nowadays?' Sure enough she was – ridiculously so – a bad bad sign. We sanctioned[3] a telegram for the *Daily Express* to the effect that Mother and I had gone to Paris to buy my trousseau. Zig-Zag was the only theatre choice as neither of the men can understand one french word. It was very bad, made indelicate for the audience, who made it more so. Its a queer race – a bogus conjurer asked for a number – so with one voice the public shrieked 600 – with the exception of a few who said 69. Rex[4] I saw – and mind him most – his line in Paris is "we've got to fight this League of Nations, that's our real danger".

I am so tired now – I've just left Crooks and V. in their luxurious

[1] Respectively – Head of the Allied Forces, President of the United States, British Ambassador, French Prime Minister, President of France and British Foreign Secretary.

[2] As Secretary of State for India, Edwin Montagu was subject to the strict guard imposed by the British on their delegates at the Hotel Majestic.

[3] i.e. vetoed.

[4] Rex Benson, 1888–1975, D.S.O. M.C., later Lt. Colonel Sir Rex Benson. Future brother-in-law of Diana's sister Letty.

nest, and expedited Ted to his Etoille. All my love sweetheart. Diana.

Duff to Diana, 16 January 1919　　　　　　　　　　　*Foreign Office*

Great joy my darling over a letter from you this morning. It took three days to come. I hope mine go quicker – or what shall we do about the articles?

I dined last night at the Garrick and read Chambonas on the Congress of Vienna – a charming book, well worth reading.[1] Then I went to a party given by the Fairbairns at his father's house in Great Cumberland Place. It was terribly dull – all the people one most expected and least wanted to see. I played Bridge and lost £4. Scatters' Marchesa[2] was there with Marconi[3] – Bettine[4] sitting about in silence with Wolkoff, Ralli[5] drunk, Nancy [Fairbairn] not noticeably so, Gilbert & Maudie,[6] John Craigie & Marjorie,[7] Lionel & Clare,[8] – but Harry the King, Bedford & Exeter, Warwick & Talbot, Salisbury and Gloster were all absent.[9]

Diana to Duff, 18 January 1919　　　　　　　　　　*Hôtel Ritz, Paris*

My darling. Just look at this pen and ink – its an imposition. I'm sitting in Venetia's room on Sunday morning. They have gone off very reluctantly to Versailles – and I can hear Crook's ablutions next door. I feel very ill and boiled – but better than I did last night when having dined with the Aga I found myself quite incapable, through excess of food, of writing to you. The menu was as follows. 1) Emerald green oysters. 2) fine soup in which excellence floated a marrow bone boiled to a shining ivory and overflowing with marrow fat. 3) Souls in sauce, and with them served on great flat silver dishes frizzling soft roes. 4) Chickens wings resting on inky

---

[1] *Souvenirs du Congrès de Vienne*, by Comte A. de la Garde-Chambonas.
[2] The Marchioness Curzon, formerly Mrs. Alfred Duggan. She was very much in love with Scatters Wilson, and lost a lot of money on a racing partnership with him.
[3] Guglielmo Marconi (1874–1937), the radio pioneer.
[4] Bettine Grant, wife of Eddie Grant, née Stuart-Wortley. They divorced in 1922, and she later became Lady Abingdon.
[5] Sir Strati Ralli, 2nd Bart. 1876–1964.
[6] Gilbert Russell, 1875–1942, who married Maud Nelke in 1917.
[7] Marjorie Trefusis (see p. 21). She divorced Captain Trefusis in 1919 and married Captain John Craigie.
[8] Lionel Tennyson (see p. 42) had married Clare Bethell, née Tennant, in 1918.
[9] *Henry V*, Act IV scene iii.

trufles couched on onion stuffing. 5) Foi gras pinker than Helen's cheeks and cut like cottage loaves – in its wake a dozen fat fresh green asparagus apiece. 6) Entremet 7) Brie cheese. I sat next Edwin and Maurice Rothschild.[1]

A Frenchman said to me *'Je suis très keen sur le sport. Tout l'hiver c'est le Rugby – et puis l'été le Vater Polo'*. South of France looks more certain I fear. I spoke to Edwin seriously about the desirability – and he against all expectation encourages it. I think he is mad keen to get rid of Venetia – who he undoubtedly loves less daily. He said she had not been happy for three years and that she might be so there – he became petitionary. Looks bad baby.   Diana.

Duff to Diana, 20 January 1919   *Foreign Office*

My darling – I went down to Taplow on Saturday evening. Rosemary,[2] Monica [Grenfell] and Eric [Ednam] were there. It was quite pleasant. After dinner we played little games – chiefly pretending to be two people. Ettie and Lord Desborough came in as Their Graces discussing our engagement. He was quite marvellous and more like His Grace than you can possibly imagine.

I had a dentist [tête-à-tête] with Ettie on Sunday afternoon. She thought we were quite right to take the line we had. She told me your Mother has been raining letters on her about us, making a great point of her absolute certainty that you don't love me, saying she has proved it by several 'tests', laying great weight on how happy you were at Belvoir at Christmas, etc. And why does she write it all to Ettie who hates her and always has? Darling I do so long for you to come back but I think you ought to go to the South of France – you would like the sun and the blue sky – London is very dark and cold and wet. Today is the Eve of St. Agnes, and bitter chill it is. I love you, love you, love you.   Duff.

[After six months of waiting, Diana tentatively broached the subject of their wedding again. The Rutlands, who had seemed so adamant about the full year's wait, gave in after a little more gentle pressure.

[1] Baron Maurice de Rothschild, 1881–1957.
[2] Rosemary Leveson-Gower was married this year to Eric Ednam, later 3rd Earl of Dudley, 1894–1969. She died in a plane crash in 1930.

The wedding was on June the second, and the excited crowds gathered outside St. Margaret's to see Diana in her pale gold, lace-covered gown. The presents they had received from their many friends and Diana's innumerable admirers could scarcely be contained in the Arlington Street house. Libraries of books there were, cellars of wine, galleries of paintings and *objets d'art*, chests full of gold and silver plate and fine linen. How satisfying if the exaggeration could be continued, 'banks full of money' – but although there were some hefty cheques, money was scarce.

Their honeymoon in Italy was idyllic, but their marriage got off to a bad start when Diana broke her leg. She was on a roof, watching the peace celebrations in Hyde Park, took a step up to get a better view, and fell two floors through a skylight. Duff pushed her around for months in her wheel-chair, to parties in the evenings and house-hunting at weekends; thus it was that they found 90 Gower Street, that was to be their home for the next twenty years.

They moved in, with the bare minimum of staff – Duff's manservant Holbrook, Diana's maid Kate Wade, a cook, a housemaid and a tweeny. Their friends could not imagine how they were going to manage with so few servants.

Duff was still working in the Commercial Department, and although he had had a rise in salary, their total income with their various allowances came to only £1,720 a year. 'Money had to be spun from somewhere,' wrote Diana in her autobiography, 'even for the life we were living.' However, she was extremely happy, and hated leaving Duff even for a weekend.]

Diana to Duff, Winter 1919   *Belvoir Castle*

Darling Mr C. You might have delivered yourself of one subtle or code word on that frozen telephone to caress me on my dread departure. I felt terribly ill on the train in spite of a full length position with the Major[1] as pillow and a lot of ostentatious fur rugs and coats and brocades. The fat rich but thrifty middle class old

---

[1] Diana and Duff had a series of Bedlington terriers, each one of which was called Major.

girl who sat opposite must have thought I was 'Sarah' or 'Melba' or an exotic eccentric of sorts. She stared pained at Wade's hand and foot ministrations – finding my book place, and offering me dope, rouge, lip-salve, scent – and pandering a lot to the pet-dog. The party is Lord Morven Bentinck[1] (half-wit – a doctor's case) – Cazalet,[2] Prince Henry[3] – Bouch – Lord & Lady Worsley for dinner. I sat next to Cazalet. Easy as can be – but he asked me if I had known Tennyson who surely died in the '80s, didn't he? We talked too of religion and the Reformation and of how it would have happened without Henry VIII and more balls & balls without end. After dinner and a desultory bit of dancing, someone made the fortunate discovery that the Prince's favourite game beyond all others was 'blind man's buff', so it was played for two hours and the young ladies dresses' were torn and liberties were taken with the King's son – a fine success.

Poor baby then staggered into her exquisite bedroom off the ball room with the topless green satin bed and gave herself up to one of the worst nervous crises I have had for a long time. It arose like this. a) Duffy not there to quiet and reproove and rock her. b) A tickle in the throat and appauling nausea and malaise. c) Dread of starting flu – ill at Belvoir, no doctors, no Duffy – pneumy death. d) A thousand supersticions that baby generally prides herself on poo-pooing gathered up to strengthen her panic. She broke the mirror, and a robin has taken up its abode in the house. A miracle, I own – it goes from room to room, sits on the heads of all, lives on Petit Beurre and water and their Graces are *delighted* with the bird – but my old wives tales tell me to prognosticate death from birds entering the house.

All the royals assembled one anniversary of Queen Victoria's death at Frogmore and as they all knelt round the tomb in reverence and love, a dove circled round them. "Dear Mama's spirit," they murmured as one man, "we are sure of it". "No, I am sure it is not so," said Princess Louise. "It must be dear Mama's spirit" again they choroused. "No, Mama's spirit would never have ruined Beatrice's hat". It's not a funny story, but rather funny as told by Prince Henry – who by the way is not half bad. I

[1] The youngest son of the 6th Duke of Portland.
[2] Victor Cazalet, 1896–1943. Politician and squash champion, he was to become Political Liaison Officer to General Sikorski, with whom he died in a plane crash in 1943.
[3] Prince Henry, 1900–1974, third son of George V and Queen Mary. He was created Duke of Gloucester in 1928.

sat next to him at deenah. The Prince arrived sans equerry, sans clothes, sans valet, sans everything. He has had to telephone to the Palace, or as Letty would say 'Buck House' for clothes, and Tommy [Bouch] has had to fix him up this morning. I am favourably impressed with him. Dear Duffy, I dread tonight, I must learn to be a better baby. I cannot wait to be back.

I am ashamed of myself when you are not with me. I have no strength to be normal without your support – last night was disgraceful. My pretty Duffy. I love you with all my life and every thought. No time to read this over – but Baby never sees the mistakes so it won't matter.   Your baby.

1920–1922

[Their working lives revolved around what they called The Plan. The point of The Plan was to make as much money as possible in a short space of time, so that Duff could leave the Foreign Office and fulfil his ambition to enter politics.

The articles for the *Sunday Express* led to other commissions, and Diana toyed with various other money-making schemes. Two of these were conspicuous failures – the first being the nominal editorship of a magazine called *Femina*, and the second the directorship of a bogus rose-essence company, which ended in a humiliating scene in court.

Early in 1920, Duff was transferred to the Egyptian Department, where he found real diplomacy a great deal more absorbing than commerce. His next post, which he held from 1922 to 1924, was that of private secretary to the Under Secretary for Foreign Affairs. His salary went up again, and the job put him in close touch with the House of Commons. More and more he longed to get into Parliament.

Diana's name and beauty put her in a far stronger position than Duff to make some money fast. They both knew this, and Diana – whose nature was adventurous and hard-working – seized her chance when it came.

A film director called J. Stuart Blackton, who had not had much success in Hollywood, asked her in 1922 to star in two films he was planning to make in England. He offered her a substantial amount of money, and she accepted with alacrity. But what of the Duchess? Would she not be appalled at the idea of her daughter providing mass entertainment? She was indeed horrified; but once she heard how much Diana was to be paid, her scruples shrank to a manageable size.

The first film was called *The Glorious Adventure*, which was a swashbuckling, bodice-ripping epic set against the dramatic backdrop of the Plague and the Great Fire of London. Diana played the distraught heroine, beating her frail fists against the massive chest of Victor McLaglen. As Queen Elizabeth in *The Virgin Queen*, there was less bodice-ripping and more pageantry; but just as much blatant disregard for historical accuracy, which Diana found exasperating.]

Duff to Diana, 21 November 1922   *Foreign Office*

What are you doing, you pretty, naughty little girl? Why don't you write or telegraph to me to let me know whether you have been burnt up like Harriet or whether you are still stamping about? Mr Charles Mendl[1] of Paris has just been to see me, raving about that baby. Says that Elsie de Wolfe,[2] whoever she may be, (he seems to expect one to know) swears that the child could make £50,000 a year very easily in America. This she swore after having only seen *The Glorious Adventure*. I think *The Virgin Queen* should multiply it by two. He wants to know whether to inform her that you will consider offers from the States. I said I would consult you.

The death of M. Proust[3] comes to me as a severe blow, and nobody seems to know whether the great book is finished or not. He was only 51 – but always delicate as one gathers.

[1] Charles Mendl, 1871–1958. In 1920 he was appointed Paris representative of the Foreign Office News Dept. He was knighted in 1924, and was press attaché at the British Embassy in Paris from 1926–1940.
[2] Elsie de Wolfe, 1865–1950. She began her career as an actress but left the stage in 1905 to become a very successful interior decorator, and she married Charles Mendl in 1926.
[3] Marcel Proust, born in 1871, died on November 18th 1922. Although he was making corrections and additions up to the night before his death, *À la Recherche du Temps Perdu* was complete.

1923–1929

[Diana's major break came in the spring of 1923. Max Reinhardt and his impresario, Morris Gest, were planning a lavish production of *The Miracle* in America.

The Miracle is a mime play, set to music by Englebert Humperdinck, that was extended and arranged for Max Reinhardt's production by Einar Nilson. Karl Vollmöller put the story together from its legendary sources, and like the mystery plays that were its ancestors, the action is set in a vast and shadowy cathedral.

Diana auditioned for the part of the Madonna, at Morris Gest's suggestion. Reinhardt was impressed: she might not have much experience, but she had great beauty, natural grace, and the taste and intelligence needed to develop them. She was accepted.

Since Diana's life was so bound up with *The Miracle* for the next few years, it helps when reading her letters to be familiar with the plot.

The play opens with a festival, in honour of the Miraculous Statue of the Madonna. A young Nun, swept up in the celebration, dances boisterously with a group of children. The Abbess scolds her, and as a punishment she is told she must spend the night alone in the cathedral.

She is locked in, and her initial fears turn to anger at her imprisonment. She tears the figure of the Infant Christ from the Statue's arms, and hurls it to the ground.

At that moment a door opens to reveal a Knight, who fell in love with her during the festival and has come to take her away. Delighted, the Nun takes off her veil and rosary and leaves them at the feet of the Madonna, before running off with her deliverer.

Then – the miracle: the stone Madonna comes to life, and puts on the Nun's habit in order to take up her life in the convent. When the sisters come in they are appalled to find the Statue missing, and they beat the disguised Madonna mercilessly.

Meanwhile the Nun is making her way up in the world. Her Knight dies and she comes under the evil influence of the Spielmann, who gradually increases her power and wealth until she is an empress. But her fortunes turn, and soon she is penniless, humiliated and pregnant by the Spielmann who has deserted her. Before giving birth to her child she recites the Lord's Prayer, the only spoken part of the play.

The Madonna, disguised as the Nun, slips back into the empty cathedral. She takes off the Nun's habit, and resumes her place as the Statue in the empty niche.

The Nun finds her way back to the cathedral, holding her dying baby. She lays it at the foot of the Statue, from whence Death lifts it up and gives it to the Madonna, in whose arms it becomes the Christ Child. When the Abbess and the sisters come in, they see the Nun – now back in her habit – kneeling at the foot of the Statue, that has mysteriously returned to its place.

Maria Carmi, Princess Machiabelli, was furious that Diana had been given the part of the Madonna. A tall, elegant, dark-haired beauty, she had been married to Karl Volmöller and had created the part in Reinhardt's first production of *The Miracle* in 1912. She thought it was hers by right, and was understandably outraged that a young society flapper with almost no experience should steal it from her.

It was finally decided that Diana and Maria Carmi would play the part alternately. The other main part, the Nun, was also going to have two actresses. The first was Rosamond Pinchot, the eighteen-year-old daughter of Senator Gifford Pinchot. The second was still unchosen. Morris Gest was an inspired publicist; he created a good deal of suspense about the second Nun, and even more about whether Diana or Carmi was to play the Madonna on the opening night.

It was November 1923 when Duff and Diana sailed to America together. In early December, Duff returned to England alone.]

Diana to Duff, 8 December 1923 The Ambassador Hotel, New York

Studio

My dear angel. My heart seems to tear my body with pain for the loss of you. I don't know how I am going to bear it. I dare not look ahead or think too precisely. I dare not go home.

12 Midnight

I am home and miserable it is & desolate & the unturned bed grins at me. I think of you through my talk and laughter and wine & work & of nothing else but you. It must get more bearable of course. I went to the studio when you left me and naturally did wonders. Schildkraut,[1] the best actor here, an old man – *cried* and Kommer[2] handed me a letter – which I copy as it is an encouraging testimonial. George [Gordon] Moore fetched me & took me to lunch at the Colony. He was appalling. He has a piece, that he repeats at every juncture or pause: "My God, is'nt it funny, I mean My God, I mean. No one here knows what you mean to me. That I love you so, I mean, God, isn't it funny." I got home at five having had my poor nut washed and the nits picked out, Duffy, I looked so dejected that the barber said – "poor kid". The woman had a hare lip. It illustrates how different and foreign we feel in America – that I felt surprise that they should have hare-lips over here. They might all have them for the obscene noise they make. I tried to sleep till 7.30, and then dressed in my black lace improved by an orchid bunched on me by Fairy.[3] Hugo [Rumbold] cavaliered me to Mrs Hearst.[4] She had a nice party at the Ritz. Private room – beautifully done, with a claret that would have made you beam, with fine cham to follow.[5]

I so adore writing to you – for a few minutes I feel you are not so

[1] Joseph Schildkraut, 1896–1964. He played the part of the Emperor in *The Miracle*.
[2] Dr. Rudolf Kommer, Max Reinhardt's right hand man, who was to become Diana's close friend and guardian angel throughout her years with *The Miracle*.
[3] Another name for George Gordon Moore.
[4] Mrs. William Randolph Hearst, wife of the famous publisher and newspaper owner.
[5] These are Prohibition days. On his first visit to a New York restaurant, Duff had nearly fainted when the waiter asked him if he would have tea or coffee with his lunch.

cruelly far away – but it it takes me sickeningly back to the war & Guy's, and writing against time before lights went out from the mains at ten. Mrs Hearst was really charming in every way and line – save for calling her intimates *Mrs* Dash, *Mrs* Egg. I love you so terribly.

Duff to Diana, 8 December 1923   R.M.S. Aquitania

My beloved – I had difficulty in not crying all the way to the station – and I have it still when I think of you. The departure was moving and would have been much too moving had you been there – Band playing, crowds waving and shouting, one stern old man with a grey moustache crying quite openly on the quay. I sympathised with him. I felt rather ill all the morning – luckily the sea was calm – but the unshaven face of the Duke of Manchester[1] which appeared to be in an advanced stage of decomposition was a high test for a delicate stomach.

Diana to Duff, 10 December 1923   *The Ambassador*

My darling. Nanny[2] has left me a sharpened pencil by my bed so I can write with pleasure, outworn though I am. They worried me to death today about playing the Nun until I agreed to try it, on the condition that they would say without embarrassment or fear of hurting that I was unsuited. I am glad I stood out, and only gave in to the trial to get them out of the difficulty of finding no one suitable. I made it clear that I was not anxious. I'll do it so far better, I know, than the understudies they have tried, and yet so much, much worse than Pinchot.

I lunched today in a still funnier and still cheaper place than 'Childs' – you take a long look at all the dishes including eggs meat, fish, veg, in appetising concoctions, you pick and carry your dish and coupon off to an armchair in a long row which sports one elephantine arm on which you place your plate glass and utensils. I had a plate of corned beef hash, a big sugar cake & a glass of milk for 20 cents.

All my beaus in the cast flew at me for going to the chair café – so I daren't go again. I took all the children [in the cast] a box of

[1] William Angus Drogo Montagu, 9th Duke of Manchester, 1877–1947.
[2] Miss Wade.

[144]

sweets to make them love me, its done the trick. I got to Hoytie's[1] at midnight and was introduced to ninety Yanks, none of which I shall know again except Mr Wiborg,[2] who has shaved his moustache, and still says 'Mr Wiborg' automatically when shaking hands.

I love you desperately. I cross off the days. As I write your face is on mine. When I cease it is 2,500 miles away. I dare not think.   Diana.

Diana to Duff, 11 December 1923   *The Ambassador*

My dearest love. This morning I rehearsed hard and well. I think I have won the cast by humbleness, and they are all out to poison Carmi. I came home, stretched myself out, & received Dickie Fellows,[3] Gordon Leith,[4] also Edward Eyre[5] also Bert Cruger[6] who has become a lover. Carmi crossed [the Atlantic] with Olga.[7] She looked I hear very savage, dressed completely in leopard – old, but tall and thin, not the dumpling. There are awful interviews from her in tonight's papers. She is referred to as royal, and she tells how God visited her, & said "play my Mother" and a lot more of her being *Reinhardt's* choice. It makes me feel so sick but one must just not read them, or anyway pretend not to. Vollmöller, the author, turned up tonight (her ex-husband,) he had travelled over on the same boat and not known she was on board. He is a charming German – specs & *Kultur* – he stroked and adulated me. I don't get his game quite. It will be interesting to see if truth and innocence wins – or whether like the sonnet Captive Good attends Captain Ill. She I fear will be more *grosartig* – that's the rub.

I do hate my loneliness. I hate it more & more & sometimes I console myself that it is good for me to be confronted with the world, and not always to cower behind you, or luxuriate in your arms. O but I want you.

---

[1] Mary Hoyt (Hoytie) Wiborg and her sisters Olga and Sarah delighted London society by singing together and playing the guitar.
[2] Mr. Wiborg was Hoytie's father, who was a partner in the printing firm of Ault & Wiborg.
[3] Dorothy Fellowes-Gordon, life long friend of Elsa Maxwell.
[4] Gordon Leith, 1879–1941, merchant banker.
[5] Edward Eyre, 1885–1962, banker.
[6] Bertram Cruger was a good looking, middle aged, quite wealthy man about town (New York). He had a job on the parole board and a long standing mistress, Mrs. Vera Whitehouse.
[7] Olga Lynn, who had come to live and work in New York for a while.

Diana to Duff, 12 December 1923   *The Ambassador*

My angel. Today has been very amusing. Carmi refused to meet Baby, said she would have but one rehearsal and that I must not be present. I assume for fear I might pick up some good business; a disappointment to me, as I had relied upon it. I lunched with Will Slater, the man we met at Caroll's[1] – who had the stuffed shirt to meet me – I fear they consider him my fancy-man. I was forbidden the studio on account of Carmi but I went later at eight after a dinner, that should have been alone with my lover Bert Cruger, but at which I hitched on to a man called Schuyler Parsons. The cast's account of her was very unfavourable, she had behaved very *grand dame* – stretched out a left hand to all the principals mouths' to be kissed, and generally put their backs up.

My Mummy sails today.[2] I shall have to pray for her too – O dear, O damn.

My lover Cruger knew Edward[3] well – its a link but Lord he is heavy and serious. I mean God! I mean I love you. Enclosed a Carmi cutting. My love, my love –   Baby.

Diana to Duff, 13 December 1923   *The Ambassador*

My dear darling. There is little to say of today. I am discouraged with my part in the show. I feel I have gone back. It is due to the fact that I never am rehearsed. They have got into a groove of "She's all right" and I'm not. My stage lover Mr. Schuyler Ladd[4] says I am much better the last two days. Is he right or am I? Anyway I am discouraged.

I gave all afternoon to concocting a glycerine tube & bulb with the help of the drug-store man on the premises to produce tears mechanically as I take off my crown – it is concealed in the folds of my drapery. It worked marvellously at home, and perfectly behind the scenes once, but failed me at the psychicological moment. I had told no one – so shame was spared me.

When you write will you always give me a short day to day political *resumé*. I cannot master their papers because they are in

---

[1] Caroll Carstairs, with whom Duff went on leave in Paris in October 1918.
[2] The Duchess was coming to America to see Diana.
[3] Edward Horner, who had visited America before the first war.
[4] Schuyler Ladd, the actor who played the part of the Prince in *The Miracle*.

sections and so dull. I dread to think what my Mummy will say to the reporters. She must have said at Soton that I went on the pictures originally because I was so desperately poor. The consequence is that all day the reporters have been buzzing & shadowing me to discover what we call poor. I think you are at Cherbourg. Will you have wired me from there? I expect not – perhaps wisely. Be good my pretty love. Think of Baby, trying to be good and so faithful. Don't let others think they can take you from me. Put Daisy[1] in her place – if you see her please. Hugo seemed to know a thing or two about her attitude to you – and me, but I would not ask him, and he only did a 'could, and if I would'. Love the good, eschew the evil – be fairly sober and don't gamble much, and keep early hours, and love your missing baby that cries for you at all time, and gets no comforting.   D.

Duff to Diana, December 14　　　　　*on board the* Aquitania

My darling love. We are just leaving Cherbourg where we were so happy together in the sunshine. Did the photographs we took on the boat deck ever come out? I am feeling very sad and sentimental – the more so after a short talk with Mr Cooper who sells autostop safety razors and who is wondering whether his wife will be at Southampton to meet him. Oh my love, however can I bear four months without you? I dread going to Gower Street. I do hope I shall have a letter from you soon. You won't get this much before Christmas. Oh my little sweetheart you will get no Kickermas present from me. I am crying.

Good bye my soul's joy. I shall write to you every day now and number the letters on the outside so that you will know in what order to open them if they arrive together.   D.

Diana to Duff, 14 December 1923　　　　*The Ambassador*

My day was rehearsal as usual. Wonderful properties arrived from Berlin. They are masters of art. Lunch with my stage-flame Mr. Ladd and two ghastly old women friends of his. A crowd of us

---

[1] The Hon. Mrs. Reginald Fellowes. She was very rich, being an heiress to the Singer Sewing Machine fortune. She was much publicized as one of the best dressed women in the world, and she and Duff were lovers, off and on, for several years. She died in 1962.

to tea, bringing two bottles of gin – one of vermouth. Dinner with Mr. George Baker, Sen.[1] and others. The old bugger asked me to stay with him – it would mean a Rolls Royce at the door always – but I'm told no hope of a cent in his will. His ground floor was a parody of an English ancestral [home] on the film – pictures of the owner in each room draped with velvet on an easel, on a background of vile tapestry (early) let into yellow gothic panelling. Rooms cluttered with *objets Allemands*. I will consider it later – but my publicity has become so colossal (thanks to Gest's machinations, and Machiabelli's gaffes) that with the help of the powerful Mr. Maury Paul[2] I hope to get a clean sheet for a hotel bill.

So you are home, my darling and made forgetful maybe by the new developments and excitements and pleasure of our London, or as I now feel, our Europe. Let my light so shine.   Baby.

Diana to Duff, 16 December 1923   *The Ambassador*

My sweet. This morning I got up terribly early and went with the *décor*-man to see a stone cloak he has made for me. It was rather wonderful I think. More the ghost breaking and tearing through its slab and cerements I shall look, than the laden, waxen, graceful Lady of Lourdes. I can't of course stoop to pick up the foundling-Christ which intensely destroys the plot of the play – so Reinhardt and Vollmöller will probably veto it. The idea is to have the light streaming through the stained windows onto all the other statues and not on me – so that when the moment of resurrection comes, there will really be astonishment. It makes the part a hundred times more dificult and risky. Carmi has refused to attempt it so I am rather fixed about it. I lunched with Hoytie and lover Cruger and Olga. Cruger took me on to a Griffith picture at a Theatre called the Capitol (where *The Glorious Adventure* was shown). The stalls are huge Chesterfields – never was comfort catered for better. I took a doze – but I don't think it cooled his ardour. I foresee an appalling, honourable declaration soon. So much more difficult to deal with than a dishonourable one.   xxxxx from B.

[1] George Fisher Baker, 1840–1931. A famous New York banker.
[2] Mr. Maury Paul, who was at that time writing the *Cholly Knickerbocker* gossip column for the Hearst newspapers.

Diana to Duff, 18 December 1923   *The Ambassador*

My darling. This morning I went to be photographed again, and was forced into ridiculous Rodin poses with fantastic arms, that will get circulated before I can veto them. I lunched (all women) with Ethel Fowler,[1] once Higgins and this afternoon I went down to meet my Mummy. I thought the *Berengaria* most squalid *qua* ship though Mother had a cabin twice the size of ours. I thought her looking very old and ill and frail – but her spirits marvellously buoyed by excitement. I made Mummy go to bed on arrival – when I came in at 12.30 she was awake talking to Wade – which maddened me. I dressed for a party under her eyes – very critical eyes they were – eyes that saw me ugly and my clothes disgraceful. I don't know how I am going to bear it especially sharing a room. I had never thought of that aspect. The party was pretty deadly – nothing to drink, and that curiously barbarous habit of changing partners in the middle of a dance rampant. They do not even respect your sitting in a corner or sitting at supper, but every two minutes men barge up and ask you to dance – and how can one refuse?   B.

Duff to Diana, 18 December 1923   *Foreign Office*

Holbrook tells me a rag and bone man has come down the area steps, got into the cellar and taken half a dozen of whiskey. Holbrook saw him going up the steps, ran after and eventually caught him. In his flight however he threw away the bottles and broke them all. When Holbrook caught him a crowd collected and, would you believe it, they all took the thief's part against Holbrook. They shouted "Let 'im go, it's Christmas," which was rather charming and Dickensian of them. The thief relying, I suppose, on the support of the crowd, wrested himself free and made off again with Holbrook in pursuit. He says however he was so puffed he couldn't catch him and he got away. He left his coat and barrow in Gower Street and these have been handed over to the police. It took Holbrook over an hour to get hold of a policeman. I wish I had been there to see the fun.

[1] Mrs. Arthur Fowler – who so closely resembled the lady Duff describes in his letter on p. 122.

Duff to Diana, 19 or 20 December 1923   *Foreign Office*

Little Girl. I dined last night with Lady Horner. When I got back I found a cablegram. Imagine with what a thrill I opened it. The very first word from you since we parted. I read *"Arrange Prudential Insurance transfer jewel policy here"*. I was a little disappointed. It appears that it can't be done – the Prudential have no agencies outside this country and do no business abroad. They suggest that you should insure your jewels with a New York firm and say that they will allow you so much off the premium you pay here in consideration of the time you are away.

By the way I heard from I forget whom that Mosley[1] got into trouble in Paris owing to his excessive attentions to Mrs Cole Porter. He went to her bedroom uninvited so that she had to complain to Cole. Adulterous, canting, slimy, slobbering Bolshie – I don't like him.

I have had a long walk today. I walked to and from the Office with Major this morning and back to the Office after luncheon with Hutchy [Sir John Hutchinson]. Alan has been very seriously ill and has grown almost startlingly thinner. I don't think Viola looks after him too well. He complained that for his breakfast this morning, which was to be his first day up, he was offered some pâté de foie gras which Lady Tree had sent round having no further use for it and some cold pork. It is bitterly cold here and is trying to snow. Good night, apple blossom.   D.

[Duff spent that Christmas with his mother, who lived in the South of France.]

Duff to Diana,   *Nouvel Hotel, Vence*
Christmas Eve 1923   *Alpes Maritimes*

Dinner was very long – the kind of dinner and the kind of company we have met so often in our travels. Old men and old women sitting gloomily about, the monotony being relieved only by an occasional hospital nurse. All speaking in whispers. Some of the English ones in evening dress. How often have we passed

[1] Sir Oswald Mosley (6th Baronet) founder of the British Fascists – 1896–1980.

through it on our gay way and said "This is the sort of life that Mother leads", and thanked God that we didn't – I remember particularly a night at Hyères and one at Carcassonne – but Carcassonne was much gayer than this, and there was a pretty woman there. However I shouldn't complain – I have only three days of it, and it does make Mother happy. She insists on paying my journey. She will be better off now. It is after dinner. *It is ten past eight!*

What a joy your letters are, my baby; You say you enclose a Carmi cutting and don't. I wish you would send me a cutting or two. When I remember how that news agency tout made me part with £10 the night of our arrival, when we came in from dining with Moore, and I was hardly in a condition to do business.

Don't worry about my infidelity nor yet about my gambling. Your letter, coming in the nick of time, has decided me against going to Monte Carlo although the tedium of this place had tempted me strongly to have a dash. Daisy I believe is there unless she has gone back to Paris – I don't know of whom else you can be jealous. I hope not of Mrs. Barrymore[1] – I'm not sure she isn't rather K.O. [keen on] me – but she would be safe from me on a desert island, so long as there were a friendly and not unreasonable turtle about. One of our subjects of conversation at luncheon the other day was an argument on whether she loved Jack as much as I loved you. She said Englishmen were cold and that everyone ought to have one great love in their lives. I said I had, thank her very much, and that she appeared not to. She said she only adored her husband. I asked her why she didn't live with him. She replied that she couldn't bear America, which was a slip as she had just been praising America at the expense of all other countries and talking a lot of Walt Whitman muck.

Of whom else are you afraid. Not Diana I hope. She at any rate is *whore de combat* until long after your return. But if you will make a little list of the people I'm to avoid, I will be careful to do so.

Goodnight my little sweetheart. Kickermas eve. On this evening for the last four years we have been together and have helped to put Isabel's[2] stocking on her bed. May we never have another one apart. My dear, dear love   D.

[1] Mrs. John Barrymore, née Blanche Oelrichs of New York.
[2] Lady Isabel Manners, second daughter of John and Kathleen (Kakoo), Lord and Lady Granby.

[151]

Duff to Diana, 31 December 1923   *Foreign Office*

My baby. I had a very pleasant journey from Paris to London. On the boat I met Roger Wright, a nice fat red-faced Grenadier to whom you once sat next when we dined at Hurlingham. You liked him. He was with two other friends and we spent the crossing sitting in their cabin, drinking champagne and talking about how brave we all were in the war.

This morning there came seven letters from Baby – seven from December the fourteenth to the twentieth. Oh what a joy they were, reflecting as they do your changing moods from day to day, from cloud to sunshine. The series ends in a dark cloud of worry about your Mother's health. I hope the next morning's sun chased it away. I find it very difficult to write an article on New York and quite impossible to write one on *The Miracle*, of which I have only a very faint idea. Sign the ones that the Hearst press write for you provided they are not offensive. Cast dignity to the winds while in New York and get the Yanks' money so that you may be able to afford to resume dignity in Europe.

Now here's an important piece of news. Tomorrow I am promoted to being a First Secretary! It means about two or three hundred more a year and it also means that I shall probably have shortly to give up my present job.[1] But they don't want to move me until my new master has been appointed and I have had time to show him about. This is all to the good as it looks as though I should be able to get leave in the Spring, come over to you, see *The Miracle* and bring you safely back. Wouldn't that be lovely? and well worth three weeks' leave.

Diana to Duff, 3 January 1924   *The Ambassador*

My beloved Love. I didn't write yesterday. It was a dull day apart from a long Nun rehearsal lasting till midders and then a party given in my honour. The enclosed is a sample of the invitations issued. Show it to the boys.[2] I know they will never believe in 'the honours done to me'. I sat up very late as I didn't get there till 1.30 and my lover left in a pet. Today I felt terribly, terribly ill as a result, and also because I am struggling with a cold, and bruised

[1] As Secretary to the Under Secretary for Foreign Affairs.
[2] Alan Parsons and St. John Hutchinson.

and battered as an old medlar. We cannot get into the theatre yet. They have forbidden fires in that studio and altogether the rehearsal was so unsatisfactory and stale that they gave me my freedom this morning for twenty-four hours or more. I dashed home and leapt into bed. My Mummy is also in bed with Potmain.[1] At four the telephone rang rudely and a peremptory message was delivered – would I be at the studio at five. I rang up Kommer for an explanation. He admitted it was to meet Carmi and draw lots – I said nothing would drag me out of bed – I disapproved of the whole thing, etc. Of course Kommer oiled me down, said Reinhardt minded it as much as I did and yet was bowing to it. So I fetched up at one of the most disagreeable seances I have ever experienced. No one present but Gest, Reinhardt, de West [the stage manager] Kommer and 24 photographers. Carmi arrived, terribly flash in gold & black and diamonds with a left handed languid greeting. I was painfully shocked by her youth and beauty, height and slimness. She was quite the woman of the world, and I was a shabby awkward bumpkin. She said *"Ora la Commedia è finita"*[2] and I said *"Spero"* which she no doubt took wrong. We were then photographed with the hat between us, and alone shaking hands, and my spirit was fainting and bursting out alternately. Just at the moment of drawing Carmi said 'Stop' and beckoned me to her, saying "before we draw I want to say that if you *want* the first night so badly I will give it to you. I protested because I created the part but if you really want it I will give it to you." I was speechless and did not realise she was guarding herself against certain failure, and it seemed generously fine, and a great lump got up in my throat and I couldn't answer anything except "I don't want the first night". She doubtless knew the fuss we had made, so I had better have said nothing. Kommer drew a paper out with my name on it and my tears got worse at the beastliness of it all. That she should lose, and that I should look so foolish winning, and rage that I should have to suffer such embarrassment and humiliation of cheating in this filthy country that can't run a good production without framing it in glistening mud. Then they all congratulated me including Carmi, and the tears were pouring down my silly old cheeks, and to cap it all Gest said "You're so human" and I felt I

---

[1] Potmain: Holbrook's word for ptomaine poisoning.
[2] The last words of the opera *I Pagliacci* by Ruggiero Leoncavallo.

[153]

wanted to behave dramatically like the nun, and cover my ears and face with my hands and arms. I refrained luckily and walked off with Kommer to oil me. My consolation is that both Kommer and Gest appeared I think a little ashamed of the proceedings, which Gest certainly would not have but for my attitude.

Duff to Diana, 3 January 1924   *Foreign Office*

What a time – oh what a terrible time letters take to come. It is now January 3rd and I have heard nothing from you later than December 20th. I see the Majestic ran aground on leaving Southampton. I'm afraid I write you dull letters now but of everything I do I only ask myself both while I am doing it or before whether it will amuse you to hear of.

I have seconded old Denison Ross[1] for the Garrick Club – the election is today – one has to write a letter to the Committee saying what you know of the candidate. I couldn't think of anything to say of Ross except that he was England's greatest orientalist. Mason[2] came up to me last night and said "Can't you say something else about him – half the old fools on the Committee don't know what an 'orientalist' is – they'll probably think you mean he's a bugger".

Duff to Diana, 4 January 1924   *Foreign Office*

My beautiful baby. I gave a dinner party last night at 90 Gower Street – Guests were Colonel Cripps,[3] Major Stuart-Wortley,[4] Captain [Eddie] Grant and Mr. Michael Herbert. I did them proud –

> Caviare (excellent – with very hot toast)
> Turtle Soup (from Fortnum & Mason)
> Homard Neuburg (cooked exactly right)
> Perdrix aux choux (couldn't have been better)
> Asperges (bought by me for £2)

[1] Sir Edward Denison Ross, 1871–1940. Among his many appointments, he was Director of the School of Oriental Studies and Professor of Persian at the University of London, 1916–37.
[2] A. E. W. Mason, the novelist, author of *The Four Feathers* etc, 1865–1948.
[3] Hon Frederick Heyworth Cripps – 1885–1977 – 2nd son of 1st Baron Parmoor. He was made Colonel of the Royal Bucks Hussars in 1917.
[4] Rothesay Stuart-Wortley, 1892–1926.

Blackberry Ice (which they all loved)
Mushrooms on toast (Very good)
Dessert (Cape plums and tangarines).
Sherry – champagne – port – brandy and coffee,
cigarettes & cigars.

Extravagant you will say, but I played Bridge afterwards and won £15 so it cost me nothing. They were all very happy and very nice and said what a wonderful cook we had got. I sent for Hilda[1] this morning and told her how good it had all been which I think pleased her. It's a good thing to give her something to do occasionally – otherwise her hand will lose its cunning.
Good bye my little love.   D.

I enclose a cutting about a ski-ing accident. I always said it wasn't safe.

Diana to Duff, 5 January 1924   *The Ambassador*

My love. Raymond[2] never said good-bye to me nor told me he was going this week so I missed sending you a letter by him. It maddens me as it's so much quicker. Please my beloved find the cheapest way of transatlantic cable. I think it is a week end letter, 5 cents a word, and send me news of yourself only, every week. I get such lonelinesses, and they are growing.

Tonight began the ten terrible days of dress rehearsals. It was worse than I feared, and I feared much when I heard them ordering coffee & sandwiches for midnight as an interval. The clothes I think will ruin all. I'd always forseen it. Krauss[3] lost his temper about his costume. Pinchot and de West quarrelled, permanently I think because she is too rude to forgive crossness in the tired and anxious. Schildkraut raged round because his dressing room wasn't on the stage level. Said his health came first whatever anybody said. Gest nearly stopped the mock wedding scene because Krauss is dressed as a joke bishop, and he said it was immoral. I quieted him by reminding him that every farce he

[1] Mrs. Wales, the Coopers' cook till 1936.
[2] Raymond de Trafford, 1900–1971, youngest son of Sir Humphrey de Trafford, 3rd Baronet.
[3] Werner Krauss, 1884–1959, played the part of the Spielmann and was one of the leading classical actors of the Austrian and German stage.

has ever put on has a mockery of a real clergyman, and this was only a pretend one. I heard Kommer reach his lowest level of calm when he said he couldn't be in two places at once. Reinhardt said "*weite, weite, de West weite*" with infinite weary rage in his lovely voice. Geddes[1] took to not answering his name and leaving the building. Pinchot cried unceasingly. I had a very bad cold but enjoyed every minute of it till three a.m. Now I'm home in bed with a newly opened endless telegram of congratulations and wishes for personal success from Lyn Harding.[2] The English on alien soil cling pathetically close. I'se very tired and I'se put Sloane's stinking embrocation all over my chest, and onto that I'se clapped some Thermogene woolly wool till I'm burning like a tiny crata. I does hope it don't turn to pneumy.

Gest repeatedly said to me, "What can you do to improve the appearance of Pinchot's breasts?" Dream of me Duffy. Eat carefully for me, drink gently for me, play soberly for me, live chastely for me, and all these things will I do for you.   Baby Wogg.

Diana to Duff, 12 January 1924   *The Ambassador*

I'm nauseated with misery. *The Miracle* is worse than ever. Nothing ready, everything wrong – myself included since they have what they call braced my stone coat with steel and only 2 more days till the opening. On the top of this Mother is of course ill, which I knew she would be. However she has gone to bed which makes it a little easier.

Its three a.m. and I'm just home having had my back broken by Krauss's last straw. He caught me in my dressing room, – looking utterly woe-begone. We groaned together a bit in pidgeon-german and he told me how ten years ago a German novelist friend of Reinhardt's had written a book with Reinhardt as the hero. It told of his rise and greatness and in the end this great artist producer goes to a *Fremdes Land* and there he creates what is to be the crown of all his genius and imagination – a super *Kolossal* production. The night comes and gradually the audience start hissing and whistling. I felt faint and had to sit down; he then told me that he thought of taking flight tomorrow – He couldn't face it he said. He felt he must disappear. He is so sadistic that he may have done all

---

[1] Norman Bel Geddes, 1893–1958 – producer and stage designer. He was designing the costumes for *The Miracle*.
[2] The actor – 1867–1952.

[156]

this to watch me writhe – he certainly succeeded and I feel haunted and desperate. Still this depression is in the best tradition of the theatre, and perhaps it's a better augury than satisfaction.

My lover has achieved an admittance to the rehearsal, so that he is there always – till any hour – I don't know whether to be pleased or sorry – it's rather ridiculous and boring but he runs out and buys milk for me and telephones and gets Mother a doctor, and even produced a bottle of cham. once – I feel sure you would get me right were you with me. I should be right if you were here – because I should be in your arms now and that would indemnify so much, but with nothing but the play – and the play wrong – poor baby is a tiny misery boo. Duff Duff, my darling love.

Duff to Diana, 14 January 1924   *Foreign Office*

My beloved, after I had finished writing to you from White's on Saturday afternoon I went home and found two more letters from you waiting for me and before I went out to dinner two more arrived, making six in one day – all apparently from the *Aquitania* and all arriving by different posts. I spent the rest of the afternoon re-reading and rearranging the letters that you wrote to me during the war. It is impossible for me to tell you all I think of them. They are most beautiful, most vivid, most witty, most touching. I laughed aloud as I read them – and I cried. I believe that if they are preserved they will live when we are dust and that this miracle will have might, that not 'in black ink' but in very pale brown pencil 'our love shall still shine bright'. I read for nearly two hours but only finished one month of them. I have five more lovely months to read that I am looking forward to. And it was best of all to turn from those letters written six years ago to new ones that were coming in even while I read and which were still as full as the same sweet love. How incredibly lucky I am – luckier far than young Mr. Ford or anyone I ever heard of. And how little have I done to deserve this great treasure of your love, except by returning it as deeply and as utterly as the capacity of my coarser and shallower nature allows.

Noel Francis had invited me to dine at the Embassy. He said it was his birthday party. I should have preferred to dine at Bucks but couldn't refuse a free meal. The 'party' consisted of only

Myrtle Farquharson[1] and Poppy Baring.[2] I was tired and bored. The only thing that amused me was that Poppy was somewhat concerned at being at the Embassy without a chaperone. She is staying with Freda [Dudley Ward] – I said I was sure that Freda wouldn't mind. She replied that Freda didn't mind a bit, but that Michael [Herbert] made such a fuss about that sort of thing – not that Michael takes any interest at all in Poppy but apparently he is cross with Freda for not properly looking after girls who are staying with her. I find it charming – the lover lecturing his mistress on her duties as a chaperone.

While Noel and Myrtle were dancing Poppy told me about Noel. He is, it appears, a terrible drunkard which I had never realised and that after a recent scandal Poots[3] has left him completely. The scandal was no later than last week when while Sheila was at Ashby poor Luffy[4] was bundled off to stay with Noel. Luffy who has just come out of an inebriates' home and Noel who had been teetotalling for months under a vow celebrated the occasion by getting gloriously drunk together. They were joined by Lois,[5] and an orgy that would have made Nero and Caligula turn in their graves with envy appears to have taken place. I begin to dance much better than I did. Alan whom I saw the other evening at the Embassy was amazed at the beauty of my dancing.

Since writing most of the above I have been out to luncheon with Hilary.[6] He dragged me to 'a little place in Soho' where of course he made me eat and drink too much. He would have been offended if I hadn't. The result is that I feel heavy and muzzy. He was very amusing – said he had been spending half the morning trying to finish his sonnet to you – and when I told him to pray for you, he said he would order masses for you and that if he could afford it he would build a cathedral to you.

[1] Myrtle Farquharson became Mrs Robin d'Erlanger in 1925.
[2] Poppy Baring, 1901–1979. Daughter of Sir Godfrey Baring. In 1928 she married Peter Thursby.
[3] Gwendolen, daughter of Charles Van Raalte. She married Lt. Col. Humphrey Butler in 1927.
[4] Francis St. Clair Erskine, Lord Loughborough (1892–1929), married Sheila Chisholm, an Australian, in 1915.
[5] Lois Sturt, 1903–1937, youngest daughter of 2nd Baron Alington. She married Evan Morgan, later 2nd Viscount Tredegar, in 1928.
[6] Hilaire Belloc, 1870–1953, poet and author.

[158]

Duff to Diana, 15 January 1924   *Foreign Office*

I can only write you a short letter today my darling because although it is your great day it is also a very busy one for me as it is the Opening of Parliament. Nor have I much to tell you.

I moved down into your room yesterday and Rothesay comes in this afternoon.[1] I felt quite guilty when I sat for the first time in your bath and thought how often I had come into the room and seen your rosy smiling little head sticking up out of that box. I am very comfortable there except that I have to go upstairs before having my bath which is a bore. Such a nice taxi driver I had. " 'Ow's 'er Ladyship?" he asked – I said you were in America. "I know that," he replied – "Is she having a great time there – going great guns?" – I said you were. "That's right," he said.

I don't know what will happen in the House today. The Labour party want to defeat the Government on Thursday and adjourn for three weeks while they form their new government. The Liberals want to go on till Monday as they all want to make speeches and endeavour to explain why, having been elected in order to keep out the socialists, they are going deliberately to put the socialists in.

How, how I wish I were with you tonight. Be brave, baby.   D.

Diana to Duff, 15 January 1924   *The Ambassador*

My darling love – I'm simply too exhausted to bear anything so this is two lines to take my love to you, and tell you it's all over, and I think successful though I dread tomorrow's papers. There were a few contretemps that ruined my hopes and performance but its possible the audience won't notice, being ignorant, and being American. I'll write at length not tomorrow, which I'm not facing – for there are two performances, and my nerves are quivering – but the day after. I love you, and think of your pride in me when the ordeal of immobility seems unbearable.[2]   Diana.

---

[1] Rothesay Stuart-Wortley was Duff's lodger at Gower Street for a few months in 1924.
[2] For the first 45 minutes of the performance, the Madonna is a Statue and therefore must hold herself completely still.

My sweetest Heart. Today has been hard to endure. No one but me is so totally wrecked but no one is half so nervous. The press 'write ups' were staggering I think. They seldom apparently mention the actors, restricting themselves to statistics of how many feet of wire cabling is used in the show and how many dollars the house held – I enclose a wad.

All day yesterday I spent trying to get a rehearsal with the finished stone coat, a thing I had never managed. I got it an hour before the show and realised that it needed a week's practise, and another week's work to perfect the carrying round of the stone figure as a finale. This didn't add to my peace. I got on to the stage ten minutes before the play was advertised to open with locomotor ataxy legs and only a glass of port as stimulus. I stand in place behind a church banner, while I get my crown on, and am handed the Christ. What was my horror when they passed me serupti-ciously a new impossible baby, made of snow white unpainted papier maché & huge & unholdable. However, being concealed I wispered my rage to the praying nuns, and in time got the property child I had rehearsed with, and in whose bum I had cut a hole to hold it by. I got through pretty well till the last great moment when I break for a second out of my monument to gather up the Nun's dead child miraculously turned into the Christ. Conceive of my horror when in Death's hand I see this obscene, enormous, snow-white repudiated abortion – impossible to hold in one hand. I managed somehow, and was surprised my stone folds kept my rage in bounds. Once off the stage I lost my temper as no temperamental prima donna has ever done – but they deserved it. It was a vile surprise, and ruined the end from an artistic point of view. The audience kept the applause on for fifteen minutes while the stage banked itself with flowers. I was too cross to enjoy anything, and outraged at being made to take calls as a Madonna *should not*. Gest was obscene, Geddes fell in a faint in the wings and remained so over an hour. Reinhardt cried which made me cross again. I had a $75 bouquet from George Baker Sr. and about thirty other bouquets – but the end of it all is that I think I hate the profession – rehearsing is heaven but acting is too painful for such as this Baby. I dread the next day – already. Tomorrow I rehearse (with Carmi) as the Nun and Saturday, I come out. So my fears seem without end. I don't know what I've written I'm too

tired. I look terrible. Such lovely cables from the Embassy – thank
all. Love love love love   G. Wog.

Duff to Diana, 17 January 1924   *Foreign Office*

What lovely news this morning. I cried when I read *The Times*
which I enclose. I enclose also the *Daily Mail*. Then came your
telegram and Malony[1] rang up to say the Duke had had one from
Her Grace, and Mr. McNeill[2] congratulated me on my wife's
success. I do so bitterly regret that I am not there with you to share
in it. You must be intoxicated with glory. I don't expect you ever
think now of me and Major and No. 90 Gower Street. I long to
hear more about it. What happened, how nervous you were and a
thousand other things. I havn't had a letter for five days, and there
is no mail due until Saturday which means Monday.

Well I must go on telling you about my tedious life. The night
before last I dined with the Vansittarts[3] – or at least with her as he
was dining with the Marquess [Curzon] but he joined us later.
Myrtle Farquharson, Chips Channon[4] and a little American
diplomat called Blair – who tries to talk in an English voice which
results in a very unpleasant drawl. When they talked of you he
said in a very condescending way – "I like her very much – I think
she's so pretty – don't you?" turning to me. I said ingenuously
"Yes I do. I think she's very pretty" which made them laugh a
good deal.

(I can't call my soul my own these days or write more than a
page of a letter in the same place.)

I lunched yesterday with E. V. Lucas[5] and Hugh Walpole.[6]
They talked about Arnold Bennett and discussed whether or no he
had behaved badly to his wife – I said that I didn't care how he
treated *his* wife but that what I did object to was the way he treated
mine.[7]

---

[1] Sister Malony had worked at the Rutland Hospital for Officers, and stayed on after the
war as nurse to the Duke of Rutland.
[2] Ronald John McNeill, 1861–1936. Parliamentary Under Secretary of State for
Foreign Affairs, 1922–1924. Later 1st Baron Cushendun.
[3] Sir Robert Vansittart, 1881–1957, diplomat, and his wife Sarita, née Ward.
[4] Sir Henry Channon, M.P., 1897–1958.
[5] Edward Verrall Lucas, the essayist, 1868–1938.
[6] Hugh Walpole, playwright and novelist, 1884–1941.
[7] In Arnold Bennett's novel *The Pretty Lady* (1918), the character of Lady Queenie Paulle
is based on Diana.

You see I had to stop this letter yesterday in the middle of a sentence. I am spending all these days in the House of Commons. It is amusing. That wicked old Squith made a good speech yesterday – with an enormous dark gold whiskey and soda clasped in his hand from which he continually gulped. The obscene Mosley made an indecent exposure. There is a very strong rumour that he is to succeed McNeill. When I sit in the House I do long to be in it – and feel that I must end there.

What is most amusing is that when the Labour Government take office which they will probably do on Tuesday they will immediately be faced by a railway strike which has been engineered largely in order to spite Thomas,[1] one of their principal leaders.

Diana to Duff, 17 January 1924   *The Ambassador*

My pretty love. *The Miracle* is an extravagant success, two editorials today which apparently is unprecedented. No seats left for 6 weeks. My fears are acute as ever, not once I am on '*die Bühne*' but for a long while before. Today was very amusing. They called a rehearsal for 'cutting' purposes and also for Carmi. She looked quite beautiful, and acted I thought well, but not I am happy to say with the simplicity that I have achieved. Her every gesture is elaborately elegant and rounded, and less gothic. Still, she was lovely – but in one hour she had got the entire cast, and staff, actually to strike. She needs must have the last act changed for her nights which is a thing supers can't do, and they all said so, and walked off the stage. It was fun for me, because they all came up to me and said they were for me – but I expect Carmi will go down twice as well with the public as she is flash and beautiful – and less anaemic than me.

I think Cruger will die of love. I was quite enjoying it until he told me he knew he would adore me till he died and that it meant, for him, a perpetual struggle to get to England. This broke my nerve with a snap. It's unthinkable. What would the boys say. He is a joke, and stands outside the stage door in a topper (tradition) even though Mother is always playing chaperone, to say nothing

---

[1] James Henry Thomas, 1874–1949. He was Colonial Secretary in MacDonald's Government.

of Wade. He has a burning desire to drive me round and round Central Park. I've stood out so far. I do the Nun not Saturday but Wednesday. Mother roves in the theatre telling people she stands behind that she is my mother. They always ask her if I am as good as I appear, then she starts off like me on Major, saying she has never heard a cross word except etc. etc. My lovely Duff no letters for so long.   B.

Diana to Duff, 24 January 1924   *The Ambassador*

My darlingest. I had a happy day today from the point of view of admiration and encouragement. The telephone this morning never ceased to be rung by members of the company, telling me how ghastly Carmi had been last night. It appears she really was a 10 cent store piece, painted brick red, elaborately studied and wobbly. This morning she rang up Geddes in a state saying she must have a stone coat. The papers were not too kind; and Gest told her she must alter her performance. I spent the day at the theatre, and ran into her once, was overcome with embarrassment and could say nothing.

Tomorrow I do the Nun, and I have a new scene put in for my first night – the tavern scene. I don't remember if you saw it rehearsed but it is the scene the parent Pinchots objected to as too 'strong'. I *adore* doing it, the Nun's lowest depth of degradation. Krauss dances with her after she admits to being with child till she faints. He dances with me in the old fashioned apache style with my feet off the ground. Krauss is marvellous to me – considers me his responsibility because he thinks it's due to his offices I got the part, it isn't but no one has disillusioned him – he never tires of giving me tuition. My greatest dread is getting blown running, and the unrehearsed Lord's Prayer. Wade is unmanned and faint with the dread of the quick changes. So am I. The snow covered New York with three white inches in a couple of hours, with the result that a party I went to with my lover, Willie Stewart and others was empty. Such a lovely letter today off the *Aquitania*, telling me of my war letters to you. I hate to hear of you doing them without me – but perhaps it is better, so long as you will edit them for my ears or eyes. What would I give to hear you read aloud, better to hear you love me   D.

Duff to Diana, 29 January 1924   *Foreign Office*

My dearest heart. Last night I dined at the Berkeley Grill with Michael, Eddie [Grant], Freda and Poppy Baring – and went to the Alhambra to see Harry Tate[1] who made me laugh as much as ever. Then we went back to Freda's house where Poppy is staying and sat and talked for some time. The unfortunate Poppy was engaged to a young man in the navy stationed in China. She recently jilted him by correspondence, and he is returning in power and wrath to claim his bride. All this provided us with suitable material for innumerable and very funny jokes in the worst possible taste – nautical references, hornpipe dancing, imitations of the Chinese accent – all ee lightee etc.

This morning I arrived here at a quarter to ten, and so for the first time succeeded in short heading Ponsonby.[2] I had a hasty meal at the Garrick where I saw the boys and showed them the telegram.[3] They were deeply impressed, and thought that Cochran's telegraphic style compared very favourably with yours.

Does this mean, I wonder, that *The Miracle* may be performed here in the autumn? I do hope so. I long to hear your views of future plans. When shall I come out and when will you come back? More every day do I incline to leave this Office and plunge into politics. I think the time is ripe. There is only the money difficulty. I should be making now about £900 a year safe. It is a lot to give up in these troublous times and I should feel myself a bit of a mackerel. But perhaps that would make me work the harder at journalism and other things. Tell me all you think.

Now don't leave this letter laying about as you always do, you naughty little girl. I love you, baby.   D.

Diana to Duff, 29 January 1924   *The Ambassador*

My sweet. I send you tonight what is better reading than my writing. I knew what would happen. My last excitement, my last

---

[1] Harry Tate, 1872–1940, entertainer and comedian.
[2] Arthur Ponsonby, later 1st Baron Ponsonby of Shulbrede, 1871–1946. He was now Under Secretary of State for Foreign Affairs, and Duff – while waiting to find out what his next appointment would be – was working for him.
[3] Duff received a telegram from C. B. Cochran, who had staged the original production of *The Miracle* with Reinhardt in 1912. "Wife's performance exquisitely beautiful unquestionable work of sensitive artist with many individual subtleties the result of thought and complete mastery of rare resources."

hope is over and successful at that which means no more fight. So now this acute longing for you and home is overpowering me and yet there are but two out of sixteen weeks gone. O God. I am brave, I have astounded Wade, it appears from Olga's evidence who received Wade's confidence – she finds me so courageous. When I use the baby voice which I very rarely do her eyes fill with tears.

I had a terrible experience tonight. The final tableau of the show is when I am lifted on high by a certain trap, worked hydraulically like a lift. Of course the platform came down, catching a man's foot in it – and no power on earth would raise it for a full two minutes. As you know there is no curtain, and the man was brave enough not to lift his voice in pain, but only to groan "my foot, my foot", in the ink darkness of the blackout. I have never felt so sick physically. There is a casualty every night and a Doctor on the premises, but nothing as bad as this has occurred before. I adore you.   Baby.

I am arranging to transfer 300 pounds to you at Paris.

Duff to Diana, 31 January 1924   *Foreign Office*

My sweet love. I have very busy days now and very little time to write. I arrive before ten in the morning and leave after 7.30. I was to have started initiating my successor in his work today but owing to other people in his department having influenza his transfer has been postponed. When I told Ponsonby he said "So much the better, as I don't think anybody could be so wonderfully useful to me as you are."[1] The work is really much more interesting than it used to be because Ponsonby has to do nearly everything that the Prime Minister ought to do. But still I shan't be sorry to get back to a Department and I should rather like once more to have a finger in the Egyptian pie – especially as the moment is very suitable for re-cooking it and Murray[2] is away so that I could have it to myself for a bit. I should refuse to go on working under him when he comes back as it is not my idea of promotion to return to exactly the same position that I occupied four years ago.

[1] Ponsonby, however, had chosen Nevile Butler to be his P.P.S. On February 13th, Duff was told he was to be Head of the Communications Department.
[2] John Murray, 1883–1937, head of the Egyptian Department of the Foreign Office.

Diana to Duff, 6 February 1924   *The Ambassador*

My sweetest. I'm in such a rage – impotent and useless, against Hugo [Rumbold] of all brick walls. He rang me up at 5.30 after my matinée to tell me he was going to see me as the Nun tonight with G. Gordon Moore. I asked him as a personal favour to be seated, since it was to be the front row, not more than half an hour late – he swore to be on the tick – because it is only my first scene of frenzy I am proud of. He drove a bargain – should he be punctual I should join him and Moore for supper. I agreed providing he came to my dressing room and pressed me. They took their seat an hour late after my frenzy – Hugo snored so loud that the audience complained, and I *heard* it from up stage. He slept solidly through it – first head forward like an animal, then head backwards over his stall like a stiff, with wide jaws. He sent Moore to fetch me to supper, and then never turned up so that I was planted with Fairy [Moore]. I never was so outraged. Really. The publicity is so bad too – *Snores in front row while Di puts Nun over.*

Mother got John's telegram saying "How are you both when are you coming home" and took it as friendly message, requiring no answer.[1] She is impossible.

I seem to get no letters from you – it's despairing though I'm sure you write every day. I never miss without saying so. I do adore you and I do want to go home. I could almost face padding it.   Wog.

Diana to Duff, [?13] February 1924   *The Ambassador*

Darling. I suppose you are in love with Poppy, & that's about the size of it. I'm sorry because she'll be so proud. O dear. I think I'll have to come home. I don't feel strong enough to stick it out. You do nothing for me about Mother – she seems absolutely stationary. My lover is good and kind, but too importunate. I didn't sleep last night for worrying about so many things. I finished a book I thought lovely, called *A Lost Lady* that I'll send you – don't laugh when you see *Bertram* in letters of fire on the fly leaf. I have some photographs to send you but must wait till I hear of someone going. We play to $55000 a week – ask if that is a lot.

---

[1] The Duchess had now been with Diana for over a month, and showed no signs of leaving.

I *am* so sad. I'll go and send a cable – that sometimes helps.
Diana.

Duff to Diana, St. Valentine's Day, 1924   *Foreign Office*

Beautiful baby. Yesterday evening I heard my official fate. I am to
be Head of the Communications Department. Bland[1] was very
apologetic about asking me to go there and said it would only be
for a year. I was expecting it and don't mind. It involves very little
and very easy work and one is one's own master – besides having
about thirty people under one. It is fool's work which any efficient
butler could perform, but as I become more and more resolved to
give up the Foreign Office at the first opportunity I don't at all
mind taking this on for a bit.

    Last night I went to Dennis Eadie's[2] new play with the Vans. I
met them at the theatre so had a sandwich first at Bucks. While I
was there came a telephone message from Holly [Holbrook] –
"Cablegram just arrived." "Please read it aloud." "Do you love
me, sir" said Holly as respectfully as possible. Naughty baby, I
thought, but couldn't help laughing.

Diana to Duff, February 1924   *The Ambassador*

Darling. Things are going too well about Mother, and I am feeling
repentant, and in mortal dread that she should ever discover that I
instigated. Please do not forget to speak very seriously to whoever
you did discuss it with before – Father or John or Letty or Sister[3] –
and tell them that her whole illusions – foundations hopes and
joys, can be shattered by a single 'I would, an' if I could'. O do
impress it. Sister is the most dangerous, as when in a temper she'll
let anything out to prove her point. Tell her for my sake and yours
– she has a hero-worship for us. It all appals me, and this
morning's letters from you telling me of Father's good spirits tears
me. She is going to wait till my chickenpox dangers are past and
her own, then I think she will actually sail.

    I have been very hard worked this week with extra Nun

---

[1] Sir Nevile Bland, 1886–1972, Private Secretary to the Permanent Under Secretary for
Foreign Affairs.
[2] Dennis Eadie, 1869–1928, actor manager and playwright.
[3] Sister Malony. See p. 161.

matinées and I am tired which accounts perhaps for my glooms lately. It is funny that I should have accused you of loving Poppy two days before I hear that Norman did the same. Don't be lechy – its dirty. My lover is so kind and so dull, and so loving, and so platitudinous. He says he can understand fighting for me, and quotes lines about eyes being like diamonds. You know the style. Still I cling to him. He lured me to his horrible little flat last night between the performances, on the bait of a cocktail which I've forgotten the taste of. When I got there I found a hot dinner on a charcoal contraption sent round from the Knickerbocker Club. I flew into a rage – but spoilt all by falling on the food. Your letters seem so far between and few. I can't think you write every day. My darling, my darling   D.

Diana to Duff, February 1924   *The Ambassador*

My dearest love. I didn't write yesterday – I felt too despondent. Sunday is worse than other days. The Doctor came and reassured us about Olga, & that was the only bright spot – her case is normal chickenpox, but it's a dreadful disease – and I am certain that I am for it. I've had a letter from you today. Alan writes me three to your one, but I'm not complaining because your one means so much more than his three. Mother has two lovers. A Russian and a Russo-Yank – so she is well pleased. I am not well pleased, my lover swoons and trembles and pants with love, but it's no good to me, and I am wretched and dead except on the stage – and I have a feeling that I cannot dismiss, that you are learning to do without me – that your pangs of separation are less sharp. Alan misses me. What am I losing to gain this miserable triumph and these few dollars. O God.

Diana to Duff, 22 February 1924   *The Ambassador*

I'm writing this in my dressing room between the acts. It's that old fool Washington's birthday so there is an extra matinée and I am weary and sick of an old passion,[1] and my eyes hurt me and I've been to the oculist, who's given me drops that make them hurt more. I'm O so bored and Valentine's boat brought no letters and

---

[1] Dowson – *Non sum qualis eram.*

I feel deserted and unmourned. Say when you think you'll come –
please do and say too you love me – say it over & over.   D.

Duff to Diana, 24 February 1924   *Buck's Club*

My heart's delight. When I got home I found two rather naughty
letters from you. In one you accuse me of loving Poppy, and in the
other you say you don't think I write to you every day. The first
accusation is so contemptible that I can only reply to it by saying
that very nasty rumours have reached me about you and Barton
French – with regard to the second it merely convinces me of what
I always suspected, that you don't read my letters. If you did and
looked at the dates on them you would see exactly how often I
write. You naughty, ugly, diseased, obstinate, perverse and dis-
obedient child.

I have played two rounds of golf today with the Herberts and
Rothesay and lunched at Juliet Duff's[1] and am now going to dine
here. Juliet had Winston who is hoping to get a seat now vacant –
Westminster. There were other people there – negligible – *not*
including Miss Baring whom I happen not to have seen for about
three or four weeks. You can verify when I last saw her by looking
at my letters *if* you keep them, or if you know the date of Miss
Myrtle Farquharson's birthday.

I must now dine because I am hungry and they are waiting for
me. But I do love my ugly little girl – not very much – but a good
deal better than all the world beside.   D.

What are your politics, baby?
Staunch Tory, Duffy.

Duff to Diana, 25 February 1924   *Foreign Office*

Well ugly – more letters from you this morning – nasty, plaintive,
whining, suspicious but ever welcome, deeply cherished letters.
You say it's dirty to be lecherous – but jealousy let me tell you is far
dirtier – because the latter is of the mind, and the former, to which
incidentally I do not plead guilty, is of the body – and 'filthiness of

---

[1] Lady Juliet Duff, 1881–1965. Daughter of the 4th Earl of Lonsdale, she was married in
1903 to Sir Robin Duff, who was killed in action in 1914. In 1919 she married Major Keith
Trevor, whom she divorced in 1926.

the mind I do hold worse'. Frankly I am ashamed of you – and your silly accusations of not writing – I never miss a day which you do often – make your case worse. What would you think of me if I were jealous of Cruger or of any of your many men friends both here and there. You would be disgusted with me. And yet you smell out a scandal in the coincidence of my having met the same creature on several occasions rather close together. By reference to my diary I find that the last time I saw Poppy was at the Embassy on February 1st but really I am ashamed, less for myself than for you, that I should have been at the pains to look it up. I haven't avoided her since and the fact that I have not seen her since is as fortuitous as the fact that for a short time I saw her frequently. In fact I feel so outraged that if I knew her address – she is no longer staying with Freda – I should ring her up and arrange to meet her. When I think of my lonely bachelor existence and your vile suspicions my blood boils. Last week I dined six nights at the Club – the seventh was in the company of my sister Sybil. If I do so again you will no doubt begin muttering about Lord Byron and Augusta Leigh. You beast, you beast, you horrid little dearly beloved beast. I must be mad to love you. It reminds me of when I was at the war and my letters, written every day, got hung up and you accused me, since there were no women there, of being carried away by military glory and of having betrayed you for Bellona.

No more of that. You ask for Hilary's sonnet. I had a very typical letter from him this morning from Alsace – "I have this day traversed the Alps and, I must say, the truth that they (& the Pyrenees) divide Europe was never better shown" etc. He is coming back to London this week and I will ask him again for the sonnet. As I have already told you – if you read my letters you will remember – when I asked him for it last he said he couldn't finish it. I will write one for you myself.

> Doubt not, sweet love, oh never dare to doubt –
> Lest doubting should conceive and bear distrust,
> Lest the pure steel of our true love show rust
> And all our hosts of joy be put to rout.
> Our citadel of love is girt about
> By envious captains – Weariness, Disgust,
> Estrangement, Disillusion, yea and Lust
> But still the traitor at the gate is Doubt.

That is only half or strictly speaking four sevenths of a sonnet – but not bad as an extempore. I will try to finish it when I can find time.

You say your Mother is really thinking of going – but her letters to the Duke, so I hear this evening, by no means confirm this. In fact he says she doesn't seem to have any intention of coming back whatever. She says she is so happy where she is and that she hasn't even told you that she has been asked to return. This being of course a lie. What is to be done?

Duff to Diana, 26 February 1924   *Foreign Office*

There is one argument which might if judiciously used spur the Duchess's return and that is the suggestion that the Duke may be ruining himself in her absence. He is putting down new carpets all over Arlington Street, recovering the chairs, has bought a Rolls Royce – is having the Duchess's car entirely done up and re-painted – he has a luncheon party every day – in fact, strictly between ourselves, he is having the time of his life. It might also be suggested that Sister, who comes in at the end of every luncheon party, looking quite pretty, very painted and beautifully dressed, is his mistress. Any outside observer would say she was. Perhaps he will leave her everything.

I have finished the sonnet which I send you and which I hope you will take to heart. Do *try* to be a better baby.   D.

> Doubt not, brave heart, oh never dare to doubt
> Lest care and calumny should breed distrust,
> Lest the fine steel of faith should gather rust,
> And we should lose what we were lost without.
> Our citadel of light is girt about
> With swords of darkness, allies of the dust,
> Jealousy, separation, lies and lust –
> And still the traitor at the gate is Doubt.
>
> Mount guard with me, beloved; you and I
> Will baffle our besiegers with disdain.
> The royal standard of our troth flies high
> As e'er it flew, and shall not dip again.
> So all assaults shall only serve to prove
> Our faith impregnable, our changeless love.

Duff to Diana, 4 March 1924　　　　　　　　　　　*Foreign Office*

My own sweet love. I got such terribly sad letters from you this morning. They made me miserable but when I got to the Office I found your telegram saying your spirits were better. I hope they still are.

You again accuse me of not writing to you, and you again ask me when I'm coming which must still depend on your return. I will come whenever you tell me to even if it means prematurely chucking the Foreign Office which I think would be silly.

Writing to me on the 22nd of February you say "It's that old fool Washington's birthday" – forgetting that it was also that young fool Duffy's. Naughty naughty Wogg.

Diana to Duff, 6 March 1924　　　　　　　　　　　*The Ambassador*

My pretty bird. I had such lovely letters from you this morning. It's made me feel so miserable to be away from you another day – and then just as I was moaning that they were writ so long ago, I get a cable saying *Vorfrühlings* that tore my heart but that made me feel close. One of the letters was most awfully cross Duffy, I got quite frightened – but Baby deserved it, and she knows it, and very very sorry that she was so dreadful naughty but the poor mite's all alone, and given to glooms, and has not a sole to talk of you to – Forgive forgive. Another one was shocking about Father's extravagances, and then there was the sonnet which I think too too lovely. O Duffy you are awfully clever – it made me so happy, and so safe, and so trusting, and so admiring and so adoring. I think I like *captains* in the original version better than the revised *allies* – allies sounds always one's own allies – perhaps I'm wrong. O it is a lovely sonnet. You have no idea how I love it.

Duff to Diana, 18 March 1924　　　　　　　　　　　*Foreign Office*

This morning I had my golf lesson. It was a beautiful Spring morning in Regent's Park – and I felt very well but when I got to the Office I started sneezing and shivering and blowing my nose so that I feared I was in for at least a cold. I thought I would stop at Pope Roach's on the way to luncheon to get a cold cure, but as I approached it I met Malcolm Bullock[1] who was going to buy wine at Berry's. It occurred to me that a glass of port would probably do me more good than anything Pope Roach could concoct so I called on Mr. Berry and discussed with him over a nice glass the prospects of the Westminster Election. He said he was going to vote for Mr. Nicholson[2] because Mr. Nicholson was a dud and the more duds you had in Parliament the better. This seemed to me an unassailable position. Fortified by the port I walked as far as White's where I repeated the treatment and where Lionel [Tennyson], my Mephistopheles, lured me to lunch in bad company. The luncheon was at Oddenino's and the party was a third member of White's and two employees of Réville's.[3] One of them was remarkably pretty, the other plain – but neither amused me and which is still more distressing I did not amuse them. Tarts don't think me funny – they never did.

Early this morning John telephoned to say the Melton Committee[4] had selected two out of eight candidates and that I was not one of the two. So may they perish in their ignorance. I am the more determined to get into that House with the least delay. But I am thrown back on the Central Office, as there is nowhere else where we have any local influence. South Norfolk would be a hard fight but it attracts me rather. It is not too far from London and – you will think this silly – it is where I came from.

I got one more letter from you last night of March 4th in which you say that £5000 from *The Miracle* and £5000 from a film would make up the £1000 a year we should lose on the Foreign Office. But baby, that only makes £500 a year – allowing nothing for taxation. However, sink or swim – the Office has got to go. I am full of confidence but should be fuller far if you were only with me all the time. I love you my baby. I do I do I do.   D.

[1] Captain Sir Malcolm Bullock, 1st Bart. (cr. 1954), 1890–1966. Conservative M.P. for Waterloo Division of Lancashire, 1923–50. He married Lady Victoria, née Stanley, widow of Neil Primrose.
[2] Otho William Nicholson, 1891–1978. Conservative M.P. for Westminster (Abbey Division) between March 1924–32.
[3] Réville & Rossiter, a fashionable dress-shop.
[4] The Melton Conservative Association needed a new candidate. It was a safe seat, conveniently close to Belvoir, and Duff and the Duke thought it would be ideal.

Duff to Diana, 22 March 1924   Swynford Paddocks,[1]
                                    Six-Mile Bottom, Newmarket

My beloved Baby. This is a gloomy business. The party consists of
Victoria, Malcolm, Lady Gosford and myself – and Malcolm has
gone out for the evening to a political meeting. How people dare?
The house is hideous, like a golf club. Poor Augusta Leigh lived
here once – I wish she lived here now. Her husband used to train
for the King. How she must have hated it. We have talked
desultory scandal from 6 to 7.30 and now they have gone up to
dress for dinner at 8.30. The only amusing moment was a gaffe by
Lady Gosford when they were discussing Princess Arthur of
Connaught, who is said to have been leading a life of flagrant
immorality in South Africa.[2] "Oh well," said Lady G. "she is bred
for it – all Fife's sisters led the most awful lives." There was a dead
silence and everybody felt very uncomfortable except me who was
amused for the first and probably the last time in this house.[3]

Diana to Duff, 26 March 1924   The Ambassador

I love you with my whole heart I do Mr. Duffy. Do you remember
the child at the gate at Lyndhurst who had a dog she called Mr.
Baby? A matinée of the Nun. Krauss started by pulling out a
whole lock of my hair, I saw him look at it in his hand with a
surprised eye that it should have come out. He then slapped me on
the back and left the red mark of five fingers so clearly defined that
I had to wear a scarf in the next scene. In the scene where he half
crucifies me on a pillar, he closed his teeth into my neck and bit
hard and long – the result is the most disgraceful red and blue scar.
The kind that Lois [Sturt] or Marjorie Craigie would have. I'm
quite ashamed. I came back and had a dreary little tête-a-tête with
Mervyn,[4] and a drink and snack with my lover in his den.

I was due to go to a musical party after the play so told my lover
I would ring him up when I started and if he was on the door-step
I'd pick him up. At 11.30 I rang him up, and to my horror got
connected to him and his mistress (Mrs Whitehouse) having the
most dreadful conversation that one knows so well – she was
whining and groaning and saying, "Don't do it for me if you dread

[1] The house of Captain Malcolm and Lady Victoria Bullock.
[2] This must have been a joke. Princess Arthur of Connaught led a very respectable life,
was a professional nurse, and Matron of the Fife Nursing Home from 1939–49.
[3] See introduction p. xiv for Lady Agnes Cooper.
[4] Mervyn Herbert, 1882–1929.

it" etc. etc. He was the ghastly surly selfish man – like Duffy never is: "Our conversations always end this way" – "Do leave me alone" – "Its no good my telling you, because you won't believe a word I say" – then a string of lies. It was a great problem for this mite, because she hates to be a Daisy Wanton Fellowes and yet I felt sure that if I saw no more of him he'd hate her doubly. So with great courage I faced him in a rage saying "how dare you say she did'nt mind your hounding me – it was a lie, I've just heard all your conversation".

He looked like a man who had seen death – so I relented and gave him the most admirable advice – which of course he'll completely bitch because he's American and they've got such leaden hands. I told him to stop his lies, and to say to her as we should or Alan would – that he is in love, and what fun it is to have a stage favourite, and that it can only last a few weeks – and say bravely 'I'm off now to the pictures with my paramour' with a light touch – but they're impossible these yanks – he'll tell her that he's got the most decent feeling he's ever had for me – that he'll love me till he dies, and that it won't interfere with his attitude towards her – peering the while with a deathly set face through those ghastly nose-nippers – that's high ideals.

Duff to Diana, 24 March 1924   *Foreign Office*

My own. I travelled up from 4 League Arse (a bad joke and my own) by the early train and was greeted by four letters from my little girl.

Your poor lover. I am so sorry for him and I am sure I should like him better than you do – although it is not quite true that *j'aime toujours les amants de ma femme.* He seems anyhow to be the only respectable person you ever speak to in New York. You must be a by-word for sapphism there I should think, as Olga seems never to leave you for a minute. I loved his reply about walking in crowds to look for people who resembled you.[1] The man's a poet. How nice I am about your real lovers and how beastly are you about my (alas) supposed mistresses. I haven't heard of the miserable Poppy – or Pop Eye as Eddie calls her – for many a long day. But Freda has just come back from the South of France, so we may be thrown together again.

[1] Diana had asked him what he would do when she went back to England.

Duff to Diana, 26 March 1924   *Foreign Office*

This morning Rosemary [Ednam] telephoned to ask me to go up to the Grand National with them tomorrow night. I couldn't resist it. They stay with somebody called Colonel Chute – She, Eric, Sidney and Betty[1] – As Mike and Freda have chucked they had two vacancies – Could I suggest a woman? Oh baby mine, I couldn't – and I did so long for you. It would have been such fun together as neither of us have ever seen the National. But I thought I ought to go. I leave tomorrow evening and get back on Saturday. 'I thought I ought to go' above reminds me of a good passage in the new Proust – a thing we know so well. I quote it. *"Ce soir elle m'avait lancé d'un air négligent ce message destiné à passer presque inaperçu: 'Il serait possible que j'aille demain chez les Verdurin, je ne sais pas du tout si j'irai, je n'en ai guère envie.'*

Anagramme enfantin de cet aveu: 'J'irai demain chez les Verdurin, c'est absolument certain, car j'y attache une extrême importance'."

I think it so funny and so brilliantly true. All Proust's genius is in that sort of perception. He catches hold of the thinnest edge of a shade of shadow of a subtlety and crystallises it for ever. But it is a pity he is so absorbed in perverted sex and snobbishness – both very good subjects in their way – but with them they become obsessions. I was told yesterday a very good, involuntary, remark of Chips Channon – à propos of some young woman, he said – "I wonder everybody isn't in love with her – I should be".

Goodbye my little freak.   D.

Major was sick on the Aubusson last night.

Duff to Diana, 29 March 1924   *Buck's Club*

My darling. I was rather drunk when I finished my letter to you last night. I do hope I didn't say anything I shouldn't. Today was again spent racing. It's no good – I don't like it – not in England anyhow. At one moment I felt as you must have felt the day you cried at Deauville. I had lost my money, lost my badge, lost my race card, lost my so called friends and my feet were cold. I met Juliet [Duff] who shared my feelings, hating it as much as I did.

---

[1] Elizabeth Viscountess Cranborne. The daughter of Lord Richard Cavendish, she married Viscount Cranborne (later 5th Marquess of Salisbury) in 1915.

The extraordinary thing is that everyone on an English race course always seems to be hurrying to somewhere, whereas I never have anywhere to go.

Diana to Duff, 30 March 1924   *The Ambassador*

I had a very amusing conversation with Mother and Olga on the subject of Mothers' loathing for all my friends on principle. I enumerated every lover I'd ever had, and although she started by denying it, it went so:

Edward – drunk and dangerous
Patrick – too, and hideous
G. Vernon – *mad*!
Charles [Lister] – just a gasp of horror
Alan – gesture of sickness
Claud [Russell] – never heard him speak, or met his eye
Gibert [Russell] – revolting and used to blush with guilt when she looked at him
Hutchie – a seducer of virgins, because she saw him with Nancy at the pictures – and anyway she can't think of him.
Dudley Coats – quite awful
Maurice[1] – mad
Raymond [Asquith] – missed my character
Michael – rude, lounging, and beastly to her.
The only 2 she passed were Ivor and the Fool![2]

If the air is balmy again tomorrow I know I shall cry. I've numbered my calendar up in a hundred curious ways – how many weeks I've done, how many to do, how many till you start how many till you get here. I do want to be gone. No boat for days. O deary deary me.   Woggy.

Duff to Diana, 1 April 1924   *Foreign Office*

My dear Baby. I don't love you any more. I meant to have told you this before – but I didn't like to hurt you. The knowledge has gradually been forcing itself on me. Of course I shall always be very fond of you but ever since I met . . .

[1] Maurice Baring, 1874–1945, poet, journalist and author.
[2] Diana cannot remember the Fool, but thinks he was an actor she knew while working for J. Stewart Blackton.

. . . Yah, bah, boo – April fool!

Talking of April fools I have just been lunching with Daisy and Fred [Cripps] at the Embassy and there was old Ralph Sneyd who was married again this morning giving a wedding luncheon to some twenty guests. Imagine a man over 60 who has been more cuckolded than most selecting April 1st for his second wedding day and giving a lunch at the Embassy. Lionel, Reggie Pembroke[1] and others were at the next table to ours and we all got cups of rice and pelted the poor old fool. Daisy, I think, is finished. Her face today was painted like a doll's with a hard clear line where the paint stopped. Once she loses her eye for that sort of thing she must be done – for she has no real beauty, as I always said even when she attracted me. Fred still seems rather in love with her. She and Fred in Monte Carlo tracked Reggie Fellowes down to a brothel and through a rough glass window – (what does one call that glass you can't see properly through) watched him performing with a poll. He didn't know of course but they told him afterwards. I was shocked.

Dina Hay[2] was at the Embasssy and told me she had had a very funny letter from Olga apologising for not coming back to her sooner, and pleading as an excuse that you had cried when she said she was going. I was shocked again.

This morning getting up early for my golf lesson, feeling cold and cross, I was sitting in my bath when the telephone rang – hopped out, ran to it in a towel, "Hold the line a moment, you're through to a call office" – buzz, bang, wallop. "Can I speak to Mr. Holbrook." I was naturally furious, spoke sharply to Holbrook – with the inevitable result – "I'm very sorry, sir, it was my brother who rang through to tell me the doctors have given up all hope of my mother's life." Isn't it typical – makes you marvel.[3]

Diana to Duff, 5 April 1924   *The Ambassador*

My sweetheart. Such a funny evening I've just spent. Valentine[4] gave a supper party in a private room here – about fourteen people – and he invited a respected old man called Charlie Macdonald,[5]

---

[1] 15th Earl of Pembroke and Montgomery, 1886–1960.
[2] Lady Idina Hay, née Gordon, later Countess of Erroll.
[3] It was impossible to get the better of Holbrook. He was always in the right.
[4] Viscount Castlerosse, 1891–1943, later sixth Earl of Kenmare. Social columnist and leader-writer for the *Sunday Express*, he was an intimate friend of Lord Beaverbrook's.
[5] Charles B. Macdonald, who introduced the game of golf to the United States.

the local Buck[1] only rather more *élite*. The old boy arrived positively plastered – really the joke stage – of having lost both the studs and starch of his shirt. Now I had taken Mother as she was so hungry, and as Rotherman and Nortons and Mrs Hearst were to be there I thought it would do – and this old boy was put next her, and I thought well and good, she never knows a drunk, she'll just find him affable and genial; unfortunately the old boy could'nt be stopped speechifying on his weak legs with a glass of cham always in each hand – two of which he poured *on Mother's head*. At last he was so frightful that Mrs Hearst rose and drawing him into the next room put his things on and told him the party was over, which luckly he believed, and so left as happy as a king. Otherwise it was a dreary little party and quite pointless. The Theatre news was more exciting. Carmi has served Gest with papers, suing him for ½ million dollars for damaging her professional reputation by inadequate publicity. Gest is of course delighted – as she has no leg to stand on and its all free advertisement.

Duff to Diana, 7 April 1924   *Foreign Office*

Five lovely letters from my baby this morning – and sunshine and warm weather and definite dates at last. I am all in favour of sailing on the *Mauretania* on May 10th and of our both coming back on the *Aquitania* on the 28th. In fact I consider it settled.

Your description of our first day together made me nearly cry with excitement. Oh baby the fun we'll have – and the journey back to Mr Hodder.[2]

Wicked Mr Krauss mustn't bite my baby. Will you tell him so, and add that he's a bloody Hun anyway – and that if he doesn't behave himself I'll fill him so full of lead that he'll think he's a pencil.

Goodbye baby – Hoobloodyray for the *Mauretania*.   D.

Diana to Duff, 24 April 1924   *The Ambassador*

My pretty. Mother will take this letter to you. Be patient with her and ask her a million questions about *The Miracle*. She is demented

[1] Captain Herbert Buckmaster, who founded Buck's Club in 1919.
[2] The purser.

[179]

on the subject and will think you do not love me if you are not as thrilled as she. Olga will tell you more of the things that you'll want to hear of – but you may not see her, as she waits in Paris and will perhaps not get to London till you have started. I am so restless with anticipation. I shall, pray God, be well – with affairs just over and my inside so well that I'll probably start a baby.

My! how I love you – be sweet to Mother – she is so upset to go. Tell her she has been missed.

loving loving loving   Baby.

Duff to Diana, 25 April 1924   *Foreign Office*

You nasty cold hearted little girl. I had little doubt but that you would wish me to come on the safer ship that sails three days earlier and takes two or three days less on the journey – so when I got your curt message last night *Sail on cheapest line* I was quite disgusted. However I went today to the Cunard Company and saw Mr. Todhunter. The *Scythia* is at present full up – they expect next week there will be something but it is very doubtful whether I could get a cabin to myself paying the lowest rate which is £45.10. It takes at least eight days over the passage. I saw plans of it and thought it looked *horrid*. I then went across to the White Star. Their charge on the *Majestic* is £57.10 – and I can have an outside cabin to myself. I have telegraphed again to you – but I have almost settled on the *Majestic*. I really do think it's worth the difference.

Duff to Diana, 1 May 1924   *Foreign Office*

My only love. This letter and the one I shall write you tomorrow will sail on the *Berengaria* on Saturday – and after that I don't think I shall write any more. "Then oh soul of my soul I shall see you again, And with God be the rest". I wonder if you will come on board at the quarantine place. Don't bother to do anything too uncomfortable which would make you get up at an unearthly hour and tire you for the day. I got a telegram from you yesterday saying *Bustle up I'se lonely* which I preferred to the one before saying *Sail on cheapest line* – and this morning I got *Glad news arrived overexcited* – So am I. I can't give my mind to anything

– can't read, can't work and nothing that I do seems worth writing about. The Duchess is due tomorrow. I have just seen Kakoo who says the Duke is in a stew about meeting her with his Rolls Royce, his new carpets and all his follies. Good bye baby – Soon Soon –   D.

[Soon it was. Duff arrived in New York in May, and saw Diana as the Nun and the Madonna, which made them both feel rather shy. They were back at Gower Street in June. Duff sent in his resignation to the Foreign Office, and the serious work of finding a constituency began.

Having tried and failed to get accepted as Conservative candidate for Stroud in Gloucestershire, he decided to try for Oldham. An industrial constituency in Lancashire would not have been Duff's first choice, but the Conservative Central Office were prepared to pay a large part of his election expenses, and for both his pride and his pocket he could not afford to be choosy. "I had become a man of leisure," he wrote in *Old Men Forget*, "with scanty means of self-support, while my wife was earning a large income."

The Oldham Conservative Association accepted him. They were doubtless impressed by his powers as a speaker, though they must have been disappointed by his lack of social ease. Duff was one of those people who, by nature, are uncomfortable with people not of their own class, and he was bad at small-talk.

Having secured his candidature, Duff sailed to America with Diana for the start of *The Miracle*'s new season, returning to England on the *Homeric* at the end of September. Also on board were Lord Louis Mountbatten, Tommy Bouch and Violet; Duchess of Westminster, formerly Mrs. George Rowley. She was returning to England to divorce her husband, Bendor, the 2nd Duke.]

Duff to Diana, 20 September 1924   *On board S.S.* Homeric

My beloved baby. Here I am on the good ship *Homeric* sitting where I used to sit to write those articles but with no fat baby and fat Mr. Kommer waiting to play with me. I have got a very nice little cabin with a private placey[1] and a private shower bath – on the same deck and with the same steward we had last time. The boat is quite extraordinarily empty. The rooms and decks are almost uncannily empty. It reminds me a little of *Outward Bound*. We positively stole out of port. There was nobody there to see anybody off. I should have thought Violet Westminster could have whipped up a bean or two and that Dickie[2] could have coerced a few snobs – but no there wasn't a soul. Violet is looking rather savage and meditating vengeance. Dickie is avoiding publicity. He told Violet that he had succeeded in arranging that their names should not appear in the passenger list. When asked why he made no reply.

Good bye Baby – be careful – mind your trotters and keep smiling.

Duff to Diana, 21 September 1924 On board S.S. Homeric

Good morning, little bird, the sun is shining so brightly on Tommy's bald head who is sitting opposite to me, and the sea is so blue and I should so like to walk round the deck with you instead of only writing to you. We have our meals at a table selected by Dickie away from the vulgar throng in a side room off the main dining room. The food is as bad as ever. After luncheon they said "We'll just have one rubber and then go and rest" – but the rubbers went straight on from then until half past seven, and from after dinner until one a.m. We play in Dickie's sitting room – which is better than anything on the *Berengaria* and better than the one old Baker had on this boat last time. It is on the opposite side. I lost a little at Bridge yesterday but I ought to win in the long run as Dickie can really hardly play at all, Tommy is extremely bad, Violet is moderate and Tony [Pulitzer] though good is nothing wonderful. Dickie has got some wonderful mechanical toys which whenever he cuts out of the rubber he plays with incessantly. They really are very good – they come from a shop called Schwartz. You might get some for Christmas presents – but I expect they're expensive. The sea is beautifully smooth at present but the boat

[1] From a French song that Diana's sister Marjorie used to sing, which tells of *la place obscure* where the writer's parents are buried. This phrase came to mean the loo, was shortened to *placey*, and can refer to parts of the body, i.e. gentlemen's placey, ladies' placey, etc.
[2] Lord Louis Mountbatten, 1900–1979. Later Earl Mountbatten of Burma.

vibrates a great deal. This is due, Dickie explains, to the fact that "she was built to do 18 and they drive her all the time to do 20". Sometimes in pauses of the conversation he says "I wish they wouldn't drive her so".

22 September

After dinner Dickie gave us a performance of his cinema. He is very pleased at being able to make it work backwards. He always selects the same incident in the Chaplin film for a demonstration of this – it is a moment when Charlie sits on the top of a step ladder which sways backwards and forwards – so that when done backwards it looks exactly the same as when done forwards. But he doesn't seem to notice this. Nor does he vary his patter which consists only of the line you noticed last time – "Extraordinary how he does without captions. You will see him in a minute describe his family and all their different sizes – simply by gesture".

But Dickie has surpassed himself this morning. He is engaged in taking moving pictures of his mechanical toys.

By the way – he says they are quite cheap – only cost about a dollar and a half. Don't forget to go to Schwartz's and look at them.

23 September

[At dinner] we had an interesting political discussion in which I questioned the greatness of Lenin, and had the able support of Dickie in combating the lightning-like repartee of Pulitzer and the subtle dialectics of Bouch. Later Dickie told us all about the Royal Family and the order in which they go in to dinner, which was awfully interesting. He also informed us more than once that his father was not a German but a Hessian. This morning I slept too long and feel liverish. I wish I had a baby to walk me round the deck.

25 September

Tommy has spent the morning talking to two Chinese boys. They haven't been in China since they can remember, have been educated in England and are now at Winchester. Tommy says that they are exactly like English boys – except in appearance. Tommy doesn't think there's so much in nationality as people make out.

[183]

Violet's appearance is beginning to wilt a little, the lines round her mouth grow more grim, but whether this is the effect of the sea air, a visitation of the curse of Eve or the thought of her approaching conflict with her husband I cannot say.

There is an argument as to whether we should ask the Captain to dinner. Dickie overwhelmed as usual with the sense of his own importance thinks we ought to, but while as a royalty he wouldn't hesitate to do it, as a junior lieutenant to an ex-naval Captain he fears it might be considered impertinent. He therefore wants Violet to. I say the Captain ought to make the first advances, and I think that he would probably think it came ill from a divorcée Duchess about to redivorce to send for him as though she were a royalty. In any case it would be a damned bore to have the old boy to dinner, and I don't let on that I met him during our last voyage in case they should ask me to approach him.

I have been going on with *Can You Forgive Her?*[1] which appears to have been accidentally packed with my things, though of course I meant to leave it for you. It is so marvellously good in parts. I want you particularly to finish it and will return it to you by the first person I hear of going to New York. (Did you ever get my shoes?) Lady Glencora becomes more and more divine, and more and more like you – and I have a great affection for Mr. Palliser – and adore Burgo.

Dear little lover, I often think of you standing there from eight to nine with the bright tears gathering in your lovely eyes. I hope you are being happy and that Bertram isn't slacking and that Hugo isn't trying to borrow money and that all is well.   D.

Duff to Diana, 4 October 1924   *90 Gower Street*

I dined last night at Claridge's with Violet Westminster, her barrister and his wife. She is a little tiresome now because, poor thing, she can think and talk of nothing but her case, which becomes a bore. I am sorry for her too as public opinion is inclined to turn on her. One can't fight a rich Duke. The reporters who met the *Homeric* asked her where she was going – She said she didn't know, as she was waiting to hear from her sister. They said

---

[1] The first of the 'political' novels of Anthony Trollope (1864–5).

"Haven't you got any home?" and she replied that she hadn't at present, which was true. The evening papers then came out with posters "Homeless Duchess" "I am the Duchess of Westminster but I have no home to go to, etc" which of course made everybody laugh at her and she is now always referred to as "The Homeless Duchess". Max did a Max – dined with her one night, said he would help her in every way he could, rang up the *Daily Express* in her presence – "Say Blum, we've got to help this poor lady all we can". The next day the *Evening Standard* produces an offensive paragraph "Homeless Duchess pigging it in a Suite at Claridges – leaves for the Newmarket meeting etc". Max explains this with his usual lie about a sub-editor.

[By the summer of 1924, the fall of the first Labour Government under Ramsay MacDonald seemed only a matter of time. Diana had insisted that she be released from her *Miracle* contract for the period of the general election, and she joined Duff towards the end of October for the last two weeks of canvassing. Duff was very grateful for her support; her warmth and zest endeared her to the voters, and made up for Duff's shyness and diffidence.

Duff won, coming in a few hundred votes ahead of Edward Grigg, the Liberal candidate. They were received at Belvoir in triumph, and were lodged, to Diana's enormous satisfaction, in the King's Rooms – the best in the house. Her choice of husband had been vindicated, and The Plan was at last a reality.

They did not have much time to celebrate. *The Miracle* called Diana back for a three-week stint in Cleveland, Ohio, and Duff – his ambition accomplished – was eager to try out his new wings in the House.]

Duff to Diana, 4 December 1924   [*90 Gower St*]

Raymond and I dined with the Guinnesses[1] – It was quite awful but so awful as to be very funny. A party of five, Beatrice, Dick and

---

[1] Richard Guinness, 1873–1949, and his wife Beatrice (d. 1942). She was previously married to Nico Jungman, and was the mother of Zita and Baby, the Jungman sisters.

the King of Portugal.[1] Filthy food and worse wine. First caviare
with toast but no butter. Then ordinary cold lobster which was not
fresh, and then quails the size of sparrows followed by cold beef –
the remains of the servants' joint overcooked and fat. Sweet, warm
champagne followed by grocer's port which Dick said was 1870. I
loathed Dick. He obviously is as mean as Beatrice makes out, and
a liar. There was a funny moment when we were playing Bridge
afterwards and Dick obsequiously approached the King and said
"Will your Majesty have a *little* more Vichy water". Raymond
and I had several *fous rires*. The King was perfect – quite exactly
like Maurice's imitation of royalty, with a Portuguese instead of a
German accent – contradicting everything very gently but very
firmly, and knowing a little more than anybody about everything.
There was a great moment when he was made to taste the vaunted
1870 port which he did with incredible pomposity – smelling,
looking at, almost listening to it before putting about a teaspoon
full into his mouth which he slowly swallowed. He then waited in
silence for at least three minutes, while we all sat round with our
eyes starting out of our heads waiting for the sentence. The poor
little devil was probably trying not to be sick. At last he said very
slowly "It is good but it is too strong". I had a successful evening
at Bridge winning about £25. When we left Raymond said "I wish
to God Diana were here so that we could go and tell her all about
it". When I got to bed I sent you a Marconigram and now I have
just got one from you. Poor mite.

Duff to Diana, 8 December 1924   *90 Gower Street*

I dined at Bucks with Raymond & Eddie. we played Bridge after
dinner – I won £3.6.0. Olga told Tallulah[2] that you told her that
Raymond told you that Gerald du Maurier asked him whether
Tallulah was a sapphist, and that he said she was – so Tallulah
came up to him and said she was going to smack his face.

This morning I rose early as I am going to do every morning
and started by writing to you as I am going to do every morning.

---

[1] King Manoel II, 1889–1932. Having seen his father and elder brother shot by
assassins before his eyes, he had reigned in Portugal only two years before the revolution of
1910 sent him into exile. He settled at Twickenham, and spent the rest of his life in
England.
[2] Tallulah Bankhead, 1903–1968. American actress of the twenties and thirties whose
sensuous beauty was enhanced by an exceptionally husky voice.

My sweet, dear, lovely little girl – I was delighted with your letter from Cherbourg which I found here last night. Mind you collect my misaddressed one.

Nothing in this morning's papers. The inhabitants of Hull are going crazy about getting a reprieve for a young gentleman of the name of Smith who cut the throat of his mistress, a married woman, in the presence of her three children because he was jealous of her relationship with her employer, an old man of 80. Good bye beloved.   D.

Duff to Diana, 11 December 1924   *90 Gower Street*

My lovely love, I didn't write to you yesterday. I had a very trying feverish ineffectual day. I woke before six and started to think about making a maiden speech. By 8 I had prepared it and I spent the morning rehearsing it and telephoning to Winston, to the Whips, to the Speaker, to Max trying to make arrangements for its delivery. All the afternoon I had to hang about in a fever of excitement and uncertainty. I went through the ordeal of standing up to catch the Speaker's eye and saw it hovering over me. I could have spoken in the dinner hour when the House was empty but I was strongly advised not to. Sidney was kind to me and took me to dine at the St. Stephen's Club. When we came back the House was still empty and I finally decided not to speak. The Speaker has practically promised to put me on on Monday next which in many ways will be a better day for me as it will be specially devoted to the discussion of Egypt. I am glad now that I didn't speak. I think I can improve what I was going to say.

Duff to Diana, 16 December 1924   *90 Gower Street*

My darling love. I never wrote to you yesterday – but yesterday was a day of storm and stress. However I will go back to where I left you on Sunday morning. I spent the rest of it sitting in the library preparing my speech. The library at Hatfield[1] is a delight-ful room. In the afternoon I went for a walk with Betty [Cran-borne] and returned for chapel. After chapel I again read Gordon[2]

---

[1] Hatfield House, Hertfordshire. Home of the Cecils.
[2] The chapter on General Gordon in *Eminent Victorians* by Lytton Strachey.

aloud to them with notable success. It was nearly however a fiasco, because towards the end I almost burst into tears. There is a terrible moment when he gives up hope. You would have sobbed.

Yesterday morning I came up by an early train with Bobbety[1] – Sidney and Betty motored. I rehearsed my speech in the morning and lunched with Sybil and Richard. Thence to the House of Commons where all the afternoon I waited anxiously. Trevelyan[2] spoke first, then Austen Chamberlain[3] spoke for an hour and a half – I thought he would never stop – then Ramsay MacDonald[4] spoke. I had got a good place by then and towards the end of his speech I saw Curzon[5] (Mary's husband who is now a Whip) nodding at me from behind the Speaker's chair so I realized that I was probably going to be put on next and yet I could hardly believe it when I heard my name called. I felt really nervous, and a thing happened to me which has never happened before – my mouth became perfectly dry. However the sound of my own voice encouraged me and I gathered confidence. What was still more encouraging was that as I went on people kept dribbling in instead of dribbling out as usually happens. It was a wonderfully fortunate moment to be put on as Ministers and ex-Ministers hadn't left the House. Ramsay was one of the few who left while I was speaking – Lloyd George[6] was there throughout and so was Baldwin.[7] Austen came in after I had been going about five minutes and I heard him say to Baldwin as he sat down "I hear he's very good". I got quite a good cheer when I sat down and Hal Fisher[8] spoke after me and congratulated me on "a really brilliant and successful maiden speech, perfect in form and distinguished by liberality and generosity of spirit and by a width of outlook which the whole House has appreciated". Arthur Ponsonby spoke

[1] Robert Gascoyne Cecil (Bobbety) Viscount Cranborne, 1893–1972, later fifth Marquess of Salisbury.
[2] Rt. Hon. Sir Charles Philips Trevelyan, Labour M.P. for Central Newcastle, 1870–1958.
[3] Austen Chamberlain, 1863–1937, Foreign Secretary.
[4] James Ramsay MacDonald, 1866–1937, leader of the Opposition.
[5] Francis Richard Curzon, later fifth Earl Howe. In 1907 he married Mary, daughter of Colonel Montagu Curzon.
[6] Then leader of the Liberal Party. Asquith held the post nominally, but had been defeated by the Labour candidate in the last election and had retired to the Lords.
[7] Stanley Baldwin, 1867–1947, Prime Minister. This was his second ministry.
[8] H. A. L. Fisher, 1865–1940, historian, statesman and Warden of New College, Oxford. He had been Duff's tutor in Modern History.

next and said it "was one of the most brilliant maiden speeches he had heard in the House". Lady Astor[1] who was sitting near me said it was the best she had ever heard and asked for your address to telegraph to you – I hope she did. Sidney said he would too. I had a letter of congratulation from the Speaker which I gather is rather an unusual honour – and also one from Winston – and one from Archie Sinclair. [2] All the evening people whom I didn't know were coming up to me and congratulating me, including members of the Labour Party and finally Philip Sassoon [3] asked me what I was doing for Christmas. In other words, baby, it was a triumph and yet I didn't speak nearly as well as I can. Oh that you had been there. I longed for you. I tried to get Letty in but failed – no tickets were to be had. Betty was there and had just telephoned congratulations. The *Express* and *Times* which are the only papers I have seen are very good. I have had a man from the *Evening Standard* later this morning.

Oh my beloved baby – this will probably reach you about Christmas – I do hope you will be having a happy time and plenty of Kickermas presents. Let us never again spend Christmas apart – never, never again. I love you so –   D.

Diana to Duff, 16 December 1924   *117 East Seventy-First Street*[4]

My little angel. This morning in bed I got the news thro' your cable that Maideners (speech) is accomplished and successful. It kind of convulsed me and left me broken. You won't know how much I hate missing these few months and it will be so long before I get the cuttings – how shall I wait? I have laid in bed an hour just wondering and speculating upon what you said, and how nervous you were, and who heard you, and how long it lasted.

[1] Nancy Astor, 1879–1964. American, née Nancy Langhorne, she became Unionist M.P. for Plymouth from 1919–1945 after her husband succeeded his father as the second Viscount Astor.
[2] Archibald Sinclair, 1890–1970, later 1st Viscount Thurso.
[3] Sir Philip Sassoon, third baronet, 1888–1939. Politician and connoisseur, he entertained lavishly and surrounded himself with artists and statesmen.
[4] The home of Mr. and Mrs. Arthur Fowler.

Diana to Duff, 17 December 1924   *117 East Seventy-First Street*

My beloved. I'm so proud of you – I'm choking with it. Nancy Astor I shall always love for sending me a cable saying "Husband made brilliant speech" and Maurice the same. The papers have been at me all day to know more, and I hear that this evening the papers were full of it, and I haven't been able to get hold of one yet. I went to a party at the Hammonds, and everybody was telling me how clever you were. I don't think I shall ever get over not being there. O my darling Duffy – I am so glad for you and so ridiculously proud and glorified. Try and say some thanks to Nancy Astor and tell her how wonderful I thought it of her.

I just come back from the party – its the second time I've written today – but I'm obsessed with the excitement of it and must tell you so adding to that all my wide love. A lot of lovely letters today from all – how sweet my friends are. I feel happy tonight and happiest in you.   B.

[After this triumph, Duff spent another quiet Christmas with his mother in the South of France.]

Duff to Diana, 28 December 1924   *Cimiez*

Little funny face – after I had written to you last night I made the mistake of going too early to bed and slept before eleven. I woke at three and hardly slept again, but made very eloquent speeches on a variety of subjects. Today has been one of clouds and rain. After luncheon I took Mother to the circus which she adored and so would you have. There were horses, elephants, acrobats, clowns and seven real tigers and it all took place in a tent. After the circus I dropped in at the Casino where I did a real Dumplings get out, winning over three thousand francs and getting away with it. I had the pleasure of giving a bank at 2,500 with a good *bénéfice* but not the pleasure of winning it. The Aga was there again. He had read my speech on Egypt and agreed with every word of it.

As for money, monkey, (you mention it in one of your letters) I wish you would tell Drummonds [Bank] to let me have some. I am overdrawn all the time although my bank doesn't seem to mind. I have a passion for paying bills, and have paid every one I've received including one from the gentleman in Hammersmith who did my room. No – there is an angry one from Selfridge's for you which I havn't paid and a large one of about £80 from Trowsers[1] – also yours – which I think can wait.

Diana to Duff, 8 January 1925   *Hotel Statler, Cleveland*

My darling. Such a funny last evening. B. and I went to the young bloods party. A great success, and we got off like hot cakes. Pinchie wouldn't come because she is what is called 'hipped on her health'. B. got rather tight on high-balls, and we were driven home by young Mr. Harvey Brown in a Chrysler. B. and I sat on the back seat and she started making advances to me – head on my neck fingers fumbling at my breast. I felt terribly embarrassed because young Mr Harvey Brown would keep on looking round, and try as I would to calm her it was vain. Once he said "You look more like a Madonna than ever" I said "What? how?" He said "I'll tell you another time" – I hope to God he meant I looked wintery. Once home B. insisted on coming to my room, and I really got a little nervous not of rape but of having to hurt and offend her. By the grace of God Kommer was standing at his door – I suppose he must have been keeping watch for hours – it was three a.m. I tore into his room with her, where she immediately retired to placey which gave me an oppotunity of putting the situation to him and of enlisting his help. He behaved splendidly, came with us to my room kept up a running conversation. Told me Bertram had finally telephoned to him, as not getting an answer off me he thought I was dead. However nothing moved B. and it was then born in upon me that all K's and my pressure to get her to go, gave her to understand he was my lover. I told him at last he'd better go, to dispel that theory anyway and then by God's good grace, and Oom's[2] infallibility – the telephone started. So I got her out on the excuse that I couldn't talk in front of her. Poor B. – I think perhaps it was more drink than lust, because I just rang her up to see if she remembered she was lunching with us, and somebody answered "she's got a pretty bad head, you see".

Occasionally ask at Oldham if those flooded houses have been dealt with & *see that they are*, using my name in fussing as I made

[1] Mr. Tom Trower, Duff and Diana's lawyer.
[2] Diana's nickname for Bertram Cruger: Johannes Paulus Kruger, 1805–1904, the Boer leader, was known to the people as 'Oom (Uncle) Paul'.

myself responsible. I thought the Xmas cards exquisite. Your face as crooked as only a stroke can make it, but *awfully* pretty. Love to Raymond.   Baby.

[Early in January 1925 Duff and his sister Sybil Hart-Davis got the news that their mother was critically ill. They rushed over to France to be with her, but by the time they got to her bedside, Lady Agnes was dead.]

Diana to Duff, 11 January 1925   *117 East Seventy-First Street*

My darling. I arrived back here this evening, & found your sad telegram. Your poor Mummy. I wish you had seen her if she was conscious – it would have comforted her – but from your point of view I suppose better as it was. I feel a delinquent at not being with you now to help you to bear all the horror of it and the grim arrangements. I've no idea why she died or how long she was ill, or whether you will bury her in that pleasant country's earth[1] or take her back to England. There was no one as thoughtful, lovingly thoughtful, of your ease and happiness as she was, more unselfish than ever I shall be; so probably she will have settled all such details for you – if she knew she was dying. I trust though she did not. I hate her to have faced fear. O Duffy my darling – I wish I was with you – because you must be a little sad, and it is as torturing not to be with you to help – as it is to be away from partaking of your triumphs. How glad I am she knew you were to be great; and also that you went to her at Christmas and that I did not force you to come to me.

Duff to Diana, 11 January 1925   *Cimiez*

Oh darling – I feel so sad. I have been going through papers and letters. The futility of the possessions of the dead is so terribly pathetic – and Mother's poor little things were all so carefully and neatly arranged – chiefly my letters, and things about me. It is terrible too to have it all happen in a hotel. I have just been interviewing the undertaker. But I mustn't darling inflict all these

[1] *Richard II*, Act IV, scene i.

miseries on you. By the time you get this remember that I shall be back in England and all this horror left behind. Yet I am glad I was here. I should have felt terribly had I been in America. So that is for the best any way. If only we could have got here a little sooner. I do wish you were with me.

Good bye my baby –　　D.

Duff to Diana,　　　　　　　　　　　　*In a café at Marseilles*
Thursday January 15th 1925

After luncheon I went to the cemetery. It was an extremely macabre performance at which I, a representative of La Maison Roblot (a quite excellent firm of undertakers with branches in every town of France whom I can thoroughly recommend to anyone dying in this country) and the head of the cemetery assisted. The details were very business-like and prosaic – too much so to be distressing. The coffin was shot into the oven which opened only for a moment to receive it. They told me that I could if I liked look into the oven by means of a peephole, but that the spectacle – they warned me – might prove *très emotionnant.* I therefore declined – having had quite enough emotion to last me for a little. The head of the cemetery proved to be a cremation enthusiast and gave us a lecture on the subject while we waited – enlarging especially on the horrors of corruption to which the buried body is subject. Then he began to boast of his cemetery and of the numbers buried there – so many English – so many Americans – so many soldiers and *des milliers des Indo-Chinois.* Also of the very extensive property they had recently acquired for future graveyards. All this, poured forth with an absurd Marseillais accent, deprived the ceremony of dignity but gave it humour.

[*The Miracle*'s winter season that year proved too ambitious and had to be cancelled. After a short holiday in the Bahamas, Diana returned to London, where in May the old Duke of Rutland died. Since *The Miracle* was next due to play at the Salzburg Festival in August, Diana had some months of leisure.

Duff, however, was working furiously. On August the
12th he wrote in his diary:
"For three months I have written nothing in this book. I
was so busy during the summer in London that I had not
time to write: What with the House of Commons, my
correspondence, visits to the constituency and other
places to speak, in addition to writing a weekly article [for
the *Saturday Review*] I hardly had a moment to myself."
    The House went into recess at about the same time as
Diana went off to work in Salzburg. Duff went rather
gloomily to Venice.]

Duff to Diana, 12 August 1925   *Venice*

Grouse Shooting and Eating begins

> No voice, no lute, no pipe, no incense sweet
>   From chain swung censor teeming
> No shame, no grave, no oracle no heat
>   No grouse nor breadsauce steaming

Dinner at the Coles[1] last night wasn't bad. No cham at all. I
played chess with Monty Woolley afterwards, the others went on
to the Piazza where we joined them later. When we arrived there
we saw there was an enormous crowd round Florians, and
immediately guessed there was a riot and that our friends were the
centre of it. Sure enough – poor old Ivor [Wimborne] and Yvonne
de Beauchamps were when we arrived receiving police protection.
She had appeared in an evening dress of the lowest possible cut
with the old familiar results. It was amusing that they should have
spotted an Italian woman. The police couldn't get the people to
disperse until somebody lent Yvonne a shawl, when they began to
lose interest. That is the only amusing thing that has happened so
far. Today is really too hot. Sirocco – stifling. I am going to dine at
the Luna with Olga and her lot. I'm not enjoying myself. But I say
to console me that this isn't holidays. It's a cure for me[2] and work
for you. I long for a letter. I got your telegram from Salzburg
today. Love love love   D.

---

[1] Cole Porter, 1893–1964, the American song-writer and composer and his wife Linda.
[2] Duff suffered from psoriasis, and sunshine was supposed to help it.

The Town looked lovelier than I remembered it. We live at the hotel, but are supposed to go to Leopoldskron[1] today – all expenses paid for all, I don't know about journeys but hotels and motors. Blow after blow hit me – first I was told we couldn't use the stone coat after all the labour and the cost, and the rumour kept reaching me all day that *The Miracle* in its new edition was beyond belief terrible. Then Maud [Cunard] got stung by a wasp and made a scene in the lounge, screaming and spitting with rage. Morris Gest was a looker on, and was disgusted, not knowing her, at her lack of breeding etc. However they met at tea in a coffee house, and today he is madly in love with her. I was at rehearsal till two a.m., all in with tiredness and despair. Nothing ready, not even the house or décor and Reinhardt uninterested and lazy. I had a good cry, and got much pampered and spoilt by the girls. A good long night made me braver, and this morning I have a suggestion, which has been accepted gleefully. The décor (by E. de Werth) is Strawberry Hill gothic gold, red and blue, the kind that goes with Sybil's kind of plaster saint. They want me to be a Lourdes Madonna with silver hearts and roses, but my argument is that all my acting and attitudes are built out of a primitive simple idea in art and that the Lourdes touch would mean a different action and line altogether – lace and curves. Now I suggest that they should paint my coat gold with touches of red and blue & have a spindly gothic bad taste crown, and it will look much more appropriate.

My sweetheart I feel so badly when your dear letters arrive so punctually and remember what a broken reed I am to you. There literally is not a moment, and the time that should be yours, alone in bed at night is made a riot by Ethel[2] and Iris[3] laughing, talking and wrestling. We moved over to the castle Wednesday, and all

---

[1] Reinhardt's *schloss* outside Salzburg, where Diana had auditioned for the part of the Madonna two years before.

[2] Ethel Russell. "she glowed with life and zest, infected you with her fun and gusto, and then loved you for these qualities". Diana Cooper, *The Light of Common Day*.

[3] Iris Tree. Although much more unconventional than Diana, Iris had the same sense of fun and love of adventure. In 1916 Iris married the painter Curtis Moffat; their son Ivan was born in 1918.

three sleep in an enormous room in the third floor. Kaetchen[1] sleeps opposite, and at 10 o'clock a beastly breakfast is brought in on a big table by four rosy girls and K. joins us. It looks very pretty with the wide windows open on the sunny lake and mist-hidden mountains. On Wednesday night we had a party at the castle. I sat next to Hofmannsthal,[2] and went down big. Perfect English scholar. A Jew I suppose, with a tongue and lisp like Maurice, quite young – 42? After dinner he told me the whole story of the *Welttheater*. He *loved* Ruby Peto. Maud Cunard is the pest. She really is unbearable, always in a towering rage and threatening to go that night if the wasps won't leave her alone. I must say they beset her. I think it must be that Oreste's unguents are concocted of wasps' vomit and they return to it. She weighs very heavily on us all. We are always trying to dodge her, and always haunted by her désoeuvréness, and spoiling our plans for her. Gerald Berners[3] is always shrieking "O I've been stung" and sucking his finger, while Maud swallows the bait without fail. Nanny [Miss Wade] is terribly cross too – I suppose it's pretty bad for her, poor Nanny. I was delighted with the story of Ivor and Beauchamp in the Piazza.

The pandemonium is appalling. I'm sitting in the stalls wait-ing. The hammering is deafening. Frau Mildenburg, a famous singer of a hundred, is practising chest notes. The rehearsal was called for 10.30, it's now 12 and they are still clearing up débris from the World-Theatre. This last took just on three hours last night – no entracte, wooden seats and unintelligible, otherwise good. Your fun doesn't sound too good. I like the cham. reports. Reinhardt's party tipple was a nice glass of beer as apperative followed by compote of peach – skins & all. Morris Gest flung Maud's cigarette case on the marble floor and chipped off some jade – the whole party went on their stomachs to look for it. Iris, Kaetchen, and Gest have gone to the Wolfgangsee and I feel tongue-tied mid these huns.   Very *very* loving Baby

---

[1] A diminutive of the German word 'Kat', it was Iris and Diana's nickname for Rudolf Kommer; so called after a cat belonging to the Austrian proprietor of the Eiffel Tower Restaurant in London: "Ach Kaetchen, Kaetchen," the proprietor would tell his cat, "it is no use for you to park und crowl."

[2] Hugo von Hofmannsthal, 1874–1929. Poet, author and librettist of several operas by Richard Strauss. He, Strauss and Reinhardt were the founders of the Salzburg Festival in 1917.

[3] The fourteenth Baron Berners, 1883–1950. Composer, author, painter and eccentric, he was the model for Lord Merlin in Nancy Mitford's *The Pursuit of Love*.

Diana to Duff, 18 August 1925 [*Leopoldskron*]

Sweet love – I've got such a cold – suppose I dribble or cough on the pillar tonight. The performance last night was a complete disgrace, I thought – and I despised Reinhardt for showing such a cobble – and let him know it. The result is that we are in the Theatre again today, for the day – and outside it is the most radiantly beautiful enticing day ever created.

We have dressed Iris up as the Nun, and she is to be tried by R. at the end of the rehearsal, to see if talent lurks.[1] Poor child she is shaking now and must shake for the next four hours.

You see it's impossible – it's half way though the performance now and this is the first moment I have not been rushing, or fussing to keep the different groups of friends and visitors mellow. Maud thank God has left us.

O my Duffy I never saw anything like "M.P. in Dreamland" – aren't you ashamed.[2] O Mr Duffy Dumpling. However I liked to see you sleeping not spooning. I like to think of you in a motorless town, where you can't be run over. I love I *love* I LOVE my Duffy.

Duff to Diana, 21 August 1925 *Venice*

My darling Baby.

How do you like Hilary's emendation of the last verse of the Ancient Mariner –

> "He serveth best who loveth best
> All creatures great and small,
> The streptococcus is the test –
> I love him least of all."

Ronald Hadow was prepared for your physical beauty in *The Miracle* – but what impressed him so much was your mental beauty. Didn't I agree? I did. Chips Channon and Cedric Alexander have arrived here now so all is well.

I dined here in the hotel last night with Maud.[3] We went to a kind of night club in the hotel called the 'Chez Vous'. I hadn't

---

[1] *The Miracle* needed another Nun, and Diana persuaded Iris to try for the part.
[2] A photograph of Duff, which appeared on the front page of *The Daily Sketch* of August 14th. It showed him fast asleep in a deck-chair on the Lido, wearing pyjamas and a striped dressing-gown.
[3] Maud Cunard. She could not bear Salzburg any longer, and had come to Venice.

[197]

been before. A lady danced wearing nothing but a sanitary towel and a live snake. Otherwise it was a dull evening. Maud is obviously suffering from what I said. She was very cross all the evening and complained of the heat, but cheered up wonderfully and showed symptoms of an incipient orgasm (perhaps the last) at the sight of the live snake. When last seen she was asking the concierge for the number of the snake's room.

Mr. Greenwood, M.P. for Stockport[1] and inhabitant of Oldham, one of my chief supporters whose face you never remembered and will never see again fell down dead in Warren Street Tube Station the other day.

"M.P. in Dreamland" was fierce. They did it to me out of spite because I wouldn't pose.

[Iris Tree got the part of the Nun, and sailed off to America with Diana and Kommer in early September. Diana was delighted – life on tour was going to be far more enjoyable with Iris for company.]

Duff to Diana,   *Danby Lodge,[2] Yorkshire*
11 September 1925

My darling joy. We had quite a nice day's shooting today – better weather although there was some rain. Holbrook is more exasperating out shooting than at any time. I shall end by shooting him in one of his moments of assumed cheerfulness in adverse circumstances. When it is pouring with rain and he is obviously half frozen and out of breath carrying both my guns and shooting stick he does a hypocritical Mark Tapley[3] that makes me see red. He will also use the wrong technical terms, call attention to something that is perfectly obvious and even after all these years he fails to distinguish between a hare and a rabbit. Today when an enormous hare was lolloping slowly towards me in the centre of a perfectly open space he hissed into my ear in a tone of tense excitement "Very large rabbit coming up in front, sir". Added to which he never marks a bird, and put the crown on everything

---

[1] Mr. William Greenwood, M.P., 1875–12th August 1925.
[2] Danby Lodge, on the estate of the Scrope family in Yorkshire.
[3] A character in *Martin Chuzzlewit*.

today by allowing a wounded bird which he had picked up to fly straight out of his hands and get clean away.

D.

Diana to Duff, 14 September 1925　　　　　[*On board ship to New York*]

I was sorting out my letters last night – Salzburg ones, and I put all yours in a methodical order, and Kommer was staggered. "He writes to you every day?" I said yes, and that I wondered at the way he didn't believe you loved me. he said he did believe it sincerely till Salzburg. So you see Mr Dimple if Kommer thought that, and I thought it and Marjorie thought it, I had some cause. After that in the small hours, (it is terribly hot and I can't sleep at all) I cross-questioned and worried out of Iris what my friends thought of you, and this was the sum total. That they, (including herself, Poots [Van Raalte], Alan, Hutchie, Phyllis [de Janzé] – those being all she can speak for – admire you and are *proud* of you – but they are all frightened, and none *loving* of you because of your deathly *coldness* to them. They think it has of course greatly developed since you married. Iris speaking for herself, who I'm sure illustrates others, feels you despise your companions of this order, so utterly. This may be true, but I hold it wrong that you should show it forth. I am very conscious and sometimes horrified at your lack of warmth to anyone, but have hugged the remembrance that to me you are different – yet sometimes lately I have felt the habit, which is all it is, on myself, and shuddered as I did at Leopoldskron.

Duffy don't be deathly proud my darling – you cannot have a completely different manner just for my group, so you probably dish out the frozen mit to all and I want all men to love as well as admire you. Don't say, "I can't be different" – I can hear it from here – and don't be bitter with poor baby who's getting terribly near the ulterior shore – it hasn't rolled once but this morning I feel as though I'd been flogged – its velly hot, and I didn't get a wink & everything sticks – I love you.

Radios pour in from friends and strangers, always asking me to join them at the opening of *The Vortex*[1] or *The Green Hat*.[2] New York is apparently on tiptoe for these epoch-makers. We are due to dock

[1] By Noel Coward.
[2] By Michael Arlen.

at nine tonight – I'm dreading it more than I can say – I'm ashamed. The dread of Oom is greatest, and that is so vile. He'll be looking so pale, and so ugly, and be speechless with emotion. O to be at Bognor[1] and all well, I'm not built for adventures – give me a harbour and you my horizon. Condé [Nast][2] gives a dinner and dance for me Thursday, I've had five cables about it, and Iris has had one asking her to meet me. My love to all around you. No, its all yours.   B.

Duff to Diana,   *Clenartney Forest, Comrie. N.B.*
16 September 1925

My dear little doe. A heavenly day – perfect weather neither too hot nor too cold – sunshine and cloud, chiefly sunshine. I had one shot and I killed one stag. It was not until after luncheon that I got my shot and I can assure you that no one since Mr. John Sargent the painter could have had a pleasanter or more painless death than my poor Stag.[3] Sitting very comfortably surrounded by his hinds, his tummy just full of fresh green grass, as I presently discovered, contemplating the beauties of his native forest and enjoying the warm weather suddenly something struck him at the back of the neck and he knew no more – he hardly altered his position. I was very pleased with myself for it seemed to me a difficult shot and I was in a terror of missing. I got back here at about half past five and had a bath having brought a change of clothes. I then had a most delicious tea and am now waiting for the others. It is nearly seven – what can have delayed them? I hope they haven't got a lot of stags. Perhaps they are pursuing a wounded one.

I wonder if you would ever care for stalking. You might. It would be rather fun to take this little lodge one year. It is so pretty and clean and so remote from all the world. But I'm afraid it would be very dismal in bad weather – lost in mist. Wherever I go I build schemes of happiness for you and me. Good bye my beloved, I think I hear them returning.   D.

---

[1] The Duchess of Rutland had bought a very pretty cottage by the beach outside Bognor, which she gave to Diana after her marriage.
[2] Condé Nast, 1874–1942. The creator of *Vogue* magazine, of which he was president and publisher from 1909.
[3] John Singer Sargent, 1856–1925, had died in April. He was found lying in bed, with his spectacles pushed up onto his forehead and a volume of Voltaire open at his side.

Duff to Diana,   *Midland Hotel, Manchester*
25 September 1925

I have been thinking about your charge against me that your friends don't love me. But why should they – that particular lot. I don't love them. I am fond of Alan and I think he does like me but the others, although I like them all very much, I should never see if it wasn't for you. I don't agree that I must, as you say, make the same impression on other people as I do on them. Take others of your friends – Katharine, Maurice and Venetia – I am sure you wouldn't find that they feel what Iris says. And if she and her lot are frightened of me, remember how frightened Eddie is of you. Anyway I will try to be better, baby dear, and don't you worry your tiny yellow nut about it or give it a single scratch on that score. I love you and you only, and can't love anyone else.   D.

Duff to Diana,   *Midland Hotel, Manchester*
26 September 1925

Well baby, dear, thank God today is over – I spent the morning reading the papers and writing a speech in my beautiful room. Then I went down stairs where I met the charming Hall Porter who asked tenderly after Her Ladyship. "I wish she was here today," he said – "Why?" I asked. "Because I could put her on to a good thing." "What is it?" "Saradella for the Newbury Cup – each way". Off I toddled to the telegraph office "£5 e.w. on Saradella".

Then an early luncheon – then the train to Oldham where I stood on the steps of the Town Hall while in extreme cold and drizzling rain two thousand boy scouts walked past – two at a time. Thence to the Blue Coat School where there were more boy scouts and thence to Greenacres Hall which we know so well. There at five p.m. (after half an hour's waiting and cheerful conversation) we sat down to the delicious meal – the menu of which you will see on the back of the enclosed programme. You can imagine how I enjoyed it. My place might have been worse – between the Mayor whom you don't like but I do and old Dr. Fawsitt whom you never remember and whose wife is always tight. The Mayor assures me that Mr. Greenwood, the former member for Stockport who fell down dead at Warren Street Tube Station, would have gone to prison had he lived and probably committed suicide. Balzac could have got so much fun and thrill out of these provincial dramas but I can't. Tea was at five, the meeting was at seven – but it came at last. Sir Alfred Pickford, a very fat man, six foot seven, dressed as a boy scout with bare hairy legs and arms, an enormous bottom, an eyeglass and a voice like G. P. Huntley was the first to address the audience of over two thousand boys. "What would you like me to talk to you about?" he asked in a jocose and fatherly manner. "Nothing!" they roared in unison. His speech never recovered from that initial blunder. I followed. I had prepared quite a good speech – but not for boys – I couldn't hold their attention. I was acutely conscious of it. It is a large hall and it was crowded. I cut my remarks short and felt what waste of time the whole thing was. I nearly always feel that when I come to Oldham. But I suppose I usually do hold the attention of the audience or I shouldn't have noticed it so much today.

Then I went on with Shepherd to a small meeting consisting of Mr Howcroft, Mr Bardsley, Mr Buntin, Mr Perkins and Dr ?. They wanted to tell me how dissatisfied they were with the Government, which Howcroft did at considerable length. I replied feebly and we had an amicable conversation after which Dr ? who was much the nicest of the lot and whom I can't remember having seen before drove me back to Manchester. I went into the restaurant to have a little supper, and then the sight of the charming Head Waiter reminded me of the charming Hall Porter; so I sent for an evening paper and like Lord Hippo,[1] saw to my astonishment that I had backed the winner – and at 10 to 1. So I enjoyed some cold grouse and two whiskies and soda and came up to bed.   D.

Diana to Duff, 3 October 1925   *Hotel Sinton, Cincinnati*

Spirits better this morning – not for any particular reason – I confess – perhaps because it's matinée day and that makes it seem less interminable. Iris was ghastly yesterday, Katzenjammer after the night out. So weak was she that she dropped her very heavily laden tray of kippered herrings and prairie oysters, butter-milk and other stomach settlers to the ground, holding up the queue in the busiest hour. In the afternoon I was taken off to a cooking

[1] From *More Peers*, by Hilaire Belloc.

[202]

demonstration – a ridiculous performance. I had been advertised to speak there so I arrived as a disappointment. A crowded theatre of women and a stage covered with ovens, refrigerators etc. I was walked on, looking just a foolish freak. A woman stood up and asked me to take my hat off, which I did with an immediate sweeping gesture like Billy Merson, and the house roared. I then tasted some whipped cream off my finger and they laughed so I thought they'd never stop. I think I must have some very exceptional comic quality that I'm wasting – after all I can always make Mr Dumple laugh, and jaded is his middle name. There was on show the Frigid-Air machine that makes ice by electricity in your house – I covet it a lot. There was one being lotteried and they gave me some tickets – so may be I'll come home with my ice-box. The woman said if I didn't win it she thought they might give me one as English advertisement. They are very expensive.

I get my pay today thank God – the whole company is on its uppers, borrowing 25 cents from each other. News goes round that Freddy has some cash – so all gravitate round him. They gave me an enormous sugar cake at the demonstration – so I've sent six or seven of them huge hunks of it for their lunch. We've all been going short and Mr. Oviatt[1] is squeezed dry.

I had four letters from Drummonds yesterday – they are coming beautifully regularly now. God bless you for it. Such sad letters from Maurice, and a life size photo of himself. Good bye dear love – Baby.

Diana to Duff, 6 October 1925   *Hotel Sinton, Cincinnati*

Darling. Kommer came back this morning, laden with presents and *foie gras* and cigarettes. In the afternoon was a woman's tea – fierce – and at 6.30 we repaired to the Radio place to have a short talk to 20,000,000 listeners. It took the form of questions and answers on *The Miracle*. Kommer had written me [a paragraph] in the breathless moments before the red light goes up, announcing that whatever you say you are telling the world. I started alright but when I got to the passage "I am now so fascinated by my work" Iris shook with laughter, and my morale deserted me, and I had to break off. Other people talked and I laughed myself dizzy for half an hour, when a pale youth rushed in saying "stop, stop,

[1] Mr. Oviatt worked on the administration side of *The Miracle*.

stop – none of it has been registering" so it's all to be done again tomorrow.

Cable me from time to time, it's instant relief.

I love you as always. There are nine kinds of angels according to the church's doctrine. Cherubim, Seraphim & Thrones, Dominations, Principalities and Powers, Virtues, Archangels and just angels. You're just an angel. When our bodies rejoin our souls, as they may do on the last and dreadful day of Judgement, we shall – if saved – be endowed with Impassivity, Agility, Brightness, and Subtlety – did you know that Mr Dumple.

Diana to Duff, 28 October 1925   *Hotel Lenox, Boston*

Opening night – huge success – mad applause, and Gest sobbing on the chancel steps.[1] [Otto] Kahn,[2] Davidson,[3] Ziegler[4] of the Metropolitan, and Oom came from New York at six and returned at midnight. One old actor fell headfirst down the steps and hurt a woman in the front row and when I pulled the bell it didn't ring – otherwise no hitches. Kahn brought me another $1000 turn over. The night wound up with the party beautifully done with yew hedges, and lit by a hundred thick church candles, really lovely – buffet and tables and a little champagne and a ghastly collection of men. Iris & I came back at 2.30, escorted by a beau called Bill Gaston, the brother of John, whom Iris is now slapping and tickling in the drawing-room, and will continue till four or five. I shall go to sleep – because I'm tired. I had an exhausting day of acute unaccountable nervousness, not relieved by John Gaston arriving with four men who he referred to as a committee formed to see we had a good time and made more hideous by a telegram from Bertram, saying would I try and meet him in the upstairs waiting room at the station – he must see me alone. I had that guilty dread, that all was discovered. However it turned out all right, and to be just a lover's ruse to see his sweetie.   Yr. Diana – I mean Miss Baby

[1] Morris Gest was in the habit of making an emotional speech from the stage after the first performance in a new town.
[2] Otto Kahn, 1867–1934, the banker. He was financing this production of *The Miracle*.
[3] Jo Davidson, 1883–1947, the sculptor.
[4] Edward Ziegler, 1870–1947, music critic and Assistant General Manager of The Metropolitan Opera House from 1920 onwards.

Diana to Duff, 31 October 1925   *The Lenox, Boston*

My own dear love. I'm so upset about myself tonight. I threw a
faint again on the pillar – didn't go right out but had to grunt and
grunt until they brought a church banner with some brandy
behind it. I'd had port and brandy before the performance so it
wasn't lack of stimulant. Every night I have a panic of it, and I can
always fight it by thinking hard of you or something – but if I get
extra tired, as I suppose I did today with playing the Nun in the
afternoon, and perhaps 'affairs' due, then I can't fight it, and I get
bathed in cold quick-silver sweat. I'm so frightened of it becoming
a habit – because I'm sure it's not heart, but nerves and thinking
about it and dreading. It may stop the Madonna for me and I'm
doing it better than ever before – 'everybody thinks so'.

Pinchie [Rosamond Pinchot] came over tonight and cried
herself sick in a box. Kaetchen said he never had such an evening,
with Pinchie hysterical by his side and me fainting on the other
side. Iris has gone off, on a two and a half hour motor drive with
her beau Bill Gaston to his country home. I refused because I'd
chucked Schuyler's beastly sister and her odious husband on the
grounds I must stay with Pinchie. I miss Iris *terribly* and am
frightened of Kaetchen's adoration without her there. My Mummy sails today. O dear O dear O dear O dear   xxxx Baby.

Diana to Duff,   *Hotel Lenox, Boston*
5 November 1925 Mr. Fawkes's day

Sweet one. I've spent rather a happy – but before that there was
last night a party given by Morris Gest in a private room with
Russians and drink and great hilarity. I sat up till four and feel
flogged today. The proprietor lent us his huge open car and the use
of his brother, and we drove off to Salem – the best example of old
colonial houses in New England. It had great charm I thought.
They burnt a lot of whiches at Salem. I got rather imbued with the
period, and thought it would be amusing and topical for me to do
up the drawing room Colonial-style. They sometimes have
wonderful 1800 hand painted wall papers, I might try and get one.
I nearly bought a 1800 bed quilt with an eagle and 17 stars made of
chinz appliquéed onto it. I chequed myself in time. Home at five,
and at six a good dinner ordered for us by the Proprietor consisting

of a baby milk-fed turkey – incomparable! Iris's Gaston and the donor and Kätchen shared it with us in our dining room and washed it down with Cham.

I've had a reporter in my room for an hour – quite tongue-tied with love and emotion. He declared himself ten minutes ago adding that I reminded him of his mother – always melancholy information from a middle-aged man.

Diana to Duff, 10 November 1925 [*Boston*]

My beloved. I've started on Napoleon III – it's awful difficult.[1] I am resigned and will take advantage of my impossibly dreary unfree nerve-eaten phase of life to get some information packed into my tiny brain. I finished *The Conqueror*[2] who I find a little like you, and now I'm running 2nd Empire and *Confessions of St Augustine* together. This latter is a typical Maurice – four hundred pages of the praise of God – unless you are a specialist – is a little tedious; I made rather a mess of the *Imitation*[3] – but I'll persevere with this. One of my bothers is not having a lover here, I'm so jealous of Iris's besotted swain, and that's the truth, not of him as an individual but as a decoration – I've never been without – but I can't let Oom come up now my Mummy's here. I've packed her off to the play tonight with the Guvenor of Masseschusets[4] and they must have gone on the tiles as it's twelve and they're not back. Iris has gone off for the night to her boy's flat with all the paraphanalia of riding equipment and a lie to Mother about going to his sister's in the country. Duffy, you remember what a glutton I is for petting – so imagine how I miss it. Do you think of your Boston Baby Bean. I hope, I hope, O I think you do. I got a panic you loved Lady Carlisle.[5] You don't, do you?

[1] Philip Guedalla, *The Second Empire* (1922).
[2] Gertrude Atherton, *The Conqueror* (1902) – an American best-seller.
[3] Thomas à Kempis, *The Imitation of Christ*.
[4] Governor Alvan Tufts Fuller, 1878–1958.
[5] Née the Hon. Bridget Hore-Ruthven, she married George Howard, 11th Earl of Carlisle, in 1918, later Viscountess Monckton of Brenchley.

Duff to Diana,   *Kildonan,*[1] *Ayrshire*
11 November 1925
Armistice Day

We have had another lovely day of cloudless sunshine – the
ground all white with frost. I forgot to tell you how lovely it was
when we arrived yesterday early morning. The frosty ground was
pink from the reflection of the sunrise. The sky was very pale,
cloudless and a thin vanishing slice of moon in it – and the sun was
just resting on the top of a hill – round and red like a toy. The
shooting was not so good today but we ended up with some
beautiful duck flighting round a frozen pond. We also got a lot of
woodcock which we in our wild, witty way call timber doodles.
The inevitable neighbour makes up our guns to eight. He is a red
faced man with spectacles, a Scots accent and a very shaky hand.
My private opinion is that he drinks too much whiskey. His name
is Dunghill or something very like it. He is always rightly put in
the worst place, and Euan, who arranges everything very scien-
tifically, is always shouting "All the guns this way except Dunghill". I have brought Holly minor with me. He is much nicer than
his brother but he has inherited the Holbrook inability to distinguish between different species of wild birds and ground game. He
continually draws my attention to a blackbird under the impression that it is a woodcock.

We play Bridge in the evening. We are quite a pleasant party – I
like them all – even Blandford.[2] He is so frank – Victor[3] came
down in a brown velvet smoking suit last night. Blandford said
"I've always been meaning to get a suit like that, but now I see it
on you I think it looks rather common".   D.

Duff to Diana, 13 November 1925   *15 Hays Mews, Mayfair*[4]

My beloved angel. A comfortable journey from Scotland last
night. The train was two hours late which was all to the good as
one had a longer sleep – I slept well. It is all up with the Foreign

[1] The house of the Rt. Hon. Euan Wallace, 1892–1941. He married Barbara, daughter
of Sir Edwin Lutyens.
[2] John, Marquess of Blandford – he succeeded his father as 10th Duke of Marlborough
in 1934.
[3] Lord Victor Paget, 1889–1952, brother of the 6th Marquess of Anglesey.
[4] Duff had let Gower Street while Diana was in America that year.

Office. The Prime Minister told Sidney [Herbert] this morning whom he means to appoint and it isn't me.[1] It is something to have been in the running at all. But I feel disappointed and the fact that I have nowhere particular to dine this evening gives me a 'nobody loves me' sensation of gloom which is increased by having had nothing to drink all day in an effort to get thin and give the psoriasis a chance. I had two letters and a telegram from you today. I'm worried about the fainting – Oh please be careful Baby dear. How I wish you were here this evening. We would have a very good little dinner together and then go to a very good play – and to bed because we're tired and it is so very cold. I can't press you to come home because it seems mad – and if you had bad crossings you would regret it – but I do want you.

You ask me to tell you politics. There aren't any. The House meets next Monday. The Locarno pact[2] is a great thing. Max and Rothermere[3] are going rather more gently. I think they realise that they have overdone the attack on the Government. I love you –   D.

Diana to Duff, 13 November 1925   [*Boston*]

Sweet dove. I telephoned Kaetchen this morning & told him to send me a wire summoning me to New York for mysterious film negotiations – I must have a respite and my spirits have risen magnificently in response to the scheme. I dreaded going to Iris's lover's. He's attractive but I've taken a violent antipathy to him on the grounds, my old grounds, that he is bad, bad. Bad-mannered, inaudible, bogus blue stocking and tonight puts the lid on it when Iris tells me that next month she will go through all the tortures of threatened and probably settled pregnancy. She is an invariable conceiver if no precautions are taken, and he refuses to take any or allow any. I flew into a passionate rage with Iris – but it will do no good. How can anyone be so selfish as him, or so wickedly wanton as her. Last time she had her 'illegal' (one of six)

---

[1] Ronald McNeill had been promoted to Financial Secretary of the Treasury, and his previous post as Under Secretary at the Foreign Office was therefore vacant. It would have been very quick promotion for Duff if he had got the job, but the *Manchester Guardian* had raised his hopes by saying that he should.

[2] This was a pact of non-aggression between Belgium, France and Germany, guaranteed by Great Britain and Italy.

[3] 1st Viscount Rothermere, 1868–1940. He took over the *Daily Mail* on his brother Lord Northcliffe's death in 1922.

she should have died, was given up in fact. Next month in all probability it will cost her her life and me £500 in specialists' bills.

Duff to Diana, 15 November 1925   *15 Hays Mews*

My only love. I was reduced last night to dining with Alan and his woman. Her name is Barbara Hamilton. Her husband has left her. She poses as pure and is so I am sure so far as Alan is concerned. She is a very pretty woman. She had been spending the afternoon with Max in the country. Last Sunday night Max gave a tremendous orgy in Stornoway House. A huge dinner party at which this lady sat on his right hand and Jean Norton[1] on his left. The rest were all stage and Alan says it was the drunkest party he has ever seen in his life – including Oxford. At one period of the evening Max performed a *pas seul*. He has been on the water wagon ever since. Oh do come back soon baby – and never go away again. Did they really burn 'whiches' at Salem?[2] Which whiches were they? And did you 'cheque' your impulse? I wish you'd cheque me.   D.

Duff to Diana, 17 November 1925   *House of Commons Library*

Margot [Oxford] had heard from Puffin,[3] and he really had done you proud. She was characteristically frank about it. "Of course I'd heard she was very good but I didn't believe it – and what's very good for others *we* might not think good. One always thinks one's friends will be bad" – but now that Puffin was convinced, she was also – he being so very critical. He was wild about it – the wonderful beauty and dignity – felt proud of knowing you – was determined to see it again before he left the country etc. She said she would send me the letter. So easily is one influenced that I find all my feelings of horror towards the little creature have quite changed. I do like people to be nice about baby.   D.

---

[1] Mrs. Jean Norton, by far the most important of the many women in Lord Beaverbrook's life.
[2] See p. 205.
[3] Antony Asquith, 1902–1968, film director; the son of H. H. Asquith and his second wife Margot Tennant.

Duff to Diana, 19 November 1925   *House of Commons*

Dear Miss Bunting. Enclosed please find warrant for fifteen shillings and one penny. Where it puts "Payee to sign here" please write "B. Bunting" – and return.

I got some lovely letters from you yesterday Baby darling. I love your habit of sending some to Bucks so that I get them in instalments. I slipped out to dine there last night after my speech and dined so happily with your letters and with your dear little mug in the *very* lovely picture which you sent me. I have put it in my pocket book where there are two others – one of you as the Madonna, very small against a huge Cathedral – and one of you in your green macintosh with the dog collar.

Raymond [de Trafford] has been in pretty serious trouble.[1] He kept paying mysterious visits to Paris which he explained to me as being in connection with a row he had had with a man at the Travellers who wouldn't pay some money that he owed him. I have now heard the whole story from Ashmead.[2] The man wouldn't pay because he asserted that Raymond had cheated and Ashmead has no doubt whatever that he did. It occurred before he came to Salzburg. The man was prepared not to make a fuss but refused to pay. He put the money in an envelope and left it at the Travellers saying that if Raymond claimed it he must have the whole thing gone into. Raymond under this accusation of cheating did nothing at all until a fortnight ago when he tried to get the money. The thing has been hushed up as far as possible but the man has neither retracted, apologised or paid and Raymond has had to promise not to play cards in the Travellers again for five years.

Diana to Duff, 17 November 1925   *Hotel Lenox, Boston*

My beloved. Today was terrific. We sat down 1100 women at the Copley Plaza. After lunch speeches began – we were at the 'above salt' table next the Guvenor. Speeches were intersected with tenors, violins, and a retired opera singer, gross and glassed and ghastly who sang *Wake my love 'tis dawn*, and I had giggles – but those giggles were smiles compared to the ones that followed

[1] Raymond de Trafford was a hopeless gambler, womaniser and drinker, and was in trouble most of his life.

[2] Ellis Ashmead-Bartlett, 1881–1931; writer, journalist and politician.

When the Chairwoman introduced us, the honoured guests, in exactly the way we used to play 'unveiling'. I was compared to Duse and Sarah,[1] and kept a grave face denoting an agreeing spirit, but when they started on Iris, and started wrong – "we are glad to give her, her right appellation, the honorable Iris Tree, daughter of that figure familiar to all our lips as Sir Henry Tree –"[2] My *fou-rire* broke me so badly that the 1100 laughed with me, and Iris's tears were rolling down her bursting face. I've just had a letter from Otto [Kahn] saying my full monnies up to today amount to $58,159. It seems a pittance to me, and will only be about $87,000 when I leave – about $17,000 – its meagre. I idolise you pretty.   Baby.

Diana to Duff, 23 November 1925   *Hotel Lenox, Boston*

Dear one. I spent a funny day visiting Harvard thoroughly. First with a dreary professor over the main buildings, halls, and library. We paused too long perhaps in the theatrical collection, and I was horrified to see the ghastly photographs of myself due to go into their shelves. Wonderful prints of plays and actors, and extraordinarily hideous photographs of poor Ellen Terry and Sarah at their best. A lot of marvellous things, and an ocean of rubbish too. The best things that I struck were original love letters from Edmund Kean to Mrs. Cox,[3] most beginning 'my dear, dear little bitch'. It read so gracefully on the old paper in pale ink.

Duff to Diana, 26 November 1925   *House of Commons*

My dear dear darling. I have had a long day. I left Charing Cross at 10.30 in fog and frost and arrived at Hastings which was bathed in glorious sunshine at half past twelve. I was met by a man who looked exactly like a corpse and who suggested that we should go for a drive as there was half an hour before luncheon and he particularly wanted me to see 'the front'. I could think of nothing to say to him during the drive, and in desperation asked him how

---

[1] Eleanora Duse and Sarah Bernhardt.
[2] His name was Sir Herbert Tree.
[3] Edmund Kean, the actor (1787–1833). His affair with Mrs. Cox, wife of a London banker, went on for many years and led to an action for *criminal conversation*, in which Kean had to pay £800 in damages.

many members there were of the Hastings League of Nations Union. He replied "If all our members were alive, we should have about fourteen hundred". The idea of his counting the dead members in struck me as so sinister and so funny that I had a *fou rire* – and the more I thought of it the funnier it seemed to me, so that I kept on all day bursting into little guffaws which upset the corpse terribly – He thought I was mad. Then we had a solemn lunch party of about nine people in the chief hotel. I sat next to the Archdeacon who was like Hutchy dressed up as a parson. He surpassed belief. Then the meeting took place in the local theatre which to my astonishment was crowded from stalls to gallery. I spoke for an hour and spoke well. They were a patient, attentive and enthusiastic audience.   D.

Diana to Duff, 4 December 1925   *Hotel Lenox, Boston*

Good afternoon Duffy. Supper last night was very funny – they sent for a man from New York, a German adventurer calling himself Baron something. He's of all buggers the greatest, and did the most shocking dances of the Macabre school semi-naked, in a Picasso-designed dress, with his naked parts covered in blood, and smelt the place out with amber scent. He wore a monocle throughout. The dances took place in a crowded dark little drawing room – and the Boston ladies didn't know what to say or think till I said I thought him extremely good, and so they all followed suit. Ruth Draper[1] was there, quite disgusted, and terribly grand – with no hope of a stunt in her.

Duff to Diana,   *Plas Newydd, Isle of Anglesey*[2]
12 December 1925

Dear Miss Bunting.

I was far too sleepy to write to you properly last night. I had had a devastating day. I left here at dawn and found myself in Manchester earlier than I expected so that I had an hour and a half there with no earthly thing to do. I walked about the streets and bought an awfully nice despatch case for a guinea. Then I had

[1] American comedienne and monologist, 1889–1956. Joyce Grenfell learnt her monologue technique from Ruth Draper, who was her cousin and life-long friend.
[2] The Seat of the Marquess of Anglesey.

luncheon with Mr Jackson, a man you've never met, not the husband but the brother in law of Mrs Jackson. He drove me down to Oldham where I opened this absurd bazaar.[1] Mr Freeman was in the chair – nice as ever. They are all gloomy there over the failure of the Belgrade Mill, connected with the death (or suicide) of Mr Greenwood. Hundreds of 'small people' have been ruined.[2] I got back here just in time for dinner having missed a glorious shoot, better than the day before and today we went to shoot the snipe marsh which owing to a partial frost was a complete one. I only fired three or four shots and killed nothing. The total bag was about half a dozen. Hartington who has a good deal of humour remarked that two pictures one representing the *Chasseurs*, and the other the Bag would be funny. The *chasseurs* were six guns, seven loaders because the Duke of Portland has two, half a dozen keepers, fifty beaters, three motor cars and a motor van – not to mention about 20 dogs. The bag was five very small snipe and a hare.

This morning I got a thoroughly naughty letter from the youngest surviving member of the Bunting family. I longed to shake the mite. I send you a cutting from one of your crapulous friend Max's papers and tell you it is a lie; that far from making a bad speech I made a good one which had considerable success[3] – to which you reply that the cutting has worried you terribly, that of course one can't expect always to make a good speech, that reverses do one good but that you only hope it didn't affect etc. etc. You little swine – do you even at this distance believe the gutter press rather than me? Or do you, which I suspect to be the case, never read any part of my letters except the printed enclosures. It is probably no good my assuring you again that the paragraph was a lie and that it had no effect whatever on the appointment. By the way I think I told you that Oliver Locker Lampson had got it, which I had indeed misunderstood from Sidney. It was not Oliver but Godfrey Locker Lampson who was already Under Secretary at the Home Office – an elderly man.[4] You met him once at dinner

[1] The bazaar was to raise money to abolish pew rents in church.
[2] See letter page 201.
[3] The Londoner's Diary section of the *Evening Standard* of November 19th had reported the debate on the Treaty of Locarno; it criticised the 'harsh partisan note' struck by Duff, and said what a disappointment this was after the brilliance of his maiden speech.
[4] The Rt. Hon. Godfrey Locker-Lampson, 1875–1943, was Under Secretary of State for Foreign Affairs from 1925 to 1929. Duff was very relieved that the job did not go to his younger brother Oliver.

with Ronald McNeill. so that no young man of whom we need feel
jealous has been promoted. I ought to be very pleased that I was
ever considered which I know that I was. According to Sidney the
one person who worked for me was Tyrrell.[1] I am sorry you
telegraphed to Winston. If one can get on without intrigue – and
I'm sure I can – it is much better not to indulge in it.

The next naughtiness in your letter was about Mrs. Hamilton.[6]
Why on earth should I get tangled in her toils? Have I ever fallen
to that type yet? If there is a thing I loathe it's the good and
common. Suspect me rather of tempting the Duchess of Portland
from the narrow path. She said to me last night at dinner – "My
secretary is so wonderful – she takes down a thousand words a
minute – no a hundred words. The Archbishop of York – no the
Archbishop of Canterbury was staying with us in Scotland this
summer and, do you know, he liked my secretary so much that he
used to have her every morning. Then he was all right for the
day".

Duff to Diana, 13 December 1925   *Plas Newydd*

You like links with the past, don't you. The man I met at the
Carlisles called Bill Coke who is three years younger than me is the
grandson of the famous Coke of Norfolk, who was born in 1754.
Portland told us that but I didn't believe it until I verified it in the
peerage this morning. The last Lord Leicester who was Coke of
Norfolk's son was born in 1822, and this his youngest son was born
in 1893. A man younger than me can therefore say "My grand-
father was no longer young at the time of the French Revolution,
and left Eton in the year that Napoleon was born". And if he lives
– and he's a great strong fellow – he will be able to say that in 50
years time.[2] I think Rose[3] and Kitty[4] are the nicest of these
children – they are both rather like you – especially Rose. I leave
here tonight by the Irish mail for London. I love you   D.

---

[1] William Tyrrell, 1866–1947, the Permanent Under Secretary of State for Foreign
Affairs – created 1st Baron Tyrrell in 1929. He was Ambassador to Paris 1928–34.
[2] See letter p. 209.
[3] Lovel William Coke, youngest son of the 2nd Earl of Leicester, was able to say that for
thirty-one years after this letter was written. He died in 1966.
[4] Lady Rose Paget, 3rd daughter of the 6th Marquess of Anglesey.
[5] Lady Katharine Paget, youngest daughter of the 6th Marquess of Anglesey, and twin
of the 7th and present Marquess.

Diana to Duff, 17 December 1925   *The Ambassador, New York*

Sunday I go to St Louis and I'm glad of it. The only hope is change when you are sick for home. I hope you're back in Gower St. I had eight letters from you in one day. I loved them but they were not very loving – don't stop – I need your love so much and only yours, unfortunately. The cheque from Lytle Hull for $5000 has not arrived, very fishy. It's funny whenever I write of loving you, I precede or follow it with a financial glint. It must read sordidly – but it is in some way connected – I wouldn't leave you except to bring you back money. I love you so.   B.

Duff to Diana, Christmas Day 1925   *Wilton House, Salisbury*

My sweetest love. A cold day – the ground covered with snow – which is all very right and proper. I have received from Juliet a nice pocket book with my initials on it – from Mrs. Beckett[1] a pocket book with my initials on it – from Patricia[2] a pocket book. In return I have given them each a pocket book – vanity case – or what you will. Lady Curzon gave me a well bound book about Lafayette. I have also received three white silk handkerchiefs from Kakoo – to whom I fortunately sent a book before leaving London. I went to Church this morning and have played Bezique with Raymond and Juliet all this afternoon. There is to be dressing up for dinner this evening – which would be such fun if only you were here, and which is no fun at all without you. I have brought my old harlequin suit but I think it's shrunk.

I'll finish this after dinner.

The dressing up was not very amusing. My old harlequin dress fitted me quite well – but I had no one to tie a black silk handkerchief on my head – so that I looked neither correct, nor funny, nor pretty. Bee[3] was dressed as little Lord Fauntleroy – black silk knickers, white lace a yellow wig. Reggie shaved off his moustache, brushed his hair forward, wore horn rimmed spectacles and a curate's clothes and really did look astonishingly different. Juliet was an Indian with a coal black face – Sidney and

---

[1] Muriel, wife of the Hon. Rupert Beckett, and 1st cousin of Beatrice Pembroke.
[2] Patricia Herbert, b. 1904, daughter of Beatrice and Reginald. She married the 3rd Viscount Hambleden in 1928.
[3] Beatrice, Countess of Pembroke. The sister of the 6th Marquess of Anglesey, she married Reginald, the 15th Earl of Pembroke in 1904.

Mike were two little girls in white nightgowns and blue bows – rouged and powdered, very funny. Raymond with a red wig and a low woman's dress was supposed to be Eloise [Ancaster]. The girls were all dressed up to look pretty. As I say it was not very amusing but might have been worse. We did some charades afterwards which were a failure. Goodnight I'se velly tired.

Diana to Duff,   *The New Coliseum, St. Louis*
Christmas Day 1925

Good christian Duffy. I'se a tiny exile. I went out and bought my feast. I bought a booful big turkey ready cooked and stuffed, I bought mince pies, I ordered 'hot dawgs' and bread and butter, and coffee and knives and foicks and glasses, I bought a huge sparkley silver candle, and a silver Kikelmas tree (small) and a fat Father Kikelmas, and with Kaetchen's delicatessen we made a câche in the dressing room along with two sheets from the hotel for cloths. The first night, (last night) was a ghastly frost, as it was bound to be if you open on K. Eve. – more than half empty, no enthusiasm, and the usual unbearable sentimental speech by Gest, through sobs, at the finish – about how he'd been picked up fourteen years ago dying on a doorstep in Olive St. and that it was thanks to a miracle he was there – delivered to a few deaf mutes.

Today was a matinée for 'the Kiddies' – supposed to be 6000 of them, 2000 turned up only and shouted and whistled and laughed and screamed at what they thought it was – a panto. It was fun, but a farce, and we only played first and last acts luckily. So by four the feast began, and a huge success it was. Three bottles of scotch consumed amongst about twelve, and a succession of good stunts – we kept it at roaring point till seven when Master Oviatt fell off his chair. That was the signal for them to go and leave us to put on our coats and lie on the bare floor for half an hour's sleep – while Mother laid a piece of paper on the floor and slept tailor wise with a fur on her head. We looked like an old pack of Russian Jews and enjoyed it. My! how the others enjoyed it – the party I mean. It was one's idea of a green-room frolic and I enjoyed it too. A great many imitations of absent members of the cast, and of Gest, dancing, banjos, singing – my style only a little cramped by Her Grace. Now it's the evening performance – equally empty, and I'm in a red rage because the paper this morning had no criticism

[216]

of the actors, and they told me that tomorrow the real criticisms
would appear. however I've just seen tomorrow's issue of the only
morning paper. Iris and I are mentioned as alternating.
Reinhardt's name is not used, and there are two long paragraphs
about Elinor Patterson who hasn't appeared yet. Gest dictates to
the press – so he shall have all the blame. I *hate* him. Sweet Duff I
love you. Be prepared to come –   Your Baby B.

Duff to Diana, 26 December 1925   *Wilton, Salisbury*

Good night, funny face, I love your letters so. It is a good thing
from some points of view that our interests should differ. How dull
we should become if I was entirely interested in *The Miracle* as
Alan would be – or if you were only interested in the House of
Commons as Letty would be. As it is it seems to me that our
interests embrace nearly all human affairs and the greater part of
the globe. I love you.   D.

Diana to Duff,   *The New Coliseum, St. Louis*
31 December 1925

I pray God that we both have a happy year in 1926. I can't
complain of this dying one. We were happy although there was
sorry in it for our *proches* – and a quarter of it away from you. Waste
waste Horatio.[1] I love you as well as ever – that matters most, and
if you love me no less I'm satisfied with the pale old year.   loving
Baby.

Diana to Duff,   *The New Coliseum, St. Louis*
14 January 1926

I didn't write to my darling Duffy yesterday it was a matinée day
and I had a tea with my old beau between, and after playing the
Nun at night I was so tired and had such a headache from the
cocktails – I could only sink into unconsciousness. All and everybody said I'd never acted so well, and I knew it was the abandon of

[1] "Thrift, thrift, Horatio! The funeral baked meats
Did coldly furnish forth the marriage tables."
Hamlet, Act I scene ii.

[217]

alcohol – so it sounded funny when it came from my poor Mummy. They had a dreadful row, Kommer and she, yesterday afternoon, over an interview in an evening paper which K. found her tearing out of the paper so that I should not see it. It was all on poverty and economy – with terrible side lights on her pinchings and clothes. It's a thing she has been begged not to do, and warned too that it is very bad for all our good names – as Americans despise poverty. We don't after all get free rooms and motors out of pity – but because we are thought grand and important. Write me ideas of improvement for Bognor. I dream them on the pillar it keeps me quieted. Write me Castles in the air to feed on.   B.

Duff to Diana, 16 January 1926   *Belvoir Castle*

My own dear darling love. Yesterday passed pleasantly as I never left the house. John and Kakoo had a row at luncheon because she had told him two people were coming and it turned out that three were. He said, "that's just what Mother used to do to Father" and she said "Well, don't get like your Father". He replied "I shall get exactly like him – and if you ever dare do it again I shall refuse to lunch at all". The luncheon guests were Kakoo's step grand-mother Mrs. Lubbock – her husband and son. Later in the day arrived the Mervyn Herberts,[1] Betty Cranborne with a child, the Colquhouns[2] with two children and Michael Tennant.[3] The number of children was another grievance for John. Kakoo suffers between him and the casualness of her relations. Michael came for a shooting party without a gun, and Ian without cartridges. John further decreed that we were to wear full dress[4] last night – rather queer for a country party of six. Luckily I had brought white tie and waistcoat. Michael of course hadn't. He said to John from the other end of the table "Don't you wear a black tie in the country?" John replied – "Yes, when I dine alone with Kakoo – in her bedroom." He is really getting rather alarming, you know. He oughtn't to be allowed to.

[1] Hon. Mervyn Herbert and his wife, the American Elizabeth Willard.
[2] Dinah, the new Duchess of Rutland's elder sister, had married Sir Iain Colquhoun of Luss 7th Bt.
[3] Michael Tennant – brother of Dinah and the Duchess.
[4] Full dress – i.e. white tie and tails.

Diana to Duff,   *The New Coliseum, St. Louis*
17 January 1926

I scolded Iris good-naturedly about her extravagence when I
got in, & this morning on waking her bill came in full of $30 long
distance calls & $10 cables, owing to neglect of writing L.C.O.
[low cost overnight] on them, & she suddenly with no warning
sprang up gibbering & screaming like a maniac, seized the baked
apple on the breakfast tray, relinquished it in favour of a cup &
smashed it across the room, bursting afterwards into a flood of
tears & paroxysms of laughter. I felt a iittle guilty but was also so
shocked – & couldn't speak or remonstrate.

Duff to Diana, 1 February 1926   *Chirk Castle, Wrexham*

Sweetest and dearest of all small creatures. The rest of yesterday
passed quite pleasantly away. I rather like Poots.[1] She is amusing
and puts vitality into this rather corpse like party. Her lover left
yesterday and she left this morning. We played a game last night
of making lists of eleven people we could bear to marry – and by
'marry' we meant go to bed with. Margot [Howard de Walden]
and Poots both put me in their list, which was rather awkward as I
couldn't put either of them in mine. You would have had no
surprises in my eleven. Dolly [Warrender][2] didn't get in. Otherwise they were the same old favourites – Betty [Cranborne],
Diana,[3] Bridget,[4] Daisy [Fellowes], Pinna Cruger[5] – and then I
had to fill up with just pretty women like Freda, Sheila Loughborough, Edvina Stuart-Wortley,[6] Peñeranda,[7] Hoebe.[8] I

---

[1] Poots – Born Gwendolen Van Raalte, she married Lt. Col. Humphrey Butler
(1894–1953) in 1927.
[2] Dorothy Warrender, née Rawson, married Victor Warrender in 1920 – he later
became 1st Baron Bruntisfield.
[3] Diana, widow of Percy Wyndham (see letter of January 1918), married the 14th Earl
of Westmorland in 1923.
[4] Born the Hon. Bridget Colebrooke, she married Lord Victor Paget (see p. 207) in
1922.
[5] The wife of Freddy Cruger, Bertram's brother.
[6] Louis Stuart Wortley (1880–1948). Rothesay Stuart-Wortley's wife, she was better
known as the soprano Edvina.
[7] Carmen, Duchess of Peñeranda – sister in law of the Duke of Alba. She sported a sun
tan when ladies never moved without a parasol, and set it off by wearing pearls and white
satin.
[8] A *mannequin* at Lucille's, a dress-shop in Paris, who Duff thought the most beautiful
woman in the world after Diana.

thought you would like to hear as in one of your recent letters you said that you dreaded the thought of my new favourites. Lady Carlisle by the way didn't get in. You may also be interested to hear that your friend B. Cruger figured on Edvina's list. I wanted to make mine more representative by including a stage favourite, and do you know I couldn't think of one. Isn't that queer? Perhaps you can remember one for me.

I have just had four letters from you my darling. Such miserable letters. I can't bear your life for you. It sounds quite ghastly – the squabbles, the intrigues, Iris's extravagance and insanity, your Mother's miserliness and insanity. I really don't know how you bear it. Be firm about returning from Chicago at the first possible moment.

Good night my poor little beast. I want you now –   D.

Diana to Duff,   *The Lake Shore Drive Hotel, Chicago*
3 February 1926

My darling dear. Who were you spooning with pray at the Sargent Exhibition. My ground scouts report. Let me know by return.

The reviews for me have been excellent – which reconciles me a little bit to Chicago. I enclose one pretty one – funny too. Is Christ the first democrat? When Gest settled to have the Patterson girl[1] play the first night here I thought it mistaken policy since an owner can't properly puff his own daughter. Wrong again, in his paper the *Tribune* there are 3 paragraphs about her art and beauty and I am actually *not mentioned*. It's a collectors' piece.

Chicago has one curious beauty – that is great puffs of white smoke everywhere, like cannon smoke in old pictures. I can't make out where it puffs from, but you'll always see one of these clouds or columns, white on a black skyscraper. No letters from you for many days my dear dear love. Its six weeks and two days till I sail. O love me well –   Baby.

Duff to Diana, 7 February 1926   *90 Gower Street*

My own dear angel. Maurice, Michael and I dined together last night and spent most of the evening discussing Raymond's affairs

[1] Eleanor Mendill Patterson, daughter of Robert Patterson, editor and publisher of the *Chicago Tribune*. Eleanor Patterson was playing the Nun while *The Miracle* was in Chicago.

which are now more serious than ever. The man who accused him of cheating at the Travellers' was only a temporary member, and when he subsequently came up for election as a real member he was blackballed. This sent his friends and others out for Raymond's blood. They sent a round robin to the Club Committee demanding that Raymond should be turned out. The Committee have summoned Raymond to appear before them in a fortnight's time and have privately recommended him to resign. Maurice's brother Hugo[1] who is on the Committee says that if he fights it he is bound to lose and be kicked out. He wouldn't of course mind resigning, but the Commanding Officer of the Coldstream has said that if he does he will have to resign from the Guards Club and every other decent club in London. He couldn't survive that. His position is really very serious. He didn't come to Brighton yesterday as he had to dine with Humphrey who went to Paris today to see if things couldn't be arranged at the Travellers'. Such lovely letters, baby darling, describing the last of St. Louis and the first of New York. Silly of me to think there was a Missouri River but in my Encyclopedia Britannica there is a page and a half about it – the river. They describe it as the principal tributary of the Mississippi which it joins 20 miles above St. Louis. They say that together with the Jefferson Fork, 'which is really the upper section of the Missouri' and the Lower Mississippi – 'the Missouri forms a river channel 4221 miles in length – the longest in the world'. However I am writing to the Editors to inform them that there ain't no such river, because Baby's been there and says there isn't and she ought to know.

Diana to Duff, 8 February 1926   *Chicago*

Good evening my darling Duffy. Two letters today from Belvoir – what a programme of work – you dear dear little nigger. Chaliapin[2] was at *The Miracle* tonight in the front row and I was so nervous and trembly and cold and sweaty, not being used to either friends or artists watching my efforts. He came to my dressing room red with love and bent on a romp. Unfortunately since

---

[1] Hon. Hugo Baring, 1876–1949, youngest son of 1st Baron Revelstoke.
[2] Feodor Ivanovitch Chaliapin, 1873–1938, the bass opera singer widely held to be the greatest singing actor of his day. Sometimes called 'Charlie Pine' or 'Tuffy Pine' in Duff and Diana's letters.

learning the English language he makes love in it, instead of the more attractive veiled Russian tongue and as his choice of erotic words wasn't too delicate, I had a wave of nausea. He said he wanted to have Baby, and I had a struggle with him in which he pressed Baby's white-washed hand on his placey. I tore it away, and in so doing left a cloud of white. So imagine my consternation when Bekefi[1] came in, he unconscious and me trying to stand between them and knowing the construction she was bound to put upon it – fly ripping. When she left I wanted to tell him and couldn't but by inspiration manoeuvred him in front of the tall glass. It worked and he laughed heartily, and seizing Iris's big bristled brush started removing it. I hesitate to tell you this anecdote, for fear of putting you off Pine – but it's too funny to resist.

This is a good impression of Chicago, arabesqued over with its smoke clouds. It would do as a picture of Pine's placey. Don't rag me for ever about fumbling gentlemen's placies – I know you will.   loving loving Baby.

Diana to Duff, 13 February 1926   *Chicago*

We had such a funny evening last night. We were taken to the studio, some little way out of town, of a certain Mr. Marshall,[2] a rich architect and hotel builder. The Prince of Wales was taken there – it's a sight, and the commonest people imaginable. The host is a lewd old satyr dressed as a French artist in velvet and a tie, and the main room is tropic out of doors, palms, grottoes, illuminated coloured fountains emitting a deafening plash, paths and turf railed off – a big swimming pool, electrically lit from inside and hideous. Then there's the bar like a ship's cabin – with a painted seascape out of a port-hole that rocks, and from another port-hole you may see a fat nude woman disporting herself in the waves. There's the Egyptian room on the roof looking over the frozen lake with a sofa in it cushioned and deep enough for thirty people. The twelve of us that composed the particularily straight-backed gloomy party lay on it, and suddenly from the floor rose a table laden with caviare and cocktails. We supped in the tropics – within sound of an unfortunate nigger at the piano in a huge

[1] A dancer in the cast of *The Miracle*.
[2] Benjamin Howard Marshall, 1874–1944.

Italian sala with nude statues, medieval church décor, a Bouguereau on an easel and a little theatre ending the room. The nigger was never allowed to pause, he'd been known to go on eight hours without a let-up. He bound his finger tips tightly with strapping, to preserve them. After supper which was filthy and without wine, macaroni served by Phillipinos – He said "Come and see the Chinese love-nest". This room the size of our library had a satin mattress floor – so shoes had to be taken off at the door – but that padded floor was good. I imagine it's an opium habit. I couldn't get going – two shows and two coming today and the appalling vulgarity of the people quite vanquished me.

I'm in great trouble today – it's entirely local but I must tell it because it will perhaps amuse me in later years. A fortnight ago I got along with three or four other principals a notice from "the Drama League of Chicago" advertising a huge dinner on Sunday 14th in honour of myself and others. I took it without delay to Dodge, the manager of *The Miracle* publicity office, and told him that I would *not* have invitations accepted without being con-sulted. Sunday my only night for rest should not hold eight speeches and a dinner for a 1000. I told him he was to get out of it. Good – he said. I told him – not to leave it till this last day so that my heart melted and I should feel obliged to go. Good – he said. Of course he did nothing and now they are all – the Theatre, the Office and the Drama League – in a state as never was – bawling at me, imploring, threatening – till I can hardly hold out. Of course I'd give in and be a damned fool in ordinary circumstances but it happens that Bertram comes that day for a few hours, and I simply wouldn't have the heart or the nerve to break it to him. It makes me furious because of course they'll say vile English manners and it's the Office who have forced me into this self-destructive position. I love you so much – . Baby.

Tomorrow is St. Valentine's Day.

Diana to Duff,   *Chicago*
14 February 1926: Oom's Day

Sweetest faithful heart – Oom was my Valentine. He arrived early and I went to meet the famous 20th Century train at ten a.m. There were four sections and as every American looks exactly like Oom, and as they all waved to people behind me, I dashed forward about four hundred times.

Now a long boring complication about which I think I've written at length all ready. The Drama League gives a party tonight. The first intimation I get fourteen days ago is an invitation to meet myself which I immediately said I could not do. O I feel sure I wrote all this. Any how when I got in after the pictures tonight at six, I found despairing letters saying I owed it to the public, and would I go for half an hour. I half setted to go but my hair was black, no dress to cut a dash in, and Bertram looked as if he'd be sick, so I packed Mother and Iris off and felt glad to have so decided as I am in my rights, and don't see why I should be so bullied. Then I dined with Bertram at the great Drake Hotel and came and sat here till now – when they returned from the feast half dead with listening to ten speeches. I was not mentioned once, whether from policy or revenge I don't know.

Diana to Duff, 15 February 1926　　　　　　　　　　*Chicago*

Well this morning brought an avalanche of abuse on my poor head. Headlines about no-one having missed me. A lot about "a dear friend from New York" – & "such things can be done in London but not here". I was furious and rang up my good friend Ashton Stevens[1] who said it didn't matter at all and also that he'd write something in justification for me. I went and had breakfast in Oom's noble appartment and who should ring me up from the Drake but old Nannie Tiffany. I'm sure she came down to see what was going on. I said I'd lunch with her. I drove Bertram to the train at twelve, and discussed with him whether to volunteer his visit here or not. Unnecessary argument because when I got to Nannie's,[2] she was chuckling and revelling over the morning papers. She's broken with Vera over it all. Vera pulled a 'showdown' with her and Nannie kicked her out of the house.

Diana to Duff, 16 February 1926　　　　　　　　　　*Chicago*

The Drama League is still stirring the Press up to write something vitriolic every day. It's a great admission of how much

[1] Ashton Stevens, 1872–1951. Dramatic critic and columnist. He was drama critic of the *Chicago Herald & Examiner*, 1910–1932.
[2] Mrs. Belmont Tiffany. A distinguished interior decorator.

I was missed. Bertram telephoned that he found a letter on arrival home from Vera saying after this last insult she couldn't travel on the yacht with him and would he call it off. He answered it was a matter of indifference to him – but a few hours later another note came saying she had been hasty and would think it over for a day or two. It's exactly the method I prophesied she would take.

Duff to Diana, 17 February 1926   *90 Gower Street*

More lovely letters from you this morning. Who was it I was spooning with at the Sargent exhibition? I think it must have been Betty. The only other person with whom I spent any time there was your sister Letty – and nobody could suspect anybody of spooning with her. However I'm afraid you need have no anxiety on that score – for even if I did love Betty she is much too faithful to her husband and still more faithful to her lover,[1] both of whom are my best friends, for anything to take place.

Diana to Duff, 18 February 1926   *Chicago*

Darling Love. I've been very extravagant and bought a magnificent 'summer ermine' fur coat. It cost $600 odd – but it certainly is some rabbit skin and she looks a velly well kept baby bunting – Duffy will approve, but it cuts into this mite's Scottish soul, and today its blizzard and she can't flaunt it. She flaunted it last night dining with Mr. Ashton Stevens and she dined in a club which was velly velly hot, and they gave the gnome cham. and quite a lot of it, and she got hotter and hotter but didn't relinquish her new glory.

3 letters today one from Chirk – with account of the copulation game. I wrote the news off to Oom at once – I've always suspected her of being an old mistress, more shame to him. I should have been sorely tried to find 11, and been driven to Celebrities as you were driven to beauties. Theres 1) Jack Barrymore, and 2) Charles Pine, 3) Michael I'd be driven to, 4) Ivor [Wimborne] – I'd hate it I suppose 5) Uncle Paul [Oom] providing the fairies [his spectacles] were drowned, 6) Reinhardt – easy. 7) Bendor[2] – phui. I've sat 10 minutes thinking hard, and can't find anyone

[1] Sidney Herbert.
[2] The 2nd Duke of Westminster.

[225]

else. D'Annunzio[1] perhaps. Of course it's much easier for gentle-men – 'cos ladies are so very pretty.

Duff to Diana,　　　　　　　　　　*House of Commons Library*
22 February 1926, my 36th birthday

Such a lovely *vorfrühling* day – and I found five letters from you awaiting me. They were all written before the one I got on Saturday which seems queer. One of them contained another moan about Biddy – whom I haven't seen since the night club night which occasioned the moan. Really if you are so naughty I shall tell you nothing. Another letter contained a dirty story about that greasy, hoarse old Bolshevik C. Pine. What would you say if I made a similar fuss about him? In another letter you contemplate another tour next year which rather depresses me. Is there to be no end to it? I suppose we need the money – but still.

I have just attended a solemn luncheon party specially sum-moned at Tommy [Bouch]'s flat to discuss the ever present problem of Raymond. Tommy, Sidney, Maurice, Freddie Bretherton (Raymond's trustee) and Humphrey[2] were the party. The chief danger now is that his London clubs will insist on an explanation and our idea is that if they do we should arrange to have it dealt with first by Bucks where he has so many friends on the Committee that we ought to be able to pull him through. Tweedmouth[3] however says that if we do have an inquiry he fears it will go against him – although he himself is quite willing to leave the matter as it is. The whole thing is complicated by Raymond's imminent bankruptcy. When that happens he has to resign his clubs anyhow. Tweedmouth says let it happen now – and he can give it as an excuse for resignation. But everybody would say that the bankruptcy was merely got up as an excuse. And what is going to become of him – sans money, sans club, sans job, sans reputa-tion sans all. Really it is tragic. Tommy had arranged as a stage effect that Raymond himself should appear at the end of luncheon. The effect was *manqué*. He slunk in looking the guiltiest thing on earth – very bloated, with tears in one eye and port in the other – Tommy and Maurice are simply worried to death.　　D.

[1] Gabriele D'Annunzio – 1863–1938. The Italian poet.
[2] Humphrey de Trafford, 4th Baronet 1891–1971, Raymond's elder brother.
[3] Sir Dudley Churchill Marjoribanks, 4th Baron Tweedmouth, 1866–1935. President of Buck's Club.

Duff to Diana, 24 February 1926   *House of Commons Library*

Today I lunched at Bucks and went after luncheon to Bedlam to see old Ralph.[1] I was shown first into a long narrow room where the loonies were all sitting about, reading papers etc. They asked me to sit down for a moment while they went to see if Ralph was ready. Presently I heard a roar from the other end of the corridor "Hooray Duffy. Come on old boy, come on Duffy" and there was Ralph dressed in a red sweater and white shorts with a towel round his waist. I advanced nervously to where he was standing the centre of a small group who were playing a gramophone. I must say he seemed the maddest of the lot – but then had one found him at any time in the middle of a little group in a club or elsewhere he would always have been the noisiest and wildest. He danced round to the tune of the gramophone, shouting "Where's the fucker who's mending my shoe", where upon a little old man danced forward keeping time to the music with a needle and cotton in one hand and an old bedroom slipper in the other. He introduced me to one of the men who was an old Grenadier, who seemed very sane and nice and respectful. Then we went into his room which led off the corridor – a small, bare rather squalid room but not much worse than he would have had at Manchester Square. I stayed with him for about an hour. He hardly stopped talking for a minute – I don't suppose I said fifty words. He said he had been in the padded cells for a week because he attacked a doctor, his reason being that they wouldn't let him see his children. I'm afraid that Ruby is right not to let them go there. It might do them no harm but on the other hand it might give them a shock for life.

He seemed happy enough, complained of nothing except of the place being badly managed, seemed to like all the attendants and whenever I asked him if I could do anything for him only gave me messages for the Prince of Wales. I fear his talk about his grand acquaintance must make them think him madder than he is. He introduced me to the Head Attendant as "once the cleverest man in the Foreign Office, won the most marvellous D.S.O. in the war. A member of Parliament (but that's only a detail) probably the future Prime Minister, married to a cousin of my wife, the famous

---

[1] Ralph Peto, the husband of Diana's cousin Ruby (see page 13). His madness expressed itself in extravagant gestures – he once burnt a pile of his mother in law's underwear in the middle of Manchester Square.

Lady Diana, the most beautiful woman in the world, known all over America." Well you know that sounded alright to me, but the keeper seemed curiously unimpressed.

Good bye, baby dear, I hopes we don't go dotty. We know what we are but we know not what we shall be.   D.

Diana to Duff, 3 March 1926   *Chicago*

My darling. I've had a bad two days of depression – couldn't bring myself to do more than lie in a heap all yesterday. I think Mother and I were both poisoned. I not badly, not worse than the usual Hanson poisoning – but my poor Mummy was terribly bad Saturday night groaning and moaning on the foor of the dressing room and when I got her home, so bad and so frightened that I had to get a doctor in the middle of the night, who gave her drastic wash-outs and emetics.

I went for a long walk this morning and bought an electric toast machine so the dumplings may have hot toast as they sit at table. Also an electric waffle iron. Please Duffy tell Holbrook to get all the information about a '*Frigidaire*' machine. I must have one – it's expensive – but I'm too spoilt for cold foods. It costs over £100 but please don't thwart me, we make our own ice and everything is made good. Also please Duffy look over the house and if there is anything that needs doing – i.e. bathroom or placey – have them painted over Easter. The shutters should be all right, but perhaps need a wash – as they were painted last year. I shall have no clothes to meet you in – but you won't mind anything will you. I won't – as long as you love me untiringly. I'm going to be shy – but travelling will make that better.   Baby.

Duff to Diana, 6 March 1926   *90 Gower Street*

You date one of your letters incorrectly "February 21st, George Washington's Birthday". He was born, poor mutt, on the 22nd and so was another great man, not a hundred miles from here, who shall be nameless.

Diana to Duff, 9 March 1926   [*Chicago*]

Letters from you today. I don't generally get them till Friday. A roaring sad one about Ralph in Bedlam. It reads strange to me –

[228]

how does he reconcile himself with the position? I can understand loonies who think themselves sane and beg to be let out, or those who think Bedlam a sty or Valhalla, but not sane consciousness and placid acceptance. Poor poor Ralph. It was very commendable of my Duffy to go – it's the sort of thing I hate doing so terribly although haunted by conscience. Tomorrow fortnight I leave Chicago. I can't count the days or my franks yet but you won't be able to answer this – but please a few cables (night letters) saying kind of plans. I'll have to know because of luggage. Shall we go first to Paris? or not. I have no predilection – only want to be led by Dumple. I'm getting frightened of course, a little more every day. Frightened of thinking you look different. I never do recognise you. Frightened of my looking *horrible*. Frightened of Cadogans, Carlisles, Wallaces, Warrenders – who never will like Baby much because she's a queer fish and rare bird in one, and a lot too good for them, and Duffy doesn't like them all that much, but he likes fleshy pots, and they tell Duffy what a clever good pretty boy he is, and think Miss Gnome is a virago.   love love love

Duff to Diana, 11 March 1926   House of Commons

Baby darling. This I am writing in the middle of an all night sitting. It will count as today's letter, the letter of this new day – so that I shan't have to bother about you again until Friday – blast your tiny neck. I dined with Winston this evening. Only he and I and Clemmie[1] and Captain Macmillan[2] – another young Tory. I discussed our Easter plans. They were so vehemently pro Seville and anti Corsica that they quite swayed me round. We can't get to Seville by Easter Sunday which is the great day when the acolytes dance before the altar. Winston described the dance at dinner very eloquently until Clemmie interrupted with "Oh Winston, you never saw it" – which he obviously hadn't.

The only thing against Seville is the time it takes to get there. It is more than a day's journey from Madrid. I am so open minded about it all that I long to know which you would really like best. I'm afraid of deciding on what I should like least simply through thinking that you would like it best. Clemmie said she didn't think

[1] Clementine Spencer-Churchill, Baroness Spencer Churchill, 1885–1977. She married Winston Churchill in 1908.
[2] The Rt. Hon. Harold Macmillan, born 1894, Prime Minister 1957–1963. At the time he was M.P. for Stockton-on-Tees.

you would like Corsica because it is very wild and the hotel would be very simple and primitive, which is of course just what you do like, poor freak, isn't it. However the main thing will be the weather and there seems no doubt that the weather is better in Spain. She said that the smell of the syringa in April was really too strong – that got me. Oh hurry along baby.   D.

[The Spanish holiday was a great success, but things in England were not going so well. In May came the General Strike. It was a time of gnawing anxiety for everyone, especially Diana who always expected the worst. She ferried workers to and fro in her car, delivered newspapers, and brooded. One morning she asked Duff when they could decently leave the country. "Not until the massacres start" said Duff brightly, which can't have helped.

It was during 1926 and 1927 that Duff really forged his reputation as a public speaker. He spoke whenever and wherever he was asked, inside and outside his constituency. Also, whenever he could, he championed the cause of the League of Nations.

Duff and Diana spent that summer in Venice, and in September they set off with Iris for *The Miracle*'s second tour of America. Duff stayed with them for the first leg of the tour in Philadelphia, and then returned to England.]

Diana to Duff, 2 December 1926   *Kansas City*

Darling love. About Mother's motor car. I've thought it all out. I want it to be a great surprise, I want you to call her up a few days before Kikermas or after, and say "Diana has sent you a Christmas present. Will you be in if I send it round" and then send it. I'd like you please Duffy to get up early one morning and go to the Fiat, or Essex, or anything good, people in Albermarle St and effect an exchange, securing a *sedan*, or limousine like Hutchie's or one with the driver sitting outside – but compact, small, and smart; if time painted that middle rather green blue, with peacock and coronet on door. Then a chauffeur must be found by Holbrook, a non-drunk, a beginner from some country motor repair shop preferably, nice appearance, all there, and willing to do odd jobs, not grand or expensive. I would like him to live in the spare room in Gower, (not Wades') and garage the car in our garage – anyway till I return. He must have a neat chauffeur's coat and cap. Later when I return, he will look after both cars when I get my new Chrysler, and it will be useful for us to have the frequent loan of a shut car for evenings. I can well afford this, and I cannot have Mother walking, and denying herself taxis which she always is doing during a cold wet winter. It must be kept a real secret and surprise or she will obstruct the plan. I feel ashamed that I have not done it before. She has given Bognor to us and squared off Portland's[1] claim upon it, I think she has got him to write off the debt. I hope she has had the sense to make him give it *me* straight as that would obviate all death duty claims. I will write to her on this score. I would like you to see several chauffeurs, and explain to them that the most important quality they must guarantee is knowledge of parts of the car, and above this willingness for unusual jobs. *The readiness is all.* If advice is needed then ask John, but don't let him tell you she has a car at Belvoir and generally deter you. She will never use that Belvoir Renault. I know her too well its too *big* and too expensive a tax, and too big an upkeep. The chauffeur can charge her with running expenses and insurance, and future tax – but I am to pay his salary. You will know how much more to spend on the exchange. I will put another £200 at your bank for the surplus, and for your own use. See that the inside looks nice, she likes straps at the side windows, and if it's possible light coloured lining. Also somewhere a mirror and place for pencil and paper. *It's not to be a big car.* I hope this letter won't make you cross and bored, I'm enjoying it so much myself. There will be no Kansas news today, there isn't any – my time on the pillar this afternoon went in a flash thinking about the car. A Citroen is too small and toyish. God bless my Duffy and keep him safe and well and loving and his heart full of this one.   B.

Duff to Diana, 4 December 1926   *Belvoir Castle*

Today has been the loveliest day's shooting of all – bright sunshine, white frost in the morning and the reservoir which is always my favourite beat.

---

[1] William Cavendish-Bentinck, 6th Duke of Portland (1857–1943). His wife Winifred was Diana's godmother, and he had lent the Duchess the money to buy the cottage.

I wish you were here baby. Some of the ladies came out to luncheon. We found them sitting inside the cottage, waiting for us like cows. I thought that had baby been there, she would have been outside stamping and waving and roaring. Dear little baby – you're the one I love.   D.

[Between the end of *The Miracle*'s run in Kansas City and its opening in San Francisco, Diana and Iris planned a short trip to the great south-western desert. Their preparations included buying themselves some very wild and western clothes.

Raimund von Hofmannsthal now began to play an important part in their lives. The son of Hugo von Hofmannsthal, the Austrian librettist and poet, he had joined *The Miracle*'s enormous supporting cast through Kaetchen, who was to rue the day he did: for Raimund was young, good-looking, intelligent and light-hearted, and soon he, Diana and Iris were inseparable. This made Kaetchen's blood boil with jealousy.

Raimund was soon passionately in love with Diana, and – although he had no money – he was determined to join them on their south-western jaunt.]

Duff to Diana, 9 December 1926   *House of Commons Library*

Beloved Baby. I probably dated my letter yesterday the 9th instead of the 8th as I got mixed. This morning I had two more letters from you and very pleased I was with them. Letters seem to come better from Kansas City than from New York – in smaller consignments, which is so much nicer. I do not much like the sound of Mr. Hofmannsthal – It is uncanny the fascination which German Jews seem to possess for you. But there's no accounting for taste – some people like Elizabeth Bibesco. She arrived the other evening to dine with Maud very late and walked round the table kissing two or three of the gentlemen, including Willy Tyrrell. She talked very loud during dinner and shortly afterwards became unconscious. Maud turned to the butler and said "I think Her Highness has fainted – give her Highness a little brandy" to which the butler replied in a resounding whisper,

"Her Highness has had seven brandies since dinner". When she came round she wanted to play Bridge but Maud insisted on her going home. "I can't go home without Willy Tyrrell" she exclaimed, whereupon no more was seen of Tyrrell than a small cloud of dust. Eventually the unwilling Edward Marjoribanks was ordered to take her home. She slept peacefully in the car and on arrival said that she had no latch key and fell asleep again on the doorstep. After much ringing Puffin [Antony Asquith] appeared and hauled her in.

The papers here are full of the mysterious disappearance of our poor Agatha Christie. She was last seen at that beautiful spot Newlands Corner which you and I once discovered by chance. Do you remember it? She left her car there in the middle of the night and has been seen no more. Ill natured people say it is a great publicity stunt. But I saw somebody yesterday who knows her husband and swears it is genuine. She was overworked and has probably gone mad.

Diana to Duff, 9 December 1926   *Kansas*

When [Iris and I] got home there was a note for Iris from our Hofmannsthal asking her to join him any hour at the Café opposite, and to come without me. I nearly fainted concocting an explanation to the effect that there was bad news for me, and that Kaetchen had telephoned him to break it to Iris first. However far from bad news it was good. His love for me, he told her, had grown to such excess that he thought he would leave the cast. She quieted him down, and I feel that there's life in the old doggie yet.

Duffy, it's very criminal to neglect your baby for 2 days on paper. *One* letter came by this mail and seeing how I count the mails, sheets and *words* of your letters even when they are lists of guests only – you shouldn't do it. You wouldn't if you thought harder – it's my only kick and therefore *mustn't* be played and tampered with.

I love you though –   Baby.

Diana to Duff, 12 December 1926   *Train*

My beloved, I didn't write yesterday. The farewell and shows and troubles were too great. Today I don't remember where I got to.

[233]

Yesterday was hell, luggage gone. Nannie had packed and locked everything three days before for that matter. We woke worrying about Hofmannsthal who is absolutely determined to come with us. It means buying a new ticket ($75 without bed) and I know he hasn't got it – so it means borrowing from the cast probably, not repaying it and general 'in wrongness'. We settled that Iris was to give it to him from me, and he was to pay back from his salary – that didn't work because he refused. If only his skin was better, he'd be ideal – because he's very intelligent, very charming and good looking – and it makes Kaetchen and Oom mad. There is 'robbing the incubator' of course, but what of it? Bertram on the phone at nine, successful.

Then a hair wash, then a visit to the Western Equipper to get the boots, then the Theatre where I cried because the altar didn't shut. Then home, for fifteen minutes peace – destroyed by Iris putting a Kotex down placey, and the whole of the unquenchable water filling the apartment and passage – gushing water 2 inches deep in half a minute. Then late for a date with Mr and Mrs Tipple, the managers.[1] No sooner up than news that Mr Parsons[2] was below – then dinner with him, me tight from tiredness and three Tipple cocktails, talking well though querelously. Then theatre and last wrangles with Hofmannsthal, who said he'd found the money. I had to play the Nun, and afterwards thought I must die of fatigue but no rest in sight, only a supper in our room for Messers Crittenden, Harkaday Baker and Mrs Baker. A fair wow, and after that again a goodnight tipple at the Tipples, Mrs Tipple plastered and hanging on Fritz's neck. I talked very long and very well to four men about oil concessions in Oklahoma. At last at four a.m. it was over and we got to bed, only to be called a few hours later, and have a dreadful rush for the train. Iris spilt a big bottle of iodine in her bag at the last second, and packed her douche half full of water so that it leaked all the way to the station. Parsons was there with twenty magazines and Hofmannsthal wildly excited, and now it 3 p.m. and we're still in the state of Kansas – shortly getting into Colorado.

[1] Mr. and Mrs. Tipple – managers of the Ambassador Hotel, Kansas City.
[2] Mr. Parsons was a sad, rich young widower who had been very attentive to Diana during her stay in Kansas.

Diana to Duff,   *La Fonda Hotel,*
14 December 1926   *Sante Fe, New Mexico*

It was a day full of success and pleasure really, and marvels for the eye and understanding. The day woke us early with blinding sun and crisp frost and at 9.30 we started for this eighty mile drive [to Taos] with the Painter Davey[1] and the unknown boy, and Hof. A fine road, snow-covered till we dropped 1000 feet imperceptibly and got into its natural ochre colour. No houses, no villages only occasional protective coloured square huts. Snow mountains in every distance, but never towering as one is on a gigantic plateau. I was very frightened in anticipation of a canyon hairpin road ahead, and sure enough when we got to it snow and ice made us stick. Iris and I leapt out and did the rest of the pass on foot, but it really wasn't dangerous. Every hour the car stopped, and a mammoth flask was opened, mugs produced, and a good whack of 'White Lightning', a sort of corn whiskey, drunk by all. The first town you pass eighty miles from Santa Fe is Taos (no railroad to it), very film like, a hundred houses all picturesque, a movie theatre and a drug store all built round a little Plaza, with fifty horses saddled hitched to a bar outside the drug store. Every face a Mexican face, every hat and boot and waistcoat and saddle Mexican. They think a great deal about clothes – show you their new boots or buttons and ask where you got yours. Occasional Redskins, the women in white suede mocassin trousers, the gents in white and grey blankets or sheets, looking more like Tuaregs on horse-back. The curious, most remarkable thing in all this is the luxury and civilisation one comes on suddenly in complete mid-desert barbary – it's really like *l'Atlantide*.[2] We had lunch at a hotel as grand as a Long Island country club – no one in it – exquisite taste, roaring fires – 'arty' rather, marble dressing rooms, with Kotex in a silver slot machine. At lunch we were joined by a charming cultivated artist who lives there from Christmas to Christmas, and was happy as people in cloisters are happy.

We drove four miles in the car to the Indian village [Taos Pueblo] – picture enclosed – and this is the most extraordinary thing I have ever seen. Along the road to it you see a lot of them on horseback. A shy people, who keep their faces almost covered.

---

[1] Randal Davey, 1887–1964. American artist who lived and worked in New Mexico.
[2] A novel by Pierre Benoit, 1886–1962.

Pueblo Indians they are. There are two big blocks like this picture with surrounding kraals for cattle and a wall and a church battered by American guns, but indestructibly mud-built and all this was built *eight hundred* years ago Duffy. There are no stairs to the different floors only those ladders outside. So it's beautiful to see them all climbing about their house and walking on different heights. About five hundred live in each block and it's the most unexploited thing imaginable, not a petrol depot, not a shop, not a road, and these funny shy people all shut away and turning their faces if you pass them. I looked into one open door, and saw a heap of very tidy and beautiful rugs as bed, and a huge picture of Christ – in whom they take no interest, and are prepared to tolerate while continuing with fire and snake rites.

The place looks very like Bethlehem to me and is almost as deserted looking as the picture, and the colour of a jersey cow.

Tea we had with a strange rich woman[1] in a beautiful house in Taos – not much better than the peasants' – but beautiful and filled with local art, and Louis XV furniture, good paintings of the Degas school – staggering? She'd been married four times – the last husband, an ordinary blanket Indian.[2] No conversation but "Ugh", his recreation playing pool. In this warm elegant room, sipping fragrant tea and eating French jams we found Brett, Lord Esher's daughter[3] – stone deaf with a trumpet. Middle-aged, fat but rabbit-faced, she lives twenty miles away in a house stark alone, no servant. She had come down while the snow lasted, because the road even on a horse was impassable to the house five miles away where she goes every other day for milk. She was perfectly happy, and wants never to leave. She goes once a week to Taos for provisions, and I suppose sees it like London and Paris and New York. She nearly collapsed when she heard Iris & I were on the stage.

---

[1] Mabel Dodge Luhan, 1879–1962, author. It was she who wrote to D. H. Lawrence and persuaded him to come to Taos, which he did in 1922, and again in 1924, described in her book *Lorenzo in Taos*.

[2] Antonio Luhan, who married Mabel Dodge in 1923.

[3] The Hon. Dorothy Brett, 1883–1977. A painter and daughter of the 2nd Viscount Esher, she came with D. H. Lawrence and his wife Frieda to Taos in 1924, and lived the rest of her life there.

Duff to Diana, 15 December 1926   *Buck's Club*

I had to speak to Lady Cunyngham's Canvassers this morning. Do you remember when I spoke there about eighteen months ago. You came with me and I jawed about the Geneva Protocol. Today my subject was the "Meaning of Toryism". I gave them very much the same stuff as I handed out to the Ladies' Carlton Club about three weeks ago. Damned good it was.

Mrs Christie has turned up at Harrogate.

Diana to Duff, 19 December 1926   *Chandler, Arizona*

My dear dear love. It is so beautiful here. I miss you so much. We ordered saddle horses and a guide and at twelve we started off for the desert two miles distant. It was divinely warm – the loveliest English May-day – not a breath of wind – glimmering light. The birds – so rare in America – singing loudly, lambs already born. Eagles – big red flowers, that I regret to say turn to Castor Oil, and this heavenly roadless limitless desert, covered with a low grey-green shrub planted into a firm yellow sand that makes one's horses feather-footed. Queer cactuses, in obscene shapes – phallic – erect themselves every few hundred yards, a canary green colour. Our guide was a cowboy philosopher of forty, with a irresistible southern poetic voice and rugged wistful face brimming with laughter. He's been a guide for 25 years all over the States and has picked Arizona to live in as the ideal. He told us stories of Indians and superstitions, and birds and plants and romances, and other cowboys, all the way, and through all the lunch which we took with us and ate in the desert. I never enjoyed a ride so much – the horse was a knockout – stirrups right. We could be so happy here though I don't see when or how, unless one of us gets consumption. There's a lovely golf course and a new one being built. The shops round the hotel are like those at Cannes. One drinks tumblers of grape-fruit juice.

Diana to Duff, 20 December 1926   *Chandler, Arizona*

Such a lovely day after a solid health-giving sleep in hammocks on the balcony – our boy swinging us to sleep. The day dawned as beautiful as a dream, and was not clouded by a bill for one night

[237]

figuring $105. We got on our horses and rode through desert and rough mountains of rock and cactus and sand and sun. At three we stopped and had a delicious meal of steaks grilled on a little fire of *mosquite* wood that gave it an extraordinary flavour – our guide regaling us the while with stories and meandering comments. One feels so well there, I'll send you snaps when they are developed. Then into a motor car and back to Phoenix, and into a train that shot us out at a junction called Barstow at four a.m. But the hours from one a.m. to three were charmingly spent listening to my Rosenkavalier's[1] declaration of love. Enjoyed it *imenzely*. He looked so sad and pretty in the faint light reflected from the snow outside into the dark of the berth – I don't mean by that he was sleeping with me – only sitting on the edge.

The day went very slowly – thro' monstrous country dead flat – cultivated – colourless Calif. We arrived cruelly late about ten p.m. and to my great surprise had an hour's ride in a glorified ferry across what looked at night the most beautiful bay, with an effect of light never before seen; like minute spangles all over the hills. The sky was moonlit but covered with fleecy white clouds and in the middle these clouds were broken into the shape of tremendous eagle, actually as distinct as that – ink black and covering half the sky. Very beautiful – my child lover breathing passion into my ear completed the beauty of it all.

I was fearful of bad news in payment for this happy week, and feared a face of doom from Kaetchen on arrival. The black face was sure enough, green-tinged from raging furious jealousy over the child-lover. We had a bad scene with him over it but it ended well enough, and he left us to sleep in our very grand apartment in the hotel, but since he's gone I've worked myself up at the way he never thinks of our *pleasure*. It's 12 o'clock now, and if he'd thought of anything but himself he'd have arranged a delectable little supper for our arrival with Reinhardt and got some hootch and some flowers as a surprise, instead of only pressing us into dreary hungry beds so that he may sprawl across them and have no competitor.   B.

---

[1] Raimund's father wrote the libretto of *Der Rosenkavalier*.

Diana to Duff, 23 December 1926   Fairmont Hotel, San Francisco

I expect it was due to a hang over, anyway we've just finished the worst row ever known with Kaetchen. He'll lose my love, and get fear and deceit in exchange if he goes on so. My young squire is the trouble and why him more than others I do not know unless it's an Austrian jealousy. But I'm in advance of the day. It began with our Noel Coward on the telephone speaking from our hotel. He is on the edge of a nervous breakdown, and to avoid it is here for two days on his way to China and Sarawak.[1] His play in America was a ghastly failure[2] but he's written a new one since. He had his minion along but he sails alone.[3] A rehearsal of principals and permanent cast at one. At four it was over and we were to rest and eat and go through some notes with Kaetchen before 7.30 when the next rehearsal began. My poor Rosenkavalier looked out of the dirty crowd so longingly, so humbly, that I said "come along and eat with us", upon which there was a scene with Kaetchen as never before. He refused to eat with us and was pretty rude on the sidewalk, making himself ridiculous in front of the boy and Reinhardt. So Iris and I had a bite with him, and came home after and sat awhile talking when our door bell suddenly rang and thinking it might be Kommer repentant we rushed the boy into the cupboard. It happened to be Noel – in a black bugger's dressing-gown – and the boy was smuggled out thinking it to be because of another lover – delightfully Mozartian. We rang up Kommer – both of us separately and could get nothing from him but "I'm through, I'm through" a fixed resolve to break all friendship and efface himself. We had been so guiltless and even if guilty what claim has he to tyrannise? His case is that originally he asked us not to take Hofmannsthal up – well, what of it? You would not ask such a thing.

I said I would not go to rehearsal, but weakened and went because poor Iris was in such a weak state of nerves. There was the Cat, half the size and black and suicidal. We had to eat with Reinhardt after. I was blackmailed into it by Kaetchen although I

---

[1] Nöel Coward never got as far as China. He was suffering from exhaustion and overwork and was too ill to go further than Honolulu, where he spent a month convalescing.

[2] *This Was a Man*, a comedy that played for a short time in New York – or possibly *The Vortex*, which had not had the same ecstatic reception in Chicago as it had had in N.Y.

[3] Jack Wilson, who had given up stockbroking to become Nöel's manager in the autumn of 1925.

pleaded a headache and great exhaustion. The dreary *parti carré* was over at last. K's brain didn't function and I was feeling physically sick with grief and rage, and by trickery we got him into our home-going motor, forced him to our room and by swallowing a whale of pride forced him to have it out. The having it out started at twelve and finished at three a.m. and now at last he has gone, a heap of repentance and shame. He says blood gushes into his brain and he does not know what he is saying or doing when jealousy grips him. It's shocking – I've told him to pray to his God. He says we both hate him subconsciously – perhaps we do – I hope not.

It's next morning. The sun is marvellous but O it's cold. Good morning, did you have a good night?   B.

Duff to Diana, 24 December 1926   *Belvoir Castle*

Sweetest and softest heart. The car has just arrived and I have just been down to the front door to look at it. I think it perfectly charming – an excellent colour, the crest beautifully done, very nice and comfortable inside with everything as you directed. I wonder what your Mother will think of it – She seems quite well today – up and about. It has cost £386 in all which includes the chauffeur's livery. Very smart and pretty he looks in it. It is really a wonderful present, and I think it wonderful of Holbrook and me to have got it here on the tick. They allow £200 for the Fiat so I have written a cheque for £186.

There is not much news here today. The chief event last night was the serving of cocktails in large quantities before dinner – which marks an epoch in the history of Belvoir Castle.

Diana to Duff, 24 December 1926   *Fairmont Hotel, San Francisco*

I've enjoyed my Christmas Eve. I can't deny it. It has been devoted to buying Christmas presents in Chinatown – which in this city isn't the slums but equivalent to Oxford Street. Needless to say I bought too many unpackable and useless things for myself and not enough for others because I *hate* to loosen up for others. We lunched, Iris, Raimund and me, in a Chinese restaurant off Chop Sueys and returned to our shopping after.

Reinhardt had been speaking all yesterday of a Chinese gong he was going to buy but couldn't afford at a famous *antiquaire*'s here. He wanted it to start his plays with in Salzburg. So Kommer and Iris and I bought it between us with the additional help of Mr. Gumps, the character *antiquaire* who took $100 off if we'd include his name. Its a very beautiful gong, chased, and may be 500 years old – you ring it from beneath and it reverberates uncannily for perhaps five minutes.

We dined with Noel Coward and his paramour in Reinhardt's room – he was dining out, and we had the gong set up, and laughed a lot rehearsing, and with false alarms to get it rung as he walked into the room. It was a great success. He was childishly pleased, said '*fabelhaft*', and '*herrlich*' and '*grossartig*' about a million times and then settled down to a too serious talk about me undertaking a theatre in London.

Everyone but me got excited about it, Volmöller in chief. It is not to be repertory or permanent at first. Kahn is to supply the money, as offered – Kaetchen to manage it. Reinhardt will produce whenever suitable. I will act sometimes. We are to secure regardless of expense the best plays – Shaw, Barrie, Lonsdale – it's policy is to be not too highbrow and not commercial. It sounds fun and I liked it when they called me *Frau director* but I showed very moderate enthusiasm and disappointed them all. We could start off with *The Miracle* perhaps in small edition. Reinhardt thinks I'm theatrically inspired, only I fear because I suggested Iris playing a paralysed girl, instead of an inexperienced Jew playing the lame beggar in the 1st act. I've bought a beautiful Chinese cat for Morris Gest and he has sent me three pairs of Chinese silk pyjamas. I shall put one aside for my child-lover and now for sleep to forget Belvoir and you for a minute, my blessed heart. This is the *fourth* Kikermas.   Baby.

Duff to Diana, Christmas Day 1926   *Belvoir Castle*

This morning after Church the car came round to the door and was admired by all. It really is a great success and reflects lasting credit on Holbrook and me. I sent a note early to your Mummie – saying "Diana has sent you a present from America which I have to give to you – so let me know at what time you will receive it and wrap up warm because it has to be given you out of doors". She said she would come down at 1 o'clock and swears she never

[241]

guessed what it was – feared it might be an animal – thought it was probably a fur coat which looked better out of doors. At one o'clock everybody was assembled to see her receive it. She walked out with me through the porter's lodge. When she realised what it was she was quite overcome, and could only press my arm very tight and bow her head to hide her tears. She was so delighted. John suggested that we should go for a turn round the terrace in it which eased the situation. Everything in it is perfect I think.

[Always hypersensitive and unstable, Sybil Hart-Davis had been suffering since November from a nervous illness that subjected her to sleepless nights and nightmarish days. Having finally sunk into an exhausted coma, she died in a nursing home in London on January the 3rd, 1927. She was forty years old.]

Duff to Diana, 3 January 1927   *90 Gower Street*

My darling – I came up from Wilton this morning and my first information was that Sybil was a little better. After luncheon I went round to the home in Queen Anne Street where she is and learnt that she was more worse. There is in fact no longer any hope. Richard [Hart-Davis] was sobbing. He took me up to her room. I was inexpressibly shocked by her appearance – shrunken and withered like an old woman. The sight of the two children[1] sitting one each side of the bed where they had been sitting all night, holding her hands and Rupert whispering to her and kissing her all the time was heartbreaking. I have never seen anything so lovely as his devotion. She was practically unconscious and breathing with difficulty. I stayed there for an hour or two then came away. Risien Russell the doctor said she might last all night. I shall go back later. It is all very painful and terrible.

I had some lovely letters from you this morning about New Mexico, Grand Canyon and Arizona. I think I should like Phoenix – but oh baby I do wish you'd come back. I just can't get on without you.   D.

---

[1] Rupert and Deidre Hart-Davis.

My darling loveliest heart – After writing to you last afternoon I went back to the home where I learned that Sybil was sinking. I didn't go up to the room again. I dined alone at the Garrick and heard on the telephone after dinner that she was dead. I can't pretend to be very unhappy. She was my favourite sister when I was a child, but for the last fifteen years she has meant very little to me. It is sad for the children. She somehow brought them up well, and they adored her. Rupert was so pathetic and so beautiful through it all yesterday. Deirdre is at the Ozanne's[1] in Paris now. We shall have to try to help her later. She is very pretty. The funeral is not until Friday.

One news straight comes huddling on another of death, and death, and death.

I have just heard that Ambrose McEvoy is dead. Pneumonia. Ellen Terry on the other hand, who was reported to be dying yesterday, is very much better.

Good bye now dear love – Keep safe.   D.

Duff to Diana, 6 January 1927   *White's*

Oyster – how are you? do you still love me best?

Are you a staunch Tory or have you become a bloody little Bolshie? Are you stamping and roaring, as you should, or wailing and whining as you shouldn't? And when, please, are you coming home?

Diana to Duff,   *Fairmont Hotel*
6 or 7 January 1927   *San Francisco*

Octavian[2] is too much for me. Last night he begged to be allowed to sit an hour in the sitting-room. I told him he'd best go to bed, and that I must go to sleep – he begged so hard that I let him. I woke an hour or so later to see his silhouette against the open door – I did not stir or acknowledge his watching but in the end fell asleep again. Next waking when the window showed dawn – there

---

[1] Marie, Alice and Lydie Ozanne ran a finishing school in Paris. Marie Ozanne was a close friend of Sybil's.

[2] i.e. Raimund von Hofmannsthal. Octavian is the hero of *Der Rosenkavalier*.

[243]

he still stood. I chased him then but he must have stood there about five hours. He's romantic, and I feel old and ridiculously ashamed. This morning was given over to reporters and an artist, and at two the boy and I went and hired a drive-yourself Chrysler roadster, and drove over the ferry into hills and woods. I found a letter on my return from Mr. Roy Pike, asking me to go out with him alone; I couldn't face that and so pressed George Moore into my service.

The boy laughed at the two old gentleman calling at the stage door – they didn't look that old to me.

Duff to Diana, 8 January 1927   *Cliveden, Taplow*

My darling. I dined last night with Clare Tennyson[1] in Gloucester Place. I arrived first. She was looking as pretty as be damned. I never saw her lovelier. She at once entreated me not to mention the fact that 'her old friend Jimmy Beck' as she called him was coming to dinner. As there were five other guests the precaution seemed hardly worth while. Maud Russell looking very middle-aged, Buffles looking like an ox and Sheila looking like a cow[2] – Beck and another American called Cox completed the party. Beck is quite a pleasant nice-looking fellow but seems to possess no unusual quality. Clare was very much *la femme delaissée* – apologising for the wine (which was quite good) saying she had had to buy it herself and knew nothing of such things. She is much worried poor little creature – Lionel has the detectives on her all the time, and Edward Grey of Fallodon is continually giving her lectures down the telephone.

I had three lovely letters from you this morning – you pretty, silly little girl. All about first days in San Francisco and your quarrel with Kaetchen and the lovers – old and young. I wonder how much I should mind if you really loved one of them. I wonder if you do. Don't tell me if you do – I'm with Othello on *pioners and all.*[3] I have no love to agitate you with – this year. Betty is still just

[1] Clare Tennyson, 1896–1960; née Tennant, she first married Capt. William Bethell in 1915, and then the Hon. Lionel Tennyson in 1918. They were divorced in 1928 when she married the American James Beck.
[2] See page 158.
[3] "I had been happy, if the general camp
    Pioners and all, had tasted her sweet body,
    So I had nothing known." (Act III sc. iii.)

[244]

a little provoking when I see her but I never think of her when I don't. The other moos[1] are all scattered and there is not one new one in the herd. Dollie in India, Mollie[2] and Biddy in the freezing North – poor Daisy dead for all I know. Poppy sleeping peacefully in the arms of Prince George.[3] I must to pastures new and see what's grazing there. Good night dear love, dear only love, sweet heart.   D.

Diana to Duff, 8 January 1927   *Fairmont Hotel, San Francisco*

Dear dear Duffy. I went this morning with George Moore to order 'chaps' as a present. We took Willie Tevis – a man I knew under Moore's Lancaster Gate roof and the only rather attractive man here. He looks like a bugger, talks like one, and is the greatest living bucking bronco rider that ever was. He was the sort of Lord Chesterfield adviser on western dress. Unfortunately I hated what was chosen – sort of black and white calf skin – but the belt inset with Spanish coins is good. Iris is back, and Pinchot arrived looking more beautiful than anything I had ever seen. She is to go down to Reinhardt tomorrow, and would cut us out root and branch I should think.

Today came some absolutely charming letters from you – about Christmas, and the motor and the children's presents. I read them with such pleasure. We must have come out well at Belvoir. Your presents sounded too lovely. I felt it was a shame you had no children, and that I ought to do more about it. I'm so sorry Duffy. Perhaps I'll pull a Sarah[4] yet. I love you all the more though so please be careful. Good-bye you dear little pumpkin.   Baby.

Diana to Duff, 13 January 1927   *Fairmont Hotel, San Francisco*

You are as bad as Kaetchen about my young page and I'm so attached to him. I live in a constant terror that Kaetchen will

---

[1] While having quite ordinary names, Diana pointed out that all the women Duff admired sounded collectively like a herd of cows: Betty, Biddy, Mollie, Poppy, Daisy etc. – she therefore referred to them as the moo-cows.

[2] Vreda Esther Mary, née Lascelles, b. 1894. Married the 8th Duke of Buccleuch.

[3] Prince George – born in 1902, he was the fourth son of George V and Queen Mary. Created Duke of Kent in 1934. He died in a plane crash on active service in 1942.

[4] Genesis, XVII, 15–19. Sarah was 90 when Isaac was born.

discover how much we have him round – he fulfils all the Kat's meanest duties, like turning the bath on or taking my shoes off – not speaking but only sitting when we sleep. It's quite a hard training for any young man, and great practice for restraint and continence, so it will do him no harm. Sweet love of youth, I should be actually with you in eight weeks. I'm so much happier than I was last year, so it will go quickly. San Francisco has only three days left – it's gone in a flash. God keep my Duffy safe is my only prayer.   B.

Duff to Diana, 14 January 1927   *90 Gower Street*

Poppy [Baring] is very thick with Prince George and there is talk of marriage. I hope it comes off. She says she couldn't bear the Royal Family. I said it wasn't much worse than other families, and that she wouldn't have to be on slap bottom terms with Queen Mary or King George. She doesn't like the Prince [of Wales] – I suppose he has been trying to put Prince George off her. The latter is really very nice and rocks with laughter at the jokes about his family which Poppy never stops making, and which rather shock my loyal nature.

Duff to Diana, 16 January 1927   *90 Gower Street*

Sweetest and Best. I had arranged last night to go to *Broadway* with Victor and Bridget [Paget]. Victor had undertaken to get another girl but no girl could he get – so we were three. I had a snack at the Garrick on my way to the theatre. During my hasty meal I sat next a man whom I thought charming. He was humble and shy. We discovered that we had both been in America and discussed that country. Because he was humble I became patronising – and when I left I casually asked the head waiter who the gentleman was I had been sitting next to – "Mr. P. G. Wodehouse". I wished I had been nicer.

Diana to Duff, 24 January 1927   *The Garden of Alla, Hollywood*

We drove for a full hour before we came to our destination in Hollywood through endless miles of these ridiculous little villas &

now we are still on the edge of this loathsome Hollywood. The bungalow that we occupy I'm bound to say is terribly charming. It's a tiny white-washed village of the Spanish-Moorish style, with tiny streets of detached two and three room houses. One can almost get lost walking in it – it has fountains, a swimming pool and arcades and white outdoor staircases, and at night it's entrancing. The inside is decorated faultlessly – palest pink washes and funny printed linens.

Diana to Duff, 24 January 1927   *The Garden of Alla*

O Duffy I feel so sunk. I'm so glad you didn't come here. I joined them after lunch in a big bungalow, not half as attractive as ours, and went with them to Marion Davies's studio – Metro-Goldwyn. The studios are a little surprising – very grand exteriors like an entrance to a dock-yard or lunatic asylum might be – with *port-cochères* only opened for the bosses, and tremendous red-tape permits to be signed often. Marion Davies has a bungalow built in the middle of all the sets and offices, just called a dressing room but it's as good as a church with the infallible Spanish gothic touch of Mr. W. R. Hearst.[1] We are all to dine with her tonight at her home. The depressing grizzly light in the studio – the snail's pace that outwears any patience – gave me a great horror of the picture profession. I drove with Bertram to look for the sea and sunset. Found it at last in a part of Hollywood another eight miles further on called Venice, Calif., the consummation of which by sea or quake is devoutly to be wished. The beautiful Pacific had lost all charm – only the sky was left and very good it was – though it could do nothing for my sad spirit. Now I must dress and my clothes have worn out on me. I hate these common blondes. Morris Gest is already togged up for the nonce, and asking me rather sweetly if I think he'll do. He is wearing his big tie and an extremely high-waisted velvet jacket tied tightly above the stumack with a black tape. He says "We all wear this in Russia, Di dear." God bless you from your miserable Baby.

---

[1] Marion Davies, 1900–1961, and W. R. Hearst, 1863–1951, had a long-standing love affair.

Duff to Diana, 26 January 1927   *Midland Hotel, Manchester*

Darling little girl. I had a grim awakening this morning at seven, was called for by a constitutent at eight and driven down to Oldham where I was conducted over a mill. All the processes and functions of the machinery which have been explained to me so often and which I never understand were explained to me once more. It was very trying. I did nothing all the afternoon – read and wrote and this evening I gave a lecture at the Oldham Cooperative Literary Society entitled *A Justification of the British Empire*. It was rather fun because my audience was composed of all the Bolshies, the socialist intellgentsia of Oldham. They spoke, several of them, afterwards and attacked what I had said and then I replied. A few of my own supporters had turned up too, and occasionally interrupted on my behalf. My supporters were far poorer and worse dressed than the other side.

Do you remember hearing about Mrs. Jagger, a woman who used, I believe, to say horrible things about you during the elections. She was there and made a very feeble malignant speech. She and her husband are quite the most revolting couple to look at I ever saw. It is remarkable how ugly one's political opponents usually are. I can hardly suppose it is God's punishment on them – but it is very queer. The very nice man to whom I sat next at the Chamber of Trade dinner last night does sincerely believe that the present condition of the Liberal Party is God's punishment on them for disestablishing the Welsh Church. It is a good thing to go among the Socialists occasionally – if only because it makes one love one's own party better – like going abroad. The propaganda also may be of some use – two or three of them said to me on the way out, "We're socialists but we're for you." Goodnight little rosebud.   D.

Duff to Diana, 28 January 1927   *90 Gower Street*

My darling – The social last night was everything that one expects a social to be. However it was soon over – and then I caught the midnight train and arrived here safely this morning. I found Rupert here. He is extremely nice – still terribly broken with misery but very simple and unaffected about it as people who are really unhappy usually are. He had for instance been to a play last night to try to take his mind off his sorrow. I personally think that the sooner he goes back to Oxford the better, as he does nothing here but brood and see and talk to people who were friends of Sybil. Lily Gilliat[1] has got very much on his nerves by excessive kindness. He loved your letter and is surprised that Iris hasn't written, so urge her to if it isn't too late. I don't think it is.

Richard is apparently in a worse state than he is – devoured by remorse – going to spiritualists to try to get into touch and all the rest of it. Rupert is remarkably sensible about all that – saying, "Let him do it if it gives him any comfort" – and refreshingly sceptical about the nonsense himself. He is very reasonable and really sees that in many ways it is for the best – altho' he doesn't quite say so – but he feels terribly lonely, poor boy, because he is just too young still to have made any great friends or formed any interests outside the family. Do you know that he and Sybil wrote to each other every single day while he was at Eton? Goodnight Cowbaby.   D.

Duff to Diana, 29 January 1927   *90 Gower Street*

The great news was that Prince George had been to his parents and told them he wanted to marry Poppy. They had taken it quite wonderfully and raised hardly any objection – whether it will come off or not remains doubtful. Freda says with truth that if he sticks to it firmly they can't stop it. Rosemary [Ednam] said to Poppy "Lengthen your skirts and stop making up your lips and you'll win the King – and lose Prince George". It is all rather amusing.

Diana to Duff, 30 January 1927   *The Garden of Alla*

Your letters are an extasy to me these days. Nicer than they've ever been – more loving, and jealous of the boy. The latter sleeps in corners and shadows of 'the Garden' and knows all our comings and goings. The other inhabitants must think the garden is haunted – he whistles different tunes and signals at his likes and dislikes as they pass.

I love being called 'poor bee' but it's so pathetic. Good-night my dear dear love – no one else means a breath to me.   D.

---

[1] Born Lilian Chetwynd, she was first married to the 5th Marquess of Anglesey, 1875–1905. She married John Francis Gilliat in 1909.

Nun again in the evening and not a drop to drink. Some Russian refugees called and stung me into buying a hideous Russian dress – but I ordered a riding shirt, in natural flannel with the name of a fairy Russian horse embroidered round the collar with advice not to stumble. So that's a little excitement. Not that there isn't enough excitement with my grouchy men but it's never pleasurable – always anxious.

The boy called at the end of the show to take me to the Schildkraut house where Reinhardt and Iris and Pinchot had dined. I had settled that I would not go as Kommer had said he would not and Bertram had gone to bed with a promise from me to wake him for a bite of supper when I came in. The boy said K. was going after all, so pressed by many Germans of the cast who wanted lifts I went. There was old Schildkraut, the former Emperor – who I love, and his jay of a son, and animated daughter-in-law and old Mama Schildkraut, fat housefrau, who had made the uneatable *strudel* and no Kommer – I stayed an hour, drank two glasses of sherry which curiously enough made me rather tight and came home with Iris and the boy.

Then the fun began. I told Bertram through his window that I couldn't have supper as I'd had to go to the party. I found a message from K. to call him up on coming in, did so to find him furious and wretched. Why had I gone to the party? because of the boy he supposed. I explained and placated and soothed and buttered him, complained of having Bertram on my hands etc. Next, that over, Bert rings up from next villa to tell me to lower my voice when telephoning, and that he didn't know before many things he'd just learnt. I tore round to him frenzied, and uncertain of how much I had said to K. on the telly. Had to admit that the boy was at that moment in the cottage waiting for me which made things no better. During the scene I heard the boy leave the garden with the tread of the disillusioned. What a night – I wasn't born for this.

I was born to be held safely in Duffy's arms, and be soothed and comforted and loved – and then to get up on sunny morning and take the winding road with him and lie sleeping in tall grass under summer trees in old countries – with an occasional visit with him to California wilds. I was born to see Duffy become great, and to treasure and never lose his love. Pray for all this –   Baby.

Here I am, sweet love. I meant to go away by the four o'clock this afternoon but was overpersuaded. The Casa Maurys,[1] Freda, Mike and Bridget [Paget] want me to go to the play with them this evening and I have given in. I am thrown into the position of Bridget's gink which is not an exhilarating one – for me or her, tho' I like the old girl well enough.

There is a marvellous story going the rounds. Victor sold some furs to old Polignac. Frieda's sister Mrs. Blew-Jones happened to be coming to Paris so it was arranged that she should take the furs. She went round to Polignac's house at eleven in the morning. She was asked by the servant at the door whether she was the lady who was expected. She said she was and was immediately shown into a large room where she was greeted by the old Princess[2] in a dressing gown and *top boots*. On a sofa in another part of the room she saw Violet Trefusis[3] and another woman, both stark naked locked in a peculiar embrace. She ran from the room in terror. It sounds incredible, may be exaggerated but can't be quite invented.

We went on to a bad Spanish place and then to a bad Russian place and finally to that cheery old nigger place where we have been before. 'Florence's' I think it is called. Everybody was depressed and cross except me. I was perfect. When we left there the taxi asked an exorbitant fare. Sidney told him to go and get the police. Taking him at his word the taxi driver disappeared. Sidney and Betty got inside – and Fred Cripps – who had joined us meanwhile – leapt on the box and drove off the taxi. When we got to the top of the hill – (I was standing on the side board) we all got off – but were immediately arrested by a posse of police and taken off to the police station, where Fred was charged with attempting to steal a taxi. It was really rather unpleasant for a moment until I said that I was a *député* [M.P.] – and Sidney too. This produced an extraordinary and instantaneous effect on the police. They immediately implored us to go away but insisted on keeping Fred

---

[1] Pedro (Bobby) Marquis of Casa Maury and his wife. They were later divorced, and in 1937 he married Freda Dudley-Ward.
[2] Winaretta, Princesse Edmond de Polignac. The twentieth century's most generous and discerning patron of music and musicians.
[3] Violet Trefusis met Princess Edmond de Polignac through her husband Denys Trefusis, who was part of the Princess' musical circle.

who had first described himself as *banquier*[1] and then seeing the effect of *député* had said he was also *Colonel*[2] – *Colonel et banquier* they didn't believe. However after some argument he got away, and then we all had to go to the Royale to discuss it over a final bottle. The result was that I didn't get to bed till five and woke at nine. Nobody seemed to want to lunch with me today so I lunched here with some of the Embassy boys and have been jawing, playing chess and drinking ever since. I'm not in very good shape baby – but I feel better now I've written to you. I'm reading *The Conqueror* which you liked so much and which disappoints me.   D.

Duff to Diana, 8 February 1927   *White's*

Sweet, dear, beautiful baby. I began to write to you in the Travellers at Paris before luncheon this morning but was interrupted by gentlemen who insisted on cocktails – so I never finished the letter. Last night I dined at the Casa Maurys – Freda and Bridget made us five. Poppy was the subject of conversation. The Prince had telephoned to Freda from London in the afternoon saying he was afraid it was all off. Unfavourable reports about poor Poppy appear to have reached His Majesty's ears. Her worst enemy has been that vile old Revelstoke[3] – who apparently has an old grudge against her father. So the girl's sunk. We went on to the *Habit Vert* – an excellent old play revived – I enjoyed it and laughed heartily. Michael joined us after the play and we went on to the latest Paris place called Le Grand Écart. It was very crowded and very hot – not a yard of space to dance and forty couples dancing. We roared at each other for an hour or so and it wasn't too bad – but I was glad to be in bed by two.

Diana to Duff,

Shrine Civil Auditorium,
25 February 1927   *Los Angeles*

I've been naughty and cross again Duffy, and I'm so sorry, though I was a little justified. You see Pinchie came today to the matinée she and the boy went and sat in my vision in the front row, and

---

[1] Fred Cripps was a partner of Boulton Brothers, dealing with the Russian end of their business.
[2] He was appointed Colonel of the Royal Buckinghamshire Hussars in August 1917.
[3] John, 2nd Baron Revelstoke, 1863–1929. Maurice Baring's eldest brother.

Pinchie had bought two extremely funny monkeys on sticks, and she jumped them up and down relentlessly, and got me laughing on my cross, shaking and sweating till I was so hysterical that I had to scream for a flag and then the nun who brought it wouldn't put it right in front to cover me, so I swore at her still shaking, and then she was so stupid she took it away – so I had to yell again and at last she concealed me and I told them to go and stop the monkey tricks, and by that time I was so cross I couldn't get my face purified and I acted badly – so I came off a flood of invective and beat poor Pinch up, and she nearly cried, and I said *"va t'en"* to the boy – *"je ne veux plus te voir"* and he left the theatre, and has not shown up since and I'm just a pulp of remorse. One shouldn't do that with children, Duffy, should one, and it's two a.m. now, and he hasn't gone home and it's quite likely he has left the city and will lose his job. I feel extremely unhappy. So I'll go to sleep if I can and forget what a bad baby I am. I shall hear your voice on the telephone in a day or two. It's too exciting. I bless this inventive age.   Diana.

Diana to Duff, 1 March 1927   *The Garden of Alla*

I've just come home from a party where some woman of the Metro-Goldwyn Studio, in fact the leading scenario writer – said I must play Anna Karenina. The arrangements were made, dresses, sets and all, and Greta Garbo was being temperamental and wouldn't sign her contract. It luckily won't come to anything – I'm sure – but if it did I should I suppose have to stay another five weeks they say – assuming the salary was tempting enough. I hate the idea though, besides I don't see how I'm to get out of Dortmund on April 14th. I wish I knew when Easter was.

I lunched today with Elinor Glyn.[1] She's unbelievably confident and horrible, her face looks like a *maquillage* that's been through a long Albert Hall orgy. She had three exquisitely beautiful young men with her, one of whom was an Austrian 6 foot 6er. Iris pinched him, took him off riding and hasn't been heard of since. Baklanova, a leading Russian actress, played the Nun tonight. Gest had been awful to Iris and me – "Imagine how the

---

[1] Elinor Glyn, novelist. Her books were very successful, particularly the novel *Three Weeks* which dealt with her idyll with Lord Curzon.

part could be played by a real actress, dear. I mean you don't kid yourselves, do you?" She made a fair mess of it, like all the Russians do at pantomime. She looked pretty but had the step of the steam roller.   Poor Bee

[Diana returned to England alone. Iris had decided to stay on in America with her six-foot-sixer, an Austrian called Friedrich Ledebur. They were married in 1934.

The next stop for *The Miracle* was Dortmund. Rosamond Pinchot was to have played the Nun, but at the last moment she broke her ankle. There were no understudies, and Diana had to take on both parts, twice a day, for a week. It put a terrible strain on her health and she was half-dead with exhaustion at the end of it. In spite of a two-week rest in London, she was not well as the show progressed through Prague, Budapest, and Vienna.

It was a *tour de force* that marked the end of Diana's *Miracle* days, although there was talk of a film, and a much less lavish production did tour England in 1932 and '33. Diana was the Madonna, and Tilly Losch was the Nun. Diana had done a great deal for *The Miracle*, and in turn it had done well for her. It had seen Duff into Parliament, provided their capital, and survived long enough for the three-year-old John Julius to see it. "Is that *real* Mummy?" he asked, looking at a statue bathed in greenish light that did indeed bear a striking resemblance to his mother.

Early in 1928, Duff and Diana were on holiday in North Africa when Duff received a letter from the Prime Minister, Stanley Baldwin, asking him to take up the post of Financial Secretary to the War Office. Duff was delighted at having achieved ministerial rank, although there were several disadvantages to being a junior minister. He was not allowed to speak or ask questions in the House except on matters that concerned his own department, nor to augment his income with any other work. He did however continue with his public speaking, which was unpaid.

Their London life was relieved by weekends at the cottage near Bognor, which had been enlarged and embellished by the Duchess. In early spring they went to the

South of France. Duff returned early to prepare for the
annual Army and Air Force Bill on April 17th.]

Duff to Diana, 15 April 1928   *The Travellers, Paris*

My darling. Here I am after a fairly comfortable journey. Bobbety
and I had to share a double berth. Knowing that it was impossible
to find out from him which he liked best, and that if I insisted on
his choosing he would take the one he liked least, I took the one I
liked best which is the upper one – and slept well. We dined with
Evelyn and Helen,[1] and had quite a cheerful dinner. The train was
of course two hours late which in conjunction with the change to
Summer time resulted in my arriving here only just in time for
luncheon. I lunched alone chez Voisin, reading *The Times* and
having a very good meal.

I am going out tonight with your friend Lady Carlisle. I didn't
tell you this before as it was very doubtful and I knew you would
rag me so if it didn't come off. I had said that I should be passing
through today and she had said that she might be – and I found a
letter here to say that she was. But I think you know how very little
you need worry about her. I am really sorry she is coming as I shall
find her terribly difficult to talk to for a whole evening – and it
would have been as pleasant and much cheaper to have dined with
Keith Trevor[2] whom I have just seen.

Darling. I cannot forgive myself for my two mad nights at
Cannes.[3] I go on and on regretting and regretting, and building
castles based on how differently I might have behaved. I meant so
firmly to do nothing of the kind and seem to have done it so
insanely without ever giving a thought to any of my resolutions. I
feel it is so humiliating and so vile to you who are always so good
and wise about money. At thirty-eight one really ought to know
better, and what makes it the more maddening is that I was so sure
that I did – and on the first evenings when the other boys lost I was
patting myself on the back for my wisdom. The only consolation
can be found in the theory of the even distribution of fortune. I

---

[1] The Hon. Evelyn Fitzgerald, 1874–1946. In 1923 he married Helen, daughter of
Lieut. Gen. C. W. Drury. She was the sister of Lady Beaverbrook.
[2] Major Keith Trevor, M.C., who was married to Lady Juliet Duff from 1919 to 1926.
[3] Diana wrote in her autobiography: "One night he made a fool of himself at a casino. I
do not remember the occasion, let alone the loss, but the reformed gambler wrote like a
shamefaced child."

have so much that some setbacks must be looked for – and in comparison with the other larger things in life – love – health – work etc – money certainly matters least. Also any loss makes one appreciate more what one has, and this loss – which has worried me perhaps more than it ought to have and spoilt my holiday – has made me realise more than ever – if it were possible – how much I love you, how much I depend upon you and how in any trouble I turn to you as a lost child looks for Nanny.

Be careful, my darling baby, and be happy. Come home soon but no sooner than you want to – and know that I am yours utterly, utterly so long as this machine etc.   D.

Duff to Diana, 16 April 1928

My darling. I am writing this in the train with the "eversharp" you gave me on paper bought at the Gare du Nord. I may not be able to write tomorrow as I foresee a hectic morning at the War Office preparing for a long night at the House of Commons.

Yesterday evening was not a conspicuous success. We dined too late to go to a play or revue. Dined at the Café de Paris. As I expected, conversation was a labour. She doesn't try – doesn't seem to. There were pauses, long ones – during which I thought of you and envied your lovers for I am sure you always help them. Yet I ought to be easier to talk to than Tommy MacD.[1] After dinner we moved rapidly from place to place as "Shall we go on somewhere else" was always something to say – Fischer's which was shut, the Blue Room which ought to have been, the Fétiche – full of sad Sapphists – the Dédé bar, full of cheery buggers – finally to Florence – club sandwiches and beer. Lady Carlisle is a poor conversationalist – but so, I begin to be afraid, am I. The difficulty of small talk increases with the years. But at least she is not coquettish like our Betty to whom during this last visit I am afraid I have taken a positive dislike. We went for a walk in the garden that last morning while you were bathing. I was not – as you may remember – feeling too good, and when she said the same thing for the tenth time with an air of discovery I could have shrieked – and nearly did.

---

[1] Captain Tommy McDougal, an admirer whom Diana called 'Captain McDougal-de-doo'.

Diana to Duff, 18 April 1928   *Château de la Garoupe,*[1]
                                        Antibes (A.M.)

My darling Duffy – I've got my first letter from you, & it's such a lovely one that I cried over it. You mustn't worry about that silly loss, only worry about your weakness, and that will strengthen by the lapse. Dear good Duffy. It was naughty not to tell me about Biddy – when you lie you encourage me to [worry], and also I can't trust you at other times. If there is nothing in the Biddy thing, why not tell me outright about a Paris date. If there's nothing in it you bet she thinks there is and is crowing. Still you must do as you like because you're a good boy and because I do love you, almost whatever you do.

[At the end of the year Sidney Herbert invited Diana to join him for a winter holiday in the Bahamas, and she accepted. This was strange, since she and Duff had not spent Christmas together for five years. But Sidney was very anxious that she should come – not only because he wanted her company, but because he needed a chaperone for his long-beloved Betty Cranborne, who was going to join them out there. Although she hated leaving Duff, she accepted out of loyalty to Sidney, then felt guilty about Duff, then thought the whole thing would be a waste of time. The truth was that the years of travel and excitement had become a habit; without them, she was restless.]

Duff to Diana, 19 December 1928   *House of Commons*

So, my darling beloved baby, you are gone, passport and all. We had a hectic moment on the platform yesterday morning when your train hove out of, and Vera into sight with the little green bag in her hands. Everybody suggested something different. Your Mother helped us with two valuable suggestions – one, that the little bag ought to be wrapped up in paper – two, that the Prime Minister should be asked to telegraph to Mr. Coolidge.

I felt very lonely and cold all night and so did Major. Luncheon today at Bucks with Ivor Churchill and a game of chess and here I

---

[1] The house of Florence McLaren, who had inherited it from her mother.

am. I miss you terribly, baby, every other minute. Nothing is fun without you – not even the crossword. The Prime Minister came up to me last night, and asked me to go to Paris to make a speech to some society or other which exists there explaining the ideals or ideas of the Conservative Party. Ramsay Macdonald has done it for the Labour Party and they wanted someone 'of equal standing' from each party. I pointed out that I wasn't of 'equal standing' but he said that didn't matter – and he added that he wanted me to get known abroad and get well in to what he called the Geneva world. So I said I would go. It is to be sometime in February – a Monday. Let me know as soon as you can even provisionally give a date for your return.   D.

Duff to Diana, 24 December 1928   *Belvoir Castle*

My little darling. Christmas Eve is just turning into Christmas Day, and I am missing you more than usual which is impossible and therefore nonsense. It has been a lovely day and we have had capital shooting – a damp, sweet-smelling, cloudy, warm day. Mildred, Betty and some of the children came out to luncheon. At dinner I sat next to your Mother and talked to her all the time. She told the story of how her engagement to Fife had been announced [presumably in *The Times*?] whereupon Uncle Harry stated that, as everybody knew, Fife's grandfather was a butler. This coarse and crude statement upset your Mummie terribly but whether she felt it more for my sake or for Nixon's[1] I cannot say.

I send you a telegram from Raymond and Tommy, and also Lord Beaverbrook's article on Mona[2] – I think the whole thing very disgusting. Poor Mona was a person not only utterly unimportant, but also very disreputable. Because Max knew her he thinks it right to give a leading column on the front page of the *Sunday Express* to writing up her death.[3] The fact that he is still further degrading his dirty newspaper doesn't matter very much; nor does it matter much more that he is insulting his public by thrusting down their throats his own sentimental twaddle about a

[1] The Belvoir butler.
[2] Mona Dunn, daughter of Sir James Dunn, the financier. In 1925 she had married Lt. Col. E. H. Tattersall, D.S.O. She was 26 years old when she died.
[3] The *Sunday Express*, December 23rd. The personal tribute by Lord Beaverbrook described her as "a genius", and that "she had not left a single enemy or critic behind her – and of how many people of genius can that be said?"

dead friend; but what does matter is that he is doing it from the best motives, and honestly thinks that Mona can have no prouder monument than a leading column in the *Sunday Express*. The thought that he would, out of the goodness of his heart, do the same for any one of his friends adds surely a new terror to death.

Good night, my baby, and a merry Kickermas, and oh I do wish you were in the next room and we were hanging up the stockings again.   D.

Diana to Duff, 6 January 1929   The Royal Victoria Hotel, Nassau

Sunday today – and my tooth a torment. The Slazengers, (Michael's girl's mother, a delightful woman) took us in a boat to an uninhabited island beach where one could bathe naked. It was a funny arrangement because fond as I am of it, it's not worth the labour of segregating the sexes, but it was done and Mrs S. and the daughter and I were left on one coral beach and the men were taken round the point and deposited on another. Cissy Slaz. had a good tall Augustus John figure and the daughter, a dream of beauty, had surprise breasts to the knee. I would have fought bathing nude at any price in her place but she seemed unconscious. There was a big chocolate poodle and a big black poodle, and a quantity of butterflies unfrightened by human beings and fluttering very slowly around and settling on one's knee. There was a lazy turtle in the sea, and an occasional darting flying fish. Photographs were taken of nudes and poodles. *Vie Parisienne* effect. We sailed back to lunch on Fitz's yacht and ate an excellent feast of fish-chowder in a tub, it laid us out as beach-combers for the afternoon. In the evening we went off to Dr. Dolly's new Arabian Nights home that the Dr. is building with his own hand where the super *élite* of the Island were gathered together for a turtle meal. When a turtle is caught the turtle cook is sent for to the house, like the undertaker. We started with marvellous turtle soup, from that to the freshest most amazingly cooked little mushrooms with a firm cream upon them. Next the turtle herself in her own hot shell and a little roof of pastry. The best food there is, I think. There were interminable pauses – the room was tiny and I saw the boys sweating and feeling as I did on the verge of passing out. Still we ate. Next a froth of coconut ice – so young that the coconuts are still unformed, served with a cake of flyaway nuts and a compote of comquats. Then a lovely Roquefort and celery, and then in a wide platter the prettiest reddest most flavoured English strawberries. It was a culinary masterpiece, and Mrs. Dolly's in the old days was the pig-sty of the community.

Everything is nearly spoilt by my tooth, and I never sleep at nights. Curse Mitchell Thompson. [the dentist]

loving Baby.

Duff to Diana, 24 January 1929   *House of Commons*

My darling – I am much annoyed. I spent the greater part of Saturday afternoon and Sunday morning and afternoon preparing the great oration I was to deliver in Paris. I raked up old Turquet, the man who used to teach French at Scoones and asked him to translate it for I had resolved on the bold project of delivering it in French – and now the whole thing is off. It is a lesson never to take trouble about anything. The Prime Minister and his secretariat between them bungled it. They had apparently consulted Tyrrell,[1] after the P.M. had asked me, and Tyrrell had said he was very much against the whole thing. They never let me know and so having told the P.M. I would go I naturally accepted the invitation when it arrived. What is more I put off going to Paris last week because I should be going later and now I shan't be able to go at all because the only excuse I can make is ill health. It is really a shame.

I came back by the midnight train, and on arriving this morning I was met by the blow that Holbrook is ill with bronchitis. It is dreadful how dependent I am on him. I could hardly get dressed and how I shall manage to go away to shoot tomorrow I don't know.

I feel tired, I have got a headache, I am cross – but I do love you –   D.

Diana to Duff, 24 January 1929   *The New Colonial, Nassau*

O Mr Dumple. I do so want to go away. It seems such waste really. I don't feel too well, that's about the size of it, and I get worried over it. My affairs are late and last time they only lasted

<hr>

[1] Sir William Tyrrell – see p. 214.

two days instead of seven, and my tummy aches, and I'm frightened that what's wrong inside me is maybe getting acutely worse.
Perhaps I'm with child – it might be from the signs, toothache is a
great symptom. Also sudden stopping of poorly time – but I don't
think it this time. I meant not to put all that bit in because I know,
my darling, to have a child is a greater desire of yours than it is of
mine but somehow everything comes out when I start telling you
anything. Nobody will think the child anything but a Herbert.
Especially Freda and Betty.

We had a quiet pleasant day yesterday – looking at the fish
hiding under coral trees thro' the glass boat and later being left on
a deserted beach to bathe and picnic and read, just Sid, Bet and I.
In the evening a dinner party at The Old Fort – very beautiful
spectacle, full moon and open patio dancing. Flit is greatly
featured – it makes me so homesick for a sun cure with you. "Flit
me please," you hear smart women saying to the waiters at dinner.
A fortnight tomorrow I sail towards you, hip hip huraah. I will
never be more pleased to come home. It's *waste*. I'm not making
money, not keeping up American relations, just being *unselfish*.

Diana to Duff, 28 January 1929   *The New Colonial, Nassau*

Today is my last day. I'm so so glad – only never say so I should
hate Sidney to hear anything to destroy his belief that it has been
heaven for all. It has been too in a way but then I'm homesick.

Sidney has his Bett, and seems very fond, and very amused by
her – calls her little Alice in Wonderland. Then poor baby fussies a
bit about her health. Her tummy pain is thank God almost well
but her affairs still lag. A fortnight late now and she's sure it's
climate or something wrong and not a baby because it never is a
baby. And if it is a baby it may be a nigger, because everybody
who went even for a trip to the West Indies have nigger descen-
dants for ever, and don't tell me the Victorian wives did funny
things with niggy wiggs so it must be the climate and air that
produces the wool and the ebony. It's a blowy day so that I begin
to fear my crossing tomorrow – it's a cockle boat about sixty tons,
once a yacht, and infested with lice. I shall sleep on deck on the
mattress I've bought for Bognor. I feel ill and nervy. I want to get
home, I want to get home.

O my darling little boy – what heaven it will really be to be by
you.   Baby.

[261]

Duff to Diana, 30 January 1929   *Hôtel Majestic, Harrogate*

Oh baby, you can 'ave 'Arrogate – you certainly can. I saw Kakoo off to Belvoir and travelled by a luncheon train hither and arrived about half past two. I strolled out to see the beauties of the town and have been walking round it for an hour. I never saw such a place for ugliness, gloom and squalor. And of course all the book shops – the only ones I wanted – shut because it's Wednesday. And I must confess to you a terrible ignorance, the greater because I have been here to speak once before – I always thought that Harrogate was by the sea. On going out I nearly asked the porter the nearest way to the sea front, but fortunately there was a map in the hall and I had a look at that first.

This hotel is the largest I have ever seen in England, with vast reception rooms and huge fires burning in all of them, and not, so far as I can see, a single other guest. It makes me quite self-conscious – I see the page boys and porters nudging each other when I appear – "Here he comes, *the* guest, poor mut". However I remind myself that I am being paid £25 for my lecture tonight – the first time I have ever been paid for speaking in England – and that is some consolation. A band has started playing – quite a big band, and still I am the only audience. It's really very queer.

Oh dear, it isn't five yet and I can't dine before seven – but I shall dine at seven and have a glass of champagne – perhaps two – my lecture is at 8. Tomorrow I have to leave early as I've got to speak at a luncheon at Liverpool and again in the evening. And I've only got a few more pages of Drinkwater's *Life of Fox* to read. It is tiresomely written but there are a lot of things in it I didn't know and am glad to know. Good bye, my pretty baby.   D.

Diana to Duff, 29 January 1929   *The New Colonial, Nassau*

I can't go to sleep Duffy for worrying about my inside. If it is a baby it must be 7 weeks old by now, and I feel enormous – if it isn't then something has got worse. I'll have to face an operation. O dear, I wish you were holding me.   B.

Duff to Diana, 30 January 1929   *Hotel Majestic, Harrogate*

I will write to you for the second time today – Baby darling – as a treat, to make up for one of the days I've missed and also because it's only 9.30 and I've nothing else to do. I had a good dinner – I drank a bottle of cham. not because I wanted it but because they hadn't got any Imperial Pints – and after a drop of brandy to aid digestion I strolled up to the Hall which is just outside the garden of the hotel. It was a little alarming because the atmosphere of the gentlemen who were receiving me was not the grovelling politeness to which one is accustomed. You see they were paying me so they hadn't got to be polite. The Chairman explained that he would introduce me, then he would leave the platform where I should be alone, that I must speak for at least an hour and that then I mustn't sit down but step off – or as it happened step back behind the curtain. So that instead of *crash* at the end of the speech it was *swish*. I was quite satisfied with my speech – and it lasted the full hour – and the moment it was over they gave me a cheque for £25 which seemed to me very easy earned. No boring speeches of thanks nor nothing – and back here by half past nine. I wonder what lecturers can make in this country. Together with journalism I should think I could make enough to keep us both warm and fed and drunk.

The hotel remains as vast and mysterious as ever. There was one other couple in the dining room at dinner. She looked like a rather hard Belgian tart and he looked like a young man from Oldham pretending he had come from Manchester. We had a huge band and hundreds of waiters.

My God – the band has started playing again, and I was just wondering whether I oughtn't to go up because I thought they wanted to put the lights out. Two speeches to make tomorrow and not a penny payment for either. There is something economically unsound in the fact that for one speech I should by paid £25.0.0. and for a hundred speeches I should be paid £0.0s.0d. If I'm beaten at the election I shall give up politics and speak only for money. Goodnight – squashy   D.

Diana to Duff, 30 January 1929   *Everglades Club, Palm Beach*

My beloved Duff I've made that naughty sea which was curiously enough calmer than oil and have got to Palm Beach. I've spent the afternoon prinking up, hair, skin, shoes etc but I look so hideous, it's discouraging – besides I lost, or rather had stolen $200 Sidney had pressed on me before starting, and that discourages too. I've dined at a spread of Vincent's and Ethel's sat next Roddy and Joe Harriman. I left them at the gambling hell and have come home feeling really so odd I think I must be with child, or is it my nerves? They will make anything for me. Betty said a blue vein on the chest was the only real sign – so I've just rubbed my poor chest till its raw to get the anti-sunburn off, and sure enough there is one. I feel so frightened and so disinclined for such things – Fancy me Mrs. Stubbs – at our time of life[1] – and yet sometimes peculiarly *exalté*. I have never felt quite this sensation since the day after I lost my virginity in your arms at Lympne.[2] I remember so well that nervous, unhappy and elated feeling – desirous too, and extremely conscious of sex. It is so naughty of me to raise your hopes when it may all be my giant nerves and my obedient imagination.

I'll never get to sleep tonight alone in this ridiculous bungalow – I've been walking up and down it for three quarters of an hour in this hysterical state. I've never needed you more to tell me it is wonderful, and that of course you'll see I get a Caesarian.   loving loving loving Baby.

---

[1] *Fancy me and Mrs Stubbs*
  Joining all the ladies' clubs
  Fancy us forsaking the pubs
  At our time of life.
[2] They spent their wedding night at Philip Sassoon's house at Lympne, Kent.

1929–1931

1929–1932

[Diana found, to her delight and even greater apprehension, that she was indeed pregnant. On the fifteenth of September, 1929, she gave birth to her only son, John Julius. He was born by caesarian section – a fact commemorated by the latter half of his name. From now on Duff and Diana are together, and their letters are written when Diana is abroad with friends, or with John Julius in his school holidays.

In the general election of May 1929, Duff lost his seat at Oldham. He took this opportunity to abandon politics for a while and to concentrate on another of his ambitions – to write a biography of Talleyrand. The book came out in October 1932, and was received with great enthusiasm. Taken seriously as a work of history, and read with pleasure as a biography, the book is a credit to Talleyrand and to Duff: it brings out the best in both of them.

Early in 1931 the safest Tory seat in the country – St. George's Division of Westminster – was looking for a new candidate, though there were two reasons why those looking for a Tory seat were not keen to champion it. The first was that the official candidate would have to support Baldwin, who was very unpopular at the time for being such an ineffective Opposition Leader. The second was that Lords Rothermere and Beaverbrook were vehemently anti-Baldwin, and were going to fight the official candidate with all the power of the press. Duff took up the challenge, won after a short, fierce fight, and was very happy to find himself once more in the House of Commons.

That summer, Duff was called back from Venice where he and Diana were on holiday: a letter from Baldwin, who was now Lord President of Ramsay MacDonald's first National Cabinet, offered him the job of Financial Secretary to the War Office. Diana stayed on in Venice, as the guest of the fabulously wealthy American hostess, Mrs. Laura Corrigan.]

Diana to Duff, 29 August 1931　　　　　　　*Grand Hotel, Venice*

My beloved Duffy. It's my birthday and you are not with me. Your letter brought me more joy than I can tell you. You seldom say serious things to me and when you do and they are tender and truly loving, it disolves me. I have missed you I cannot tell you how much – have felt miserable and terribly nervous and determined to leave and yet I'm still here and it's Saturday already.

Now about you – I was a little disappointed that it was War Office. I suppose it's the same job or is it what was Geordie's[1] in your day? Anyway, now I think it's very good because there aren't so many billets this time, and as Lord Crewe[2] is in the House of Lords it means, does it? that you have all the House of Commons work.

I long for a letter telling me more and saying if you are pleased. I am dreadfully in the dark. They are all good to this poor baby. Chips and Hubert[3] particularly. The weather is lovely – not too hot but sunny. There is too much drinking, and I think I have found "just the thing" for next year – a three roomed flat on Granders [the Grand Canal] belonging to Landsberg.[4] I love you my beloved.　　D.

Diana to Duff, 31 August 1931　　　　　　*Polazzo Mocenigo, Venice*

Darling Love. I do want to come home – the purposelessness is obsessing me. Today has been most characteristic – Everybody on

---

[1] Lt. Col. the Rt. Hon. Sir George Frederick Stanley, 1872–1938, 6th son of 16th Earl of Derby. He was Financial Secretary to the War Office 1921–22.

[2] Robert Crewe-Milnes, the 1st Marquess of Crewe, 1858–1945. Secretary of State for India, 1910–15, Ambassador to Paris, 1922–8. He had been Minister for War for a few months before the 1931 General Election.

[3] Hubert Duggan, 1904–1943, M.P. for Acton, Middlesex, since 1931, son of Mrs. Alfred Duggan, who became the second wife of Lord Curzon.

[4] Bertie Landsberg, an Argentine, who also owned the Villa Malcontenta.

the beach told Jane[1] her gala was ghastly – badly organised – raté –
with the result that when the dear English congratulated and
praised her she broke into a flood of tears. Mason's heart has gone
wrong and he's lying in the Grand and I go and see him twice
daily. Tonight I dined with Mrs Toulmin and Elsa [Maxwell][2] in
a very pretty palace next door to Helen's.[3] 50 couverts.

1 September Clare cried on the balcony. Jimmy Beck took a bad fall
at the Gondola landing – unfortunately – not in the water. The
whole of our Palace and the servants were kept awake by yells,
sobs, screams from the Beck room. At one moment it was thought
we ought to interfere. All the noise and hysteria was on Clare's
side and the cause was straight jealousy – isn't it unbelievable.
That paunched horror. They kept it up till six and poor Clare was
heard to say "how can I face them all tomorrow, I know they've
heard everything." Christopher of Greece and wife[4] arrive at the
Moncenigo today. Mrs. Corrigan is in a frenzy of thrill. She
bought a huge new bed for Victor Cazalet, a dog, pillows or cousans
as she calls them and 50 'scrap-baskets'. At all hours of the day
new scrapbaskets arrive. I'm writing this on the beach and it's
impossible. But it's never impossible to say I love you, not even if I
were on a grid like St Lawrence, or without a tongue or in hell
itself.   B.

Diana to Duff, 1 September 1931   *Palazzo Mocenigo*

My darling. I'm sitting on my balcony (Byron's) and it's seven
a.m. and a faultless sky above and nothing much on the canal and
it's altogether intolerable to my eyes because you are not breathing it with me. Kaetchen has just telephoned from Munich and I
have arranged to meet him Sunday or Monday with or without
Iris. I don't know where, maybe Cortina. Chips will take me that

---

[1] Jane, Princess di San Faustino, an American. She was one of the great hostesses of
Venice.
[2] Elsa Maxwell, 1883–1963. International party-giver and socialite.
[3] Lady Helen D'Abernon, daughter of the 1st Earl of Feversham who married the 1st
Viscount D'Abernon, 1857–1941, in 1890.
[4] Prince Christopher of Greece. The sixth son of King George I of Greece, brother of
King Constantine, and uncle of Prince Philip, the Duke of Edinburgh. In 1929 he had
married his second wife, Princess Françoise of France.

far. You will be sorry to hear that he has become my inseparable, follows me like a little dog and is a great solace and an excellent fellow laugher. We get absolutely hysterical over things, la Corrigan first and then Victor Cazelet. He told us a story last night, (V. did) the clue of which was that one couldn't possibly not say something about one's gloves, when shaking hands with some one ungloved. He said he'd never heard of anyone who didn't, when Chips expostulated. To which he replied that one could of course waive it with men, but with Ladies!! Chips appealed to me and I couldn't speak for *fou-rire*. Mrs. Corrigan of course is the best mirth provoker. The scrap-baskets still arrive – a spate of them. She went to meet the Christophers of Greece yesterday, and curtseyed on both knees. She took a retinue of men guests and footmen and gondoliers. She said "But sir, where are the servants?" – "We have none," they answered. It was sad as the house had been turned upside down to lodge them as befitted their service rank. She couldn't help but exclaim, "but why, mam, I have 2 bodymaids, and Mr Corrigan never crossed the Atlantic without 2 bodymen." Christopher has become a tall thin bald professor-like type with idiomatic colloquial English; up to date coarsness like, "If you don't mind, I should call that 'balls'." Everybody pretends they have birthdays since mine.[1] Colin[2] pulled it yesterday, and got a shagreen pull-out watch. The Weymouths[3] gave him at dinner an inkstand made of shell on which they had written, "this ink-well" (it was very small) "should just fit your old man" – also an imitation human turd on which they wrote "a piece of shit from 2 shits to another shit". These were read aloud at dinner and the turd passed round to the 14 diners, and then you have the cheek to tell me fashions don't change. The Beck fracas has been going on hot and strong. Jimmy lunched with his first wife and daughter yesterday and some think this was the cause of Clare's hysteria. She cried again during lunch at the Taverna – Jimmy came back in the evening waving two

[1] When Mrs. Corrigan discovered it was her birthday, she gave Diana a diamond clip that fell into the canal as she was leaning over a balcony.
[2] Colin Davidson. He wore a patch over one eye, which had been spiked out by a cactus in Spain.
[3] Henry Frederick Thynne, Viscount Weymouth and later 6th Marquess of Bath. He married Daphne, daughter of 4th Baron Vivian, in 1927 – now better known as the biographer Daphne Fielding.

photographs of himself and daughter smothered in pigeons. He'd already got them framed in collapsible Venetian leather and was bucking round. Clare seemed so happy at dinner, smiling and singing and we thought all was well – but she had another bit of a cry on the Piazza because Jimmy didn't want to go home and she did. She won but when we got in an hour later he was still up not with her, and he stayed playing the piano another hour. So by now she may have murdered him or him her. At five a.m. a diver went in after baby's diamonds. I *do* hope he finds them.

The canal is filling up – the gondoliers are all coming out and tending their boats. An English tourist has just passed with a shooting-stick across his knees – very incongruous. I hope all will be well.   love from Baby.

Diana to Duff, 6 September 1931   *Palazzo Mocenigo, Venice*

My darling Duffy. I missed writing to you yesterday – because I was in my typical fancy dress frenzy from dawn till eve. I was also turned out of my Byron bedroom and put in the dressing room so as to allow forty people to dine in it. There were two tables of forty, everyone in white. A Cartier bag prize for the Ladies, and links for the lucky man. I went big, Duffy, the dress (Ghost of Byron's Glamour for the Levant) was greatly admired both by the artists, represented by Lifar,[1] Oliver[2] and Madame Sert[3] also by my old lover Charles de Polignac[4] and by my new ones Chips, Hubert and Francesco Mendelssohn. Pata[5] looked *lovely* and asked after you. Hubert did a terrific pounce when the others had gone to bed, but the party had no *entrain* – there are complaints of it on the beach this morning. The funnier complaint is one that is going round the bars this morning where the hangoverees were having hairs of dogs. They put their headaches all down to too many tuberoses.

---

[1] Serge Lifar, 1905–1954, dancer and choreographer with the Diaghilev Ballet Company, and Diaghilev's lover and biographer
[2] Oliver Messel, 1904–1978, theatrical designer.
[3] Misia Sert, 1872–1950. Born Misia Godebski, she was loved by Renoir, Bonnard, and Toulouse Lautrec among others; as Diaghilev's closest confidante and adviser, her biographers describe her as 'the *éminence rose* of the Ballet Russe'. José Sert, the painter, was her third husband.
[4] Comte Charles de Polignac – born 1884.
[5] Pata – the American wife of Charles de Polignac.

Kaetchen arrived this morning. Very nice mood and we shall start Tuesday or Wednesday via Germany. Why does Eden get the Foreign Office under sec. ship? I saw red, maybe unnecessarily, and Billy Gore[1] as Post Master General irritates – pretty picture in the *Mail* of Mr Dimple M.P. Max I see is out again with a new photograph minus the impish smile.

I love my Duffy more than all the world beside.   D.

Duff to Diana, 27 November 1931   *House of Commons*

My darling – I had just finished writing to you yesterday when I was seized by Gilbert [Russell] with renewed invitations to Blickling. I eventually said we would go there for two days shooting on the 28th and 29th of December. This would mean leaving Belvoir the Sunday after Christmas. I thought we might be glad of the excuse. Hutchy is to be there.

Luncheon at Emerald's was much better than usual. Round the table were Lord Crewe, Clemmie, Valentine [Castlerosse], Randolph [Churchill], Mrs. Ralph Glyn, Bob Boothby,[2] myself, Sheila,[3] Ralph Glyn.[4] The last named is the Prime Minister's p.p.s. and Maud never ceased abusing the P.M. "Of course we all hope we'll get rid of that dreadful Ramsay MacDonald as soon as possible." In the afternoon I went to that tea at St. George's Hospital. They were pathetically pleased at my going. It was the first time that the Member for St. George's had ever been to the hospital. Lord Greville[5] seemed to be the moving spirit. We met him, though I had forgotten it, at Oldham. I rather let you in for helping them with their flag day.

The baby was divine this morning. When we went to the gramophone he said pointing to each record in turn "I don't like that one". I said "You silly little boy, you don't like any of them

---

[1] William George Ormsby Gore, later 4th Baron Harlech. He was Postmaster General in 1931.
[2] Lord Boothby, author and politician, b. 1900.
[3] Sheila divorced Lord Loughborough in 1928 and married Sir John Milbanke, 11th Bart.
[4] Parliamentary Private Secretary to the Prime Minister, 1931–35.
[5] 3rd Baron Greville, 1871–1952.

and you don't know which is which". He then pointed to one and said "I like that one". While I was putting it on, he added "I like Boo again". To my astonishment, for I didn't even know there was such a record, it proved to be *Blue Again*. How does he do it?

There's a division now – so I must stop – sudden. I do miss you.   D.

1932–1950

[In 1932 *The Miracle* was revived, produced by C. B. Cochran (who was also responsible for its first production with Max Reinhardt in 1911). The costumes were by Oliver Messel. The production opened at the Lyceum in London, toured the country, and finished at the Golders Green Hippodrome in January 1933.]

Diana to Duff, 25 March 1932   *90 Gower Street*
[Duff was on a short trip
to the South of France.]

My darling Duffy. I have worked my silly self up. Black cats walk across the rehearsing stage, and all the actors shriek with superstitious apprehension. I'm so frightened that some harm may befall you. It is 11.15 and I've just come home, promising myself the treat of writing you this letter at *your* comfortable writing table. I light my way into your room and find it all decked in white, not for Eastertide, like the cherry tree, but for the sweep. I rush to my own library and find it dressed for the same nonce. The baby increased my apprehensions by informing Mother that "Papa *will* come back. I *know* he will, in a few days" – My blood ran cold!

Duff to Diana, 22 February 1933   *House of Commons*

Beautiful baby. This is my birthday. My forty third. Only one person in the word remembered it – that was your faithful Cat who sent me a telegram from the Western hemisphere – "May you live

[277]

long" he wrote "and brilliantly, star of three stars, one wife, one son, one book – Kaetchen" which proves that in telegraphese he is rapidly approaching the Bertram standard. At 43 Napoleon was starting on the campaign to Moscow – more behind him than I have – but very little in front. At the same age Talleyrand was a discredited and penniless exile – and Shakespeare was thinking of retiring to Stratford – I could give you more forty threes but the Westminster Housing Association are waiting for an interview. So goodnight, my beautiful baby, good-night.

I have got two men experts to stick the book plates into the books at 2/- an hour. Isn't that cheap?   D.

[In January 1935, Diana set off for Brazil, as the guest of Lord Beaverbrook.]

Diana to Duff, 17 January 1935   *Paris*

My beloved. It was awful seeing the last of you – but since then I've been quite calm and resigned and almost cheerful.

Max settles one's gestures even. One is parked or activated to order – very relieving – so Valentine [Castlerosse][1] and I found ourselves seated opposite Max and Walen[2] and from Victoria to Dover. I sat fascinated by listening to Max going through his household bills. How unlike me and Miss Towler.

"What's this? 3 doz eggs, 1 doz eggs, a further 2 doz eggs. Will you tell me what the hell I keep a chicken farm for? Tell the staff for the hundredth time that they are not to take Mrs Campbell's[3] orders. Tell the Leatherhead Gas people I'm not going to pay 10d a therm for my gas – the gas is not worth that money. Tell them Ld Beaverbrook is very unsatisfied with their rates. Mrs Campbell's telephone calls are not to be charged to me, and Max[4] is not to charge me up with calls to that black bastard bitch". Walen has to shorthand every word. It gives you no idea how funny it was, and

---

[1] See p. 178.
[2] Lord Beaverbrook's secretary.
[3] The Hon. Mrs. Campbell – Janet, daughter of Beaverbrook by his second wife. She married Ian Douglas Campbell, later 11th Duke of Argyll, in 1927 and they were divorced in 1934.
[4] Max Aitken – eldest son of Lord Beaverbrook, b. 1910.

the tinyness of the items queried. "What are Canadian Tabs, Walen. I'm not going to be charged 1/3 for Canadian Tabs whatever they are." They were calendar refills. "I will *not* have the bidets repaired until they have been estimated for". The joy of it all was that the books are always 'up' every month, just like mine. It was very rough on the Channel, we had a bottle of cham. and then I sat on the deck talking to Nancy Astor about you – and she gave me love messages for Max and said that she could never forget how good he'd been to her, and I asked why, and with tears in her eyes she said "Bobby".[1]

We're drawing in now. I'll write from my Wagon-Lit but I thought I must write you a word of love from Paris and tell you that it's only you I love in the whole world – nothing else and if you were with me now I'd be in heaven. God bless you my dear dear –   love Baby.

Duff to Diana, 22 January 1935   *Treasury Chambers, Whitehall*

My darling – It seems a very long time since you went away – but little has happened. I miss you terribly and I think the baby does too. He loved your letters, and enjoyed being shown on the map where you had gone to and were going to. He is very nice and I see a good deal of him. The French woman[2] has started to come again. I played 'lotto' with him on Sunday – a game she teaches him – and I was surprised to find how much French he knew. I don't want him to go to Eastwell[3] for more than a fortnight as he learns nothing while he's there. He's a good little boy – and so am I.

This has been a very busy day. I went off to Greenwich at 9.30 to lecture to a lot of Admirals, which I didn't enjoy – but I liked seeing over it afterwards – the uniform Nelson was wearing when he was killed and lots of very touching Nelson relics – I think you would have cried. Then I had lunch with the Chief Admiral in his lovely house looking over the river. Since then I have received a deputation and attended a Cabinet Committee and in a few

[1] Robert Gould Shaw, Lady Astor's son by her first marriage, who had been imprisoned in 1931 for homosexuality. Lord Beaverbrook suppressed reports of the trial in his newspapers.
[2] Mlle. Perrier-Gentil, who had started teaching French to the five-year-old John Julius three days a week.
[3] Eastwell Manor, near Melton Mowbray, then occupied by his grandmother the Duchess.

minutes I have got to go to a meeting of the Constituency Executive. You will know long before you get this the result of Randolph's by-election[1] which is a topic of some amusement. He never consulted Winston who is not best pleased. I have bet Cardie[2] £5 to £10 that the Socialist gets in. I gather from this morning's issue that the *Express* is going to guy Randolph. He seems to have made a most offensive speech coupling the Prime Minister's name with Lady Londonderry's.[3]

Diana to Duff, 22 January 1935

Conversation was on what the plans are to be. I am very adverse to going to B.A., [Buenos Aires] it takes three days each way, but I said nothing. At one o'clock the bar – for buckets of tomato juice – lunch up again on deck, but Max can't stand it for more than half an hour. "Damned cold up here, isn't it?" just because of a cloud. So he goes back to his stuffy little cabin, and the sun comes out again. No endurance for anything.

I stayed up reading – not unhappy – rather longing for a Radio,[4] but curiously calm.

At five we go to a film about Frederick the Great. Jean Norton's grovel is alarming. They talk a good deal – when discussing plans about air-routes, they are all recorded in the *South American Handbook*. Sometimes I'm asked what I think. I say, it doesn't affect me in any way as I'm not flying myself. They argue on the old safety statistics line. Walen comes in with the Daventry[5] news bulletin, which seems only to record air disasters. I say to Jean later that I will not be blamed for them not taking a plane to where they want to go. I made it clear from the day I was invited that I am happy to be left in Rio, but that I would not be bullied or shown up as a drag. She quite seriously begged me to allow it. Max doesn't the least want to fly – is very frightened of it, but *must* be allowed to say it's my fault that they don't soar over the Andes. If only they would go. I should be bird. I'd go and stay with

---

[1] Randolph Churchill, 1911–1968; journalist, author and politician. He had independently challenged the Tory candidate for Wavertree, and as a result the Tory vote was split and the Labour candidate won, to the rage of the Tory party.

[2] Lionel 'Cardie' Montagu, youngest brother of Edwin Montagu.

[3] *The Daily Express* called Randolph Churchill 'The Fat Boy of Wavertree'. He had made a speech in which he said that those in power in the Conservative Party spent too much time at social events in London. Lady Londonderry's 'political' parties were famous.

[4] i.e. a radiotelegram.

[5] The BBC short wave transmitter.

strangers in *estancias*, or get someone nice to let me down a gorge, three days' trek away, to find an orchid or butterfly.

It was funny tonight. Jean told me Val was writing his auto-biography. I asked him about it when he came to see me resting in my cabin before dinner. He said it was a novel, and he'd written 8000 words and not to tell Max. I asked to read it. No no it isn't sufficiently developed. At dinner it crops up. Max's eyes glint. "Send for my secretary." Walen comes to the table. "Have you been typing Lord Castlerosse's book? What's it like? Is it any good? When I get up from dinner I want you to bring that typescript up to me, and you'll read it aloud to us." Very good. "Can Walen read aloud?" I said. "Like hell he can – the worst in the world." Well it was done – in the open bar. Walen spluttered through it to us jeerers. It was pretty bad too. "Not worth a damn, is it?" – Val never winced.

Diana to Duff, 22 January 1935

Val, F. Owen[1] and I retire ultimately to Val's fine cabin and drink beer and talk the day over. We agreed tonight that Max is not enjoying himself – but the warm weather (now postponed by the stewards for another two days) may improve things. Jean said to Val, "Do you know that I'm almost beginning to believe that Max when he's not trying is capable of being almost a bore." Val shook and laughed till the tears ran down his cheeks.

[Duff remained a junior minister from 1931 to 1935. During this time he also accepted a commission to write the official biography of Field Marshal Earl Haig. He was correcting the final proofs of the second volume, when he was promoted to the cabinet as Secretary of State for War, in November 1935.

The Spanish Civil War began on July 16th, 1936, when the Spanish Generals and the army they controlled mar-ched into Madrid. The cause of the war was the general election of February, which brought the left wing coalition

---

[1] Frank Owen, 1905–1979. Journalist, author, and editor of the *Evening Standard*, 1938–1941.

called the Popular Front to power. Diana was in Spain briefly at the time, on her way to Morocco via Gibraltar.]

Diana to Duff, 19 February 1936   *Madrid*

As I was saying Sid [Sidney Herbert] is in excellent spirits, so are Miss Wade and the poor Welsh footman from the Embassy who beamed at the English faces, but who admitted to loathing Spain. It is loathable too, I think, no one smiles at you or tries to understand your desires. They seem but half alive and dirty. No one travelling, unexpectedly. Excellent food. Sid's description (at endless length) of Madrid is very grim, but very like what we knew of it before they de-Kinged it.

Empty gloomy Ritz, empty gloomy bars, nothing doing generally. As a matter of fact there was a lot doing because it was general election time and the streets were swarming with armed men and tanks and little riots were being carried on and a few men were being killed and the votes were going to the Left instead of to the expected Right. Now we are arriving at San Roque and it's 11.30 Wednesday and tomorrow we shall cross the sea and I'm going to make a bold bid for a destroyer or something as I hear the daily boat is lousy. What more shall I say but that I love you. You know I do more than ever I can say or show. Don't get knocked about till I return.

Diana to Duff, 20 February 1936   *Government House, Gibraltar*

The house is poverty stricken and *scuola di* Grand Guignol Theatre in Paris, naves and cloisters and gothic bones poking through the photographs and mascots and shields. All bedroom furniture is old 'servants'. But the perfect climax is Lady Harington,[1] to look at a good mixture of Lois Sturt and Sister Malony, Irish and uninhibited, a heavily-built woman of forty-eight, glowingly but not ridiculously painted, grey nigger hair *en brosse*, dressed always in jodhpurs, no affectation. Everything nice is unexpectedly 'sweet', everything bad 'foul' – talking incessantly and singing quite loud when not talking. The General has picked up this last habit but doesn't do it so loud. His pride and love of her is touching, and I'm sure he's right because she's never discour-

---

[1] Gladys, Lady Harington, wife of the Governor, General Sir Charles Harington, 872–1940. He was Governor of Gibraltar from 1933 to 1938.

aged and loves everything and body. It's *pouring* with rain and a thick mist covers the Rock.

Friday. After lunch an afternoon sleep. H.E. took us in a motor through pouring rain to look at 'The Cottage', a minute bungalow fifteen minutes away clinging to the rock, quite sweet for me, *awful* for you. It is the Gov's summer residence. Water pours through the roof. It smelt asphyxiatingly of must and decay, and he showed it off as though it had been a dream-house. "She painted all this furniture blue, and there's a red suite in here, and this is the yellow one. Glad did it all. The dogs love it here." After this drenching expedition for which I wore a mac. (kindly offered me quite easily by the butler – personal property) we joined Glad at the Rock Hotel. Very gay bar life, no hat for Glad, salutes for the Gov, no alcohol for Glad, whisky for the Gov.

Then home to have a grand tour of the house. They talked a great deal about the ballroom – how they'd done it up and how beautiful it looked. They'd relit it: new picture of King Edward to boot, but to my surprise when seeing the room I found it transformed irrevocably into a badminton court – floor *indelibly* marked but in black lines. He told me "it would all come out", but she told me laughing and singing that she'd been assured it wouldn't, and wasn't it foul.

I got a telegram from you about the revolution in Spain, which I may say I never anticipated nor was I conscious of it till Sid said he'd seen some tanks and guns. Here they take it rather seriously. The place is packed on account of refugees fleeing frightened from Spain. It worries their Exs terribly, because for the moment they are on very good terms with the Spanish Government and General, but they fear under the new Gov. these may be changed and some bad fellows put in their place. "It's tremendously serious for us, you see," he said – "It's such a small hold and we're so hemmed in, we've very few resources; if anything went wrong with the Spaniards I don't know what we should do. We're totally dependent on them for" – (I felt he must mean for food, trade, defence, Empire) – "the hunting, polo, shooting and racing."

22 February

[I'm writing to] tell you that the heaven-sent representative Harington must be made a Field Marshal. Everyone speaks of how he missed it by bad luck or enmity or something. Look into it,

[283]

Duffy. You must be lavish and untapey about honours and influence. Nobody *really* minds though they automatically object, and recipients are happy and grateful for ever. There's nothing weaker than red-tape users unless it's the tape.

Diana to Duff, 23 February 1936   *El Minzah Hotel, Tangier*

I'm thinking all the time if you would like it – some of it you certainly would. Dining at Menebhi's[1] you couldn't have failed to be amused by. He sent a smart car with an ordinary plain-clothes gangster as chauffeur. We'd all tanked up at the hotel bar knowing there would be old Mahommedan customs. We were ushered into an immense white Moorish hall, with all round the walls and darting out in T and E shapes were hard kind of Wagon-Lit divans, with the hard Wagon-Lit bolster and cushion all uphol-stered in the violent Midland Hotel cretonne. The party consisted of us 4,[2] Miss Green[3] the interpreter and old Gye,[4] sweating dreadfully. His Consulate servant Allal was on the job and doing most of it with the help of two fat bare-footed women, who clearly despised activity. My practised eye caught the glint of four gold-necks[5] glinting in the corner and then the host sailed down to meet us off a raised alcove, where we were set to eat. A man of rare charm, with a twinkling dark European face. His arms wide open, something of a black Chaliapin about his grace. He led us to our seats – low corner banquettes, him in the middle and the others quite comfortable on individual W.L. divans. Menebhi did the piling up of cushions round our bums and elbows and took one comfortable little fall in doing it.

We were each handed a large towel for our lap and on a six-inch high table were laid in rapid succession the most delicious foods ever I tasted. The first a boiling dish of pastry, so light you could not get it to your mouth, in which were hidden quails. Between every three people was a shallow plate of clear honey and another

[1] His Excellency Mehedi ben Arbi el Menebhi, G.C.M.G., who had been Special Ambassador from the Sultan of Morocco, 1901. He had stayed at Belvoir, and played tennis in his robes.
[2] Diana, David Herbert, Elizabeth Ann 'Poppet' John and A. E. W. Mason.
[3] Miss Jessie Green, the niece of Sir George Kirby Green who was Minister in Morocco at the turn of the century. She lived all her life in Morocco and spoke Arabic fluently.
[4] Ernest Frederick Gye (1879–1955) Consul General in Morocco, 1933–36.
[5] Bottles of champagne.

plate with a block of butter on it, also each person had a large hunk of bread to dip into the dishes and honey and butter, and also to keep their fingers dry upon. The dishes were so large that although we ate liberally of each, one made no impression on them. They were all rather the same, and there seemed little reason why the meal should ever stop or why it should come to the abrupt conclusion it did. Then there was a good deal of washing at a stand-up centre brass ablution arrangement – a slave pouring hot water from a smart kettle and soap too.

Conversation never lagged and of course there is no greater fun than talking to each other about the house and host in his presence. Miss Green was very good at the interpretation – an unchangeable drone of a voice that in the same tone passed you on an oriental compliment or said "Of course the old man finds it frightfully difficult to get his daughters off". There were 5 grand-father clocks in a row in the hall and endless photographs of the Royal family and the Ripons and Gladys and Lord Lonsdale and Juliet.[1]

After dinner we moved to an identical room, only smaller, leading from the main hall. Same W.L. divans and bolsters propped round us. The old darling found it very difficult to get up off his divan and always offered us a hand each to crane him up, but he was so heavy we could only just do it. Gye, who tried once single-handed, failed but the Moor laughed through everything. Whenever Mason put his hand into the common dish, he pulled out mistakes such as bones. "What do I do with this?" he yelled. "Lay it on the table", came Miss Green's drone. Another time he got involved with a skewer and to our shame, he made such a fuss that a slave brought a plate and *fork*. We flew at him for letting us down and Menebhi had it explained to him that Mason was the 'butt' from which time he took a violent fancy to him, and at parting suddenly started tickling him and saying "Good man, good man". In three of the *Hammam* rooms that lay off the hall the centre *pièce de Musée* was an English wardrobe, like those to be seen in a Grantham hotel bedroom, stained deal with two mirrors and drawers in the middle. In the fourth was a painting of himself by Lavery. It was a great night for me.

---

[1] The 2nd Marquess of Ripon (1852–1923) and his wife Gladys, widow of the 4th Earl of Lonsdale, and mother of Juliet Duff.

Diana to Duff, 25 February 1936   *Palais Jamai, Fez*

Again dinner was a whizz, and after dinner the Sherif, a remarkably common descendant of the Prophet but good-looking, threw a Moroccan stew in an upper room here – a glorious room – and it was all lovely. Very smart stomach-dancers and men dancers and delicious mint tea, and O so funny, they sprinkle you with rose water and also bring along a silver brazier of incense and cedar, and put it under the ladies' skirts. You are then invited to put your nose under your dress between your breasts and inhale. You can imagine how some of the old English girls dealt with the situation and what an extraordinarily indecent effect the operation gave.

God bless you, my beloved Duffy. I'll add to this from Rabat. I love you more than all the world beside – I do indeed.

[Summer holidays at Aix-les-Bains, 1937. Diana took John Julius alone (without Nanny) to improve his French. She hired a youngish but highly unreliable Frenchwoman, Simone Laurent, to help her look after him and to engage him in what she hoped would be a ceaseless flow of French conversation.]

Diana to Duff, 12 August 1937

J.J. has unfortunately palled up with an English family – but certainly his French is easier today. The English family is like a stage one – rather young and pretty Queen Victoria-fat mother with crimson hair, and three children also violently red-headed with skins burnt a brilliant light pink. Pig-tailed thick girl of fourteen, and two thick boys. J.J. told me today that he could *never* make friends, he didn't know how it was done. I told him when he was shy he looked cross, and that made children not meet him half way. Then I saw him Malvolioing the English family so I could not discourage him.

Diana to Duff, 19 August 1937

Yesterday was a glory and we rowed seven kilometres across the lake. J.J. and I came back by steamer and left Mademoiselle to row the boat seven kms. back. Of course the wind got up and of course we couldn't spot her anywhere, and I got a panic that she was drowned and the child adored every minute of the anxiety. She came back at last, having had a ghastly time and is black and blue today. Tomorrow they choose a Venus, on the beach – it will be better than the baby show. Lord and Lady Baldwin have arrived. She sent me a P.C. signing herself L.B. of B. – aren't we grand.[1] I get no reading done, it's crosswords and bawling the baby out.

Diana to Duff, 21 August 1937

I went to Annecy – alone – and it was far more beautiful than I remembered – after [Lac du] Bourget which is lovely and one gets used to – the other on a fine day robs one of breath. I walked alone up the dear Street and bought some Corn Flakes and tooth paste, and was just going to have 'one' to help me face the Kocks,[2] when I met them and we motored to Talloires and had an A.1. lunch at the other Bise[3] in blazing sun. I found myself in a delicious haze of sun and wine and reaction from asceticism. I was home by four to see the Venus of the beach chosen – but alas it didn't come off.

We've made the child a *cache-sexe* instead of what seems to him his rather stuffy trunks – it's made of the cotton Manchester makes for natives in the Conrad country. It's so attractive you wouldn't believe – it allows his hips and behind, now snow-white, to brown up to match his body.

This morning brought the immense treat of seeing Mrs. Baldwin coming out of the *Bains*. She was looking fascinating, much improved by no hat. She wore the *de rigueur* Jaeger overalls – in a brilliant peacock shade. White woolly jacket superimposed, a peacock goblin's peaked hood, and the daintiest of red slippers. I did not speak to her. Truth to tell I was ashamed of my raggermuffin great-coat, espadrilles and handkerchiefed head, my bottle for J.J.'s milk under one arm, the *Express* and a packet of Lux under the other. Think I'll bunch her.

---

[1] Stanley Baldwin had just been made 1st Earl Baldwin of Bewdley.
[2] Gerald Koch de Gooreynd and his wife.
[3] Georges 'Pèze' Bise, hôtelier and restaurateur at Talloires on the Lake of Annecy.

[In August of 1936, Diana and Duff joined a party of guests – including Mrs. Simpson – on the King's yacht *Nahlin*, for a Mediterranean cruise. On December 11th Edward VIII formally abdicated the throne.

Baldwin retired in 1937, having regained his popularity by the tact and firmness with which he handled the Abdication. He was succeeded by Neville Chamberlain, who appointed Duff First Lord of the Admiralty.

It was considered an enviable job, since with it went the use of Admiralty House, and the thousand-ton sloop *Enchantress*. Diana was delighted with them and Duff's romantic title, but grief came in December with the death of her mother. Early in 1938 they sold their house in Gower Street.

They did not stay at the Admiralty for long, since events were moving towards the Munich crisis, that was also to be the crisis of Duff's career. It was brewing for most of September, the first weeks of which Diana and John Julius spent in Geneva where the peace talks were being held.

Hitler invaded Czechoslovakia on September 30th 1938. Duff felt that the Government had betrayed the Czechs, that its idea that there could be peace with Hitler was a dangerous delusion, and that he could no longer be a part of the Cabinet. He resigned the following day.]

Duff to Diana, 9 September 1938   *Admiralty*

My darling. I got your earlier letters this morning and was glad to learn that the journey had been such a success. But from your last one I fear you are a little bored and lonely with the silly brat and the foolish frog. Never mind, the Captain[1] will be joining you on Sunday and you will be surrounded by delegates. The Captain won't much care for his ex-brother-in-law Buck[2] acting as his boss. The said Buck is much concerned with the international situation. He came to see me yesterday afternoon – he thinks we are not taking a sufficiently firm line – and I think he's right.

Meanwhile as you have probably seen *The Times* has thrown

[1] Captain Euan Wallace. He first married the 9th Earl De La Warr's sister, Myra Idina.
[2] Herbrand Edward Sackville, 9th Earl De La Warr, 1893–1976. At that time Head of the Peace Mission in the place of Lord Halifax.

away our case and done everything possible to encourage Hitler, by suggesting in a leading article that the Czechs should hand over all the territory the Germans want. So things go from bad to worse, and I hardly know whether I ought to be off to Plas Newydd this afternoon by that 5.20 train, which I was prevented from catching with you last year owing to a panic in the Foreign Office. There is a Cabinet meeting on Monday and Hitler makes a speech on Monday so that I don't think anything can happen before then. I shall have to come back by the night mail on Sunday.

I have just been lunching with Seymour Berry[1] and Bobbety at Bucks. The Berry press are delighted with *The Times'* gaffe and rub it in every morning. I met Mary Marlborough[2] in the street – she had been lunching with Ivor [Churchill] who had so frightened her about the war that she was putting off taking her children to France. I asked why? They would be quite as well off in France as in England in any case. You'll do best in a neutral country. Give my love to J.J. and say I shan't love him if he won't speak French. But I shall love you whatever you speak – my darling.   D.

Diana to Duff, 10 September 1938   *Geneva*

Darling love. Geneva is the place for any girl who wants confidence in her sex appeal bucked up a bit. After a week of strictest detachment from the world I know, suddenly men grow up from the ground as though dragons' teeth had been sewn. I take every meal now with five. Last night it was the same as Thursday plus Fish Butler[3] – a man I could not much take to. Tonight it is to be Chips, [Peter] Loxley, a man called Foster[2] (law) another called Makins[4] & Peake[5] again.

The little boy has a snively cold but not a 'nasty snively cold' and is very gay and sweet, and very like you in so much prefering the bar of the Carlton with billiards and drinks and other chaps than a romantic wander through old streets or dappled woods.

---

[1] John Seymour Berry, b. 1909, Deputy Chairman of the Daily Telegraph. Became 2nd Viscount Camrose in 1941.
[2] Mary, Duchess of Marlborough, 1900–1961; born Mary Cadogan, she married the 10th Duke in 1920.
[3] Richard Austen Butler, 1902–1981, later Lord Butler of Saffron Walden.
[4] Sir John Foster, Q.C.
[5] Sir Roger Makins, now Lord Sherfield.
[6] Sir Charles Peake, 1897–1958, diplomat.

Today we had lunch on the pavement with Chips and Peter Loxley and after we rushed off on foot across the lake to pick up the car. In it I found a note from my Swiss[1] saying could he come to the circus with us, and off he came – if only I could understand him a little better – his mind processes, his articulation, his pressure (very high pressure) of thought leave me treading water.

Duff to Diana, 11 September 1938   Plas Newydd, Isle of Anglesey

My darling – We had a pleasant day yesterday. We all went to the Bay in the afternoon and lay in the sunshine sleeping and reading. It was not quite nice enough to bathe. In the evening I went duck flighting with Charley [Anglesey] and Henry[2] and the tutor, who is a very nice boy and has only just left Eton. It was an evening of memorable beauty – a remarkable sunshine followed by a huge full moon soaring like a rocket from behind some low trees. So that although I shot no duck I enjoyed myself. We came back and had a good meal at 10 o'clock – and I played bezique with Liz,[3] and we listened to the wireless news and a pouch arrived from the Admiralty which kept me busy until half past one.

I was haunted all yesterday by war fears. It still seems to me more likely than not. This morning's papers however have left me rather more cheerful – although perhaps on insufficient grounds. There is a unanimity about their tone which must impress Germany if the people who matter there take the trouble to read them. Garvin,[4] my pet abomination, has an excellent article. If only *The Times* hadn't sold the pass last Wednesday. So much depends upon what Hitler says tomorrow that it is difficult to wait for it. Here we are so peaceful and remote. Charley doesn't even unfold a newspaper – and Marjorie occasionally asks rather petulantly why we need to bother about the Czechs. So that although I am very happy here as usual and adoring the girls as ever I am glad that I have to go tonight for tomorrow's Cabinet. Geneva must be fairly humming – Liz showed me a very sweet letter from you that she got yesterday. If there is war there will probably be a coalition Government and I shall be out.   D.

---

[1] Carl Burckhardt. League of Nations High Commissioner from 1937 to 1939, historian, biographer (Richelieu) and essayist. He was Ambassador to France after the war.
[2] Henry, Lord Uxbridge, now Marquess of Anglesey. Born 1922.
[3] Lady Elizabeth Paget, daughter of Lord and Lady Anglesey.
[4] James Louis Garvin – journalist. Died 1947. Editor of *The Observer*, 1908–1942.

The weather is sublime – misty at sunset with a clear pink Mont Blanc shimmering above the mist. The rumour and panic in the Carlton is not quite what you might expect it to be. Only Charles Peake the head of the journalists acts like a melodrama. He's always tearing in with a typewritten paper – that seems to say nothing new – always equally bad. O dear, O dear when will it end.

I'm really rather ashamed of our heads of delegation Buck, Euan, and Bernays.[1] The underlings make a more intellectual show. Tomorrow I am to be hostess to the British Empire banquet. I was to have had a night on the tiles with Carl the Swiss but Chips is very firm with me. I've just been to see Maurice de Rothschild in his appalling chateau. He'd got oil all over his nose and upper lip but was quite unselfconscious with it. I have to lunch with him and his bosom friend Litvinoff[2] tomorrow in exchange for which *supplice* he will give all my boys dinner Thursday and Chateau Yquem. On Friday I throw my romantic fête in the Villa Byron.[3] The chairs are covered with stuff chosen by him, and I have collected up to date holders for 60 candles. I've ordered the collation. Hot soup. *Langouste. Pâté de Canard au Périgord. Entremet – Friandises et fruits* – yum yum.

Wednesday a.m. It's blazing hot and we're sitting on the beach. I've got to go and dress for Litvinoff. J.J. refuses to lunch up at the Rothschilds so I've had to lie for him. Maurice wanted us all to move in to his monstrous mansion for the rest of our days. I had to explain as best I could that I'd rather die. So I'll leave J.J. and Mad.[4] to eat ham and eggs in the sun. I chucked dining with the Captain last night in order to have my dinner with my new lover. Semi-duty, semi-choice. It was a fantastic evening of sight-seeing after dark. First to an old Swiss town called Aubonne and then because there was no nice inn there on to Lausanne to a nice bar restaurant – just what you like, with an exquisite *truite flambé à*

---

[1] Robert Hamilton Bernays, 1902–1945. Liberal member for Bristol since 1935.

[2] Maxim Litvinov, 1876–1951, Russian Foreign Minister 1930 to 1939. He also headed the Russian delegates to the peace conferences of the twenties.

[3] Diana had been so well entertained by the peace conference delegates, that she planned to give a party for them in the Villa Diodati, where Byron had lived from June to October of 1816.

[4] Mademoiselle, John Julius' French governess hired in Paris.

l'Armagnac for me, and a *chateaubriand saignant* pour Monsieur. Then all the way home the story of his life – but of course he wouldn't listen to mine – they never will. What is amusing is that his advances of courtship are identical with Raimund's. The latter must have asked Carl as a boy for lessons and tips – but my new lover has it over Raimund every time, for one reason his hand is not like a hippopotamus's tongue. I could almost fall for him if I wasn't always in an agony of not understanding. Hanging over this fantastic evening were the spectre words *état de siège* and ultimatum – in Lausanne we heard them over the strains of the Lambeth Walk. My Byron fête threatens to be another Brussels ball. O God tonight I am hostess, Buck is host. Hiding the skeleton will be the game's name. Mr. Bruce[1] I shall get and who? Bless you for lovely letters Ever very loving   B.

Duff to Diana, 13 September 1938   *Admiralty*

My beloved. I am glad you have plenty of boys to look after you at Geneva. I had a nice cheerful letter from you this morning. Here temperatures are pretty high and life is pretty hectic. I dined with Oliver[2] at Buck's last night. He and I see alike – and so does Buck [De La Warr] who flew to Geneva yesterday and whom you may meet there. Unfortunately his support in Cabinet is, between ourselves, rather more a liability than an asset. He is not powerful in Council – nor is Eddie Winterton[3] who also argues with us. George Carlisle joined us at the end of dinner – and welcome – because our tête-à-tête resources were beginning to give out.

And then Anthony Winn[4] rolled up fresh from *The Times* offices. He told us they were running today a so-called 'balanced' correspondence on the advantages and disadvantages of handing over the complete Sudeten territories to Germany. Nothing could be more mischievous at this moment – tending as it must to persuade

---

[1] The Rt. Hon. Stanley Bruce, later Viscount Bruce of Melbourne – 1883–1961. Head of the Australian delegation to the League of Nations.
[2] The Rt. Hon. Oliver Stanley, 1896–1950, at that time President of the Board of Trade. He married Lady Maureen Vane-Tempest-Stewart in 1920.
[3] The 6th Earl Winterton, Chancellor of the Duchy of Lancaster.
[4] Anthony Winn, Lobby correspondent of *The Times*. His article praising Duff's resignation speech was suppressed, and was replaced by a piece that called the speech a 'damp squib'. It was signed 'from our Lobby correspondent', and Anthony Winn resigned in protest.

the Germans that England is divided on the issue. I got on at once to 10 Downing St. where the Big Four – Neville, John Simon,[1] Halifax[2] & Sam H.[3] were in conclave and told them about [it]. Halifax got on at once to Geoffrey Dawson and spoke to him, I am told pretty strongly. But it was too late – the first edition was out. Oliver and I walked home across the park.

Today I had Hilary [Belloc] to luncheon at Admty Ho. His moustache is thicker, his teeth are fewer and farther between and his appearance is gruesome. We had an excellent luncheon which he wouldn't eat – but otherwise he was very nice and rather pathetic – much occupied with the problem of mortality. Good bye – my pretty love –   D.

Duff to Diana, 14 September 1938   *Admiralty*

Well, my beloved, here we still are, enjoying all the pleasures and suffering all the horrors of hysteria. For indeed it is a state of mind which produces pain and pleasure just as the physical phenomenon produces tears and laughter. One enjoys the excitement while one trembles at the cause of it. Yesterday afternoon they told me you would ring me up at 7.30 but at that hour I was attending a conference of Service Ministers and Chiefs of Staff at No. 10. When I got back to Admiralty House I did speak to somebody at Geneva who said you had already gone.

I dined with Oliver and Maureen. We dined under the impression that all was over and the war had started, for it seemed to us that Hitler would march last night. It was a fortunate impression in some ways for it made Oliver prodigal with his champagne. There was one embarrassing moment when he tried very mildly and very sweetly to persuade Maureen to forego her fourth kümmel. However she remained on the whole fairly sober. It was an exciting evening and you would have enjoyed it. This morning we had a Cabinet meeting, where we were informed of decisions of

---

[1] Sir John Simon, Chancellor of the Exchequer.
[2] Lord Halifax, 1881–1959 who had become Foreign Secretary after Anthony Eden's resignation in February.
[3] Sir Samuel Hoare, the Home Secretary.

which we all approved.[1] And for the moment everything is paralysed – every action held up. By the time that you get this you will know why.

I have just thrown a fortuitous luncheon party at Admiralty House. My old friend Walford Selby whom you met in Vienna and who is now Ambassador in Portugal – Winston and Venetia. It went well – Winston in rollicking form and Selby playing up well to all his opinions.

Good bye – much haste – much love –   D.

Duff to Diana, 15 September 1938   *Admiralty*

Beloved – my dinner for eight was quite successful last night except when Mrs. Blackman sent up roast partridges without bread sauce. I nearly had a stroke. Seymour Berry and Anthony Winn came in afterwards with the latest from *Telegraph* and *Times*. I sent out for sandwiches and Holbrook procured some heavenly ones from Lyons Corner House – a thing to know of. Then the best part of the evening was hearing your squeak on the telephone – and getting the latest from Geneva. I hope my little boy had a happy birthday today.[2] Tomorrow I hope to go to Lavington – It looks like a quiet week-end for I don't suppose the P.M. will get back till Sunday. Will it be a) peace with honour? b) peace with dishonour – i.e. the Czechs deserted and betrayed, or c) bloody war? I shouldn't like to bet. I love you.   D.

Duff to Diana, 16 September 1938   *Lavington Park, Sussex*

Darling. I have come down here for the night. I shall have to go up to London tomorrow morning for the Cabinet, but I felt that I wanted to get away – it was a lovely evening and I was feeling sick of London and of the anxious hanging about and the endless discussion of the eternal topic. Between ourselves I was getting rather sick also of Oliver and Maureen, whom I seemed to be seeing almost exclusively. I love them both – but his gloom and

---

[1] That Chamberlain would fly to Munich the following day and see Hitler at Berchtesgarten. This was his first meeting with Hitler, where Chamberlain offered the separation of Sudetenland from the rest of Czechoslovakia.

[2] He didn't. He was stung by a wasp.

her slightly assisted gaiety were, between them, getting me down. Of the three alternative possibilities that I gave you in my last letter I should now back the second pretty heavily – and the result, though more satisfactory in the immediate future, must, it seems to me, be worse in the long run.

The great joke here is that you and Euan are the only people who don't know there's a crisis. Apparently he rings up Barbie continually to say that all is well as they have got through clause 18 without opposition.

Diana to Duff, 17 September 1938   *Geneva*

Darling the party was a whizz. JJ., Mad. and I worked at it all day – flowers, carting candelabra from *antiquaires*, even putting in a big chandelier of candles for the nonce. four tables and chairs still covered in Byron's choice of *toile*. Two waiters, a chef, a barman, and a Radio – this last impossible to find because of no electricity. My lover produced five *indigènes*, the vice-consul's wife, another two Swiss *hochgeboren*. We were thirty-two strong and I'm sorry to say forty-two bottles of wine were drunk *ex*cluding hundreds of cocktails and thirty armagnacs. It cost a fortune – but was worth it. They danced to the radio till about one (it began at 7.30) and then everyone moved on to somebody's ball – which is all rather blurry – 'I can't remember how I went to bed'[1] I can really. The Swiss deposited me relatively intact at two a.m. I enclose you two Collins's received this morning. Stationery has run out. I start tomorrow or the next day. I can't settle which, the weather is so lovely. I don't know whether to have three short days on the road or two long ones and another day here from J.J.'s point of view.   Love me my darling

[After his resignation, Duff was commissioned to write a weekly political article on a year's contract for the Evening Standard. He and Diana now lived at 34 Chapel Street, a house that the Duchess had bought after the sale of her house in Arlington Street. She had done it up

---

[1] The punch line of a *ballade* by Maurice Baring.

magnificently to leave to Diana, but it was too large. It was sold soon after the war.

In January 1939, Diana took John Julius ski-ing at Sestrière.]

Duff to Diana, 5 January 1939   34 Chapel Street, Belgrave Square

I lunched with Caroline[1] at the Jardin. Raimund has got his divorce and the only question now is how soon they will marry.[2] I read Marjorie's letter which you left for me. I do think there are faults on both sides. Young people in love are bound to be selfish and can sincerely love their mothers and fathers without wanting to be with them all the time. Caroline says that Marjorie is terribly unreasonable which we know her to be. She argues, "How can Liz pretend to love me when she wants to marry a foreigner, knowing that I hate all foreigners." Nor does she ever miss a chance of saying something rude about foreigners and Jews in front of Liz.

Then I came back here and did some work. My room is beautifully warm but I want to sit in a comfortable chair and go to sleep – but there isn't a comfortable chair to sit in. Holbrook seems as gay as a grig about going – only suggests staying on a few days next week to show the new man round. I understand that they have started work on the library – and Rex was seeing a man this morning about the measurements which he says are still wrong.[3]

Only three words from you so far – "happy and sunny" – perhaps I shall hear more tomorrow. I love only you.   D.

Diana to Duff, 8 January 1939   Sestrière

I overdid it yesterday and was so exhausted today that I could do no good – a rumour arose that there were no [ski-ing] lessons or classes Sunday. I knew it to be untrue, but accepted it and stayed till later in bed. Mad. picked up some young men and went out on a half-day excursion while J.J. and I walked to the frontier and read the tablet on the monolith which comemorates Napoleon's

[1] Caroline Paget, the eldest daughter of Lord and Lady Anglesey.
[2] Raimund von Hofmannsthal had stayed in America after *The Miracle*, and married Alice Astor, the daughter of John Jacob Astor, by whom he had two daughters. They had just got divorced, and Raimund was now free to marry Elizabeth Paget, Diana's niece and Caroline's sister, with whom he had been in love for some time.
[3] The walls of the library at Chapel Street were going to be painted by Rex Whistler. Work began but was never finished, and Rex Whistler was killed in action in 1944.

crossing of the Alps. I remember Harry Cust in the Hotel at Turin pointing to where I am today – a col in the range of Alps – and telling me of Napoleon's army coming through.

Hannibal took this route too with all his ellies. Poor Babars – goaded across, by cruel soldiers – still it's not steep.

In the afternoon we skied down to the next village – Clavière – being assured we could get a taxi back – of course we couldn't and had to walk carrying skies. J.J. was maddening and I was so cross he cried. He will not attend or concentrate, that is his only fault I think. It's a monkey mind. He cannot keep up with the others walking, however much you remind him not to stop and look and play. He cannot carry his skis without dropping them or muddling them, because even after a bad scolding he'll juggle or play with them or forget them, in fact he is impressionless of reproof and *won't* use his mind. Sometimes he asks questions of such a magnitude of idiocy I am horrorstruck – poor little boy he's so good and sweet really. The little frogs have gone. We still have one retiring plucky little Belgian.

I can't call on Deirdre, it's too far. Mad.'s throat of course was nothing, now it's a bad knee, that has to have groans and perpetual massage – she says it's like a melon from swell. I've looked at it, it's not even puffy. I make her a warning of health fuss and pain fuss to J.J. It's been a day of reaction today. Tomorrow I feel rested – I shall recover my *extasie* – the following day have a blow out at Sestrière and Sunday it's home to work we go.

I've had a letter every day from you. They delight me so. God bless my darling love   D.

Duff to Diana, 11 January 1939   *34 Chapel Street*

My darling, I was delighted to get two letters from you when I got back from Himley – one complaining of J.J.'s failure to concentrate. Poor little boy, he isn't very old. Challis the new butler has arrived but Holbrook has not yet left. With his customary acumen he is behaving exactly like Jesus Christ – never a bitter word or a reproach – says he thinks Challis seems a very good man and should do well etc.

I enclose an account of my *conférence* which appeared in *La Dépêche de Brest* and which was sent me by the author. I like '*solide gaillard*'. Only this minute since cutting it out for you do I see that '*d'apparence plébeienne*' refers to my *name* – not to me – which spoils the joke. I shouldn't have bothered to send it – however *solide gaillard* is good. I also send you yesterday's arti., which you will see is very mild and pro-Government.

Good bye – my darling. I don't know what to write my next arti. on. Kisses   D.

Duff to Diana, 11 January 1939   *11.15.p.m. 34 Chapel Street*

Darling. I think I'll write to you again today because I didn't write yesterday and it won't go off till tomorrow. And then I think I shall write no more because you start home on Sunday and I remember that last time you went abroad most of my letters only reached you after you had come home. This has been a political day for me. I gave Liddell Hart[1] luncheon at Buck's. His views, you know, are sound[2] but he's such a shamble and I can't like him. I went to see Sidney in the afternoon. Mrs. Miller was there – with her husband who it appears is a judge, but obviously not a judge of women. Her views are superlatively sound and she says South Africa is behind me to a man, or to a Boer. And Sidney says that at the Academy Cinema the other evening my appearance on the screen was cheered and that nobody else's was. Then I went to see George Lloyd.[3] His wife – that miserable Tommy Lascelles's sister – is so sound that she is suffering from nervous breakdown. "She never got over Munich," he said. "Women feel these things more than we do." I implied 'didn't I know it', and gave it to be understood that you were very near mental collapse on account of the Coroner's[4] foreign policy.   D.

[On September 1st Germany invaded Poland, and two days later England was at war.

Duff's main concern then was that he had nothing to do. After much hesitation, since he knew he would be criti-cised for leaving his country in time of war and there was

---

[1] Sir Basil Liddell Hart, 1895–1970, the military historian.
[2] i.e., anti-appeasement.
[3] George Lloyd, 1st Baron Lloyd, 1879–1941. In 1911 he married Blanche Lascelles.
[4] Neville Chamberlain.

always a chance that a job might turn up, he accepted an invitation to do a lecture tour of the United States. This was a great success, and he and Diana were in America from October 1939 to the following March, when Winston Churchill became Prime Minister. On May 11th, he appointed Duff Minister of Information.

It was not a happy appointment, and Duff described himself caught between the 'gifted amateurs' of which the department was full, and an impatient press, with whom he was not popular. He asked to be transferred if possible, and in 1941 he was succeeded by Brendan Bracken.

John Julius had been sent to Canada in 1940. The house in Chapel Street was rented out to Daisy Fellowes, and Duff and Diana lived with a minimum of possessions in the Dorchester Hotel.

At about the same time that Duff left the Ministry of Information, Diana began her small-holding at Bognor. Here she milked her cow, chased her goats, fed her chickens and fattened her pigs. She also made 20 lbs. of small-holder's cheese a week, and was blissfully happy.

As 1941 wore on, Churchill became increasingly uneasy about the Far East. Duff was made Chancellor of the Duchy of Lancaster and sent to Singapore – but he barely had time to write his report on the situation and make his recommendations before the Japanese invaded.

Back in England Duff, still Chancellor of the Duchy of Lancaster, was employed on secret work until October 1943, when he was made British Representative to the French Committee of Liberation, with the prospect of becoming Ambassador to Paris after that. He was to fly to Algiers, where Harold Macmillan was already installed as Minister Resident with the Allied Headquarters. This marked the end of Diana's days as a small-holder, and very sad she was to see them go; but the little farm continued, under the capable administration of Miss Wade.

Diana and Duff arrived in Algiers in January 1944. At that time, relations between the British, the Free French and the Americans were precarious to say the least. The British had faith in de Gaulle's leadership of Free France, but the Americans were highly suspicious of him. With his unbending pride and his unshakeable belief in his own destiny and that of France, they saw in him a potential dictator.

They had been backing General Giraud, who was far less troublesome. He outranked de Gaulle, having five stars on his sleeve where de Gaulle only had two, and he had no political ambitions whatsoever. He was a brave and distinguished soldier and, they thought, an ideal figure-head for France until after the Liberation. That he was no match for de Gaulle had become obvious to everyone, by the time Diana flew back to England for John Julius's Easter holidays in 1944.]

Duff to Diana, 29 March 1944   Algiers

I had a fair but rather restless night. I think that when you are there I lie still because I subconsciously don't want to disturb you. I've noticed before that I toss much more when I'm alone.

I walked to the Office with Raymond Mortimer[1] this morning. There has come a letter for you from your Swiss lover, Carl [Burckhardt]. It arrived with great solemnity, heavily sealed and accompanied by a covering letter to me from the Belgian Ambassador. Freddie[2] said, "You had better open it. You may have to send a wire to Lady Diana" – so all his precautions ended in his letter being laid open under the eyes of me and Freddie. 'The best laid schemes of mice and Carl – gang aft a-gley.'[3] I didn't read it because Carl's letters always bore me.

Duff to Diana, All Fools Day 1944   Algiers

My darling – soon after my letter left for the bag old Maitland Wilson[4] came puffing along to see me. Giraud[5] wants to visit London, which is not convenient – but how are we to stop him?

[1] Raymond Mortimer, 1895–1980, author and critic. He was Literary Editor of the *New Statesman* between 1939–47.
[2] Freddy Fane. Erstwhile Secretary of the Travellers' Club in Paris, he had been appointed Comptroller of Duff and Diana's household in Algiers.
[3] cf. Robert Burns, *To a Mouse.*
[4] Lt. General Sir Henry Maitland Wilson, 1868–1940, known as 'Jumbo'. He was in command of British troops in Algiers.
[5] General Henri Honoré Giraud, 1879–1949, became High Commissioner of French North and West Africa after the assassination of Admiral Darlan in 1942, and on formation of the Committee for National Liberation became co-president with de Gaulle, and Commander in Chief of the French Forces until his retirement in 1944.

Say it's all Eisenhower's[1] fault, was the astute decision at which we eventually arrived.

[Lunch] was quite fun. Langier was quite amusing – and I like the Kessels – but she isn't the least attractive – like Emerald younger – but not much. Apparently St. Exupéry[2] has written a charming book for children called *Le Petit Prince*. Of course one can't get it. *Le Petit Prince* meets a drunkard, and never having seen one before he says '*Mais pourquoi buvez vous?*' The drunkard replies '*Pour oublier*'. '*Mais pour oublier quoi*' asks the prince – '*Pour oublier que je bois*'. The English speakers faded away first. The French sat on until half past eleven. I think they enjoyed themselves.

This morning came your telegram to say that all was well – and glad I was to get it.

2 April. It is really hot at last – quite different from anything we have ever known here before and I am sitting in the window seat surrounded by lilies. Old Catroux[3] sent you a vast bunch which arrived just after you left. Yesterday was almost as lovely but not so hot. I saw Madame Flandin[4] and Miss Tamara in the morning, the former asking the same old questions and me making the same old replies. Tamara – Russo-Franco-American correspondent of the *Herald Tribune*, was splendidly tough about Pucheu[5] – said she couldn't understand her colleagues of the New York and London *Times* – she said they seemed quite sorry for the man just because he spoke so well and behaved with so much dignity. She herself had been moved by his last speech – but she would never allow sentiment to interfere with politics. The female of the species is certainly more deadly than the male.

Oh I do wish you were here. I can't tell you how lovely the garden is. I never saw so many arum lilies and the drive is lined with white irises in two ranks. The wistaria is full out, and near it is

---

[1] General Dwight D. Eisenhower, 1890–1969. Allied Commander in Chief.

[2] Antoine de St. Exupéry, 1900–1944.

[3] Gen. Georges Catroux, 1887–1969. Commissioner of Moslem Affairs in the National Liberation Committee, and afterwards Ambassador to Moscow, 1945–48.

[4] The wife of Pierre-Etienne Flandin, 1889–1958. He had held posts in the Vichy government, and was prime minister from 1944–5. Flandin was currently under arrest, following a purge on Vichyites by the National Liberation Committee.

[5] Pierre Pucheu, 1899–1944. Vichy Minister of the Interior, 1941–1942. He defected to Algiers, fearing nothing since he had a safe conduct from Gen. Giraud. But was taken prisoner, tried and sentenced to death by the National Liberation Committee. He said "My death will be more useful to France than my reprieve", and insisted on shaking hands with every member of the firing squad.

a lovely white wistaria that I never saw before, which smells divine. And purple Judas trees a many.

Oh and I forgot to tell you, Freddie caught an Arab thief. He arranged a drive with all the staff taking part – and Smith, the second chauffeur, who is also an expert Rugby player, caught the Arab on the run – and Freddie had him tied up to a tree for two hours and then gave him a kick on the bottom and let him go, which seems to me a very good way to treat thieves.

Diana to Duff, 2 April 1944   *Bognor*

I got to London, distributing bananas to porters on the way, and came to the Dorchester. The staff had not realised I'd been away – I heard myself telling everyone – they told me John Julius had gone to Bognor the day before. I called him at once – his gay voice was joy to my ears and heart – he said Conrad[1] and Katharine were waiting for me at Bognor. I was in rip-snorting form all evening, couldn't stop talking – no one else had a chance – but Katharine and Conrad are ideal for listening and they have little to vary the monotony of their lives. I feel sometimes ashamed of knowing so much of Mells and Mells life – of Billy Jolliffe[2] and Trim,[3] and Katharine *not* knowing how informed I am. We had a curious conversation about Billy's *dolce-far-niente* – with me asking naive questions, Conrad listening and Katharine answering in lies out of loyalty.

It's dreadfully cold – cold as early Algiers – the primroses are here looking a little pale – the daffodils too, a bit *abattus*. The place as a whole is wickedly Kelly'd[4] up – never saw such disorder – Irish blood, I expect, every farm or garden tool shed is broken, roofless, a receptacle for rusting iron bits, dead syphons, uncleaned buckets, rat's bodies – lids, and rotting sacks – everything that should be oiled and greased, laid away preserved through the winter, is out and unable to resist the depredations and attacks of the elements. I feel a little hopeless and quite helpless.

[1] Conrad Russell, 1878–1947. 4th son of Lord Arthur Russell, his life was spent farming his land, cultivating his mind, and writing long and entertaining letters to his friends. He and Diana corresponded regularly from their meeting in 1933 till his death.
[2] The Hon. William Jolliffe, 1898–1967, 4th Baron Hylton. He married Katharine Asquith's daughter Perdita in 1931.
[3] Julian, b. 1916, 2nd and present Earl of Oxford, only son of Raymond and Katharine Asquith.
[4] Kelly was the gardener-handyman at Bognor.

J.J. has *Kim* as a holiday task, we read a chapter last night. Katharine left for a bumper Palm Sunday and Conrad read aloud. It's nearly incomprehensible I should think, to any boy of fourteen not brought up in India and no background of Moslems, Hindoos, Urdu, Rajputs and Sahibs. We all three had a big tussle with it. The ban[1] is a cruel nuisance – because there seems nothing cut and dry – no passes – a great many exceptions – but apparently one has to satisfy the police at the guichet. I'll to go bore the War Office when I get 'up' [to London] Tuesday.

Edith hasn't calved. The hens are in generous lay – ducks too – 1 goosy gander sitting the other laying – the gander protective – but I'm out of touch with it all and discouraged by the disorder and decay, and feel I can't get into the old soothing routine for three weeks of freezing spring weather. Everything is late – no birds even – in other words I long to be back with you, and the friesias and the African hills and vines and siren shores.

Sunday Mrs. Kelly is going to have a baby. She has chosen August to lie in, the month we had hoped to work her to the bone – she looks like death and told me she would have liked to drown herself when she discovered her condition. I make no comment.

Duff to Diana, 5 April 1944   *Algiers*

Then the meeting with the Generals. Wilson, Devers and Rooks.[2] Not much sense in them. They decided that I should ask Giraud to withdraw his resignation – so I said I would ask to see him but when I got to my office I found he had asked to see me. So the old fool came at 11.30. He was charming as ever and I argued in vain. He always fell back on "You know that if you were in my position you would resign" – which I certainly should. He had come to ask me to telegraph for permission for him to go to England and live there as a private citizen. I persuaded him to promise that he would not actually send in his resignation until he had seen Murphy,[3] who is due from America this afternoon and who is supposed to have influence with him. Curiously enough I

[1] For military and security reasons, the Sussex coast was out of bounds to those who did not actually live there.
[2] General Jacob L. Devers and General Lowell Rooks, both U.S. Army.
[3] Robert Murphy, 1894–1978, Roosevelt's personal representative in French North Africa.

had previously asked to lunch today Generals Devinck[1] and Chambe[2] who are Giraud's principal buddies. Eric[3] brought one and Frank[4] brought the other. Virginia[5] lunched off her typewriter so we were six. Food excellent – buttered eggs, delicious tournedos, jam tart with real cream. Jaw, jaw, jaw – we worked out a possible scheme for keeping Giraud – *if* the P.M. and the President will make a fuss, *if* de Gaulle will issue a statement defining Giraud's powers – *if* Giraud will accept it – *if* he will withhold his resignation meanwhile – I doubt very much that it will work.

6 April Before dinner I went to see Murphy who had just arrived. I took an immediate and grave dislike to him. There is a strong suspicion that he had been influencing the President against the Committee and I have no doubt that it is justified. I hope he won't stay here.

After lunch. My instinctive dislike of Murphy has already been justified. The son of a bitch in his interview with Giraud did not urge him to remain although I had told him that I had done so. Little, sweet Chapin[6] came to me this morning in some distress. He doesn't know what Murphy is going to do here. It is obviously ridiculous for Murphy and Macmillan both to remain merely as Jumbo's advisers.

Massigli[7] came to see me this morning – delighted by the agreement the Russians have made with the Czechs about civil administration in Czechoslovakia after the liberation.[8] If only we would make a similar one with the French all would be well. The

[1] General Paul Devinck, 1892–1960, General Giraud's Chief of Staff, 1942–43.
[2] René Chambe, b. 1889, Général de Brigade Aérienne. He was Commissioner of Information in Giraud's government.
[3] Eric Duncannon, later 10th Earl of Bessborough. b. 1913. Second and subsequently 1st Secretary of the British Embassy, Paris – 1944–49.
[4] Colonel Frank Raphael.
[5] Virginia Cowles, war correspondent for the *Sunday Times*, now Mrs Aidan Crawley.
[6] Selden Chapin, 1899–1963, U.S. Chargé d'Affaires.
[7] René Massigli, b. 1888. Commissioner of Foreign Affairs in the National Liberation Committee, he became Ambassador to London after the war.
[8] Edouard Beneš, the Czechoslovak Resistance leader, made strong ties of alliance with the Russians. They recognised Czechoslovakia's sovereignty and said they would not interfere politically after the liberation. When the Communists took over in 1948 Beneš' pro-Russian policy was criticized – but in the interests of a united Czechoslovakia, he did not have much option at the time.

fact is that the Russians are getting away with everything – winning the war and carrying out a sane and practical foreign policy while we are handcuffed to an obstinate old cripple[1] and cannot move a yard in any direction.

General Juin[2] came to lunch (last of the old brandy.) Giraud had sent for him to hold his hand. Juin a nice, tough soldier, the best of the lot – doesn't care much whether Giraud goes or stays but thinks it better he should stay and had told him so. Only Freddie and Frank at lunch. Frank is very useful – He had nobbled Juin for lunch and he is off again this afternoon.

Jumbo came up to the villa before dinner to say it had been proposed to him that he should send Giraud to London to join Eisenhower with the title of Commander-in-Chief – and that he should resign when he got there. We both agreed that it was an idiotic suggestion.

Duff to Diana, 9 April 1944 – Easter Day   *Algiers*

At about eleven-thirty we reached the first stopping place where we were supposed to be received by a Boushaga [local commander] and entertained with what Freddie first described as a *'petit dejeuner'* – he had later changed it to 'just a *collation*' but as we approached the spot he said it was a *'vin d'honneur'*. We were all very thirsty and hungry but of course there was nothing there – the Boushaga had gone away for the day and nobody had ever heard of us. Voisin looked very embarrassed, Freddie was very cross and Teddie [Phillips] roared with laughter. After another hour and half's driving we found ourselves in gloomy desert, a high wind blowing, no sun nor sign of human habitation. We had driven through swarms of locusts and been obliged to shut the windows to prevent them from coming in. The wind screen and radiator were covered with their corpses. Then we noticed far away on the right a dingy sand coloured fort like the one in *Beau Geste* and a small blue car coming from it toward us across a track in the desert. It was the French *Administrateur* of the district who told us that that was where we were expected. Our hearts sank as we

---

[1] Franklin D. Roosevelt, 1882–1945.
[2] General Alphonse Juin, 1888–1967, had been captured by the Germans in 1940 and was released at the request of Marshal Pétain, who offered him the post of Minister of War. Juin preferred to join de Gaulle in North Africa.

followed him across the bumpy track and arrived at the squalid outhouses of the fort where three bearded Arab chieftains awaited us. We followed them into the fort and found ourselves in a lovely patio with apple trees in blossom, a fountain in the middle and a tame gazelle ambling round. They led us into a room furnished according to the taste of Louis Philippe, heavy carpets, family portraits and numberless bottles of drink. We were led into a bedroom to wash our hands. It was as clean as a whistle, a large satin-wood double bed, good linen, unused cakes of *Savon Cadum* wrapped in paper. Followed a variety of apéritifs – (none of the three old boys who were brothers drank anything but water.) Then lunch – hors d'oeuvres really variés – including foie gras – cold turkey in delicious mayonnaise with white and red wine of the country. Then chicken and mushrooms, quite first rate and I felt I had had enough. But not at all. 'Would you mind coming into the next room?' In the next room was the *méchoui* [local dish] – two sheep roasted whole – and to help us with them they handed round Chambertin 1921. When we staggered back again we were greeted by an exceptionally good dish of fonds d'artichauts and petits pois. With this we drank iced sauterne. A compote of prunes followed – I don't like prunes as a rule but these were exceptional. Then couscous. "It is our local dish so we hope you will take a little". After that there was only dessert accompanied by champagne – Roederer 1921 – very good little home made cakes which one couldn't refuse – and oranges. Coffee and of course Courvoisier brandy or Armagnac whichever one preferred. What a snack! And what an end to a week's banting!

We left in high spirits not minding if it snowed ink, which it seemed likely to do for there was a gale blowing and the sky was black. On the outskirts of Djilfa, where there is a telephone, we were stopped by a messenger (all laid on by Freddie) *"Prière a M. l'Ambassadeur de rentrer à Alger aussitôt que possible"*. It was a blow – but I thought at the time how much more you would have minded it than I did. Already I was feeling doubtful of sleeping under a tent in that windy desert and the prospect of my own comfy villa was not unpleasing. You are the fearful adventurer, I the courageous stay at home.

---

[1] The writer Enid Bagnold, Lady Jones, 1889–1981, who had a house at Rottingdean. Their close friendship began when they both – "we two old farm wives" – would meet at Barnham Market.

[306]

My new friend (Enid)[1] came over for the night – rather depressed – her son is out of the battle for the time being, so she has no cause. I guess there is a general war depression – pendulum swung – Italian impasse – cold and sickness. At 5.30 we met Venetia and Victor[1] and motored down to Tring [to Victor Rothschild's house] for the night, and such a lovely night to be there because it was to be announced the next day that he was to expect the George Medal. He was childishly, and unconcealedly delighted but a little nervous because no word had come from Downing St. The press were constantly on the telephone which led us to expect the announcement on the nine o'clock news. We were all tuned in only to be disappointed – for no mention of Lord Rothschild. Victor was heavenly to J.J., – had him to sleep in his room, took him out to fetch bumbles.[2] He asked a million questions about you – he misses you miserably – asks me if you enjoy his letters – I lied 'yes'. J.J. and Victor sat up hopefully for the twelve o'clock programme. We left before the morning papers arrived and bought them at Berkhampstead. In them the glad news was nicely headlined. Isn't it glorious. I am so madly glad. Fine for Jewry, fine for his friends. Splendid for him who has a nervous system like mine.

Downing St. from my angle was a complete failure. The butler greeted me with a "Lord Beaverbrook wants to see you before you go in". Max appeared with a warning that there was a certain Adolf Berle,[3] – U.S. V.I.P. lunching, who when told I was due fresh from Algiers for my son's holidays, mumbled something

---

[1] Nathaniel Mayer Victor, 3rd Baron Rothschild, b. 1910. Biologist. In 1939–45 he was attached to Military Intelligence – he won the George Medal for his services as a bomb disposal expert.
[2] Maurice Baring invented a language that consisted of taking the first letter of any word, and attaching "umble" to it. So "bumbles" could be anything from bread to bootlaces.
[3] Adolf Berle, 1895–1971. Assistant Secretary of State, 1938–44. He was in England to talk about civil aviation after the war. He was extremely intelligent, and had apparently passed the Harvard Entrance Examination at the age of thirteen.

about American women not flying around for their son's holidays.[1] Clemmie had retorted that for all she knew I'd come in a freight boat. So, said Max, would I keep to that lie. I said I'd keep to the freight part but couldn't say ship for fear he checked up – but that anyway the subject could easily be avoided, and what the hell had it got to do with him. Lunch was a complete failure from my point of view. We were just the five, and Winston talked exclusively to Berle. Max spoke twice in the most ingratiating way, having told me outside that "the fellow was a bastard". Duckling's[2] talk was on a very high global theoretic level – not saying much, very well, and very ingratiating too. All he said about France was to the effect that Charlie [de Gaulle] had done himself no good by his last move. Clemmie was bored and we left the dining-room. Duckling made as to come too but Max mumbled "one thing more" and the door closed on us. We jawed away till twenty past three when she said she must go, and I had a date with Moura[3] at 3. So I got no word with Duckling. The Baroness was sad – H.G. [Wells] is condemned – cancer of the liver (a secret) and in pain. He doesn't know. I thought he should be told, for he might prefer to make his quietus. She said, "O he would never do that – he would think it uncourageous". I was surprised – without church religion, at that age, when slow dying can only disquiet your friends and dog the war effort by using food and doctors and nurses, it's surely better.

At the Bognor station there were barriers, and soldiers and Police and queues formed to deal with these unfortunate residents – it took me fifteen minutes to get through. Next day, Friday 7th, we left for Rottingdean,[4] and after dinner youth returned to the old 'uns and we played 'clumps' and 'the game', and to wind up – as the Jones children had *never heard of it* – Hunt the Slipper. "Cobbler cobbler mend my shoe and get it done by half past *two*" I shouted, tapping my morocco slipper on the boards. Then followed the scramble, and the yells and giggles, and "Let's have one more go" as the slipper was dragged out of Enid's fork. Great larks.

---

[1] She had in fact flown to England, without a permit and with the help of Air Vice-Marshal Grahame Dawson.

[2] Winston Churchill.

[3] Moura, Baroness Budberg, sometime Benckendorff, 1892–1974. Author, translator and linguist, she had been the mistress of Robert Bruce-Lockhart, Maxim Gorky and H. G. Wells.

[4] Where Enid Jones lived.

April 8th. Conrad got through quite easily. He was able to satisfy the Police that he was a resident here practically. The weather isn't up to much. It looked lovely early but it's all grey now. No answer to my *wire* to you fretted me but I got a *letter* on my return, which soothes me though of course it had no cause to – as it's twelve days old. Perhaps you are hunting the gentle gazelle or harnessing birds of prey. I do hope you are happy enough, and missing me, but not too much. The freak ticket-collector always tells me to remember him to his Lordship.

Diana to Duff, 11 April 1944   *The Dorchester*

Dearest dear. Edith today, in the small hours, gave birth to an 80 lb. calf. She's a dear girl, fat and calm. A great relief to all and a bit of butter for the weekend. I'll never again complain of people not noticing one's absence or being uninterested in one's exploits. Interested questions are worse when you see a lot of inquirers – I'm so sick of hearing my own stories – my stale jokes thro' the old rasp. I just long to take the next plane back to you. They all say I look well – they'll say anything. I look like hell.

Duff to Diana, 13 April 1944   *Algiers*

Yesterday was uneventful. Jumbo wanted to see me in the morning. He had had what he described as 'a rocket from the P.M.' It was a telegram which ran something like this. "Ambassador Cooper informs me that you have spoken slightingly of General Giraud to Mr. Murphy. You might at least inform your own Government of your views before expressing them to others." Fortunately I was able to prove to Jumbo that I had done nothing of the kind. I had merely reported that from a strictly military point of view Jumbo had agreed with the Yanks that Béthouart[1] would be an improvement on Giraud. I left him happy – but it occurred to me afterwards that it was very unlike Winston to refer to me as Ambassador Cooper and that it was probably a de-cyphering error for Ambassador Winant.[2]

---

[1] General Antoine Béthouart, 1889–1982. Chief of Staff for National Defence.
[2] The American Ambassador to England, John Gilbert Winant, 1889–1947.

It's torture talking to Daisy [Fellowes] in Chapel St. My eye uncontrollably is picking out depredations and dilapidations of my furniture, carpets, *objets*. These I lay at her door, and it affects my conversation. She looked lovely, but not so lovely as she did at Chips' that night – the few candles – the Carcanos[1] to show off to, Shakes[2] on one side of her. Never have I seen her in such glamorous looks. The women were startled, the men looked avidly. She adores Compton Beauchamp – Oxford and Gerald [Berners] within reach and an amorous American group to strengthen her morale.

[Back at the Dorchester:] I went to see Betty [Cranborne], full of beans and sympathtic. True, she asks you a new question while you are answering a previous one. She had cobalt hair and was uncommonly common – but I enjoyed it a lot. Next I dropped in on Annie[3] – the double beds were covered with Peter Quennell,[4] Philip Toynbee[5] covered in turn with angry spots, Alastair Forbes,[6] and Esmond.[7] Whiskey whizzing round – atmosphere of a pub. All U.S. soldiers were confined to barracks so I was chucked by Raimund and Liz,[8] who was to arrive from Wales. So I was flung back upon Emerald.[9]

At eleven or so I groped my way torchless to Max's – on invitation, and there I found him supine in a huge armchair – Brendan[10] equally supine in another, miles apart. I sank supine into the sofa – supine from horror of their manners. Two more graceless louts I've never seen. "How do you like Algiers, Diana," Brendan said, but nothing else. Max I thought was asleep and said so – but he wasn't – though he'd closed his eyes and folded his

---

[1] Dr. Miguel Angel Carcano, the Argentine Ambassador, and his wife.

[2] William Shepherd Morrison, 1st Viscount Dunrossil. Then Minister of Town and Country Planning, and Speaker of the House of Commons, 1951–1959.

[3] Ann O'Neill, 1913–1981. Wife of the 3rd Baron O'Neill. She married the 2nd Viscount Rothermere in 1945, and became Mrs. Ian Fleming in 1952.

[4] Peter Quennell, b. 1905, poet and critic.

[5] Philip Toynbee, 1916–1981, novelist and critic.

[6] Alastair Forbes, journalist.

[7] Esmond Rothermere, 1898–1978, second Viscount Rothermere. Newspaper proprietor.

[8] Raimund was a G.I. in the American army.

[9] Emerald Cunard had also set up house in the Dorchester, where she was to live until she died in 1948.

[10] Brendan Bracken, 1st Viscount Bracken, 1901–1958. Minister of Information, 1941 –45.

hands on his stomach. I made no pretence of affection or enjoyment, and left as soon as possible. Perhaps they had much on their minds.

Duff to Diana, 16 April 1944   *Algiers*

Sunday morning – sitting in the window – lovely weather. Haven't written since Friday. That afternoon there was a last flutter about Giraud. Winston sent him a personal message urging him to accept post of Inspector General. It was too late and this morning his farewell message appears in the press. So that is over.

Raymond Mortimer has gone this morning – at least he has gone to Maison Blanche[1] which we know doesn't mean gone for good. He improved steadily and I almost liked him in the end. He gave me a copy of his book and wrote in it "with deep gratitude to the Ambassador and friendly admiration to the Man of Letters". I liked the last bit.

I'm sorry your luncheon at Downing Street was such a flop. As you don't mention anything that Winston said of me I feel that he must have said something unpleasant. I should have been interested to meet Adolf Berle. He doesn't seem to have made much impression on you.

[The plans for the Normandy landings had been made without consultation with General de Gaulle, and without any part for the Free French, which was a sad disappointment for them. The British sought to mitigate this by inviting de Gaulle to London just before the beginning of the operation, and he accepted. Because of the intense security that surrounded D-Day, no one knew exactly when de Gaulle and his entourage would leave.

The summons came on June 2nd, and Duff and the General's party flew to London on June 3rd. This left Diana – for whom any flight spelled certain death, quite apart from the dangers of war – in a frenzy of terror.]

---

[1] The Algiers airfield.

Diana to Duff, 3 June 1944   *Algiers*

Darling Love – How shall I sleep without you? I dare not face it without two of Piggy's malignant looking yellow pills – I cannot tell you how desperate I am – if you ever get this shriek it will be over – the torture – only to begin again if I am to get you back. Something enough! I've been dining with Adrian and Betty Holman[1] – a grisly affair – and done O! so badly. Eric Duncannon escorted me and dined too – the other *convives* were Paul-Boncour, nephew of old silver locks[2] who I *think* used to pinch my "bit the boys love" in Paris – (can't be sure), and Billotte.[3] Adrian would *tutoyer* Paul-Boncour, a thing that suits Englishmen as ill as kissing women's hands does. Betty (to me) speaks French worse than I do and with no *plunge*. Paul-Boncour spoke English, Billotte *had none. I* was the only one who spoke out of civility. Adrian said "I can't think why you are speaking in French". I pointed out to the trained Diplomat that it was rude to leave an enforced mum chance at a chatty table. He only spoke French occasionally to air the *tutoyage*. I stuck it out with the stone in my soul, (the thirty years training of jabber at dinner tells) till a quarter to eleven when Eric brought me home.

Duff to Diana, 4 June 1944   *The Dorchester*

Here I am – safe and sound – and twenty-four hours ago I didn't know whether we should start. Five of us in the plane you know – Wormwood,[3] Frank, Gaston [Palewski][4] and [Lt.] Teyssot. Frank of course felt frightfully sick and, I think, still more frightfully frightened, so sought the seclusion which one of the bunks gave and lay prone till Rabat. There the Bird[5] met us – I flew off to his nest for a couple of quick ones as Charlie [de Gaulle] thought best for security reasons to dine on board the plane. The female Birds were happy to see me and still happier to be brought back and

---

[1] Adrian Holman, 1895–1974. Counsellor on Duff's staff, April–Sept. 1944, and subsequently Minister at the British Embassy in Paris, 1944–1946.

[2] Joseph Paul-Boncour, 1873–1972. Prime Minister of France, 1932–33.

[3] General Pierre Billotte, b. 1906. Armoured Brigade Commander of the Leclerc Division, and a close member of de Gaulle's entourage.

[4] General de Gaulle.

[5] de Gaulle's *chef de cabinet*, b. 1901.

[6] Sir Hugh Stonehewer Bird, 1891–1973, Consul General for the French Zone of Morocco, 1943–45.

shown the plane and presented to Wormwood,[1] who was all that there is of most affable. Followed a fairly gloomy dinner – just the five of us – two quite silent – Gaston breaking in occasionally. It was slightly enlivened by a bottle of cham. Three cham meals in two days. A record for this epoch. Then half an hour walking up and down the air field – just Long Charlie and I. We talked of everything – except, I was glad to say, the present situation and it wasn't too bad.

We left at 10.25. They said "we shall be there at 6" and as the clock struck 6 we struck the ground. That sort of thing impresses the French. They can never even leave at the appointed time – let alone arrive at it. The great secrecy of our arrival was enhanced by the presence of the massed bands of the Air Force who played the *Marseillaise* a good deal better than they play it in Algiers, and a guard of honour fifty strong. A host of Foreign Office and French Embassy people.

I was looking forward to a day divided between White's and the girls. But not at all – I'm off at ten a.m. for you-know-where and not back till tomorrow. Got on to Wade at Bognor. "Good gracious!" she said, recognising my voice at once. "Is her ladyship over?" No – deep disappointment registered.   D.

Diana to Duff, 6 June 1944   *Algiers*

The moment I closed my letter came the news of the landing.[2] O dear O dear. It's Wednesday now and one gets such a little snippet of news blazoned in press, bawled out on the Radio – without pause and one feels frustrated. I'm so glad you were there – are there through all my longing for you to be safe back – one can make no guess at the measure of success or failure. The frightful party the Naval Mission took me to was given by a pretty vulgar Algerienne in the local Bayswater. The two *vedettes* [stars] were Brigadier Bourbon's father and Josephine Baker.[3] He was there on time, so was I. The hostess was flat on her stummack begging Monseigneur to *daigne* to be seated. We waited over an hour for Josephine. I had to admit rather loudly to my jealousy, when we finally sat down without even news of her – jealousy for her

---

[1] Wormwood and Gaulle. A joke of Alastair Forbes'.
[2] D-Day. By that evening, 156,000 men had been put ashore.
[3] The American-born black singer, star of the French cabaret.

sanction of unpunctuality. I said it was not allowed *me*. Why? they said in defence of her, and in the face of what, I fear, they thought was racial discrimination. – I said my husband would never allow me bad manners, and when he was not there my conscience shouted at me. She arrived at coffee with charming unconcern. Her appearance is Barnum and Bailey – but I warmed to her.

7 June. The great news came – I had the joy of telling them at the packing centre.[1] They gathered round me quite *affoléed*. The war was over – no point in packing any more parcels – when would *they* land? how soon Paris – (the Mustaphas took it more calmly) I had to damp, or try to damp them.

From packing I went on to the French hospital – new, stream-lined and filthy – wards of patients speckled with flies – then I gave my blood to others. It's amusing to have done it in several countries, the methods are so different. Singapore the most interesting and all round the best. England over-solicitous – un-theatrical with obligatory tea and twenty minutes rest. France, a spirited group round the bed – babbling and gesticulating and telling me that I was saving a man's life tonight – up you get quick – hurry to the bar – whacking great cup of ersatz Port – cigarettes and marmalade and off for a tour of inspection of entire hospital unit – basements and all.

Duff to Diana, 7 June 1944   *The Dorchester*

My love. I am having a wild time and can only give you a schedule since I stopped writing at 10.a.m. on Sunday morning.

4 June

10.15. a.m.	Ten minutes at White's on the way to Carlton Gardens to remind myself of the taste of port.
10.30–12.50	Drive in car alone with Wormwood through country very familiar to us.
12.50.	Arrive Dumpling's[2] H.Q. He playing at soldiers and living in a train to everybody's inconvenience.

---

[1] Diana was working there, packing biscuits and pyjamas.
[2] Winston Churchill.

	Of all the inhabitants of the British Empire whom had he chosen to meet Wormwood?
	Smuts!![1]
1.	Conference.
2.15.	Lunch – heated arguments – almost rows. cham.
4.5	Drive to Ike's H.Q. Friendly talks between soldiers.
	Back to Dumpling's.
	Leave with Donkey[2] and Dixon[3] for Donkey's stables.
	Heaven. *The* house we were looking for.
	Never liked Donkey so much. V. pleasant evening. Early to bed. Deep sleep.

5 June

10.30.	leave with Dixon for London.
12.	arrive Dorch.
1.	Hair cut at White's. Everyone says 'How well you're looking. Bronzed and thin. Diana said you were enormously fat.'
1.30	Lunch with Martha [Gellhorn] and Virginia [Cowles] at Claridges.
3.	An hour with Pierre Viénot. (Frog Ambassador)[4]
3.40	F.O.
5.30	Whites
6.	Barbie Wallace
7.	Emerald.
7.45	Caroline [Paget]. dine Savoy.

6 June
D. Day.

9.a.m.	J.J. on telephone.
10. ,,	General Willoughby Norrie.
11. ,,	Ernie Bevin at M. of Labour.

[1] Field-Marshal Jan Christian Smuts, 1870–1950. South African statesman and soldier. He had made a speech during the winter of 1943, in which he said that France would never be a great power again. He also said that England wouldn't be either, but this did not make it any better in French eyes.

[2] 'Donkey' – Anthony Eden, 1st Earl of Avon, 1897–1977. Secretary of State for Foreign Affairs (1940–45). Duff spent the night at his house near Midhurst, Sussex.

[3] Sir Pierson John Dixon, Principal Private Secretary to Anthony Eden.

[4] The French Committee of Liberation's Ambassador to London, 1941–1944.

11.30	F.O. learn of terrible ructions last night.
	Wormwood doing the mule.
	Duckling the mad baby. The York told to be ready for immediate departure.
	Fearful complications.
	Long conversation. Donkey, Viénot, etc.
1.	Lunch with Freda [Dudley Ward] at Bon Viveur.
3.	An hour with Wormwood. Great diplomatic triumph for D.C. "Only you could have done it" etc. etc.
	Storm abates.
4. 5.15.	Foreign Office. Congrats – dictating account etc. getting late for
5.25	Our Tart who has to leave for theatre at 5.40.
6.	Brendan at Ministry of Information. B.B. very sensible. On our side – pro frog.
6.40	Glorious Lady Cunard *chez elle*.
7.20	Victor at the Dorchester – jabber jabber, jabber.
8.	Dine with Daisy at Coq d'Or.

7 June

Am now awaiting arrival of Alphand,[1] after which I go to F.O. lunch with Victor at Wilton's – dine with Wormwood having been obliged to chuck farewell party for Biddy who is a brigadier and is leaving for India tomorrow to hold the A.T.S. of all the golden east in fee. Wormwood seems to like me. Nobody can understand it. I least of all.

The future all unknown. We want to get the other boys over[2] – but it seems doubtful. Here's Alphand. No more time – Bag shuts at noon.

    hugs and x x x   D.

[Duff was Ambassador to Paris from 1944 to 1947; it was the culmination of his political career. He was a

---

[1] Hervé Alphand, b. 1907. Director General of the Ministry of Foreign Affairs in Paris.
[2] The Free French.

passionate francophile and spoke French fluently, and he and Diana were enormously popular in Paris. At first Diana dreaded the formal entertaining and the restrictions of protocol, but soon the parties were spiced with poets and artists and the protocol had to fit itself in as best it could. In the rebuilding of Europe, Duff thought it was vital that the French and the British conclude a treaty. His efforts bore fruit in 1947 with the Treaty of Dunkirk, of which he was one of the main architects.

They moved to Chantilly after their term was over, to the lovely Chateau of St. Firmin, which they had already been using as a weekend retreat. Here they lived and entertained for the rest of their life together.

Diana adored North Africa and often went back there. In 1949, her companions were Mary Tessier and Paul Louis Weiller. A close friend since the Embassy days, he had been a heroic aviator in the first war, and had become a great industrialist after it.]

Diana to Duff, 4 March 1949   *Marrakesh*

Paul-Louis [Weiller] was anxious to see boys or girls dance in the *Quartier Reservé*, but the concierge here was so discouraging that the plan was renounced, so while he wrote some letters we ordered dinner for three at my bed side. I dressed up as an yashmaked odelisk on my bed. The lovely Mary Tessier padded her bosom and hips out with my sachets and jerseys, veiled her face, kohled her eyes and played castanets (*à la danse du ventre*) with two bedroom keys. Drian[1] put on a Fez and a mackintosh and a carpet rug over his shoulder so when Paul-Louis came back, the *Quartier Réservé* had come to him. This story has very little interest but it serves to show what infantile high spirits still obtain in our *parti-carré*.

Mine are failing today thanks to Papa's[2] cruelty. If it's not J.J who tortures me with silence, it's Papa. Yet you both know what suffering and anxiety you cause me. I sent a telegram for news yesterday – of course no reply. I buy the *Daily Mail* of three days before to see if there is a headline or an obituary about Papa. This

[1] A. Drian, the French painter and illustrator.
[2] Duff. This letter is addressed both to him and John Julius.

morning I got Paul Louis to ask his secretary in Paris to make enquiry about a husband – the humiliation was a little mitigated by Mary being in the same position. The answer from the factotum was that Lord Duff Cooper was in perfect health but that M. Tessier was *grippéed*. Since this news I have had a telegram. Not having my address is no excuse, since I gave Papa the sec's telephone number.

Duff to Diana,   *Château de St. Firmin,*
8 March 1949   *Chantilly, Oise*

Darling – I've had six lovely letters from you since you left. You must forgive me if I find your movements a little difficult to follow as you give no details about plans and your dates are confusing. You left Paris on February 23rd. Your first letter, written in the train, was dated Feb. 16. Your second letter, still travelling, was dated 25 March. You no doubt gave it to somebody in the embassy to post, for it arrived two days after the third letter and was correctly addressed in a neat clerk's handwriting, so that I put off opening it as long as possible. The third letter – (you had obviously given more care to the question of dating) bore the superscription 27th or 28th March '49. You got the year right any way. In number four you are less meticulous, heading it "no idea of the date it's Monday", which internal evidence leads me to suppose was February 28th. In number five you temporarily abandon the problem of time, but in number six I gather from the heading that you are in Africa, that it is March 4th and still 1949. However the upshot of it all is that you are, or were, having fun, which makes me very happy, but that your knee is not better but much worse which makes me very sad.

Now for how I've spent my time. The greater part of it has been taken up with dealing with replies to the invitations you sent out to all your friends to come and stay, just before you plunged into darkest Africa. That was a good idea of yours. I forget what it is that one sows to reap the whirlwind, but you have certainly sown it. I don't think you'll ever be allowed to take a rest-cure again. You get too active. You might start an international war next time.

[Duff had returned to his writing. In 1949 there appeared a small volume of his *Translations and Verses*. This was followed by *Sergeant Shakespeare*, and in 1950 his only work of fiction, *Operation Heartbreak*. In 1953 he published his autobiography, *Old Men Forget*, and had the satisfaction of seeing it received with as much praise as his first book, *Talleyrand*. He died a few months later, on New Year's Day, 1954.

Diana hated growing old, hated the gradual erosion of her beauty and the incessant search for her spectacles. "Please don't mind being sixty-three," she wrote to Duff. "I can't bear you to mind." Nobody likes seeing themselves age, but Duff was happy during his few years of retirement. He cultivated the more intellectual and reflective side of his nature, and when he wasn't writing he was enjoying the pleasant company of his friends and his books. Sixty-three was not so very old. Besides, Diana was still with him, and his love for her was as young as ever.]

June 2nd 1949

Once more to you a wreath I bring
To lay your golden brow above –
Once more to you a song I sing
To celebrate our changeless love.

Another year's return to store –
I think that now, in common tact,
We shouldn't add them any more,
Beginning rather to subtract.

Thus every year will make one less,
Until the night when we shall say,
"Tomorrow – oh the happiness –
Will bring us back our wedding-day".

INDEX

Baldwin of Bewdley, Lucy, Countess, 286
Baldwin, Stanley, 1st Earl Baldwin of
    Bewdley, 188, 208, 254, 257, 258, 260,
    267, 268, 286, 288
Balfour, Arthur James, 1st Earl, 101, 131
Balkanova, 253–4
Balzac, Honoré de, 108, 202
Bankhead, Tallulah, 186
Baring, Sir Evelyn, 83
Baring, Sir Godfrey, 158
Baring, Hugo, 221
Baring, Maurice, 177, 186, 190, 196, 201,
    203, 220, 221, 226
Baring, Poppy (later Mrs Peter Thursby),
    158, 164, 166, 168–70, 175, 245, 246,
    249, 252
Barrie, J. M., 105, 241
Barrymore, John, 225
Barrymore, Mrs John, 151
Beardsley, Aubrey, 19
Beatrice, H.R.H. Princess, 135
Beau Desert (house of 6th Marquess of
    Anglesey), 3, 120
Beaufort, 9th Duke of, 102
Beaverbrook, Gladys Lady, 255
Beaverbrook, Max Aitken, 1st Baron,
    launches appeal, 76; shows German
    film, 88; in case of emergency, 101–2,
    103; and Orpen, 121, 124; commissions
    Diana for *Sunday Express*, 127, 130; and
    Venetia Stanley, 131–3; and Duchess of
    Westminster, 185, 187, 208, 209, 213;
    and obituary of Mona Dunn, 258–9,
    267; takes Diana to Brazil, 278–81; at
    Downing Street, 307; at Dorchester, 310
Beck, James, 244, 269, 270–1
Beckett, Muriel, 215
Beckett, Hon. Rupert, 215
Bedlam, 227
Belloc, Hilaire, 158, 170, 197, 293
Belvoir Castle, xiv, 12, 16, 53, 135, 185,
    221, 231, 240, 241, 272
Beneš, Edouard, 304
Bennett, Arnold, *The Pretty Lady*, 161
Benoit, Pierre, *L'Atlantide*, 235
Benson, Lady Violet formerly Lady Elcho,
    xiii; and Lord Elcho's death, 29, 70, 128,
    136, 167, 189, 217, 225
Benson, Lt. Col. Sir Rex, 131
Bentinck, Lord Morven, 135
Beresford, J. D., *God's Counterpoint*, 92
Berkeley House, Hay Hill, 3, 12, and
    passim
Berle, Adolf, 307, 311

Bernays, Robert, 291
Berners, Gerald, 14th Baron, 196, 310
Bernhardt, Sarah, 134, 211
Berry, Seymour, *see* Camrose
Bethell, Capt. William, 244
Béthouart, Gen. Antoine, 309
Bevin, Ernest, 315
Bibesco, Antoine, Prince, 83
Bibesco, Elizabeth, Princess, 83, 85, 92,
    122, 232–3
Billing case, the, 66, 67, 69, 71
Billing, Pemberton, 66, 71
Billotte, Gen. Pierre
Bird, Sir Hugh Stonehewer, 312
Birrell, Augustine, 61, 94
Blackton, James Stuart, 136, 177
Blair, 161
Bland, Sir Nevile, 167
Blandford, Marquess of, later 10th Duke
    of Marlborough, 207
Blew Jones, Mrs, 251
Blumenfeld, R. D. 'Blum', 128, 185
Bognor, the cottage at, 200, 218, 261, 291,
    302–3, 308
Bonar Law, Andrew, *see* Law
Bonham-Carter, Sir Maurice, 24
Bonham-Carter, Violet, 24
Boothby, Penelope, 69
Boothby, Robert, 1st Baron, 272
Bouch, Thomas, 103, 124, 128, 135, 136,
    181–3, 226, 258
Bourbon, Brigadier, 313
Boushaga, Duff's feast with the, 305–6
Boyd, Phyllis, *see* de Janzé
Bracken, Brendan, 1st Viscount, 299, 310,
    316
Brassey, Lt. Gerald, 108
Brazil, voyage to, 278–81
Breccles, Norfolk (house of Edwin and
    Venetia Montagu), 79, 81, 91, 95, 97,
    124
Bretherton, Freddie, 226
Brett, Hon. Dorothy, 236
Brighton, 21, 22, 64
Brooke, Rupert, 32, 42, 59, 92, 96
Browne, Harvey, 191
Browning, Robert, xiv, 58, 75
Bruce, Stanley, later Viscount Bruce of
    Melbourne, 292
Bruce Lockhart, Robert, 308
Brummell, George 'Beau', 52, 86
Buccleuch, 8th Duke of, 245
Buccleuch, Mary Duchess of, 'Mollie', 245
Buchanan, Capt. J. N., 54–6

Winn, Anthony, 292, 294
Winterton, 6th Earl, 292
Wodehouse, P. G., 246
Wolkoff, Count Gabriel, 28, 88, 132
Wolverton, Lady, 77
Woolley, Monty, 194

Worsley, Lord and Lady, 152
Wyndham, Diana, *see* Westmorland
Wyndham, George, 45
Wyndham, Percy, 42

Ziegler, Edward, 204

JOHN ROBERT MANNERS
7th Duke of Rutland 1818-1906
m. 1. CATHERINE MARLAY
  d.1854
  2. Janeta Hughan
  d.1899

COL. CHARLES HUGH LINDSAY
1816-1889
m.
EMILIA BROWNE
d.1873

EDWARD
1864-1903
unmarried

KATHERINE
1866-1900
unmarried

CECIL
1868-1945
unmarried

ROBERT
1870-1917
m. Mildred Buckworth

WILLIAM
1873-1897
unmarried

VICTORIA (Queenie)
1876-1933
unmarried

ELIZABETH
1878-1924
m. Lord George
Montagu-Douglas-Scott

HENRY, 8th Duke m. VIOLET
1852-1925   d.1937

CHARLES
1862-1925
unmarried

HENRY
1866-1939
m. Norah Bourke

MARJORIE
1883-1946
m.
Charles, 6th
Marquess of
Anglesey
1885-1947

CAROLINE, 1913-1976
m. Sir Michael Duff

ELIZABETH, 1916-1980
m. Raimund von Hofmannsthal

MARY b.1918
unmarried

ROSE b.1919
m. Hon John Francis McLaren

KATHERINE b. 1922
m. 1 Lt Col. Jocelyn Gurney
   2 Charles Farrell

HENRY b.1922
7th and present Marquess
of Anglesey
m. Shirley Morgan

ROBERT,
Lord Haddon
1885-1894

JOHN, 9th Duke
1886-1940
m.
Kathleen Tennant (Kakoo)
b.1894

URSULA b.1916
m. 1 Lt Col. Anthony Mar
   2 Robert d'Abo

ISABEL b.1918
m. 1 Loel Guinness
   2 Sir Robert Throckmo

CHARLES b.1919
10th and present Duke
m. 1 Anne Bairstow
   2 Frances Sweeny

JOHN b.1922
m. Mary Moore